THE GARDEN-FRESH
VEGETABLE COOKBOOK

1⁰⁰

The Garden-Fresh Vegetable Cookbook

Andrea Chesman

Illustrations by Margaret Chodos-Irvine

Storey Publishing

*The mission of Storey Publishing is to serve our customers
by publishing practical information that encourages personal independence in
harmony with the environment.*

Edited by Dianne Cutillo and Andrea Dodge
Art direction by Kent Lew and Cynthia N. McFarland
Cover design by Kent Lew
Cover illustration © Ted Wright
Cover author photograph © Natalie Stultz
Interior illustrations © Margaret Chodos-Irvine
Text design by Cynthia N. McFarland
Text production by Jessica Armstrong and Jennifer Jepson Smith

Printed in the United States by R.R. Donnelley

10 9 8 7 6 5 4 3 2 1

LIBRARY OF CONGRESS CATALOGING-IN-PUBLICATION DATA

Chesman, Andrea.
   The garden-fresh vegetable cookbook / Andrea Chesman.
      p. cm.
   Includes index.
   ISBN-13: 978-1-58017-534-0 (hardcover: alk. paper)
   ISBN-10: 1-58017-534-1 (hardcover : alk. paper)
   1. Cookery (Vegetables) I. Title.
TX801.C438 2005
641.6'5—dc22
                                        2005004049

To Richard, Rory, and Sam,
always

CONTENTS

THERE ARE TWO TYPES OF GARDENERS, I think. There are gardeners who cook, and there are cooks who garden. I happen to be a cook who gardens. You can recognize my type by my less-than-photogenic garden, my casual attitude toward weeds, my hatred of thinning (throwing away good food!). I spend winter evenings with cookbooks, not with treatises on soil building. I am unlikely to plant vegetables that are reluctant to grow in my northern garden just to prove that I can. I have never grown a prizewinning anything. I have never even set aside space in my garden for a carving pumpkin.

Don't get me wrong. I have tremendous respect for those who put gardening first. Their gardens are gorgeous! These gardeners are often so adept in the outside world that they are capable of building beautiful trellises and amazing bean tepees. They never fail to properly put the garden to bed in the fall, and their peas are inevitably two weeks earlier than mine. They often lead the way with planting new varieties or experimenting with old heirloom varieties. They save seeds, and they have opinions on compost.

But here's the big difference. Cooks who garden are thrilled by the harvest. We believe every overflowing basket of vegetables is an opportunity for a crispy fresh salad, a fragrant harvest stew, a terrific new pasta sauce. On the other hand, gardeners who cook will spend hours in the garden, making everything look perfect, and then find themselves stricken with guilt. Oh no, they suddenly realize, someone has to cook all those vegetables!

Of course, not everyone who enjoys vegetables has the chance or the inclination to grow her own vegetables. Some of my very best friends buy all of their vegetables. And why not, with farmers' markets, produce stands, and CSA (Community Supported Agriculture) farms distributing wonderful fresh produce to rural, suburban, and urban markets? Once these shoppers get their vegetables home, however, there is still the problem of what to do with them.

Well, not to worry. Cooks like me have fun in the kitchen, making recipes that are quick, easy, and delicious and honor the vegetables we have worked so hard to bring into our kitchens.

But whether you are a gardener who cooks or a cook who gardens, we undoubtedly share the thrill that comes with the start of the gardening season. My garden lies uphill from my house on a plot that has been a garden as far back as anyone remembers, which is more than 50 years. Each spring, the snow melts from the garden plot early and, before my lawn is snow-free, garlic shoots poke through the dark soil of the raised beds. Within a few weeks, I plant peas and spinach, then more spring greens. I begin to harvest fresh chives, oregano, and thyme to enhance my cooking. Then it is asparagus season, and the harvest has truly begun.

Because I live in the North (Zone 6), my gardening season is limited. I have often been able to get two sowings of peas as well as green beans out of my garden, but some years I have very few tomatoes. I have never been successful with peppers or eggplant. Although this cookbook follows the harvest, the particulars of my harvest seasons may be different from yours. I know that my brother in Alabama harvests his first tomatoes when I am reveling in the first asparagus. Still, he gets in a crop of spring greens, just like I do, though the month of the harvest is different, and my season lasts longer than his. So I have organized this book by season, and within each season, I have organized the vegetables alphabetically, since variations in number of days to harvest various vegetables make it impossible to predict the exact order of the harvest. What is possible to predict is that you won't find certain vegetables growing together, and you won't find

recipes for unlikely combinations of vegetables in this cookbook. No stews with winter squash and peas, no green bean and asparagus salads.

There are some flaws to this system. Take carrots. You could easily plant short-season carrots, harvest them young, and enjoy in the summer. Or you could plant a long-season variety well suited to long-term storage. So are carrots a summer or fall vegetable? Well, I've chosen to put them with other fall storage crops, because I don't usually cook with summer carrots. Those early carrots are just perfect as they are. Carrots from the root cellar can and should be enhanced by cooking. If you can't find a vegetable in its "proper" season, look for it in the index.

What I've tried to accomplish with my seasonal organization is to present simple recipes that feature in-season vegetables, recipes that let the unique flavor and texture of each vegetable take center stage. I hope you enjoy them.

ACKNOWLEDGMENTS

There is no way this book could have been written without the help of all the farmers who supply my local farmers' market and food co-op with delicious vegetables. I am simply too limited as a gardener to grow enough vegetables — and enough variety of vegetables — to provide myself with all the produce needed for the recipe tests that went into this book. My special thanks to Will and Judy Stevens of Golden Russet Farm in Shoreham, Vermont, and Marion Pollack and Marjorie Sussman of Orb Weaver Farm in Monkton, Vermont, for veggies, inspirations, and recipes. My thanks also to all the folks at the Middlebury Natural Foods Co-op for keeping such a terrific store going, and for inspiration, conversation, and making my regular shopping trips so much fun.

I'd also like to thank all the people who gave their time to be interviewed for profiles in the book. Thanks also to my sister for help with recipe testing and profile leads, and to Annie Harlow for her fabulous potato recipe.

This book would never have been started without the encouragement and advice of Dianne Cutillo, a wonderful editor, and it would never have been finished without the help of Andrea Dodge. Thank you to all the other hands at Storey Publishing, including Jessica Armstrong, Pam Art, Kent Lew, Cindy McFarland, Jennifer Jepson Smith, and Sarah Thurston.

THE WELL-STOCKED PANTRY

Nothing beats the simple pleasure that comes from eyeing a basket of freshly harvested vegetables — be it from your own garden or a CSA or a farmstand — and cooking whatever appeals to you at that moment. If your kitchen is well stocked with staples, you'll be able to whip up a delicious dish at a moment's notice.

PANTRY STAPLES

A well-stocked kitchen contains an assortment of oils, vinegars, and soy sauce. Chicken broth, pasta, rice, flour, nuts, canned beans, salt, pepper, and spices are also items you should never be without.

Broth

Chicken or vegetable broth is a pantry staple, needed for braised vegetables and some soups, stews, and sauces. I try to keep a supply of homemade chicken broth (see page 9) in the freezer. But to guarantee I am never without it, I also stock a quart or two of store-bought broth in the cupboard. You'll have to taste a variety of chicken broths before you can settle on your house brand; quality and availability vary tremendously. I usually stock organic free-range chicken broth. It comes in shelf-stable aseptic boxes and keeps longer in the refrigerator once opened than homemade broth.

Vegetarians can substitute vegetable broth for chicken broth, but commercial vegetable broths are tricky. Often one flavor dominates, especially carrots or tomatoes, making the broth unsuited for some applications. Or the broth's flavors are muddy and unpleasant. Taste before you use; generally ones labeled "un-chicken" are the most neutral in flavor. A recipe for vegetable broth can be found on page 8.

Oils

Many recipes start with sautéing garlic or onion in oil. I stock extra-virgin olive oil as my daily cooking oil and salad oil. It is a heart-healthy monounsaturated oil. It is also the oil of choice for coating vegetables that are to be grilled or roasted. To add more flavor to the oil, you can infuse it with herbs (see page 5).

When a neutral-tasting oil is needed, I use canola oil, another monounsaturated oil. For stir-fries or deep-frying, I might use peanut oil because it has a high smoking point, but canola oil is fine to use. I also use toasted dark sesame oil in stir-fries for flavor.

Vinegars

Vinegar isn't just for salad dressing and pickles. A drizzle of vinegar finishes roasted vegetables to great effect. It is also used in sauces when a sharp contrasting flavor is needed. I regularly use several different vinegars when I cook.

If you are buying vinegar for making pickles,

make sure the vinegar contains 4 to 6 percent acetic acid and has a 40- to 50-grain strength.

Balsamic Vinegar

True *aceto balsamico* is made only in Emilia-Romagna, Italy. It has been aged for at least 12 years, resulting in a vinegar that is fruity, thick, rich, and dark brown. This is an expensive vinegar; you can pay anywhere from $15 for 250 ml (about 1¼ cups) aged 6 years to more than $200 for vinegar aged for 200 years. If you are paying less, you probably are getting vinegar that has been flavored and colored with caramel syrup. Do yourself a favor: Buy the best you can afford and use it sparingly. White balsamic vinegar is actually clear, and it adds sweetness without color to salad dressings.

Cider Vinegar

Cider vinegar is made from apples and is great for using in sweet pickles. Its cidery flavor is rather pronounced. It is also good in some tomato-based salad dressings.

Red Wine Vinegar

Made from red wine, red wine vinegar is sharp and slightly fruity in flavor. The best red wines are aged in oak casks. One can find varietal vinegars as well as less expensive blended red wine vinegar.

Rice Vinegar

Used extensively in Asian cooking, this vinegar is mild and sweet. It is sometimes called rice wine vinegar. Rice vinegar does not always have the same acidity of other vinegars, so it cannot be used for preserving foods. Buy the unseasoned kind so you can control the flavorings you add.

Sherry Vinegar

From Spain, sherry vinegar is a distinctively flavored red wine vinegar that works well with most vegetable dishes. Its flavor tends to be milder and sweeter than red wine vinegar and has a nutty undertone.

White Vinegar

Strong but neutral in character, white vinegar, or distilled white vinegar, is used mainly in making pickles. It is also used in certain sauces from Southeast Asia.

White Wine Vinegar

White wine vinegar may be made from a single wine or from blended wines, as with red wine vinegar. Quality varies with price. White wine vinegars range from fruity to dry. The advantage of white wine vinegar is that it does not color foods, as red wine vinegar will.

Condiments and Sauces

I have a cupboard near my stove filled with bottles of oils, vinegars, soy sauces, fish sauces, hot sauces, and the like. I have a refrigerator likewise filled with opened bottles of mustard, chili sauce, chutneys, and pickles. If I had to start over, the following is what I would stock first.

Asian Fish Sauce

Fish sauce is used extensively in Southeast Asian countries, much the same way soy sauce is used. It is a clear liquid, ranging in color from amber to dark brown. Salty and pungent, its flavor is less strong than its odor. Fish sauce is made by layering salt and fish in barrels and allowing the fish to ferment. The liquid that accumulates from this process is the fish sauce. In Thailand, the sauce is called *nam pla;* in Vietnam it is called *nuoc mam.* Buy imported fish sauce from either country.

Mustard

Made from ground yellow, black, or white mustard seeds, mustard adds a distinct spicy flavor to many dishes, especially a classic vinaigrette.

Mustards are a popular condiment, amenable to so many different styles and flavorings that one can belong to a mustard-of-the-month club. For the recipes in this book you will need **American ballpark mustard,** the ubiquitous bright yellow mustard made from a smooth blend of yellow mustard seeds, vinegar, and turmeric, and **Dijon mustard,** made from mustard seeds, wine, salt, and spices. Dijon mustard is creamy in texture, gray-yellow in color, and has a clean, sharp flavor, which makes it perfect for vinaigrettes.

Buy mustard in small jars, keep opened jars refrigerated, and use within 6 months, before the flavor fades.

Soy Sauce

Soy sauce is made from fermented soy beans and a grain, usually wheat, and aged for a few years.

The best soy sauces have no additives or artificial color. **Tamari** is a pure Japanese dark soy sauce. It is slightly less salty than many Chinese soy sauces. Kikkoman is a very reliable brand of soy sauce that is available in most supermarkets. Pearl River Bridge is another good brand, but is not as widely available.

Salt and Pepper

Salt and pepper are the most important seasonings in your cupboard. Treat yourself to some coarse sea salt or kosher salt for sprinkling on grilled and roasted vegetables especially. Sea salt is made from evaporated seawater. It contains minerals in addition to the sodium chloride found in table salt and kosher salt, and hence has more flavor. Black pepper should always be freshly ground.

In the Refrigerator

Lemons are a necessary item for many recipes. Select fruits with glossy, fine-grained skin, and store in the refrigerator for 2 to 3 weeks. A lemon will yield 2 to 4 tablespoons of juice.

Parmesan cheese is another refrigerator staple. Buy authentic Parmesan from Italy and grate it as needed. The best are labeled Parmigiano-Reggiano.

It's amazing how much a sprinkling of nuts can spark up a ho-hum vegetable or add crunch and texture to a salad. Almonds, cashews, pine nuts, walnuts, pecans, and peanuts all have their uses. Because nuts have a high fat content, they should be kept in the refrigerator to prevent rancidity. Shelled nuts can be refrigerated in an airtight container for up to 4 months or frozen for up to 8 months. Unshelled nuts will keep twice as long.

RECIPES

The recipes collected here are for basic ingredients — flavored vinegars, broths, and herb combinations — that you may want to stock up on when you have the time. It will make cooking from the garden much easier.

herb vinegar

The best time to collect herbs is before they go to flower. Collect in the morning, after the dew has dried from the leaves but before the hot sun has evaporated the essential oils from the leaves. It is easiest to begin the process in a regular canning jar. After the vinegar is infused with herbs, you may want to transfer it to a better bottle for pouring. Recycled wine bottles work well, and can be used as gift bottles as well. Corks are available from many hardware stores.

MAKES 1 QUART

1½ – 2 cups fresh, firmly packed herbs (a single type or a mixture of herbs), plus additional herbs to identify the finished product

3 – 3½ cups red wine, white wine, or sherry vinegar

1 Wash the herbs in a basin of cool water. Remove any discolored or insect-damaged leaves. It is fine to keep the leaves on the stems. Dry the herbs in a salad spinner or pat dry. Be sure the herbs are completely dry before proceeding.

2 Pack the herbs into a clean canning jar. Pour the vinegar over the herbs.

3 Store in a cool, dark place for 2 to 6 weeks, shaking the mixture every few days. Begin tasting after 2 weeks. When the vinegar is flavorful, it is ready.

4 Pack a single fresh herb into a clean storage bottle to identify the flavoring in the bottle. This is optional, but very helpful.

5 Strain the vinegar through a coffee filter to remove all herbal debris, and pour into the storage bottle. Cork or cap, label, and store in a dark cool place. The vinegar will keep indefinitely.

pesto

Pesto — the heavenly paste made from fresh basil, Parmesan, olive oil, and pine nuts — is an incredibly versatile flavoring agent. It is worth the space in the garden to grow as many basil plants as you can, so you can make many batches of pesto to freeze and have it available year-round. This is the recipe I use.

■ MAKES ABOUT ⅔ CUP ■

1½ cups tightly packed fresh basil leaves

2 garlic cloves

3 tablespoons toasted pine nuts, almonds, or walnuts (see page 7)

¼ cup extra-virgin olive oil, plus additional oil for sealing the top

3 tablespoons freshly grated Parmesan

Salt and freshly ground black pepper

1 Combine the basil, garlic, and pine nuts in a food processor fitted with a metal blade. Process until finely chopped.

2 Add the oil through the feed tube with the motor running and continue processing until you have a smooth paste. Briefly mix in the cheese and salt and pepper to taste.

3 Set aside for at least 20 minutes to allow the flavors to develop if you are going to use the pesto immediately. Otherwise, spoon it into an airtight container and pour in enough oil to completely cover the pesto and exclude any air. Seal and store in the refrigerator for up to 1 week, or in the freezer for up to 6 months.

herbes de provence

Herbes de Provence is a blend of dried herbs characteristic of the cooking of southern France. Typically, the blend will contain dried basil, fennel seed, lavender, marjoram, rosemary, sage, summer savory, and thyme. The herb mix can be bought wherever herbs are sold, or you can make your own.

■ MAKES ABOUT ¾ CUP ■

3 tablespoons dried basil
3 tablespoons dried marjoram
3 tablespoons dried thyme
2 tablespoons dried summer savory
1½ teaspoons dried rosemary
½ teaspoon dried lavender flowers
½ teaspoon dried sage
½ teaspoon fennel seeds

Combine all the ingredients and store in a covered jar.

toasted nuts

Toasting brings out the flavor in nuts.

■ MAKES 1 CUP ■

1 cup almonds, cashews, pine nuts, pecans, or walnuts

Toast the nuts in a dry skillet over medium heat, stirring occasionally until golden brown, 7 to 10 minutes. Alternatively, preheat the oven to 350°F, spread out the nuts on a baking sheet, and bake, stirring occasionally, for 10 to 15 minutes, until golden brown.

vegetable broth

The distinction between broth and stock is slight — broth is salted to taste at the end of the cooking, whereas stock remains unsalted. It is easier to cook with broth because the flavors are more easily discerned once the salt is added. But when using broth in a recipe, be sure that any additional salt is added to taste.

YIELD: 3½–4 QUARTS

2 carrots

2 leeks

1 large onion

¼ small head cabbage

1 fennel bulb

4 garlic cloves

1 bunch parsley

4 sprigs fresh thyme

1 cup dried porcini mushrooms

4 quarts water

1 cup dry white wine

1 tablespoon black peppercorns

Salt (optional)

1 Quarter the carrots, leeks, onion, cabbage, fennel, and garlic. Combine with the parsley, thyme, and mushrooms in a large soup pot. Add the water. Cover, bring to a boil, then reduce the heat and simmer for 30 minutes.

2 Add the wine and peppercorns and continue to simmer, covered, for 10 minutes. Strain and discard all the solids.

3 Season to taste with salt, or leave unsalted and use as a base for soups and grain dishes. Use immediately or cool, then refrigerate. It will keep for about 5 days in the refrigerator or 4 to 6 months in the freezer.

chicken broth

Save chicken parts, such as wings, backs, and necks, for making broth. If you are buying chicken specifically to make broth, buy dark meat. It is less expensive than white meat and more flavorful. The additional fat in the dark meat will be skimmed off and discarded.

YIELD: 2–3 QUARTS

3–4 pounds chicken parts
1 large onion, quartered
4 stalks celery
4 garlic cloves
1 bunch parsley
4 quarts water
Salt (optional)

1 Combine the chicken, onion, celery, garlic, and parsley in a large soup pot. Add the water. Cover and bring just to a boil. Immediately reduce the heat and simmer gently for 2 hours with the lid partially on. Do not allow the soup to boil.

2 Strain and discard the vegetables. Remove the meat from the bones and save the meat for another use, such as chicken salad.

3 Chill the broth for several hours. Skim off the fat that rises to the top and hardens.

4 Season to taste with salt, if desired. Use immediately or cool, then refrigerate. It will keep for about 3 days in the refrigerator or 4 to 6 months in the freezer.

basic pie pastry

This recipe can be used for two single-crust pies or free-form tarts or one double crust.

■ **MAKES PASTRY FOR 9-INCH OR 10-INCH PIES OR TARTS** ■

2 cups unbleached all-purpose flour

1 teaspoon salt

⅔ cup butter or vegetable shortening

6–7 tablespoons cold water

1 Mix together the flour and salt in a food processor. Add the butter and process until the mixture resembles coarse crumbs. With the motor running, add the water. Alternatively, stir together the flour and salt in a medium bowl. Cut the butter into the flour with a pastry blender or two knives until the mixture resembles coarse crumbs. Sprinkle the water over the flour mixture and stir together. Press the mixture into two disks, wrap in plastic wrap, and refrigerate for 30 minutes.

2 Lightly flour a surface and roll out one ball of dough on the surface, working from the center out in all directions until you have a 12-inch round. If you are making a single-crust pie, fold the dough in half and ease into the pie pan with the fold in the center. Unfold the dough and trim it to the edge of the pie pan. If you are making a tart, transfer to a baking sheet by partially rolling the dough onto the rolling pin, then unrolling it onto the baking sheet. The tart shell is now ready to bake.

3 If you are making a double-crust pie, roll out the second piece of dough in the same manner, but make into a slightly larger circle. Place on the filled pie. Trim the dough ½ inch beyond the edge of the pie plate. Fold the extra under the bottom crust. Crimp the edges. Prick holes into the top piece of dough in several places to allow steam to escape. Bake as directed.

4 To bake the dough for an unfilled single crust, preheat the oven to 450°F. Fit the bottom crust into the pie pan as directed in step 2, and trim and crimp the edges. Prick the dough with a fork, covering the surface with tiny holes. For a partially baked crust, bake for 5 to 10 minutes, until barely colored. For a fully baked crust, bake 10 to 15 minutes, until browned. Let cool or use as directed.

prosciutto chips

Consider these bacon bites done right. Prosciutto chips make a terrific topping for a salad, without the greasiness of bacon. Also, the process of making chips will not leave your kitchen smelling like a diner during the breakfast rush.

■ **MAKES 2 CUPS** ■   4 paper-thin slices prosciutto (about 2 ounces)

1 Preheat the oven to 400°F.

2 Cut the prosciutto into ½-inch strips and lay them out on two rimmed, ungreased baking sheets in a single layer.

3 Roast for 5 to 8 minutes, until crisp and darkened but not burned.

4 Use immediately or store for a few days in the refrigerator. To restore the crisp texture, heat in a 300° F oven for 3 to 4 minutes.

basic pizza dough

I make pizza fairly often, and there are several pizza recipes throughout the book. To turn this dough into pizza, spread tomato sauce over the dough, sprinkle with grated cheese, and top with lightly cooked vegetables or other toppings. Bake at 500°F for 12 to 15 minutes.

MAKES TWO 10-INCH TO 12-INCH ROUND OR TWO 12 X 15-INCH RECTANGULAR PIZZAS

4 cups unbleached all-purpose flour
1 tablespoon salt
1½ cups warm (110° to 115°F) water
1 packet (¼ ounce) or 1 tablespoon active dry yeast
3 tablespoons olive oil

1 In a food processor fitted with a dough hook or in a large bowl, combine 3¾ cups of the flour and the salt. Measure the warm water into a glass measure, add the yeast, and stir until foamy. Stir in the olive oil.

2 With the motor running, pour the water mixture into the food processor and process until the dough forms into a ball. Continue processing for 1 minute to knead the dough. Alternatively, add the yeast mixture to the dough and stir until the dough comes together in a ball. Use the remaining ¼ cup to lightly flour a work surface. Turn the dough onto the surface and knead until the dough is springy and elastic, about 5 minutes. The dough should be firm and just slightly sticky — not dry.

3 Grease a bowl with oil and place the dough ball in the bowl, turning the dough to coat with the oil. Cover and let rise in a warm, draft-free place until doubled in bulk, about 1 hour.

4 Divide the dough into two balls. Brush two baking sheets or pizza pans with oil. Stretch the dough to fit each pan. The dough is now ready for topping with sauce and vegetables.

basic cheese sauce

I find most kids are delighted when asparagus, broccoli, Brussels sprouts, cauliflower, or green beans are served with a cheese sauce. You can use this sauce to make a gratin (see page 26) or crêpes (see page 28). You can also make a white vegetable lasagna with this sauce, layering sautéed or grilled summer vegetables (bell peppers, summer squash, cherry tomatoes, eggplant, green beans, spinach, broccoli, broccoli rabe) with sheets of lasagna and cheese sauce. Use this sauce to make macaroni and cheese, and fold in blanched asparagus, broccoli, broccoli raab, cauliflower, green beans, or spinach. Or fold in diced and drained tomatoes or halved cherry tomatoes.

MAKES ABOUT 2½ CUPS

4 tablespoons butter

¼ cup unbleached all-purpose flour

2 cups milk

1–1½ cups grated Cheddar, Fontina, Swiss, Gruyère, or Jarlsberg

Salt and freshly ground black pepper

1 Melt the butter over medium heat in a medium saucepan. Blend in the flour with a wooden spoon to make a smooth paste. Cook for 2 minutes, stirring constantly.

2 Stir in the milk, a little at a time, until the sauce is thick and smooth. Bring to a boil, stirring constantly. Stir in the cheese and cook until smooth and melted, about 2 minutes longer.

3 Season to taste with the salt and pepper. Serve hot.

herbed croutons

When I make fresh croutons, I'm lucky if I end up with enough to use in whatever recipe I'm planning to make because little (and big) hands constantly try to steal these irresistible morsels.

Have a kid who doesn't like salad? Top the salad with croutons. Have another one who doesn't like broccoli? Nap it with cheese sauce and top it with croutons. Croutons can form the crumb topping on a casserole, make a quick stuffing for a chicken, enliven the filling of a stuffed eggplant, or turn a quick vegetable sauté into a treat for all ages.

■ **MAKES ABOUT 5 CUPS** ■

1 pound slightly stale Italian, French, or other white bread
⅓ cup extra-virgin olive oil
3 garlic cloves, minced
2 teaspoons herbes de Provence (see page 7)
Salt and freshly ground black pepper

1 Cut the bread into ½-inch cubes. (It is more tedious to make small croutons, but they have more uses in a small size; if you are just using them to top a salad, ¾-inch cubes are fine.) You will have about 6 cups of cubes.

2 Heat the oil in a large skillet over medium heat. Add the bread cubes, garlic, and herbs. Season with salt and pepper. Fry, stirring occasionally, until cubes are crisp and golden, 20 to 30 minutes.

3 Let cool in the pan. Store in an airtight jar at room temperature for 3 to 4 days.

roasted peppers

Peppers — both sweet bell peppers and chiles — are often roasted before they are added to a recipe. This can be done in quantities, in which case a grill or oven is used, or one at a time, in which case a gas burner can be used.

Bell peppers or fresh chile peppers of any color or variety
Extra-virgin olive oil to store, if necessary

1 Preheat the broiler and lightly grease a baking sheet with oil.

2 Place the peppers on the baking sheet with space between each one. Broil 4 inches from the heat until charred all over, turning several times, 10 to 20 minutes.

3 Place the peppers in a covered bowl, plastic bag, or paper bag. Seal and allow the peppers to steam for about 10 minutes to loosen the skins.

4 Slit the peppers to catch the juice that runs from them. If possible, incorporate the juice into the dish that requires the pepper to enhance the pepper flavor. Scrape or peel the skins and discard. Scrape and discard the seeds and membranes.

5 Leave the peppers whole or slice, as the recipe requires. To store, place in a jar and cover with the olive oil. Refrigerate for up to 2 weeks.

Gas Burner Variation

If you have a gas burner and wish to roast only one pepper at a time, simply char the pepper over the gas flame, holding the pepper with tongs. Rotate the pepper so that it chars evenly, 10 to 15 minutes. Then place in a covered container and proceed as above.

Grill Roast Variation

To roast the peppers over a grill, prepare a medium-hot fire in a grill or preheat a gas grill on high. Place the peppers on the grill and grill until charred all over, turning several times; this will take 10 to 15 minutes. Proceed with the recipe as above.

MASTERING THE BASICS: METHODS & RECIPES

My mother taught me a great deal about cooking, but I don't recall her ever consulting a cookbook. She learned from her mother, who learned from her mother, and so on. I did learn some techniques from formal courses, a lot from on-the-job training in various sweaty commercial kitchens, and even more from kibitzing in friends' kitchens. For those who haven't had the same opportunities, here are a few basic techniques and master formulas.

BASIC COOKING METHODS

One rule of thumb applies to all cooking with vegetables: Use your judgment as to when your vegetables are done. Vegetables are not uniform from garden to garden or from day to day. Rainy seasons produce vegetables with higher water content than dry seasons. Stressed vegetables tend to be woody or fibrous. Overripe vegetables may be extra tender or waterlogged. A vegetable held for a week in the refrigerator is not the same as a freshly harvested vegetable. When cooking, judging when a vegetable is done is never simply a matter of using a timer accurately.

Boiling and Blanching Vegetables

Boiling or blanching vegetables is easy. Both are done in a large pot of generously salted boiling water. Blanching vegetables means adding the vegetables to rapidly boiling water and boiling until just barely tender. They are cooked just long enough to set the color and partially soften the texture. The vegetables are then drained and plunged into a bowl of ice water to stop the cooking process. Vegetables that are blanched may then be dried and frozen to preserve them. Or they can be quickly finished in a sauté. Boiled vegetables are cooked until tender, drained, and eaten.

- Large root vegetables and potatoes do best if they are started in cold water to cover. Bring the water to a boil over high heat, then boil gently until the vegetables are tender.
- Most green vegetables and cauliflower should be added to already boiling water and boiled vigorously.
- Don't cover the pot when blanching or boiling.
- Check the vegetables for tenderness by removing a piece with a slotted spoon and biting into it. Large vegetables, such as potatoes and beets, are done when you can easily pierce them with a fork or skewer.

Steaming Vegetables

To steam vegetables, bring a few inches of water to a boil, place the vegetables in a steaming basket or colander, place the basket over the boiling water, cover the pot, and cook the vegetables until tender. Here are the general guidelines.

- Steamed vegetables are similar in taste and texture to boiled vegetables.
- Steaming takes slightly longer than boiling vegetables.
- Steaming works best with small quantities of vegetables.

- Steamed vegetables are fine served plain, but a pat of butter and a sprinkling of fresh herbs or chopped nuts go far in enlivening the flavors. Steamed vegetables are also enhanced with a drizzle of vinaigrette or browned butter, or a dollop of cheese sauce (see page 13). Steamed vegetables dipped in aioli (see page 380) are heavenly. Toasted bread crumbs also can be used to add flavor and crunch.

Sautéing and Stir-Frying Vegetables

Sautéing and stir-frying add flavor to vegetables by cooking the vegetables in butter or oil, often with the addition of garlic, onions, ginger, or other aromatics. Flavor is also added when the vegetables are browned, a process that caramelizes the sugars on the surface of the vegetables. Sautéing and stir-frying are quite similar in that the food is cooked over intense heat with just a little fat. Stir-fried foods are always cut up, and stir-frying is best done in a wok. Sautéed foods may or may not be cut up, and sautéing is usually done in a skillet or sauté pan.

- Choose a heavy-bottomed pan for even heating.
- Don't crowd the vegetables or they will steam rather than sauté or stir-fry.
- A pan that is too large is better than a pan that is too small.
- A little bit of butter or oil is essential, even with nonstick pans — mainly for flavor. Extra-virgin olive oil is my oil of choice for most sautés, but canola oil can be used for a more neutral flavor. Like olive oil, it is a monounsaturated fat, one of the so-called good fats.

- The addition of minced garlic, chopped onions or shallots, or chopped bacon or prosciutto adds considerable flavor to sautéed vegetables. For an Asian stir-fry, minced garlic and ginger often are essential additions.
- For quick and even cooking, keep the vegetables moving in the pan or wok.

Braising Vegetables

Braising involves slowly cooking vegetables over low heat in a small amount of broth or another aromatic liquid. The resulting vegetables are meltingly tender and very flavorful, and the braising liquid becomes the sauce that is served with the vegetable.

- Braising is perfect for slightly tough or overripe vegetables, such as overgrown green beans.
- Use a high-quality vegetable or chicken broth for the braising liquid (see recipes pages 8 and 9). Additions of dry wine or sherry enhance the flavor.
- Usually, the vegetables are briefly sautéed in olive oil, butter, or bacon fat to add flavor, then they are simmered in the braising liquid until tender.

Grilling Vegetables

Grilling is an excellent way to cook vegetables. The high heat caramelizes the sugars in the vegetables and enhances the flavor. Grilling vegetables lets you prepare a feast without heating up the kitchen during the hot summer. It is also wonderfully convenient to grill vegetables when you are also grilling meats. Here are a few tips.

- Grill vegetables over a hot fire.
- With vegetables, the question of charcoal versus gas is not particularly relevant in terms of flavor. Because vegetables cook quickly, the fire does not impart much in the way of smoke flavor. However, unless you have a large gas grill that puts out a lot of BTUs, you are better off with a charcoal grill because it will cook the vegetables more quickly and evenly.
- A vegetable-grilling rack is a relatively inexpensive and very useful piece of equipment. It is a flat metal plate drilled with holes. Place the grilling rack on top of the grill grate, and it prevents small pieces of vegetables from falling into the fire. This enables you to chop vegetables into bite-size pieces before grilling and to cook mixtures of vegetables together.
- When grilling bite-size pieces on a grill rack, toss the vegetables frequently for even cooking. A pair of long-handled tongs works best. You can also use a flat metal spatula or a pair of spatulas — one in each hand.
- A grill wok has less surface area directly in contact with the grill than a vegetable grilling rack. Vegetables tend to cook more slowly and to steam rather than grill. Grilling baskets are less effective than grilling racks because fires are rarely even, so one area cooks faster than another, but the entire basket must be turned or removed from the heat at the same time. Also, people tend to crowd vegetables into a grilling basket, making it likely that the vegetables will cook via steam rather than the dry heat of the grill.

- Vegetables should be slicked with oil before they are grilled to enhance the browning process and prevent the vegetables from drying out. I don't advise using butter unless the vegetables will be served hot; the butter will start to congeal as the vegetables cool.
- Vegetables can be tossed with marinades for added flavor before grilling, but lengthy marinating times are not necessary. With the exception of eggplants, garden vegetables do not absorb marinades, so time spent in a marinade has no impact on the final dish.
- Grilled vegetables can be used to top pasta and pizzas, folded into omelets and frittatas, stuffed into sandwiches, and tossed into salads.

Roasting Vegetables

Roasting is an excellent way to prepare vegetables. The dry heat coaxes out and concentrates flavors. Even vegetables that have few fans, like parsnips, can be surprisingly delicious when roasted. Roasted green beans are so delicious, they can be served as a snack.

- To prepare vegetables for roasting, cut into uniform-size pieces and slick with oil.
- Spread out the vegetables on a lightly oiled large sheet pan (preferred) or shallow roasting pan. The sheet pan is preferred because its low sides allow better air circulation. Shallow roasting pans will do the job, however. In either case, do not crowd the vegetables or they will steam rather than roast.
- Generally, vegetables are roasted at 450°F.
- Shake the pan, or flip the vegetables with a spatula, once or twice during roasting to ensure even cooking.
- You can roast mixtures of vegetables as long as they are cut to uniformly small pieces.
- Roasted root vegetables are delicious and beautiful; roasted green vegetables are equally delicious but somewhat less than beautiful.
- Roasted vegetables can be served with a sprinkling of coarse sea salt or kosher salt and a drizzle of balsamic vinegar or a squeeze of fresh lemon. Vinaigrettes make a fine topping for roasted vegetables.

FOR THOSE NIGHTS when the bounty from the garden or farmer's market is just too overwhelming to try a new recipe, here are fourteen master recipes to use throughout the year. There's not much difference between making a quiche with broccoli and making one with spinach, or stir-frying green beans and stir-frying cabbage. A gratin of Swiss chard is assembled just like one made with potatoes. Most recipes require blanching the vegetables first, and cooking times for blanched vegetables can be found at the start of the individual vegetable chapters. Blanched greens, such as spinach, should be squeezed to further remove excess water.

sautéed vegetable medley with fresh herbs

A side dish of sautéed vegetables is welcome with almost every meal. The trick is to blanch the vegetables, then finish in the pan. All of the vegetables are optional — use whatever you have on hand.

■ **SERVES 4** ■

1 medium zucchini or other summer squash, julienned

2 teaspoons salt

2 tablespoons extra-virgin olive oil

1 shallot or 2 garlic cloves, minced

1 bell pepper or 1 small fennel bulb, cut into strips

1 cup shelled peas, sugar snap peas, snow peas, or corn kernels

1–2 cups mix of blanched vegetables, such as julienned asparagus, broccoli stems, carrots, celery root, snap beans

Salt and freshly ground black pepper

2 tablespoons chopped or torn fresh herbs (basil, mint, oregano, rosemary, sage, summer savory, tarragon, thyme, alone or in any combination)

1 If you are using zucchini or summer squash, toss with the salt in a colander and set aside for 30 minutes. Squeeze dry.

2 Heat the oil in a large skillet over medium-high heat. Add the shallot or garlic and sauté until fragrant and very slightly colored, about 1 minute.

3 Add the uncooked vegetables (bell pepper, fennel, peas, snap peas, snow peas, and/or corn) and sauté until slightly softened, 1 to 2 minutes. Add the blanched vegetables (asparagus, broccoli, cauliflower, carrots, celery root, and/or snap beans) and continue to sauté until heated through, 2 to 3 minutes.

4 Season generously with salt and pepper. Sprinkle with the herbs. Sauté for 1 minute longer. Serve hot.

mixed roasted summer vegetables

The lemon-garlic marinade is baked into the vegetables while they are roasting, brightening the rather bland flavors of summer squash.

SERVES 4

2 garlic cloves, minced

¼ cup chopped or torn fresh herbs (basil, mint, oregano, parsley, sage, thyme, alone or in any combination)

Zest of ¼ lemon, minced

2 tablespoons fresh lemon juice

3 tablespoons extra-virgin olive oil

Salt and freshly ground black pepper

8 cups diced or julienned summer vegetables, such as baby artichoke halves, bell peppers, broccoli, carrots, cauliflower, chiles, corn kernels, eggplant, fennel, green or wax beans, leeks, okra, onions or scallions, summer squash, and zucchini

Coarse sea salt

1 Preheat the oven to 425°F. Lightly grease a large sheet pan (preferred) or shallow roasting pan with oil.

2 Pulse the garlic, herbs, lemon zest, and juice in a food processor to blend. With the motor running, slowly add the oil and process until it is fully incorporated. Add salt and pepper to taste.

3 In a large bowl, combine the vegetables. Pour the lemon-herb mixture over them and toss to coat. Transfer the vegetables to the pan and spread out in a single layer.

4 Roast for 15 to 25 minutes, until the vegetables are lightly browned and tender, stirring or shaking the pan occasionally for even cooking.

5 Transfer the vegetables to a serving bowl or platter. Sprinkle with the sea salt. Serve warm or at room temperature.

mixed grilled summer vegetables

Flame-kissed vegetables are worth the effort to start a fire in the grill. The perfect accompaniment to any meal — vegetarian or otherwise — grilled garden vegetables are delicious. Enjoy them as a side dish, a topping for pizza or pasta, or stuffed into a pita with cheese. A vegetable grill rack is necessary for this recipe.

SERVES 4

⅓ cup extra-virgin olive oil

2 tablespoons fresh lemon juice or red wine vinegar

2 garlic cloves, minced

1–2 tablespoons chopped or torn fresh herbs (basil, mint, oregano, rosemary, sage, summer savory, tarragon, thyme, alone or in any combination)

8 cups mixed uniformly cubed or sliced vegetables, such as baby artichoke halves, asparagus, bell peppers, broccoli, cauliflower, chiles, corn kernels, eggplant, fennel, garlic cloves, leeks, okra, onions or scallions, snap beans, summer squash and zucchini, and halved cherry tomatoes

Coarse sea salt and freshly ground black pepper

1 Prepare a medium-hot fire in the grill with a lightly oiled vegetable grill rack in place.

2 Combine the olive oil, lemon juice, garlic, and herbs in a large bowl. Add the vegetables and toss to coat.

3 Lift half the vegetables out of the marinade with a slotted spoon and transfer to the grill rack. Grill, tossing frequently with tongs or two spatulas, until the vegetables are tender and grill-marked, about 10 minutes. Transfer to a serving platter, keep warm, and repeat with the remaining vegetables.

4 Drizzle the remaining marinade over the vegetables, if desired, and sprinkle with the salt and pepper to taste. Serve warm.

Anytime you fire up the grill, consider making garlic toasts as an accompaniment. They add a lot to a meal, with very little effort. On a hot summer night, garlic toasts with marinated garden tomatoes, some grilled zucchini, and perhaps some cheese make a perfect meal.

SERVES 4   1 loaf coarse-textured Italian or French bread
2 garlic cloves, peeled and halved

1 Prepare a medium fire in a charcoal grill or preheat a gas grill on medium.

2 Slice the bread ¾ inch thick.

3 Grill one side of the bread until lightly toasted, about 2 minutes. Turn and rub the toasted side with the garlic. Grill the second side until lightly toasted, about 2 minutes. Rub that side with garlic. Serve warm.

herb-roasted root vegetables

Of all the possible ways to prepare root vegetables, roasting is probably everyone's favorite. The vegetables hold up well on a buffet table or in a covered dish, if you cannot serve them immediately. Be warned, however, that what starts out looking like a huge amount of food reduces down to a fairly small serving size. The roasting time is longer for this large quantity than it would be for a smaller amount. Winter squash is not a root vegetable, but has similar cooking properties and works well with root vegetables.

SERVES 4–6

3–4 pounds winter squash and mixed root vegetables, such as beets, carrots, parsnips, rutabagas, sweet potatoes, turnips, and white potatoes, peeled and cut into 1-inch cubes

1 cup pearl onions or shallots, peeled and left whole (cut shallots in half or quarters if large)

1 head garlic, cloves separated and peeled

3 tablespoons extra-virgin olive oil

2 tablespoons chopped fresh herbs (rosemary, sage, thyme, alone or in any combination)

Coarse sea salt or kosher salt and freshly ground black pepper

1 tablespoon chopped fresh parsley

1 Preheat the oven to 425°F. Lightly grease a large sheet pan with oil.

2 Combine the mixed vegetables, pearl onions, and garlic in a large bowl. Add the oil, herbs, and salt and pepper to taste. Toss to coat. Transfer the vegetables to the pan and spread out in a single shallow layer.

3 Roast for about 1 hour, or until the vegetables are lightly browned and tender, stirring or shaking the pan occasionally for even cooking.

4 Transfer to a serving platter, taste, and add more salt and pepper if needed. Sprinkle with the parsley and serve.

cheese quiche with vegetables

If you like, add ½ cup diced ham or smoked turkey to give the quiche more substance.

SERVES 4-6

1 unbaked crust for a 9-inch or 10-inch single-crust pie (page 10)

¾ cup grated Swiss, Gruyère, or Jarlsberg cheese

1–1½ cups chopped or diced blanched mixed vegetables, such as artichokes, asparagus, broccoli, broccoli rabe, cauliflower, chard, corn kernels, fennel, leeks, snap beans, and spinach

2 tablespoons chopped fresh chives or scallions

3 eggs

Milk or cream

Salt and freshly ground black pepper

1–2 tablespoons finely chopped fresh basil

Tomato Quiche
If you'd like to use tomatoes, use 2 cups seeded diced tomatoes. Combine the tomatoes with 2 teaspoons salt in a colander and let drain for at least 30 minutes. Toss the tomatoes with 1 tablespoon flour before transferring to the crust.

1 Preheat the oven to 425°F.

2 Bake the crust for 5 minutes, until lightly colored. Remove from the oven and let cool. Reduce the oven temperature to 375°F.

3 Sprinkle ½ cup of the cheese in the crust. Make a layer of the vegetables on top of the cheese. Sprinkle with the chives.

4 Beat the eggs in a glass measuring cup. Add enough milk to make 1½ cups. Season with salt and pepper. Pour over the vegetables. Sprinkle the remaining ¼ cup cheese and the basil over the quiche.

5 Bake for 30 to 35 minutes, until puffed and browned. Let stand for at least 10 minutes. Serve warm or at room temperature.

vegetable gratin

Vegetable gratins are generally considered side dishes, but I think they make a fine main course for a vegetarian meal. Leftovers are a personal favorite for breakfast. Gratins can be assembled several hours in advance and baked at the last minute.

SERVES 4

2½ cups Basic Cheese Sauce (page 13)

4 cups diced or chopped blanched mixed vegetables, such as artichokes, asparagus, Belgian endives, broccoli, broccoli rabe, Brussels sprouts, cauliflower, celery, chard, corn kernels, fennel, leeks, okra, snap beans, spinach, and winter squash

1 onion, halved and thinly sliced

Salt and freshly ground black pepper

½ cup grated Swiss, Gruyère, or Jarlsberg cheese

⅓ cup dried bread crumbs (optional)

1 Preheat the oven to 425°F.

2 Lightly grease a 2-quart baking dish with butter or oil. Spread a little cheese sauce in the dish. Layer the mixed vegetables and onion in the dish. Season generously with salt and pepper. Cover with the remaining sauce. Top with the grated cheese and bread crumbs, if using.

3 Bake for 20 to 30 minutes, until heated through and browned on top. Serve hot.

fettuccine alfredo with vegetables

Luxurious and rich are the only ways to describe fettuccine Alfredo. You can justify this indulgence by adding heaps of vegetables.

SERVES 6

2 tablespoons extra-virgin olive oil

1 garlic clove, minced

4 cups blanched, julienned vegetables, such as artichokes, asparagus, bell peppers, broccoli, broccoli rabe, carrots, cauliflower, chard, Belgian endives, fennel, leeks, spinach, and summer squash

1½ cups half-and-half

Salt and freshly ground black pepper

1¼ pounds fresh fettuccine, or 1 pound dried

1 tablespoon butter

1 cup freshly grated Parmigiano-Reggiano cheese

5 fresh basil leaves, cut into ribbons, for garnish (optional)

1 Begin heating a large pot of salted water for the pasta.

2 Heat the oil in a large skillet over medium-high heat. Add the garlic and sauté until fragrant, about 30 seconds. Add the vegetables and sauté until heated through, about 3 minutes. Transfer to a saucepan with a slotted spoon.

3 Place the saucepan over low heat. Add the half-and-half. Season to taste with salt and pepper. Keep over low heat.

4 Cook the pasta in the boiling water until al dente. Drain briefly.

5 Transfer the pasta to a large serving bowl and toss with the butter and cheese. Pour the vegetable sauce over the pasta and toss again. Taste and adjust the seasoning, adding more salt and pepper as desired. Garnish with the basil and serve at once.

cheese and vegetable crêpes

Crêpes are much easier to make than you might expect, provided you have a good nonstick or well-seasoned crêpe pan. Crêpes can be made in advance, layered between sheets of waxed paper, and refrigerated overnight or frozen for up to a month. If you've never made crêpes before, consider making a double batch of batter, to have extra for throwing out the crêpes that don't come out right. Also, the most common mistake is making the crêpes too thick, which means you will be short on batter. You can substitute Cheddar for Swiss, but omit the nutmeg.

SERVES 4–6

Crêpes

- ½ cup unbleached all-purpose flour
- ½ cup milk
- ¼ cup lukewarm water
- 2 eggs
- 2 tablespoons butter, melted, plus additional butter to grease the pan
- ½ teaspoon salt

Filling

- 2 ½ cups Basic Cheese Sauce, made with Swiss, Gruyère, or Jarlsburg cheese (page 13)
- 1 egg, lightly beaten
- 1 tablespoon dry sherry (optional)
- 2 cups finely chopped blanched mixed vegetables, such as artichokes, asparagus, broccoli, broccoli rabe, cauliflower, chard, Belgian endives, fennel, leeks, and spinach
  Salt and freshly ground black pepper
  Pinch of freshly grated fresh nutmeg
  Milk, as needed
- ⅔ cup grated Swiss, Gruyère, or Jarlsberg

1 To prepare the crêpe batter, combine the flour, milk, water, eggs, butter, and salt in a blender and process until smooth. Set aside at room temperature for 30 minutes or refrigerate for up to 2 days.

2 To make the crêpes, have waxed paper ready. Melt a little butter (about ½ teaspoon) in a nonstick or well-seasoned crêpe pan over medium heat. Swirl the pan to distribute the butter. When the butter foams, stir the batter and pour in about 2 tablespoons, lifting the pan off the heat and swirling the pan until the batter forms a very thin, even layer. Place the pan over the heat and cook until the top is set and the bottom is browned, about 1½ minutes. Turn the crêpe over using tongs, your fingers, or a spatula and cook until the second side is lightly browned, about 30 seconds. Transfer the crêpe to a piece of the waxed paper. Continue cooking crêpes, adding a little butter and stirring the batter before starting each one.

3 To make the filling, reserve 1 cup of the cheese sauce. Beat the egg and sherry into the remaining 1½ cups sauce. Fold in the vegetables. Season generously with salt and pepper. Add the nutmeg.

4 To fill the crêpes, grease a baking dish with butter. The dish should be large enough to hold twelve rolled crêpes in a single layer. Place a crêpe, attractive-side down, on a work surface. Spoon 2 to 3 tablespoons of the filling on the bottom third of each crêpe and roll up. Place seam-side down in the prepared baking dish.

5 Preheat the oven to 400°F.

6 Reheat the reserved cheese sauce until hot. Stir in a little milk, 1 tablespoon at a time, to thin the sauce to a pouring consistency. Pour over the crêpes. Sprinkle with the grated cheese.

7 Bake for about 25 minutes, until the sauce is bubbling and the cheese is melted. Serve hot.

fettuccine with vegetables in a light tomato sauce

For such an uncomplicated dish like this, it is best to use fresh pasta and real Parmigiano-Reggiano from Italy. Vegetarians take note: This is best made with chicken broth, but you can substitute half water and half white wine.

■ SERVES 4–6 ■

3 tablespoons extra-virgin olive oil

3 tablespoons butter

2–4 garlic cloves, minced

4 cups blanched, julienned vegetables (pages 16–17), such as artichokes, asparagus, bell peppers, broccoli, broccoli rabe, carrots, cauliflower, chard, corn kernels, Belgian endives, fennel, leeks, peas, sugar snap peas, snap beans, snow peas, spinach, or summer squash, alone or in any combination

¼ cup chopped or torn fresh herbs (basil, mint, oregano, parsley, alone or in any combination)

2 ripe tomatoes, seeded and diced, or 1½ cups halved or quartered cherry tomatoes, or 1½ cups canned diced tomatoes

1 cup chicken broth (see page 9)

Salt and freshly ground black pepper

1¼ pounds fresh spinach fettuccine or half spinach fettuccine and half egg fettuccine, or 1 pound dried fettuccine

1 cup freshly grated Parmigiano-Reggiano, plus additional for serving

1 Begin heating a large pot of salted water for the pasta.

2 Heat the oil and butter in a large skillet over medium-high heat. Add the garlic and sauté until fragrant, about 30 seconds. Add the vegetables and sauté until heated through, 3 to 5 minutes. Stir in the herbs, tomatoes, and broth and season to taste with salt and pepper. Keep warm.

3 Cook the pasta in the boiling water until al dente. Drain briefly.

4 Transfer the pasta to a serving bowl. Add the vegetable mixture and toss to coat. Add the cheese and toss again. Season generously with salt and pepper. Serve the dish hot, passing additional cheese at the table.

pesto pasta with vegetables

No summer is complete without pasta dressed with pesto. But why limit yourself to summer? Pesto freezes well, so you can enjoy pesto pasta anytime. Use whatever vegetables you have available.

SERVES 4–6

1 medium zucchini or other summer squash, julienned

1 large tomato, seeded and diced, or 1½ cups halved cherry tomatoes

2 teaspoons salt

3 tablespoons extra-virgin olive oil

1 green, red, or yellow bell pepper or 1 small fennel bulb, cut into strips

1 cup sugar snap peas, snow peas, or corn kernels

2 cups blanched asparagus or green beans cut into 2-inch lengths, or chopped broccoli or cauliflower florets

1 cup blanched julienned artichokes, carrots, green beans, celery root, alone or in combination

1¼ pounds fresh linguine, or 1 pound dried

⅔ cup pesto sauce, store-bought or homemade (page 6), at room temperature

Salt and freshly ground black pepper

Toasted pine nuts (see Note), to garnish (optional)

1 If you are using zucchini, summer squash, and/or tomatoes, combine the vegetables with 2 teaspoons salt in a colander. Toss to mix and set aside to drain for 30 minutes. Pat dry with paper towels.

2 Begin heating a large pot of salted water for the pasta.

3 Heat the oil in a large skillet over medium-high heat. Add any uncooked vegetables (bell peppers, fennel, snap peas, snow peas, corn, zucchini, summer squash, and/or tomatoes) and sauté until tender-crisp, 3 to 5 minutes. Add the blanched vegetables (artichokes, asparagus, green beans, broccoli, cauliflower, carrots, and/or celery root) and sauté to heat through, another 3 to 5 minutes. Keep warm.

4 Cook the pasta in the boiling water until al dente. Reserve about ½ cup of the pasta cooking water and briefly drain the pasta.

5 Return the pasta to the pot. Add the pesto and as much as the reserved cooking water as needed to create a sauce. Toss to coat. Add all the vegetables and toss to mix. Season with salt and pepper.

6 Transfer the pasta to individual serving bowls or a large serving bowl. Garnish with pine nuts, if desired, and serve.

note To toast pine nuts, pour a handful of nuts into a small skillet over medium heat. Toast, stirring frequently, until the nuts are fragrant and very lightly browned, about 5 minutes. Watch carefully and do not let the nuts scorch.

basic stir-fry

If I had my druthers, I'd probably make stir-fries on most nights. It is important to have all the vegetables prepped and all the ingredients assembled before you start cooking. And don't forget to start cooking the rice first. I have an electric rice cooker, purchased years ago. It is an appliance that gets regular use and more than justified its purchase price.

SERVES 4

1 pound boneless, skinless chicken, beef, or pork, sliced into matchsticks, or 1 pound extra-firm tofu, pressed and cubed (see Note)

5 tablespoons soy sauce

3 tablespoons oyster sauce

2 tablespoons rice wine or dry sherry

1 tablespoon sugar

2 teaspoons dark sesame oil

¼ teaspoon freshly ground black pepper

½ cup vegetable or chicken broth (see page 8 or 9)

1 tablespoon cornstarch

3 tablespoons peanut or canola oil

1 onion, halved and cut into slivers, or 1 leek, white and tender green parts only, thinly sliced

4 cups chopped or diced firm vegetables such as asparagus, broccoli, carrots, baby corn, snap beans, snow peas, snap peas, corn kernels, and shelled peas, alone or in any combination

8 cups slivered greens (cabbage, bok choy, broccoli rabe, chard, escarole, or kale)

1 piece fresh ginger (1 inch long), peeled and minced

3–4 garlic cloves, minced

Hot cooked white rice

note Pressing tofu releases excess moisture. Wrap the tofu block in several layers of paper towels or a clean kitchen towel. Place a weight on top of the tofu, such as a heavy cutting board. Leave for 10 to 30 minutes. The tofu will compress and excess water will be forced out. Cut into cubes. Then proceed with the recipe as above.

1 Combine the meat or tofu, 2 tablespoons of the soy sauce, the oyster sauce, 1 tablespoon of the wine, and the sugar, sesame oil, and pepper in a medium bowl and set aside to marinate.

2 To make the sauce, combine the broth, 1 tablespoon of the soy sauce, the remaining 1 tablespoon of wine, and the cornstarch. Whisk until thoroughly combined and set aside.

3 Heat a large wok or skillet over high heat. Add 1 tablespoon of the peanut or canola oil and heat until very hot. Add the meat or tofu and marinade and stir-fry, stirring constantly, until well browned, 4 to 8 minutes. With a heatproof rubber spatula, scrape out the contents of the wok into a medium bowl and keep warm. Return the wok to high heat.

4 Heat 1 tablespoon of the remaining oil in the wok over high heat until very hot. Add the onion and firm vegetables and stir-fry until slightly softened, about 3 minutes. Add 1 tablespoon of the remaining soy sauce, cover, and let the vegetables steam until soft, 3 to 4 minutes. Remove from the wok and add to the meat or tofu mixture.

5 Return the wok to high heat and add the remaining 1 tablespoon of oil. Add the slivered green vegetables and stir-fry for 1 minute. Add the last 1 tablespoon soy sauce and continue to stir-fry until limp, about 2 minutes longer. Push the vegetables to the sides of the pan and add the ginger and garlic. Cook until fragrant, about 45 seconds. Stir into the vegetables.

6 Return the meat or tofu mixture with the vegetables to the wok and toss to combine. Whisk the sauce and pour into the wok. Stir-fry until the sauce is thickened and evenly coats the vegetables, 1 to 2 minutes.

7 Serve immediately with the hot rice.

basic lo mein

Lo mein doesn't take much effort, uses up loose odds and ends of vegetables in the refrigerator, and everyone loves it. It lends itself to many variations and can be made as a vegetarian dish with tofu.

SERVES 4

Meat or Tofu and Marinade

1 pound boneless, skinless chicken, beef, or pork, sliced into matchsticks, or 1 pound extra-firm tofu, pressed and cubed (see Note)

1 piece fresh ginger (1 inch long), peeled and minced

2 garlic cloves, minced

2 tablespoons soy sauce

1 tablespoon oyster sauce

1 tablespoon Chinese rice wine or dry sherry

1 teaspoon dark sesame oil

1 tablespoon cornstarch

Noodles and Vegetables

1 pound Chinese egg noodles or thin spaghetti

3 tablespoons peanut or canola oil

1 onion, halved and cut into slivers, or 1 leek, white and tender green parts only, thinly sliced

2 cups chopped or julienned firm vegetables (asparagus, broccoli, baby corn, snap beans, snap peas, snow peas, or sugar snap peas, alone or in combination), corn kernels, or shelled peas

1 carrot, cut into matchsticks

2 tablespoons soy sauce, or to taste

4 cups slivered greens, such as bok choy, broccoli rabe, cabbage, chard, escarole, or kale, alone or in any combination

⅓ cup oyster sauce, or to taste

1 cup mung bean sprouts

1 To marinate the meat or tofu, combine it in a bowl with the ginger, garlic, soy sauce, oyster sauce, wine, and sesame oil. Toss to mix well. Add the cornstarch and toss to mix. Set aside while you prepare the remaining ingredients.

2 Cook the noodles in plenty of boiling salted water until al dente. Drain well.

3 Heat a large wok over high heat. Add 2 tablespoons of the oil and heat. Add the meat or tofu and marinade and stir-fry until the meat is cooked through (or the tofu is browned), 4 to 8 minutes. Use a heatproof rubber spatula to scrape out the mixture from the wok and into a bowl, and keep warm.

4 Reheat the wok over high heat. Add the remaining 1 tablespoon oil and the onion and stir-fry until tender, about 4 minutes. Push to the sides of the wok and add the firm vegetables. Stir-fry until slightly tender, about 2 minutes. Add the carrot and 1 tablespoon of the soy sauce. Continue to stir-fry until the carrot is almost tender, about 3 minutes. Add the slivered greens and the remaining 1 tablespoon of soy sauce and stir-fry until all the vegetables are tender, 3 to 6 minutes.

5 Add the noodles, meat or tofu and marinade, oyster sauce, and bean sprouts to the wok. Continue to toss and stir-fry until all the ingredients are thoroughly mixed and heated through, 3 to 4 minutes. Taste and add more soy sauce and oyster sauce, if desired. Serve hot.

tempura

Deep-fried, batter-coated vegetables are a treat, especially when you use a variety of vegetables — and maybe some shrimp as well. This recipe also works for squash blossoms.

SERVES 4

Tempura Batter

- 2 cups unbleached all-purpose flour
- 4 egg yolks
- 1 cup flat beer
- 1 cup cold water
- 1 teaspoon salt

Dipping Sauce

- 6 tablespoons soy sauce
- 6 tablespoons water
- 1 tablespoon minced peeled ginger
- 1 large garlic clove, minced
- 1 ½ teaspoons rice vinegar

Vegetables

- Oil for deep-frying
- 1½ – 2 pounds mix of firm vegetables, such as bell peppers, broccoli, carrots, cauliflower, eggplant, green beans, and summer squash, cut into bite-size pieces
- 1 cup unbleached all-purpose flour

1 To make the batter, combine the flour, egg yolks, beer, water, and salt in a blender. Process until smooth. Allow to sit for at least 30 minutes.

2 To make the dipping sauce, combine the soy sauce, water, ginger, garlic, and vinegar. Set aside.

3 Begin heating 3 to 4 inches of oil in a large, deep saucepan over medium-high heat.

4 When the oil reaches a temperature of 365°F, begin frying. A few pieces at a time, dip the vegetables into the flour, then into batter. Then slip into the hot oil. Fry until the pieces are golden, 3 to 4 minutes.

5 Drain on paper towels or on wire racks set over a baking sheet. Serve immediately, accompanied by the dipping sauce.

spring into summer

ASPARAGUS

PEAS

SPINACH

SALAD GREENS

THE DAY MAY BE DARK AND DREARY with mud or snow, or both, but inside, growlights are humming quietly and the smell of moist earth pervades the air. Tiny green garden plants are poking their heads through the soil of their pots, their temporary homes until the ground outside warms up.

Cooks like myself are getting ready to garden. At least a few dreamy afternoons have been spent poring over seed catalogs. I once asked Ruth Page, one of Vermont's foremost gardeners, someone who is known for her down-to-earth gardening and environmental commentary heard regularly on Vermont Public Radio, how she decides what to grow each year. "Why, we just grow what tastes good," she said, chuckling.

Obviously, anything you grow yourself and eat quickly after harvest is going to taste *good;* the question is, how can you coax the most flavor out of your garden? Many will tell you the place to start is with the seeds. Others will tell you the answer lies in building up the soil. Starting good seeds and building up the soil are both chores for spring. Then comes planting and first harvest.

Between planting and first harvest comes one of my favorite times of the year: the time when the garden is neat and in order. It is a time before the explosion of weeds and bugs, before drought or floods or hailstones. The garden is all promise.

And soon it is time for the first harvest.

A Perennial Favorite

EVERY GARDENING BOOK you'll ever read will tell you that asparagus is not a fussy plant, but it took me three tries in my current garden to establish a bed of it. I'm glad I was persistent, because each spring I am rewarded with an abundant harvest.

Because the asparagus harvest is so early in the season, there is little to distract you from enjoying this elegant vegetable. It is delicious served hot, cold, or at room temperature and requires little in the way of fussy preparation. My favorite way to serve asparagus is to roast the whole stalks lightly and dress with a little lemon juice. It also holds its own in salads, stir-fries, and even soups.

King Louis the XIV of France loved asparagus so much, he built special greenhouses so he could enjoy it year-round. The season for garden-grown asparagus begins as early as February in California and as late as June in New England. Although imports make it possible to buy asparagus all year, it is more than worthwhile to grow your own. Age affects the flavor of asparagus enormously — the fresher it is, the sweeter and more tender the stalks.

The harvest season will last 4 to 8 weeks, depending on how quickly the weather warms up. You can expect 8 to 10 spears from each root, once the plants are well established.

GROWING Asparagus is a perennial plant that can be expected to be productive for about 20 years. It does best in sandy, well-drained soil with generous water and at least 8 hours of sun.

SOWING Plant outdoors about 3 weeks before the last frost (when daffodils bloom). In very warm areas, such as the southwestern part of the United States, fall or winter planting may be preferred. Plants started from root crowns will be productive 3 years before plants started from seed.

CULTIVATING Asparagus is a heavy feeder, so apply compost or well-rotted manure throughout the growing season. Keep the bed well weeded. A mulch of straw or hay will help with weed control and keep the soil moist.

HARVESTING Starting the second spring after planting root crowns, harvest spears that are at least as thick as a pencil when they are 6 to 8 inches tall. You want the tips to have tight buds, so check for harvesting every day during the season. Cut the stalks with a knife or snap off with your hands. Let skinny spears develop into ferns. Stop harvesting when most of the emerging spears are thin and the tips are loose and open.

ASPARAGUS MATH

1 pound = 20 spears
1 pound = 3 cups chopped asparagus

Like many fresh vegetables, asparagus begins to convert its sugars to starches the moment it is harvested, so asparagus will taste best freshly cut. But sometimes you need to harvest the stems to prevent bolting, even if you aren't ready to cook them. So place the stems in a glass of warm water, tips up, and refrigerate.

To prepare asparagus for cooking, snap off the woody ends. If you hold a stem in both hands and bend it, it will snap off at just the right spot. Fresh asparagus usually doesn't need peeling, despite the best advice of many cookbooks. Take a bite of raw asparagus. If the skin chews easily, don't bother to peel. If the skin is fibrous, then peel off the outer layer with a swivel-bladed vegetable peeler. Leave whole or cut into uniform 1- or 2-inch lengths.

ASPARAGUS NUTRITION NOTES

Asparagus contains more of the antioxidant glutathione — one of the most potent cancer fighters — than any other fruit or vegetable. It's also an excellent source of folic acid, a B vitamin that helps protect against cervical cancer, heart disease, and some birth defects. It is a good source of vitamin C, thiamine, vitamin B_6, potassium, and dietary fiber. Plus, asparagus is low in calories, with only about 4 per spear.

TIMING

Boiling: 3 to 5 minutes
Steaming: 5 to 7 minutes
Sautéing or stir-frying: 3 to 5 minutes
Grilling: 8 minutes
Roasting: 15 minutes at 450°F

roasted asparagus vinaigrette

My kids are generally happy to eat vegetables, but they drew the line at asparagus — until I started roasting it. The roasting mellows the grassy flavor of asparagus, while the vinaigrette adds just the right amount of zest. I use 1½ pounds of asparagus for this, because many spears get devoured in the kitchen. You can cut the recipe down to 1 pound, but keep the vinaigrette amount the same and save any leftover dressing for salad.

■ SERVES 4–6 ■

1½ pounds asparagus (about 30 medium-thick spears), bottoms trimmed

5 tablespoons extra-virgin olive oil

2 garlic cloves, minced

1 tablespoon red wine vinegar

Salt and freshly ground black pepper

1 Preheat the oven to 450°F. Lightly grease a large shallow roasting pan or half sheet pan with oil.

2 Arrange the asparagus in a single uncrowded layer in the prepared pan. Drizzle 2 tablespoons of the oil over the asparagus and roll to coat evenly.

3 Roast the asparagus for about 15 minutes, until the asparagus is lightly browned, shaking the pan occasionally for even cooking.

4 Meanwhile, combine the garlic and vinegar in a small bowl. Whisk in the remaining 3 tablespoons oil until it is fully incorporated. Season to taste with the salt and pepper.

5 When the asparagus is done, transfer to a serving platter. Drizzle with the vinaigrette. Sprinkle with additional salt and pepper, if desired. Set aside for at least 30 minutes to blend the flavors.

6 Serve at room temperature.

breaded asparagus sticks

Asparagus stems that are breaded, then baked to golden tenderness are irresistible. I like to use panko — *Japanese-style bread crumbs — for the breading because they add so much texture. You can find panko wherever Asian foods are sold. The crumbs are white (not toasted) and seem to be grated rather than ground, so the texture is coarser, which allows for a lighter coating. The asparagus spears can be served hot or at room temperature; just don't skip the lemon — it brings the flavors together.*

SERVES 4

- 2 eggs
- ½ teaspoon Dijon mustard
- Salt and freshly ground black pepper
- ¾ cup freshly ground Parmesan (use the fine side of a box grater or grind to a powder in a food processor)
- ¾ cup panko or other dried bread crumbs
- 1 lemon, cut into wedges
- 1–1½ pounds asparagus (20–30 medium-thick spears), bottoms trimmed

1 Preheat the oven to 400°F. Lightly grease a baking sheet with olive oil.

2 In a shallow bowl, beat the eggs with the mustard. Season with a generous pinch of salt and a few grinds of pepper. In a second shallow bowl, combine the Parmesan and panko and mix well. Dip each asparagus spear first in the eggs to coat, then in the crumb mixture. Place on the prepared baking sheet. Continue until all the asparagus is coated.

3 Bake for 12 to 15 minutes, until golden on the bottom. Turn the asparagus over and bake for another 12 to 15 minutes, until golden brown.

4 Arrange on a platter with the lemon wedges. Serve hot or at room temperature.

creamy asparagus fettuccine

It's spring! The sun is out! The garden calls! Who wants to stay indoors cooking? Here's a quick vegetarian main dish. If you have any greens, make a green salad, and dinner is complete.

SERVES 4–5

1 pound asparagus (about 20 medium-thick spears)

1 pound fettuccine

1 large red bell pepper, roasted and cut into strips (see page 15)

1 pound ricotta cheese, at room temperature

¼ cup freshly grated Parmesan, plus more for serving

⅓ cup chopped fresh chives, garlic chives, or scallions

Salt and freshly ground black pepper

1 Begin heating a large pot of salted water.

2 Snap off and discard the woody ends of the asparagus. Cut off the tips of the asparagus spears and reserve. Cut the spears into 1½-inch lengths.

3 When the water comes to a boil, add the asparagus and cook for 2 minutes. Add the tips and cook until the asparagus is just tender, about 2 minutes longer. Using a large skimmer or slotted spoon, remove the asparagus and transfer to a bowl. Cover and keep warm.

4 Cook the fettuccine in the water until al dente. Remove ½ cup of the cooking water. Briefly drain the fettuccine in a colander and return it to the pot, along with the asparagus.

5 Add the roasted pepper, ricotta, Parmesan, and chives. Toss well, adding the reserved cooking water as needed to make a creamy sauce. Season generously with salt and pepper.

6 Serve hot, passing additional Parmesan at the table.

"IT ALL BEGAN when I was a member of a CSA (Community-Supported Agriculture) farm in upstate New York."

Kathy Wolf takes a deep breath and begins to explain how she came to have the unusual hobby of starting hundreds of seedlings every year for friends and acquaintances:

"The farm had a work requirement, and I volunteered for the greenhouse. We started everything with seeds in trays. Then we transplanted the seedlings to pots. I really liked the work. Eventually we quit the CSA because my own garden was giving us too many vegetables, but by then I was bit by the bug. It doesn't make it to plant just six tomato seeds.

"We lived in a small town, right on the main street. And every year there was a Memorial Day parade right by our house. My kids would sell their lemonade, and I would sell my plants. I was also selling plants at our local food co-op. At one point I was selling twenty-one different types of basil.

"Then we moved. I didn't want a greenhouse business. But I still loved the meditative aspect of starting seeds. But without a CSA or food co-op or lemonade stand, I found myself overrun with tons of tomato, pepper, and basil seedlings. So I started taking them to the folk 'sings.' That's just a club that moves from one house to another — we get together and have a potluck and sing all night. I made sure that the May sing was always at my house and invited people to just take whatever plants they wanted.

"Then I started sending out e-mails to everyone in the folk song club, asking for requests. I send out a list of all the varieties I have seeds for." The folks on her e-mail list respond by telling her how many plants of each variety they can use.

Wolf is especially excited by some heirloom tomato varieties she recently discovered. "This year I ordered from a new seed house — Sand Hill Preservation. They have lots of European varieties. There's an early variety, Moskovich, which is very promising. And I love Ukrainian Heart — it is pink and heart-shaped and very big, about four to five inches long. It's meaty like a plum tomato," she said.

Among the peppers Wolf plants, she particularly recommends Italia, Golden Bell, and Sunrise Orange. She likes to see a variety of different peppers growing together. Mrs. Burns lemon basil, Wolf says, is an outstanding basil, but nothing beats the classic Genovese.

Starting seedlings, Wolf says, is repetitive work, but not monotonous: "It requires focus but not problem solving. There's nothing frustrating about it. I think it may be a bit like a mantra in Yoga in that it allows or necessitates a clearing out of all the worries that chase themselves around in a mind. I come away from it calm and refreshed.

"Yes, it is an expensive hobby. But it is better to have people take the seedlings than to have them all go to waste. It's how I became integrated into my community. I do this for my community. People do other things for me."

thai-style asparagus and crab salad

Sweet, tart, and salty — the flavors of this light, light salad supper are harmoniously balanced. Because the dressing contains no oil, the salad tastes like a pure indulgence, but it is very good for you. It's a great way to celebrate the early harvests of asparagus and greens.

◾ **SERVES 4** ◾

Salad

1½	pounds asparagus (about 30 medium-thick spears), trimmed and cut on the diagonal into 1½-inch lengths
1	package (3.75 ounces) bean threads or cellophane noodles
1	pound crabmeat, picked over
1	carrot, grated
2	scallions, white and tender green parts, trimmed and chopped
4	cups arugula leaves or watercress
4	cups mesclun or baby lettuce
½	cup cilantro leaves
½	cup mint leaves
⅓	cup chopped peanuts, toasted

Dressing

¾	cup fresh lime juice (approximately 6 limes)
½	cup fish sauce
⅓	cup sugar
2	garlic cloves, minced
1–2	jalapeño chiles, minced
1	tablespoon minced peeled ginger
	Freshly ground black pepper

1 Steam the asparagus over boiling water until tender, 4 to 5 minutes. Drain; plunge into cold water to stop the cooking; drain.

2 Soak the noodles in hot tap water to cover for about 5 minutes. Drain.

3 To make the dressing, combine the lime juice, fish sauce, and sugar in a medium bowl, stirring to dissolve the sugar. Mix in the garlic, chile, ginger, and pepper to taste.

4 Pour about ½ cup of the dressing over the noodles. Toss to mix and set aside.

5 In a large bowl, combine the crab, carrot, and scallions. Add about ½ cup of the dressing. Toss to mix. Set aside to allow the flavors to blend, at least 15 minutes, or longer in the refrigerator.

6 Just before serving, toss the arugula, mesclun, cilantro, and mint in a large bowl. Add a few tablespoons of the remaining dressing and toss to mix. Add more dressing if desired.

7 To serve, line a platter or individual plates with the greens mix. Top with the noodles, then the crab mixture, and finally the asparagus. Sprinkle on the peanuts and serve, passing the remaining dressing at the table.

ASPARAGUS IN HISTORY

ASPARAGUS IS BELIEVED to have originated somewhere in the Mediterranean or in Asia Minor, though it has been found wild in so many places, there is some disagreement as to where it actually originated. It thrives along riverbanks, shores of lakes, and even close to the salty waters of seacoasts, tolerating considerable salt in the soil in which it grows.

The Greeks were happy to enjoy wild asparagus, but left behind no instructions for cultivating it. As early as 200 BC, Romans were cultivating asparagus in gardens for eating fresh and drying for later use. Pliny recorded methods of producing especially large stems. The first cookbook ever published, *De Re Culinaria,* written by Marcus Gavius Apicius in the first century, featured a recipe for asparagus tips pounded with herbs, wine, oil, eggs, and onions and then baked. Asparagus was on the menu for a feast to be served in Pompeii on the day the explosion from the volcano on Mount Vesuvius buried the city.

Northern Europeans have been eating asparagus for as long as there are any records about them, and the Puritans brought seeds for "sparagrass" with them to the New World.

grilled asparagus and chicken salad

Keep cool with a quick meal made from grilled chicken and vegetables atop a bed of salad greens. Grilled toast rounds out the meal.

■ SERVES 4 ■

Juice of 1 lemon (about 3 tablespoons)

2 garlic cloves, minced

1 shallot, minced

1 teaspoon Dijon mustard

2 teaspoons chopped fresh thyme, or 1 teaspoon dried

6 tablespoons extra-virgin olive oil

Salt and freshly ground black pepper

4 boneless, skinless chicken breast halves, cut lengthwise into ½-inch strips

1 pound asparagus (about 20 medium-thick spears), bottoms trimmed

8–12 cups mesclun or mixed salad greens

Garlic Toasts (see page 23)

1 Prepare a medium-hot fire in a charcoal grill and let the coals burn down until they are covered with white ash, or preheat a gas grill on high.

2 To make the marinade, combine the lemon juice, garlic, shallot, mustard, and thyme in a small bowl. Whisk in the oil until it is fully emulsified. Add salt and pepper to taste.

3 Place the chicken in one bowl and the asparagus in another. Pour half the marinade in each. Toss the chicken to coat with the marinade. Toss the asparagus to coat with the marinade.

4 Lift the chicken out of the marinade and arrange on the grill. Grill the chicken for 4 to 6 minutes, until cooked through, turning once. Set aside and keep warm. Discard any remaining marinade in the bowl.

5 Grill the asparagus until limp and lightly grill-marked, about 8 minutes, turning once. Reserve the remaining marinade.

6 To serve, divide the greens among the dinner plates. Arrange the chicken and asparagus on top. Drizzle with the reserved marinade. Place two garlic toasts on each plate and serve.

lemony grilled asparagus

Have you set up your grill for grilling season? Asparagus is the first spring vegetable suitable for grilling. If you like roasted asparagus, you'll probably like it grilled as well. Add grilled salmon and you have a springtime feast.

■ **SERVES 4** ■

1½ pounds asparagus (about 30 medium-thick spears), bottoms trimmed

2 tablespoons extra-virgin olive oil

Salt and freshly ground black pepper

½ lemon

1 Prepare a medium fire in a gas or charcoal grill.

2 Place the asparagus in a shallow dish. Drizzle the oil over the spears and toss to coat.

3 Grill the asparagus, turning occasionally, until tender, about 8 minutes.

4 Arrange the asparagus on a serving platter. Sprinkle with the salt and pepper to taste, squeeze the lemon over the spears, and serve.

Always Sweet, Always Welcome

I'LL NEVER FORGET my first harvest. I had a community garden plot in Ithaca, New York, a few miles from my apartment. It was a hot June morning, and I walked for about an hour, trowel and a quart of orange juice in my backpack. The first peas were ready! Fresh shelling peas, right out of the pod, washed down with cold orange juice — it was one of the finest feasts I have ever enjoyed.

I never tire of peas! Green beans can be become an overwhelming burden, tomatoes can accumulate on the counter, and let's not even mention zucchini. But the first peas of the season fulfill a need for green food that isn't quickly sated.

Until very recently, garden-fresh shelling peas were a treat that mainly gardeners could enjoy. About 90 percent of the American fresh pea crop goes directly into the freezer. Even those who found fresh shelling peas at a farmers' market were not able to fully enjoy what a garden pea has to offer. Within 6 hours of harvest, a pea will convert roughly half of its sugar to starch at room temperature. So the grower who harvested peas at five in the morning was selling a reduced-flavor product by eleven. In the past couple of years, supersweet varieties of shelling peas have been offered in seed catalogs. Like supersweet hybrid corn varieties, these peas are touted to hold their sweetness longer. Whether they are as full-flavored as older heirloom varieties remains to be tasted.

Sugar snap peas and snow peas hold their flavor and texture better in the refrigerator than shelling peas, so most of my crop goes to sugar snap peas. They don't need any fancy preparation; we enjoy them raw as snacks. What more could one ask for?

GROWING Peas are a cool-weather crop. They do best in fertile, well-drained soil. Yields are increased if trellises are provided, but dwarf varieties can be grown without supports. Space seeds about 1 inch apart in narrow bands on both sides of a trellis, or space 1 inch apart in wide rows or raised beds without supports.

SOWING Sow outdoors as soon as soil can be worked. In some climates, a second sowing in late summer will produce a fall crop.

CULTIVATING Keep the beds moist until blossoming occurs. Fertilize lightly with a complete fertilizer when seedlings are 2 to 4 inches tall.

HARVESTING For the best yield, it is important to stay on top of the harvest. Leaving mature pods on the vines signals the plant to stop producing more peas. For best flavor and texture, harvest shelling peas as soon as the pods have filled out but aren't bulging around the peas. Harvest snow peas as soon as the pod reaches its mature length and before the peas start to develop. Harvest sugar snap peas when both the pods and peas are plump and the pods snap like a bean pod.

PEA MATH

1 pound fresh pea pods = 1 to 1¼ cups shelled peas

1 pound fresh sugar = 4 to 5 cups pods snap or snow peas

During pea season, a bowl of freshly picked sugar snap peas finds it way to my table every night. The only preparation required is rinsing and stringing the pods. Raw sugar snap peas make a fine addition to salads and platters of crudités. I find that kids generally prefer raw sugar snaps; they also enjoy standing in the garden and grazing on shelling peas.

To strip the strings from sugar snap peas and snow peas, start at the tip and strip toward the stem on the concave side of the pod, then over the top and down the convex side. To shell peas, press along the seam to pop open the pods, then strip out the peas by pushing with your thumb. Shelling peas are a good candidate for freezing; they don't hold up well in the refrigerator.

To freeze, blanch (pages 16–17) for 1½ to 2 minutes, then immediately plunge into an ice bath to stop the cooking. Drain well in a colander, then dump onto a double layer of absorbent cotton towels on your countertop. Let the peas dry for a few minutes, then bag in resealable freezer bags, making sure all air is removed from the bags, label, and freeze. Snow peas and sugar snap peas can be handled the same way (increase the blanching time to 2 minutes for sugar snap peas); snow peas make an acceptable frozen product but sugar snap peas lose most of their crispness and charm.

Peas are delicate and require very brief cooking. They can be blanched or steamed. Snow peas are excellent in sautés and stir-fries. All types of peas are fine added to soups and stews and other slow-cooking dishes in the last few minutes of cooking.

TIMING
Blanching: 2 to 4 minutes
Steaming: 3 to 4 minutes
Sautéing or stir-frying: 2 to 3 minutes

risi e bisi

When shelling peas are finally ready for harvest, this is the dish I am most likely to make first. Rice with peas is a specialty of Venice; it was supposedly a banquet dish served to the doges there to celebrate the Feast of St. Mark. It contains very few ingredients, so it should be made with the finest ones — including homegrown peas and homemade broth. Although cookbook writer Marcella Hazen says it should never be made with frozen peas, I have been known to enjoy a bowl of this pure comfort in winter with frozen peas.

SERVES 4

4 cups high-quality vegetable or chicken broth (page 8 or 9)
2 tablespoons butter
1 tablespoon extra-virgin olive oil
1 shallot, diced
¾ cup uncooked medium-grain or arborio rice
   Salt (optional)
2 cups fresh shelled peas (about 2 pounds in the pod)
½ cup freshly grated Parmesan
   Freshly ground black pepper

1 Heat the broth to simmering in a saucepan on top of the stove or in a heatproof container in the microwave.

2 In a large saucepan, heat the butter and olive oil over medium heat. Add the shallot and sauté for 2 minutes. Add the hot broth and rice, stir well, cover, reduce the heat, and simmer until the rice is just tender, 15 minutes.

3 Taste and add salt if desired. Stir in the peas and cook gently until the peas are done enough to suit you, about 5 minutes for fresh peas (less for frozen peas). Stir in the Parmesan and season with pepper. Serve at once.

"IF YOU CAN'T GROW A BIG GARDEN, grow a small one. Stay connected to the earth by learning to feed yourself with the foods you grow. Teach kids to garden. Food is not a commodity you buy at the supermarket. Somebody has to plant that seed."

A few sentences sum up Ellen Ecker Ogden's mission. Ogden is the co-founder and spokesperson for The Cook's Garden, a seed company, and she lives by what she preaches.

Ogden started out as a market gardener near Londonderry, Vermont, on a 10-acre farm. The farm specialized in greens. After a few years of growing specialty vegetables such as romanesco broccoli, haricot verts, and arugula, The Cook's Garden started importing seeds in bulk from Europe and repackaging the extras. In 1984, The Cook's Garden published its first catalog — a two-page newsletter featuring lettuce and other salad greens — and the seed company was off and running.

Ogden's work has always been as much based in the kitchen as in the garden, creating recipes to encourage customers to try something new in their gardens: "There is always a culinary basis to the vegetables chosen for the catalog. We don't just offer zucchini, for example. We offer Ronde de Nice zucchini because it is best for stuffing."

At one point Ogden went to Venice to study cooking under Marcella Hazen. "I would go to the market before each class and bring back greens. 'What's this? How do I prepare that?' There are just so many greens — all the different chicories, puntarella, dentarella — Americans know so little about. We are all familiar with radicchio shredded into salads, but Treviso radicchio is so good cooked, especially grilled."

Fennel is another vegetable Ogden learned more about, solving the mystery of why some fennel bulbs are flattish while others are more rounded. Fennel plants may be male or female. The male plants produce rounded bulbs ones, and they are more tender and succulent. The flat female bulbs are tougher, more likely to be stringy.

In 2003, Ogden collected 21 years' worth of recipes she had developed for the seed company in a cookbook she titled *From the Cook's Garden* (William Morrow). It contains "recipes for cooks who like to garden, gardeners who like to cook, and everyone who wishes they had a garden to cook from." Since then she has also appeared as the "salad lady" on TV, with 2-minute cooking spots, and toured the country to give cooking classes.

These days her garden has shrunk. All she has time to tend are her herbs, sunflowers, and salad greens. "I couldn't live without those," she says.

For the rest, Ogden has joined a community-supported agriculture farm. Each week a box of vegetables is delivered to her home. "I love the surprise of box. It's like a Crackerjack box. You never know what you'll find inside. I love feeling like the Iron Chef, rising to the challenge of figuring what to do with all the lovely vegetables."

stir-fried shrimp and snow peas in black bean sauce

There's no finer way to greet the snow pea harvest than with this flavorful stir-fry. Have everything prepped and ready to go before you start cooking; the actual cooking time is less than 10 minutes. Fermented black beans add a subtle flavor to the stir-fry. You can find them wherever Chinese foods are sold, usually in small plastic packages, shelved with other dried foods. They aren't exactly optional, but you can omit them if you must.

■ SERVES 4 ■

Shrimp and Marinade

1½ pounds medium shrimp, shelled and deveined
1 tablespoon rice wine or dry sherry
2 thin slices fresh ginger
1 teaspoon sesame oil
1 teaspoon salt

Sauce

½ cup chicken broth (page 9)
1 tablespoon soy sauce
1 tablespoon rice wine or sherry
1 teaspoon cornstarch
½ teaspoon sugar

Stir-Fry

4½ tablespoons peanut or canola oil
1 pound snow peas, tails and strings removed
2 teaspoons Chinese fermented black beans, minced
2 garlic cloves, minced
2 teaspoons minced fresh ginger
1 scallion, minced
Hot cooked rice

1 Rinse the shrimp and pat dry. Place in a medium bowl. To prepare the marinade, add the wine, ginger, sesame oil, and salt to the bowl. Toss several times. Set aside for 20 minutes to marinate.

2 To prepare the sauce, combine the broth, soy sauce, wine, cornstarch, and sugar. Mix well. Set aside.

3 When you are ready to cook, heat a large wok over high heat. Add 1½ tablespoons of the oil and heat for a few minutes. Add half the shrimp to the wok and stir-fry for 2 to 3 minutes, until the shrimp change color. Remove from the wok and set aside in a bowl to keep warm. Add another 1½ tablespoons oil, heat, and repeat. Add the shrimp to the bowl with the other shrimp and wipe out the wok.

4 Add the remaining 1½ tablespoons oil to the wok and heat until very hot. Add the snow peas and stir-fry until almost tender, about 1 minute. Make a well in the center of the peas and add the black beans, garlic, ginger, and scallion. Stir-fry until fragrant, about 10 seconds. Stir into the peas. Add the shrimp and stir-fry for 1 minute to heat through. Add the sauce and stir-fry until the sauce thickens and clears, about 2 minutes longer.

5 Serve hot over rice.

spicy tofu with peas

Ma po tofu is a popular Sichuan dish of contrasting flavors and textures. It is more of a stew than a stir-fry, with the sweet flavor of the peas and the smooth silken tofu providing relief from the spicy chili paste.

3 squares soft tofu (about 3 pounds)

½ pound ground pork

5 tablespoons soy sauce

2 tablespoons rice wine or dry sherry

2 teaspoons Chinese chili paste with garlic, or more to taste

1 teaspoon sesame oil

2 tablespoons peanut or canola oil

2 garlic cloves, minced

1 piece (1½ inches long) fresh ginger, peeled and minced

2 cups chicken broth (see page 9)

2 cups fresh shelled peas (about 2 pounds in pods)

1 carrot, diced

1 can (8 ounces) sliced water chestnuts, drained

2 tablespoons cornstarch dissolved in 2 tablespoons water

2 scallions, white and tender green parts, chopped

Salt

Hot cooked rice

"How luscious lies the pea within the pod."

—Emily Dickinson

1 Wrap the tofu in paper towels, place under a heavy weight, and let drain for about 30 minutes. (The tofu will release a lot of liquid, so you may want to do this in a colander in the sink.) Unwrap and cut into ½-inch dice.

2 Meanwhile, combine the pork, 2 tablespoons of the soy sauce, 1 tablespoon of the rice wine, the chili paste, and sesame oil in a small bowl. Mix well.

3 Heat a large wok over medium-high heat. Add the peanut oil and heat. Add the pork mixture and stir-fry until brown, about 4 minutes, breaking up any clumps as it cooks. Push the meat to the sides of the wok and add the garlic and ginger. Stir-fry until fragrant, about 30 seconds.

4 Add the broth, remaining 3 tablespoons soy sauce, and remaining 1 tablespoon rice wine. Bring the mixture to a boil. Add the tofu, peas, and carrots. Lower the heat and simmer for 5 minutes, until the liquid reduces somewhat. Increase the heat and return the mixture to a boil. Stir in the cornstarch mixture, stirring until the mixture clears and thickens, about 1 minute.

5 Stir in the scallions and season with salt. Serve hot over rice.

arroz con pollo with peas

Saffron and green olives give this classic combination of chicken and rice its Cuban signature. If you are looking for a quick stovetop, one-dish meal in spring, seek no further.

◾ SERVES 4 ◾

2 cups long-grain white rice

2½ cups chicken broth (see page 9)

½ cup dry sherry

¼ teaspoon crushed saffron threads

2 tablespoons extra-virgin olive oil

1 pound boneless, skinless chicken breast, cut into 1-inch cubes

1 onion, diced

2 garlic cloves, minced

2 cups fresh peas (about 2 pounds in shell)

1 roasted red pepper (homemade, page 15, or bottled), diced

20 pimiento stuffed green olives, sliced

¼ cup chopped fresh parsley

Salt and freshly ground black pepper

1 Place the rice in a sieve and set in a bowl. Run cold tap water over the rice until the rinse water runs clear. Drain well. Set aside. (This step is optional. It does wash away vitamins that have been sprayed onto the rice, but it greatly improves the texture of the final dish.)

2 Combine the broth, sherry, and saffron in a small saucepan and warm gently over low heat.

3 Heat the oil in a large skillet over medium-high heat. Add the chicken and sauté for 2 minutes, until the chicken is partially cooked. Add the onion and garlic and continue to sauté until the chicken is white and firm, 2 to 4 minutes. Add the rice and sauté until the rice appears toasted, about 3 minutes.

4 Stir the chicken broth mixture into the rice. Bring to a boil, cover, and reduce the heat to maintain a gentle boil. Cook for 3 minutes. Add the peas to the skillet (do not stir) and continue to cook until the liquid is absorbed and the peas are tender, about 10 minutes. (If your peas are "mature," they may take a few minutes longer.)

5 Fluff the rice with a fork. Stir in the red pepper, olives, and parsley. Season with salt and pepper. Serve at once.

A BRIEF HISTORY OF PEAS

THE GROWING OF GARDEN PEAS stretches so far back that no one really knows where this ancient food originated. According to Norse legend, peas were sent to earth by Thor in the talons of dragons to fill up the water wells of unworthy humans. Some of the peas were dropped accidentally on the land and sprouted into plants. The Norsemen dedicated the plant to Thor and vowed to eat peas only on Thor's day (Thursday).

There is evidence that the ancient Egyptians, Greeks, and Romans all ate dried peas. The Greeks enjoyed pea soup, and the Romans sold fried peas at the circus (popcorn having to wait until the discovery of the New World). Probably peas were enjoyed only in their dried state until the Italian Renaissance, when the Italians developed *piselli*

novelli, a type of pea eaten unripe and fresh. They quickly became wildly popular. It took a famine year (1555) for the English peasantry to discover that peas taste as good green as they do dried.

Columbus planted peas in his 1493 garden on Isabella Island. The Pilgrims brought peas with them to New England, and Jefferson claimed that peas were his favorite garden vegetable.

Edible pod peas, or snow peas, also called *mangetout* (eat-all), were first developed by the Dutch and English in the early 17th century. Sugar snap peas, which are a cross between English and snow peas, were probably developed in the late 17th century, but they did not become widely available in the United States until the 1970s.

shells with peas and prosciutto

Peas and pasta are a natural combination, and any pasta shape can be used. I particularly like using the very small shells, but this classic dish is often made with orzo or linguine. If you have a steamer insert that fits into your pasta pot, this is a very fast dish to whip up. Even if you have to heat water in two separate pots — one for the pasta and one for the peas — this is a no-fuss dish that makes a fine meal with the addition of a green salad and bread.

SERVES 4

2 cups peas (about 2 pounds in pods)

3 tablespoons extra-virgin olive oil

4 ounces prosciutto, cut in one thick slice and diced

1 small onion, diced

2 garlic cloves, minced

1 cup freshly grated Parmigiano-Reggiano, plus extra for serving

Salt and freshly ground black pepper

1 If you have a steamer insert, bring a large pot of salted water to a boil. If you don't have a steamer insert, bring a large pot of salted water to a boil for the pasta. Bring a second, medium pot of salted water to a boil for the peas.

2 Add the peas to the salted water and boil just until tender, 3 to 5 minutes, depending on their age. Drain well.

3 In a large Dutch oven, heat the olive oil over medium heat. Add the prosciutto and onion and sauté until the onion is softened, about 3 minutes. Add the garlic and sauté until fragrant, about 1 minute. Reduce the heat to very low and stir in the peas.

4 Cook the pasta until just al dente. Reserve a cup of the pasta liquid and drain the pasta.

5 Add the pasta to the pea mixture and toss to coat. Add the cheese and toss well. Add the reserved pasta water as needed to moisten the pasta. Season generously with salt and pepper.

6 Serve at once, passing additional cheese on the side.

peas and new potato salad

Marble-size potatoes are best for this early-summer salad, where the peas and potatoes are equal partners. If your potatoes are larger than bite-size, cut them down to size.

SERVES 4–6

1½ pounds tiny new potatoes (about 4 cups), scrubbed
  Salt
2 cups shelled peas (about 2 pounds with pods)
1 cup sour cream (reduced-fat sour cream is fine)
1 spring onion, bulb and tender greens, sliced, or 2 scallions, sliced
¼ cup chopped fresh dill
1 tablespoon horseradish
  Freshly ground black pepper

1 In a medium saucepan, cover the potatoes with cold water and add salt generously. Bring to a boil. Allow the potatoes to boil for 3 minutes, until almost tender. Add the peas and cook another 3 minutes, until both peas and potatoes are tender. Plunge immediately into ice water to stop the cooking, then drain.

2 In a large bowl, stir together the sour cream, onion, dill, and horseradish. Season to taste with salt and pepper. Add the peas and potatoes and mix gently with a rubber spatula. Taste and adjust the seasoning.

3 Allow to stand for 30 minutes before serving, or refrigerate for up to 4 hours, then bring to room temperature and serve.

A Very Compliant Green

I DON'T LIKE TO BRAG, but I have an ideal spot for spring spinach. It is a spot that stays cool and gets plenty of moisture, so my spinach often refrains from bolting for a solid couple of weeks. Don't envy me for it — it also means that my tomatoes are slow to grow, and forget about peppers.

Spinach is a very compliant green; it takes well to many different styles of cooking without protest.

A very lovely aspect of spinach is that once cooked, it will hold up amazingly well in the refrigerator — better in the refrigerator, I think, than in the freezer. So if your spinach is threatening to bolt, or if you received pounds of these vitamin- and mineral-rich greens from your CSA and you don't have the space in the refrigerator, cook the spinach in a large pot of boiling water for about 30 seconds, just until wilted. Immediately plunge the spinach in cold water to stop the cooking, then drain well. Store the cooked spinach in an airtight container in the refrigerator for up to 5 days. Then use it in any recipe calling for cooked or wilted spinach; the flavor will still be fresh and bright.

GROWING Spinach grows best in cool weather at the beginning and end of the growing season in rich, moist soil. This cold-hardy crop can withstand hard frosts with accompanying temperatures as low as 20°F. Spinach can be overwintered for early-spring production in many areas.

SOWING Sow every 2 to 3 weeks from early to late spring. Sow again in late summer or early autumn.

CULTIVATING Keep soil moist with mulch and light, regular watering.

HARVESTING With kitchen scissors, cut off the outer leaves as soon as they are big enough to use in salads. Cut the entire plant about an inch off the ground to encourage another crop of leaves. When the plant begins to send up a tall central stem, it is time to harvest the entire plant because the spinach is about to bolt (produce seeds).

SPINACH MATH

1 pound spinach = anywhere from 12 to 24 cups of loosely packed, washed, and trimmed leaves depending on variety (crisp, fully mature savoyed leaves will measure about 24 cups to a pound; baby spinach will measure about 12 cups per pound)

1 pound raw spinach = 2 to 3 cups cooked

Spinach requires careful washing. The best way to do this is to fill a very large bowl, or your sink, with cold water. Add the spinach leaves and swish, pressing down to submerge the leaves and dislodge the soil and debris. Allow the dirt to settle to the bottom, then lift the spinach out of the water into a colander. Clean out the bowl, fill with fresh water, and repeat. If you are serving the spinach fresh, dry the leaves in a salad spinner. Otherwise, you can usually cook the leaves with the water still clinging to the leaves.

If the spinach has large stems, you may wish to remove them. Just hold the stem in one hand and pull off the leaf with the other.

Because spinach gives off a great deal of water as it cooks, it is often blanched in boiling water for about 30 seconds, until wilted. Then it is drained. To eliminate even more water, squeeze it with your hands. This step makes a huge difference in the final texture of a dish.

TIMING

Blanching: 30 to 60 seconds
Steaming: 3 to 5 minutes
Sautéing or stir-frying: 4 to 6 minutes

SPINACH NUTRITION NOTES

Spinach is exceptionally rich in carotenoids, including beta-carotene. It is rich in vitamins and minerals, particularly folic acid, vitamin K, magnesium, and manganese. To get the full nutritional benefit of this leafy green, it is best to eat it cooked. Two cups of raw chopped spinach contains only 13 calories.

spinach salad with feta and pecans

Everyone has a version of spinach salad she loves. I love this version because of the contrasting sweet and salty flavors. The fact that it does not contain raw mushrooms (who ever decided raw mushrooms were edible?) is a bonus.

■ SERVES 4 ■

1 cup pecan halves

6 tablespoons extra-virgin olive oil

2 tablespoons white balsamic vinegar

1 tablespoon honey

Salt and freshly ground black pepper

1 pound spinach, tough stems removed and large leaves torn

1 cup dried sweetened cherries or cranberries, or dried apricots snipped into tiny pieces

6 ounces feta cheese

FACT FICTION

New Zealand spinach is often touted in gardening books as a hot-weather spinach crop. This is fiction from a culinary point of view. In fact, New Zealand spinach has an unpleasant texture and can't be enjoyed raw. Some people do enjoy it cooked.

1 Toast the pecans in a dry skillet over medium heat until they are fragrant and very lightly colored, about 5 minutes. Remove from the skillet and set aside.

2 To make the dressing, combine the oil, vinegar, and honey in a small bowl. Whisk until well blended. Season to taste with salt and pepper.

3 Combine the spinach, pecans, and dried fruit in a large salad bowl. Toss to mix. Crumble the cheese into the salad, add the salad dressing, and toss again. Serve immediately.

curried spinach and shrimp

Despite the long ingredients list, this is a fast dish to make. If you prefer a mild curry, then substitute a bell pepper for the chiles.

■ SERVES 4–6 ■

1½–2 pounds spinach, washed and trimmed
2 tablespoons canola oil
3 onions, thinly sliced
3 garlic cloves, minced
1–2 fresh or canned green chiles, minced
1 piece fresh ginger (1½ inches long), peeled and minced
1 tablespoon curry powder
1 teaspoon ground cumin
½ teaspoon fenugreek seeds
½ teaspoon ground coriander
1½ pounds medium shrimp, shelled and deveined
1½ cups buttermilk
Salt
Cayenne (optional)
Hot cooked rice

1 Bring a large pot of salted water to a boil. Add the spinach and cook about 30 seconds. Drain well and roughly chop.

2 Heat the oil over medium-low heat in a large saucepan. Add the onions, garlic, chiles, ginger, curry powder, cumin, fenugreek, and coriander. Sauté until the onions are golden, about 10 minutes. Do not let the mixture burn, or you might as well start over.

3 Stir in the shrimp, increase the heat to medium-high and cook until the shrimp are just white and firm, about 5 minutes.

4 Reduce the heat to low. Stir in the buttermilk and spinach. Season with salt. Add cayenne to taste. Cook over low heat until the spinach is heated through. Serve hot over rice.

spinach cheese custard

There's just enough egg and cheese to bind together this crustless quiche. The dish can be served as a main dish, side dish, or brunch dish. Sometimes I make this to have on hand for quick, healthy breakfasts and lunches. If you like, you can make a richer version using two whole eggs instead of three whites and one whole egg.

SERVES 4

1½–2 pounds fresh spinach, tough stems removed
1 tablespoon extra-virgin olive oil
1 onion, diced
3 egg whites
1 egg
1½ cups milk
1 cup grated Gruyère
Salt and freshly ground black pepper
½ cup freshly grated Parmesan

1 Bring a large pot of salted water to a boil. Stir in the spinach and cook until wilted, about 30 seconds. Drain well. Press out the excess moisture. Transfer to a cutting board and finely chop.

2 Heat the olive oil in a sauté pan over medium heat. Add the onion and sauté until fragrant and softened, about 2 minutes.

3 Preheat the oven to 350°F. Lightly grease a 7- by 11-inch baking dish with oil.

4 In a large bowl, beat the eggs with a whisk until smooth. Add the spinach, onions, milk, and Gruyère. Season with the salt and pepper to taste. Pour into the baking dish. Top with the Parmesan.

5 Bake until the custard is set and a knife inserted comes out clean, about 30 minutes.

6 Let sit for at least 5 minutes before serving. Serve warm or at room temperature.

creamed spinach

My requirement for creamed spinach is that it be creamy and hold up well without becoming watery. So I like to start with a flour-stabilized cream sauce, a béchamel, rather than a pure cream. This is a good basic recipe that you can flavor in many different ways. A classic flavoring is to forgo the shallot and add nutmeg (a grating of fresh nutmeg is best). Garlic can replace the shallot. Garlic, shallot, and curry powder make a delicious and colorful variation.

SERVES 4

2 tablespoons butter

1 large shallot, minced

2 tablespoons unbleached all-purpose flour

1 cup milk

Salt and freshly ground black or white pepper

1½ pounds spinach, tough stems removed

1 Bring a large pot of salted water to a boil.

2 Melt the butter in a medium saucepan over medium heat. Add the shallot and sauté until soft, about 3 minutes. Whisk in the flour until you have a paste. Increase the heat, pour in the milk, and whisk to combine. Continue whisking until the sauce thickens, about 3 minutes. Season with the salt and pepper to taste. Reduce the heat to low.

3 Add the spinach to the boiling water and cook long enough to wilt, about 30 seconds. Drain well. Place the spinach on a cutting board and roughly chop.

4 Add the spinach to the cream sauce and stir to thoroughly combine. Taste and adjust the seasoning. Serve hot.

greek-style baked
spinach and shrimp

When you add shrimp, any rustic dish becomes company fare. This dish has the added advantage of lending itself to advance preparation. The casserole can be assembled and held in the refrigerator for several hours. Just before dinnertime, make the rice and pop the casserole in the oven. A crusty baguette and a crisp white wine round out the meal.

■ SERVES 4 ■

1½ pounds spinach, tough stems removed
2 tablespoons extra-virgin olive oil
2 shallots, minced
2 garlic cloves, minced
1 can (15 ounces) diced tomatoes, drained
2 tablespoons chopped fresh dill
½ pound feta, crumbled
   Salt and freshly ground black pepper
1½ pounds medium to large shrimp, shelled and deveined
   Hot cooked rice

1 Wash the spinach and place in a large pot with the water still clinging to its leaves. Cover and steam over high heat, until completely wilted, about 5 minutes, stirring occasionally. Drain well, pressing out any excess water with a spoon.

2 Preheat the oven to 400°F. Lightly grease a 1½-quart casserole dish with oil.

3 Heat the oil in a large skillet over medium-high heat. Add the shallots and garlic and sauté until fragrant, about 3 minutes. Stir in the tomatoes and dill. Then stir in the spinach and half of the cheese. Season to taste with the salt and pepper and remove from the heat. Stir in the shrimp.

4 Transfer the spinach mixture to the prepared casserole. Crumble the remaining cheese over the top.

5 Bake for about 30 minutes, until the shrimp are white and firm. Spoon over the rice and serve hot.

wilted spinach salad with chickpeas

The spinach is cooked, but the dish is served at room temperature, hence it is called a salad. If you are running out of space for your spinach, consider cooking it for this salad. It can be served as an appetizer with other antipasto-type dishes, or it makes a fine side dish. Because it is served at room temperature, and because the spinach is already cooked, it holds up well on a buffet table — much better than a "fresh" spinach salad.

■ SERVES 4 ■

1½–2 pounds spinach, tough stems removed

1½ cups cooked chickpeas or 1 can (15 ounces) chickpeas, rinsed and drained

1 small red onion, halved and sliced

3 tablespoons extra-virgin olive oil

1½ tablespoons red wine vinegar

1 garlic clove, minced

Salt and freshly ground black pepper

1 Bring a large pot of salted water to a boil. Stir in the spinach and cook until wilted, 30 to 60 seconds. Drain well. Press out the excess moisture. Transfer to a cutting board and chop.

2 Combine the spinach, chickpeas, and onion in a large bowl. Toss to mix.

3 Whisk together the oil, vinegar, garlic, and salt and pepper to taste in a small bowl. Pour over the spinach mixture and toss to mix well. Taste and adjust the seasoning. Serve at once.

pasta with green clam sauce

We love pasta with clam sauce — so much that I discovered it was convenient and useful to rely on canned clams and bottled clam juice so that I always had a quick "pantry meal" available for a spur-of-the-moment meal. Adding fresh spinach to the clam sauce makes it a quick one-pot family supper that everyone loves. In the winter, frozen spinach can be substituted for the fresh.

■ **SERVES 4–6** ■

1½–2 pounds fresh spinach, tough stems removed
⅓ cup extra-virgin olive oil
4 garlic cloves, minced
1 bottle (8 ounces) clam juice
1 cup chicken broth (page 9) (or substitute another 8-ounce bottle clam juice)
2 cans (6 ounces each) chopped clams in clam juice
½ cup dried bread crumbs
1 pound vermicelli
Salt and freshly ground black pepper

1 Bring a large pot of salted water to a boil. Add the spinach and cook until wilted, about 30 seconds. Remove from the water with tongs or a slotted spoon and let drain in a colander. Let the water return to a boil.

2 Meanwhile, heat the olive oil in a medium saucepan over medium heat. Add the garlic and sauté until fragrant but not browned, about 1 minute. Add the clam juice and broth. Strain the clam juice from the cans of clams into the saucepan. Add the bread crumbs and let simmer.

3 Squeeze the excess water from the spinach. Transfer to a cutting board and coarsely chop.

4 When the water returns to a boil, cook the pasta until just al dente. Drain the pasta, reserving 1 cup of the pasta-cooking water.

5 Return the pasta to the pot. Add the clams, spinach, and simmering sauce. Toss to mix. Add enough of the reserved pasta cooking water to make the pasta very moist. Season lightly with salt and very generously with black pepper. Serve at once.

sautéed spinach with garlic and pine nuts

There's nothing exceptional about this recipe. It is just a very good, very basic way to prepare a tender green. The water clinging to the leaves of the freshly washed spinach is all the liquid necessary. If you like, throw in a handful of raisins with the spinach.

■ SERVES 4 ■

3 tablespoons extra-virgin olive oil
1 garlic clove, minced
¼ cup pine nuts
1½–2 pounds spinach, tough stems removed and large leaves chopped
Salt and freshly ground black pepper

1 Heat the oil over medium-high heat in a large wok or Dutch oven. Add the garlic and pine nuts and sauté until the garlic begins to smell fragrant and color, about 1 minute.

2 Add the spinach, cover, and cook, stirring occasionally, until the spinach is wilted, about 3 minutes. Uncover, season with the salt and pepper to taste, stir well, and continue to cook until the liquid evaporates, 2 to 3 minutes. Serve hot.

S HAPPINESS WITH THE QUALITY of your vegetables possible if you don't grow them yourself?

Yes, says Diane Travis, a member of the Food Bank Farm, a Community-Supported Agriculture farm in western Massachusetts. "We get loads of fresh vegetables every week. It's incredible."

CSAs are supported by members, who buy a share in the farm and, in exchange, receive organic produce throughout the season.

The Food Bank Farm, to which Travis belongs, is one of the largest CSAs in the country. It is also unique because its primary mission is to provide healthful, organic produce for the Food Bank of Western Massachusetts. Over the last five years, the farm has produced more than 900,000 pounds of food for the food bank and its member agencies.

Meanwhile, members of the Food Bank Farm, including Travis, go to the farm each week and pick up their share of fresh vegetables, flowers, herbs, and fruit. Travis describes the experience as similar to going to a green market. All of the produce is displayed in bins in the big produce room. It is all washed and ready to be brought home.

"Each week I go to the farm," explains Travis, "and I see what's available and in what quantities on a big board. A lot of times there's tons of greens — kale, collards, Swiss chard — and you can take as much as you want. Then there will be a variety of vegetables of which you can take a

certain quantity, and usually you can mix or match. You get a bag that's about the size of a five-pound potato bag and you can fill it with what's available — like eggplant, carrots, peppers, tomatoes. You can take all of one vegetable, or some of each, or you skip one type of vegetable because you don't want any."

The harvest begins in late May or early June with greens. As the summer progresses, there are more and more vegetables to choose from. The farm grows more than 250 varieties of vegetables, flowers, and herbs. In November and December, members receive a month's supply of storage crops, including carrots, beets, winter squash, cabbage, leeks, and rutabagas.

Throughout the season there are some crops that members can pick themselves. These vary from year to year but always include green beans, strawberries, sugar snap peas, more than 20 types of herbs (including three kinds of basil), and plum and cherry tomatoes. At this particular farm, they also offer unlimited harvesting of more than 50 different flower varieties.

Because the Food Bank Farm includes building community as part of its mission, the farm also makes available a wide assortment of fresh local products: organic sourdough bread baked in a brick oven, local and organic eggs, tofu, goat cheese, tempeh, miso, bottled salad dressings, granola, baked goods, fruit, beef, lamb, chicken, fresh pasta, and biodegradable detergents. They even sell a soap that is made locally with bicycle-powered equipment. "The prices are really good," offers Travis, "like half of what you pay in a grocery store." The shares are reasonable, too. In 2004, a $420 farm share could feed a family of three to five for the season.

At some CSAs, members are required to put in a certain number of hours of work each month, but this particular farm has no work requirement. Are there no challenges to belonging to a CSA, I ask? What about getting stuck with an unfamiliar vegetable?

"Well, I had never seen pattypan squash before. This was about ten years ago. But we tried it and fell in love with it."

"What about kohlrabi?" I ask, thinking surely kohlrabi would stump anyone.

"I cook it just like my godmother in Austria," she replies. "I peel it, cube it, steam it, and throw in lots of butter. In any case, the farm also publishes a great newsletter with recipes and tricks about using different vegetables."

"When the kids were little," Travis comments, "they loved to go out to the farm with me and pick the vegetables. Now I go out on my own. It's really beautiful there. I really love picking flowers. There's the Holyoke Range in the background. It's so beautiful at the farm."

Belonging to a CSA sounds like having a garden without the chore of weeding or turning over the soil. Travis says, "It's on par with going to a really great market, except you know a lot of the people there. And you are where the food is grown. Picking your own tomatoes and basil and flowers — it's a very direct experience."

grilled teriyaki chicken strips with sesame spinach

"Grillicious," my kids called this dish the first time I made it. The white-meat chicken sears quickly over the hot fire, sealing in moisture. The chicken, combined with the wilted Japanese-style spinach salad and rice, makes a delicious meal. You can double the amount of chicken without needing to alter the rest of the recipe. The leftovers can be used in a salad the next day, or rolled up in a wrap with grilled or tamari-flavored sautéed onions.

SERVES 4

Marinade

2 garlic cloves, peeled

1 piece (1 inch long) fresh ginger, peeled

½ cup tamari (see Note)

¼ cup sake or dry sherry

3 tablespoons dark sesame oil

2 tablespoons brown sugar

Chicken and Vegetables

4 boneless, skinless chicken breast halves, cut lengthwise into ½-inch strips

1½ pounds fresh spinach, tough stems removed

1 large carrot, grated

1 tablespoon rice vinegar

Hot cooked white rice

3 tablespoons sesame seeds, toasted

1 To make the marinade, mince the garlic and ginger together in a blender or food processor. Add the tamari, sherry, oil, and brown sugar and process until well mixed. Alternatively, mince the garlic and ginger. Mix in a small bowl with the tamari, sherry, oil, and ginger.

2 Place the chicken in a nonreactive bowl. Add half the marinade and toss to coat. Cover and refrigerate while you prepare the rest of the dinner, or up to 2 hours.

3 Wash the spinach and place in a large pot. Add an inch or so of water. Cook over high heat until the spinach is completely wilted, 3 to 5 minutes, stirring once or twice. Drain well. Transfer the spinach to a medium bowl and add the carrot. Toss to combine.

4 Stir the vinegar into the remaining marinade. Add to the spinach and toss lightly. Refrigerate until you are ready to serve.

5 Prepare a hot fire in a charcoal grill and let the coals burn down until they are covered with white ash, or preheat a gas grill on high.

6 Grill the chicken for 4 to 6 minutes, until tender and no longer pink, turning once.

7 To serve, place a bed of rice in the center of a platter or on individual plates. Arrange the spinach over half the rice. Place the chicken on the other half, sprinkle the sesame seeds over all, and serve at once.

note When a recipe calls for tamari rather than soy sauce, it is fine to substitute soy sauce, but use a little less. Many people do use the two interchangeably, but the flavor really does differ. It is hard to conduct a tasting plain, but if you sprinkle a little tamari on white rice and compare it to rice sprinkled with soy sauce, you will taste the difference. Tamari is less salty and the flavor is more rounded. Soy sauce is much saltier and the flavor is more dominating.

SPINACH IN HISTORY

SPINACH ORIGINATED IN PERSIA (Iran), but it was not known outside its native land for quite some time. The earliest written record of spinach is in Chinese; the King of Nepal introduced it to China in AD 647. The Saracens brought it from North Africa to Italy in the 9th century. It reached Spain in 1100. By the 14th century it was a fairly common sight in European monastery gardens where it was used for medecinal purposes. Spinach didn't reach England until 1568, where it rapidly gained popularity as an early-spring crop when most vegetables are scarce. Its popularity in the United States hit an all-time high in 1929 with the introduction of Popeye the Sailor, whose strength came from spinach. ("I'm strong to the finish 'cause I eats me spinach.")

The Spring Tonic

A FEW YEARS AGO, I found myself in the middle of a field of lettuce in Monkton, Vermont. Every few feet, grower Marjorie Sussman offered me a different leaf, a new taste, a new texture.

"Here, try this one." She handed me an inner leaf from what looked like a head of Boston lettuce, only it was red on the outside. "Carmona. My favorite this year. Isn't it wonderful?"

It was wonderful: rich and buttery, full of flavor — the best Boston lettuce I had ever tasted. Carmona, Rosalita, Kalura, Lolla Rossa. The names were no less beautiful than the flavors were exciting. Here were lettuces so tasty they didn't even require an anointing of oil.

I had spent the previous year immersed in the creation of salads for a book entitled *Salad Suppers*. I had spent countless wintry hours cooking off-season foods in the kitchen. Finally it was summer — time for real field research. I arranged to visit some farms in the hope of expanding my gardening palette beyond the familiar oak-leaf and black-seeded Simpson lettuces I was in the habit of growing.

My first taste of Lolla Rossa was inspiring. The deeply curled leaves concealed a pale frosty-green interior with rose tips, and the flavor was richer than most any other lettuce I had had. Merlot — named after the wine — was beautiful and rich tasting. These lettuces now follow the early-spring mesclun mix and arugula I always grow. Every year I try new lettuces. My garden may not produce prizewinning tomatoes, but my greens never let me down.

GROWING Greens do well in a seedbed that has been prepared with some finished compost mixed into the top 3 inches. Most greens do best in full sun but will tolerate partial shade. Arugula needs only a few hours of sun every day. Garden cress is so easy to grow, it will grow indoors in windowsill containers.

SOWING You can sow seeds outdoors as soon as the soil can be worked. Make additional plantings every 3 weeks as long as the cool weather lasts. Greens do very well in cold frames and unheated greenhouses.

CULTIVATING Greens do not need a lot of water, but they do like a constant supply. Dry conditions lead to bitterness in the leaves and early bolting.

HARVESTING Begin harvesting as soon as the leaves are of edible size. If you cut the leaves and stems as needed, the plants will continue to grow and produce. The leaves are best when young, but these peppery greens are good until the plant starts to bolt. The flowers can be tossed into salads. Claytonia flowers are also good in salads.

It's best to harvest lettuce and other salad greens in the cool of the morning, before the leaves have wilted in the heat of the day. But if this isn't possible, or if previously harvested greens have gone limp, you can easily revive them with a brief soak in very cold water. Or several changes of water, if you need to wash them as well. Lift the greens out of the water, leaving behind any sandy residue in the bottom of your bowl or basin. Then dry them in a salad spinner. If you don't plan to use them right way, wrap them in a cotton kitchen towel or lightly dampened paper towels and seal them in a plastic bag. They should be fine for another day or so.

GREEN MATH

1 pound greens = 6 cups, loosely packed

warm mushroom salad

Arugula makes a tasty, pungent bed for the warm mushrooms in this salad, but you can substitute another green, such as watercress, if needed. The theme of the salad is contrast — of textures and flavors.

SERVES 4

8 cups arugula leaves

4 tablespoons extra-virgin olive oil

2 teaspoons fresh lemon juice

Salt and freshly ground black pepper

1 pound mixed mushrooms, quartered or cut into wedges

2 garlic cloves, minced

1 teaspoon chopped fresh thyme or ½ teaspoon dried

1 tablespoon red wine vinegar

Freshly shaved Parmesan (see Note)

note Use a swivel-bladed vegetable peeler to shave the Parmesan.

1 Put the arugula in a large salad bowl. Drizzle in 2 tablespoons of the olive oil and the lemon juice. Toss to coat. Season to taste with salt and pepper. Divide among four salad plates or arrange on a large platter.

2 Heat the remaining 2 tablespoons oil in a large skillet over medium-high heat. Add the mushrooms and let cook undisturbed until golden on the bottoms, about 4 minutes. Add the garlic and thyme, stir, and continue to cook until the mushrooms are tender throughout, about 4 minutes longer.

3 Stir in the vinegar and let cook until the vinegar is mostly absorbed. Season to taste with more salt and pepper.

4 Spoon the mushroom mixture over the arugula. Top with a few curls of shaved Parmesan. Serve at once.

ARUGULA With a distinctively peppery and slightly bitter flavor, arugula stands out in a salad mix. People either love it or hate it. Deemed an aphrodisiac, arugula was banned from monastery gardens in the Middle Ages. It has small, lobed, dark green leaves on stems that should be discarded if tough. Arugula becomes progressively stronger-flavored as the weather warms. If grown under stress — particularly without enough water — it will be very sharp-tasting. Arugula is the Italian name; look for it also under the names "rocket" and "roquette." Wild arugula, sylvetta, or *rucola selvatica,* is smaller, more pungently flavored, and slower to bolt.

CRESS Both garden cress and watercress have a peppery tang that makes them a good substitute for arugula.

ESCAROLE In the chicory family, escarole has broader leaves than frisée but tastes similar. The leaves on the outside of the rosette are darker and more strongly flavored. The leaves on the inside should be blanched.

FRISÉE Also know as curly endive or chicory, frisée has a loose head with dark frilly leaves on the outside of the head and paler ones toward the center. The flavor is bracingly bitter. A properly grown head has a large area of blanched leaves, achieved by placing a "blanching cup" over the center of the head.

LETTUCE There are dozens of different lettuce varieties, but they fall into four general types. Crisphead lettuces, such as iceberg, form a firm round head. Each head contains about 90 percent water by weight, which accounts for its insipid flavor. Alone these lettuces make a bland salad, but when placed in a mix of greens, they add a juicy texture and sweet flavor.

Romaine or cos lettuces have long, narrow leaves that are dark on the outside and lighter and crisper toward the interior of the head. They offer more flavor than crisphead lettuces while still being crisp and sweet. Red romaines are now available, as well as the standard greens.

Butterhead lettuces include Boston lettuce, butter lettuce, Bibb lettuce, and Kentucky limestone lettuce. Their leaves are distinctively soft and crumpled, with a mild, sweet flavor and buttery texture. Butterhead lettuces are quite delicate and wilt almost as soon as they are dressed. A salad that includes butterhead tastes richer and more luxurious than usual. Carmona, a red Boston type, is unusually sweet and flavorful.

Loose-leaf lettuces offer the most variety in shape and color. In general, these lettuces are mild, sweet, and somewhat crisp, with colors ranging from pale green to deeply red. Oakleaf, with its distinctively lobed leaves, is lovely to look at and reasonably flavorful. Lolla Rossa and Lolla Bianco are exceptionally tasty with deeply frilled leaves.

MÂCHE Mâche also goes by the names corn salad, field lettuce (because it is found growing wild in cornfields), and lamb's lettuce (because the small, tender, velvety leaves are said to resemble a lamb's tongue). The flavor is delicate and rather nutty; salads that feature mâche are good choices for dressings made with walnut or hazelnut oils.

MESCLUN From a French word meaning "mixture," mesclun is a combination of baby greens and herbs. The mix may include butter lettuce, mâche, arugula, red leaf lettuce, baby mustard leaves, spinach, dandelion, and herbs. Often mesclun mixes will include Asian cabbages and greens such as mizuna, pac choi, and tatsoi. Red Russian kale is another nontraditional green that is fine for salads when the leaves are "baby," and is often found in mesclun mixes.

MIZUNA This Asian green has glossy, dark green feathery leaves and a fairly mild flavor.

RADICCHIO Not a green at all, radicchio is a type of chicory that adds both color, texture, and flavor to a salad bowl. Radicchio forms heads that are snowy white with deep maroon markings. The texture is like a very tender cabbage and the flavor is more tart than bitter. Guilio is a good variety for spring crops, producing bright red heads about 90 days from sowing.

pasta with arugula pesto

If only basil could be made into pesto, then spring and early summer would be diminished indeed, for inevitably the supply of pesto in the freezer runs out a few months shy of the next basil crop. But, as it turns out, arugula makes a fine pesto. Just warn your diners ahead of time; otherwise the first forkful will cause no end of confusion.

SERVES 4

Pesto

- 8 cups arugula leaves
- ½ cup pine nuts
- 2 garlic cloves
- ½ cup extra-virgin olive oil
- ½ cup freshly grated Parmesan
- 8 sun-dried tomatoes packed in oil, minced
  Salt and freshly ground pepper
- 1 pound vermicelli
- ½ cup pitted cured black olives

1 Bring a large pot of salted water to a boil. Add the arugula and blanch until wilted, about 30 seconds. Remove the arugula with tongs and transfer to a bowl of ice water to stop the cooking process. Let cool, then drain. Keep the water hot in the pot for the pasta. Alternatively, if you have a steamer insert, place the arugula in the insert, set it into the pot of boiling water, and blanch the arugula until just wilted, about 20 seconds. Lift the insert out of the water, transfer to the ice-water bath, and continue as above.

2 Drain the arugula and squeeze out as much moisture as possible.

3 Chop the pine nuts and garlic in a food processor. Transfer the arugula to the food processor and process until finely chopped. Add the oil and Parmesan and process until the mixture has the consistency of a thick paste. Transfer to a bowl and stir in the sun-dried tomatoes. Season to taste with the salt and pepper.

4 Return the water in the pot to a boil. Add the pasta and cook until al dente. Reserve ½ cup of the cooking water and drain well.

5 Transfer the pasta to a heated serving bowl. Mix the arugula pesto and olives with the pasta, adding the reserved cooking liquid as needed to moisten the pasta. Serve at once, passing additional Parmesan at the table.

SALAD SPINNER: A WORTHWHILE GADGET

NORMALLY, I DON'T ENDORSE owning a space-taking, single-use tool — but I make an exception for a three-piece salad spinner, which costs between $15 and $20. Spinners have round perforated baskets that are set in an outer basket. The perforated basket is loosely filled with greens and covered. Then the gears in the lid are cranked to spin the basket rapidly. Centrifugal force pulls the greens to the sides of the inner basket while the water is flung out through the perforations, resulting in freshly washed and dried greens, ready for salad or storage.

Spinners come in a few different styles, with a hand crank or a pull cord. The pull cord models work more efficiently, but the cords tend to break with heavy use. You can greatly extend the life of your cord by making sure it is completely dry before putting it away (my current model is 9 years old). Some models have drainage holes on the bottom and an opening in the top to allow you to wash under running water, spin dry, and drain all in one container. The washing action only works with small loads of greens that are not excessively dirty.

chicken taco salad

Taco salad is what I make when I need to whip up a meal quickly. Tortilla chips replace the fried tortilla bowl served at restaurants. Beyond lettuce and avocados, the vegetables vary with what is in the garden: radishes and snow peas early in the season, tomatoes, peppers, cucumbers, and corn later on. Use whatever you have on hand. Instead of the chicken mixture, you can make your usual ground beef chili mixture.

■ SERVES 4 ■

2 tablespoons extra-virgin olive oil or canola oil

4 cups chopped cooked chicken (to use leftovers from making broth, page 9)

1 onion, finely chopped

1 fresh green chile, seeded and finely chopped

4 teaspoons chili powder

1½ teaspoons ground cumin

1 cup unseasoned tomato sauce

Salt and freshly ground black pepper

10 cups chopped or torn lettuce

1–2 avocados, peeled and sliced

2–4 cups sliced or chopped vegetables, such as carrots, corn, cucumbers, jicama, sweet onion or scallions, bell peppers, radishes, and tomatoes

½ cup Lime Cilantro Vinaigrette (page 93)

Tortilla chips

Grated Monterey Jack or pepper Jack, sour cream, heated refried beans, sliced black olives, and chopped sweet onion, to garnish (optional)

1 Heat the oil in a large nonstick or cast-iron skillet over medium-high heat. Add the chicken, onion, chile, chili powder, and cumin and cook, stirring frequently, until the onion is soft and the chicken is slightly crispy, about 8 minutes. Add the tomato sauce and salt and pepper to taste. Keep warm while you prepare the salad.

2 Combine the lettuce, avocado, and vegetables in a large bowl. Toss with the dressing. Place the tortilla chips in a bowl. Put whichever garnishes you are using in separate bowls.

3 Serve buffet-style, allowing each diner to assemble his or her own dish. There is some controversy as to whether the tortilla chips should be placed in the bowl first or crumbled on top.

THE ACCENT IS ON RADISHES

ONE OF THE REWARDS of clearing and cleaning the garden in the fall is having a blank soil canvas for starting a quick crop of radishes before any other vegetable seems possible. Radishes like French Breakfast, Cherry Belle, and Easter Egg all germinate quickly, grow best in cool weather, and are ready for harvest in 3 to 4 weeks.

Vegetable expert Elizabeth Schneider calls radishes multicolored, multipurpose, and multicultural. She notes that throughout Asia, radishes are a staple food, often cooked or pickled. In this country, radishes are usually a colorful afterthought to a green salad or crudités platter. In Asia, the radishes grown, like the daikon radish, are especially good pickled. Our "table" or red radishes can be sautéed but are really best served raw.

So what can you do with table radishes? Start with appetizers and do what the French do — eat them (rinsed off right out of the garden) with unsalted butter. Or take dense artisanal rye bread, smear thickly with unsalted, creamery-fresh butter, top with thinly sliced radishes, and sprinkle with coarse sea salt. Multicolored radishes on a crudités platter disappear fast. And, of course, radishes add color and snap to spring salad greens.

Asian radishes tend to have a longer growing season than spring radishes. They are often planted for fall harvest and storage in root cellars. Fresh Asian radishes can be sliced and served as a "cracker" with spreads. Or they can be cooked any way you would cook a turnip. They make terrific pickles.

pan-seared chicken on a bed of greens

Composed salads make incredibly easy and elegant dinners. They are family favorites, and my kids never fail to compliment me on the presentation. Searing the chicken over high heat gives it a lovely crust and seals in the juices. Adding anchovies to the dressing adds depth and richness but no fishy flavor, and the dressing is low-fat because it is based on defatted chicken broth — all in all a flavorful, healthful dish.

■ **SERVES 4** ■

Anchovy-Shallot Sauce

¾ cup chicken broth (see page 9)

3 anchovy fillets

1 large shallot, chopped

2 tablespoons chopped fresh parsley

1 tablespoon best-quality balsamic vinegar

1 tablespoon extra-virgin olive oil

Salt and freshly ground black pepper

Salad

4 boneless, skinless chicken breast halves

2 tablespoons extra-virgin olive oil

Salt and freshly ground black pepper

8–12 cups torn mixed lettuces and greens

2 cups chopped vegetables (see Note)

¼ Vidalia or other similar sweet onion, cut into thin rings

1 To make the sauce, combine the broth, anchovies, shallot, parsley, vinegar, and olive oil in a blender. Process briefly to mix. Season with salt and pepper.

2 To make the salad, place the chicken breasts between two pieces of plastic wrap and pound lightly to even out the thickness of each piece.

3 Heat the oil in a large nonstick skillet over high heat. Add the chicken breasts, season with a generous pinch of salt and a few grinds of pepper, and cook on both sides until tender and no longer pink, about 8 minutes. Remove from the skillet and keep warm.

4 Return the skillet to high heat and pour in the sauce. Bring the sauce to a boil, stirring and scraping up any browned bits that cling to the bottom of the pan. Continue to boil the sauce until it is until reduced by a third, about 3 minutes. Transfer the sauce to a small pitcher.

5 Arrange the greens and vegetables on individual plates. Slice the chicken on the diagonal into thin strips and arrange over the greens. Drizzle the warm sauce on top. Scatter onion rings over the salads and serve.

note The vegetables you choose for the salad should be whatever looks good in the garden — or in the refrigerator. In the spring, you might want to add lightly steamed cut asparagus, snow peas, sliced radishes, or sugar snap peas. Later in the season, it might be steamed broccoli or green beans, or wedges of tomatoes or roasted beets.

vietnamese chicken salad

There's no cuisine lighter and fresher than Vietnam's. This salad is distinguished by its full flavor and very low fat content. Serve with crusty French bread for mopping up all the delicious dressing. If you like, substitute shrimp or thinly sliced roast beef for the chicken.

SERVES 4

Dressing

¼ cup water

¼ cup sugar

½ cup fresh lime juice (about 4 limes), or to taste

6 tablespoons Asian fish sauce

3 garlic cloves, minced

1 teaspoon crushed red pepper flakes

Salad

4 boneless, skinless chicken breast halves

1 cup chicken broth (see page 9)

1 piece (2 inches long) fresh lemongrass, chopped, or zest of 1 lemon (1 tablespoon)

1 teaspoon minced fresh ginger

2 teaspoons Asian fish sauce

3–4 ounces dried rice vermicelli

4 cups shredded red leaf or green leaf lettuce

1 carrot, grated

⅓ cup roughly chopped fresh basil leaves

⅓ cup roughly chopped fresh mint leaves

⅓ cup cilantro leaves

1 head Boston lettuce, leaves separated

¼ cup chopped roasted peanuts, to garnish

Lime wedges, to garnish

1 To make the dressing, combine the water and sugar in a small bowl. Heat in a microwave until the sugar is completely dissolved, about 1 minute. Stir in the lime juice, fish sauce, garlic, and red pepper. Taste and add more lime juice, if desired.

2 Cut each chicken breast into five diagonal strips. In a medium saucepan, combine the broth, lemongrass, ginger, and fish sauce. Bring to a simmer, add the chicken, stir, and cover the pan. Cook over low heat for 5 minutes. Turn the heat off and let the chicken steam for 5 minutes. Remove the chicken from the pan and shred it.

3 Bring a large pot of water to a boil. Remove from the heat and add the rice vermicelli. Leave in the water for 3 to 5 minutes, until al dente. Rinse in cold water and drain well.

4 Combine the chicken in a large bowl with the shredded lettuce, carrot, basil, mint, and cilantro, and toss to mix.

5 Line four dinner plates with the Boston lettuce leaves. Separate the rice vermicelli into individual strands and layer over the lettuce. Spoon the chicken mixture over the vermicelli. Pour the dressing over the salads. Garnish with the peanuts and lime wedges. Serve at once.

LETTUCE BE HONEST

Regardless of what grown-ups put on the table, kids will always prefer iceberg, or crisphead, lettuce. Let's be honest. In hot weather, nothing beats a salad made of crisp, light, well-chilled iceberg. Yes, this is one of the most nutritiously light-weight of all the greens, offering little in the way of vitamins, minerals, or fiber. It may not be good for you, but it isn't bad for you either. So every once in a while, it is a good thing to treat yourself to a salad made of a wedge of iceberg lettuce topped with Blue Cheese Dressing (page 99) or Catalina Dressing (page 98). And if the salad is accompanied by juicy, garden-ripe tomatoes and fresh-picked corn, you'll have the makings of a memorable summer meal.

classic vinaigrette

A classic vinaigrette is made of oil and vinegar, bound together with a touch of mustard and flavored with a little garlic, shallot, or herbs. The best-quality extra-virgin olive oil and the best-quality vinegar will make all the difference. Which vinegar to use — red wine, white wine, sherry, herbal, raspberry, balsamic — depends on the salad you are dressing. All work equally well with a salad of mixed greens. This recipe is easily multiplied when a large quantity it desired, but for best flavor, make it fresh each time you need it.

MAKES ABOUT ¼ CUP

1 tablespoon balsamic, herbal, raspberry, red wine, sherry, or white wine vinegar

1 small garlic clove, minced, or 1 tablespoon minced fresh herbs or shallot

½ teaspoon Dijon mustard

3 tablespoons extra-virgin olive oil

Salt and freshly ground black pepper

Combine the vinegar, garlic, and mustard in a small bowl. Whisk until smooth. Slowly pour in the oil. Whisk constantly until the oil is fully incorporated. Season with salt and pepper. Use immediately.

herb vinaigrette

The emphasis here is on fresh herbs. This salad dressing is ideal for vegetable and pasta salads — the herbs give the dressing great clinging capacity. It also makes a great marinade for vegetables, poultry, and fish that are about to be grilled.

MAKES ABOUT ⅓ CUP

4 garlic cloves, minced
¼ cup chopped fresh basil
2 tablespoons chopped fresh oregano
2 tablespoons red wine or white wine vinegar
1 teaspoon salt
½ teaspoon freshly ground black pepper
¼ cup extra-virgin olive oil

Combine the garlic, basil, oregano, vinegar, salt, and pepper in a small bowl. Slowly pour in the olive oil, whisking until the oil is fully incorporated. Use immediately.

DRESSING SALADS IN THE BOWL

If you have high-quality ingredients on hand, there is no need to carefully follow a recipe to make a delicious dressed salad. Here's what you do. Start, if you like, by crushing a garlic clove and rubbing it in the inside of your salad bowl for a very subtle garlic flavor. Discard the clove. Fill the bowl with greens and whatever chopped vegetables you choose. Drizzle on some of the finest olive oil you have on hand. How much? Not much — a few tablespoons, depending on how heavily you like your salad dressed and how big a salad you are preparing. Then sprinkle (more lightly) some vinegar or fresh lemon juice. Add a bit of crunchy sea salt or kosher salt and a few twists of a peppermill and toss. Taste a salad leaf. If the balance of flavors is off, add a little more of whatever is missing to even it out.

CLEANING OUT MY PERENNIAL HERB BED, which is located in the back row of my kitchen garden, is a satisfying spring chore. Chives are unquestionably the earliest spring "vegetable" and I snip a few stems to munch on, just to say I started my harvest season in March (or April). Here are some perennial herbs I recommend for their ease and versatility in the kitchen.

CHIVES Chives can be grown from seed, but they are easiest to grow from live plants, purchased at a garden center or dug up from a friend's garden. Since they grow so prolifically, most people divide their chives often and replant or give away extras.

In cool climates, chives die back to the ground in the winter, but in warmer areas, they remain green throughout the year. Harvest leaves with scissors to snip individual stems, or give the entire clump a trim. The flowers make a beautiful addition to salads. Use chives fresh in salads or as a delicate onion alternative added to dips, salsas, or sauces. They are also good in quickly cooked dishes, such as scrambled eggs and omelets.

MINT Mint spreads vigorously and some people don't recommend having it in a vegetable garden at all. But it is an easy weed to pull up, so I don't mind the inconvenience of its spreading as long as I have a steady supply when I need it in salads. Mint brings fresh flavor to salads and sauces; I couldn't live without it. Also, mint supposedly discourages cabbage moths and ants.

There are many different mints and many different flavors, so be sure to taste before you plant.

OREGANO Sometimes called Greek oregano, *Origanum vulgare* is used extensively in Mediterranean cooking. It is closely related to marjoram *(Origanum majorana)* and the two are sometimes confused. Oregano has white flowers and it is thicker stemmed and more robust in growth habit and flavor.

In the garden, oregano is an aggressive spreader. It does best in full sun and well-drained soil. Shear the plants about 2 inches from the ground just before they flower in early summer and you'll have another harvest at the end of the season.

ROSEMARY A perennial in warmer climates, this herb is an annual in Zone 6 or colder. Rosemary likes full sun and well-drained soil. It doesn't need cutting back after flowering. You can try potting rosemary and bringing it inside for the winter.

SAGE Fresh sage is less potent than dried sage, which makes it more versatile in the kitchen. It goes very well with sweet root vegetables, as well as poultry and meat. The plant likes full sun and well-drained soil.

TARRAGON Tarragon has a distinctly aniselike flavor, so use with caution. French tarragon is not grown from seed, so purchase this plant. This drought-tolerant plant likes full sun and well-drained soil. Pinch back the growing tips to keep the plant bushy and well mannered.

THYME Thyme is highly aromatic and indispensable to many dishes. There are many different species of thyme, including ones that are flavored with lemon, orange, and nutmeg. Thyme likes full sun and well-drained soil. Cut back after flowering.

lime-cilantro vinaigrette

The delicate floral flavor of lime makes this dressing perfect for lettuce or cucumber salads that accompany a Mexican- or Thai-inspired dinner. The vinaigrette also makes a delicious baste for grilled shrimp or fish.

MAKES ½ CUP

1 teaspoon lime zest
2 tablespoons fresh lime juice (about 1 lime)
1 teaspoon white balsamic vinegar
5 tablespoons canola or grapeseed oil
2 tablespoons finely chopped fresh cilantro
2 tablespoons chopped fresh chives
Salt

Combine the lime zest and juice and vinegar in a small bowl. Whisk in the oil until completely blended. Stir in the cilantro and chives. Season with salt. Use immediately.

black & green olive vinaigrette

When I made this dressing, I was in the mood to eat olives, and rather than add them to a salad, I decided to make the dressing out of olives. The result was more than pleasing — salty, sharp, earthy, a sensational contrast to a mix of sharp-tasting greens. This dressing is also wonderful on a pan-seared or grilled chicken or fish. And it is terrific in a pasta salad or a warm potato salad.

MAKES ABOUT ¾ CUP

1 garlic clove
1 tablespoon fresh oregano leaves
¼ cup pitted black olives
¼ cup pitted green olives
3 tablespoons red wine vinegar
6 tablespoons extra-virgin olive oil
Freshly ground black pepper

1 In a blender or food processor, process the garlic and oregano until finely chopped. Add the black and green olives and process to finely chop. Scrape down the sides of the container, pour in the vinegar, and process until mixed.

2 With the motor running, slowly pour in the oil and process until the mixture is thick and smooth. Season to taste with pepper.

3 Serve immediately or store in an airtight jar in the refrigerator for up to a week. It will need remixing before serving.

miso vinaigrette

Miso is a fermented soybean paste that is a basic flavoring ingredient in Japanese cooking. It comes in many colors and flavors, with "white miso" lighter in flavor and color than some of the darker kinds. It is fine to substitute another miso, if you already have some on hand. Miso lasts forever in the refrigerator, and since it is bought in 1-pound tubs, it takes forever to use up a batch. Likewise, the pickled ginger used in sushi is just perfect in this salad dressing, but if you prefer, you can substitute fresh ginger.

MAKES ½ CUP

2 tablespoons fresh lemon juice

1 tablespoon tamari

1 tablespoon miso (white is recommended)

1 tablespoon minced pickled ginger or 2 teaspoons grated fresh ginger

1 teaspoon dark sesame oil

1 garlic clove, minced

¼ cup canola oil

Freshly ground black pepper

1 In a small bowl, combine the lemon juice, tamari, miso, ginger, sesame oil, and garlic. Whisk to fully combine the miso with the other ingredients. Whisk in the oil. Season with pepper.

2 Use immediately or store in an airtight container in the refrigerator for up to 4 days.

tahini dressing

Tahini is a paste made of sesame seeds, and it makes frequent appearances in Middle Eastern cooking. This dressing is delicious on spinach salads and grilled or roasted vegetables, and is terrific in a pita pocket with falafel (chickpea patties).

MAKES ABOUT 1¼ CUPS

1 garlic clove
⅔ cup tahini
6 tablespoons fresh lemon juice (about 2 lemons)
2 tablespoons honey
¼ cup water
Salt

1 Mince the garlic in a food processor or blender. Add the tahini, lemon juice, honey, and water and process until well blended.

2 Season to taste with salt. Serve immediately or store in an airtight jar in the refrigerator for up to a week. It will need remixing before serving.

mustard crème fraîche

The combination of mustard and horseradish gives this salad dressing tremendous presence, making it a terrific foil for assertive greens, such as arugula. I love it as a dip for a platter of raw vegetables, a topping for baked potatoes or raw beets, and a spread for a tomato sandwich. This is an incredibly versatile sauce. You can substitute sour cream for the crème fraîche if you prefer.

■ MAKES 1 CUP ■

1 cup crème fraîche
1 tablespoon prepared horseradish
1 tablespoon Dijon mustard
   Salt and freshly ground black pepper
   Milk, for thinning, if needed

1 Combine the crème fraîche, horseradish, and mustard in a small bowl and stir until well blended. Season to taste with salt and pepper.

2 Serve at once or store in an airtight container for up to 4 days. It will thicken in the refrigerator, so it may need to be thinned down with a little milk to serve as a salad dressing.

catalina dressing

The sweet-and-sour dressing of my youth, wonderful on a wedge of iceberg lettuce, a Cobb salad, or a green bean salad. It's not for delicate spring greens, but it is terrific later in the season. This recipe makes a reduced-fat version.

MAKES 1¼ CUPS

½ cup ketchup

⅓ cup water

3 tablespoons red wine vinegar

2 tablespoons extra-virgin olive oil

2 tablespoons finely chopped onion

2 tablespoons sugar

2 garlic cloves, minced

Salt and freshly ground black pepper

1 Combine all the ingredients in a blender and process until smooth. Taste and adjust the seasonings.

2 Serve at once or store in an airtight container for up to 2 weeks in the refrigerator. Stir or shake well before using.

blue cheese dressing

Pungent and lively is the only way to describe a blue cheese dressing. If you use low-fat buttermilk, it is also a good-for-you dressing, perfect for pairing with raw vegetables, green salads (especially spinach salad), even roasted carrot and celery root sticks.

MAKES ABOUT 1 CUP

½ cup buttermilk
¼ cup crumbled blue cheese, such as Roquefort
3 tablespoons mayonnaise (reduced-fat is acceptable)
2 tablespoons chopped fresh parsley
1 garlic clove
Salt and freshly ground black pepper

1 Combine the buttermilk, blue cheese, mayonnaise, parsley, and garlic in a blender or food processor. Process until thick and fairly smooth. Season to taste with salt and pepper.

2 Serve immediately or store in an airtight container in the refrigerator for up to 5 days.

lemon-soy dressing

If you were to peek into my refrigerator at any point in the year, this is the salad dressing you would be most likely to find. It is a pleasing blend of flavors, is low in fat, keeps forever, and is very, very good.

MAKES 1 CUP

½ cup soy sauce

¼ cup water

¼ cup dark sesame oil

6 tablespoons fresh lemon juice (about 2 lemons)

4 garlic cloves, minced

1 Combine all the ingredients in a glass jar and shake well.

2 Serve at once or store in an airtight container for several months in the refrigerator. Stir or shake well before using.

HEIGHT OF THE SEASON
SPRING

Cooking from the garden is almost a novelty each spring. It is a pure pleasure to cook each vegetable in its time — to fully enjoy the fresh green flavor each vegetable presents. But there is also joy in combining vegetables, in truly recognizing the abundance that the garden represents. The few recipes presented here combine spring vegetables to make dishes that celebrate the season.

A recipe for garlic scapes is included. Scapes are the flower stems of garlic plants. They don't deserve their own chapter, perhaps, but they are a spring green that should not be ignored.

pasta primavera

Primavera *means spring, and what better way to celebrate the first harvests than with this luxurious pasta dish. The vegetables listed below are typical of my early harvests, but if your garden or CSA or farmstand has different offerings, then substitute what looks best. If you don't have leeks, consider using scallions, spring onions, bunching onions (added with the spinach), or wild leeks. If you don't have asparagus, substitute wild fiddleheads or even broccoli florets. Arugula or dandelion greens can stand in for spinach. Mature carrots can replace baby carrots, or substitute red bell peppers, added with the peas.*

SERVES 4–5

1½ cups vegetable or chicken broth (page 8 or 9)

8 ounces baby or mature carrots, cut into 1-inch pieces (about 1 cup)

6 asparagus spears, cut into 1-inch pieces (about 1 cup)

1 leek, trimmed and thinly sliced

4 ounces sugar snap peas or snow peas (about 1 cup) or ½ cup shelled peas

2 tablespoons extra-virgin olive oil

2 large garlic cloves, minced

1½ cups half-and-half or light cream

1 pound fettuccine, linguine, or penne

10 ounces spinach, large leaves torn and stems discarded (about 8 lightly packed cups)

Salt and freshly ground black pepper

1½ cups freshly grated Parmesan

1 Begin heating a large pot of salted water for the pasta.

2 Bring the stock to a boil in a large skillet. Add the carrots and cook for 3 minutes. Add the asparagus, leek, and sugar snap peas, if using, and cook for 1 minute. Add the snow peas, if using, and cook for 1 minute.

3 Add the oil, garlic, and half-and-half and bring just to a boil. Cover and turn off the heat.

4 Cook the pasta in the salted water until just tender. Drain.

5 Over medium heat, stir the spinach into the sauce. Cook, stirring frequently, until the spinach is wilted. Season to taste with salt and pepper.

6 In a large heated serving bowl, toss the pasta with the sauce. Add 1 cup of the Parmesan and toss again. Season with salt and pepper. Serve immediately, passing the remaining ½ cup Parmesan at the table.

risotto primavera

I've specified the vegetables to use in this risotto, but feel free to make substitutions with what you have on hand. I've used storage carrots in place of baby carrots, sugar snap peas in place of snow peas, arugula in place of spinach. It's just a lovely dish with any fresh vegetables.

SERVES 4

8 asparagus spears, cut into 2-inch lengths

1 cup snow peas

4 baby carrots, cut into narrow spears

2 cups baby spinach

5½ cups high-quality vegetable or chicken broth (page 8 or 9)

½ cup dry white wine

2 tablespoons extra-virgin olive oil

2 shallots, minced

2 cups uncooked Arborio rice

Salt and freshly ground black pepper

¼ cup chopped fresh chives

¼ cup chopped fresh basil or sun-dried tomatoes

1 Bring a medium saucepan of salted water to a boil. Add the asparagus, snow peas, and carrots and boil for 30 seconds. Stir in the spinach, then immediately drain. The vegetables should be barely cooked.

2 Heat the broth and wine to simmering in a medium-size saucepan.

3 Heat the oil over medium heat in a large nonstick skillet. Add the shallots and rice and toss to coat with the oil. Sauté for 3 to 5 minutes, until the rice appears toasted.

4 Add 1 cup of the simmering broth to the rice. Stir until the liquid is mostly absorbed. Continue adding more broth, 1 cup at a time, cooking and stirring as the liquid is absorbed. It will take a total of 20 to 30 minutes for the liquid to be absorbed and the rice to become tender and creamy.

5 Stir in the vegetables and allow to heat through. Stir in the chives and basil. Season generously to taste with salt and pepper. Serve hot.

chicken lo mein with mushrooms and garlic scapes

Garlic scapes are the flower stems of the garlic plant. They look like curly scallion greens, though they are firmer and tougher. The flavor is mildly garlicky. Stir-fries are an excellent way to prepare them.

SERVES 6

1–1¼ pounds boneless, skinless chicken, cut into matchsticks
4 tablespoons soy sauce
2 tablespoons rice wine or dry sherry
2 teaspoons dark sesame oil
1 pound vermicelli
½ cup chicken broth (page 9)
¼ cup oyster sauce
1 tablespoon cornstarch
2 tablespoons peanut or canola oil
1 pound white mushrooms, sliced
¼ pound shiitake mushrooms, stems discarded and caps sliced
5 cups roughly chopped garlic scapes
1 tablespoon minced peeled fresh ginger

1 Combine the chicken, 1 tablespoon of the soy sauce, 1 tablespoon of the wine, and 1 teaspoon of the sesame oil in a medium bowl. Mix well and set aside to marinate.

2 Bring a large pot of salted water to a boil. Add the pasta and cook until al dente. Drain well. Rinse lightly under warm running water and drain. Toss lightly with the remaining 1 teaspoon of sesame oil and set aside.

3 To make the sauce, combine the broth, 2 tablespoons of the remaining soy sauce, remaining 1 tablespoon wine, the oyster sauce, and cornstarch. Whisk until thoroughly combined.

4 Heat a large wok or skillet over high heat. Add 1 tablespoon of the peanut oil and heat until very hot. Add the chicken and marinade and stir-fry, stirring constantly, until tender and no longer pink, about 6 minutes. Transfer the chicken to a medium bowl and keep warm. Wipe out the wok.

5 Heat the remaining 1 tablespoon of peanut oil over high heat until very hot. Add the white and shiitake mushrooms and the remaining 1 tablespoon soy sauce and stir-fry, stirring constantly, until the mushrooms give up their juice, about 5 minutes. Push the mushrooms to the sides of the pan and add the garlic scapes. Stir-fry until tender, about 4 minutes. Push aside the mushrooms and garlic scapes. Add the ginger. Cook until fragrant, about 45 seconds. Toss with the scapes and mushrooms.

6 Return the chicken and marinade to the wok. Add the pasta. Whisk the sauce and pour into the wok. Cook, stirring constantly, until the sauce is thickened and the pasta, vegetables, and chicken are evenly mixed, about 2 minutes.

7 Serve immediately.

GARLIC SCAPES

When the garlic starts to flower, snip off the flower stems, called scapes, before the flowers open. The scapes can be discarded or used as a green. The texture of these scapes is a little tougher than a scallion green, but good in a stir-fry.

early to mid-summer

BEETS

BROCCOLI

CUCUMBERS

SNAP BEANS

SWISS CHARD

ZUCCHINI & SUMMER SQUASH

NOW THE GARDEN IS producing well — too well some-times. Weeds proliferate — and if you don't stay ahead of them, they will overwhelm you. Now is the time to weed, mulch, thin, and side-dress. And harvest. There is always something in the garden that you can enjoy, even if you can't harvest a full meal quite yet. In addition to the vegetables in this chapter, most gardens also offer baby vegetables — baby carrots, tiny potatoes, slender leeks — at this time.

Upbeat About Beets

VEGETABLES DON'T OFTEN INSPIRE NOVELS, but the beet inspired Tom Robbins to write *Jitterbug Perfume,* in which the beet provides the base note for a perfume. People who haven't read Robbins's floral prose may wrinkle up their noses. Beets, they say, smell like the earth. Well, that's his point.

They also can taste like the earth. At least, that's the opinion of some. There is a mineral tang to beets. Their high sucrose content makes them extraordinarily sweet, but a concentration of certain chemicals that leach into beets from the soil causes an earthy flavor. You can find the same chemical influences in spinach and Swiss chard (a close relative of beets). Fans love that flavor; detractors say beets just taste like dirt.

It is the cook's job to discipline that earthy base note in beets while celebrating their brilliant color and uncommon sweetness. Few plants are as beautiful in the garden, or as spectacular on the dinner table.

GROWING Give beets deeply dug, loose soil, so the long taproot has plenty of room to grow. Beets grow best in cool weather with full sun and moderate, even watering.

SOWING Sow 3 to 4 weeks before the last frost.

CULTIVATING Because each beet seed is actually a dried fruit containing a cluster of seeds, thinning is always necessary. After the seedlings emerge, thin each cluster by cutting with scissors. Don't pull out unwanted plants, because you are too likely to disturb the ones remaining. Provide even moisture and don't let the soil dry out. Fertilize every 3 to 4 weeks with a low-nitrogen fertilizer; too much nitrogen will encourage growth of the greens at the expense of the roots.

HARVESTING Harvest when the beets are 1½ to 2½ inches in diameter. Although there isn't the same urgency for harvesting as there is, say, for beans, don't leave beets in the ground for too long, or the roots will become woody and flavorless. To store, twist off the greens. Place the greens and roots in separate plastic bags in the refrigerator. Or store the beets layered in damp sand in a root cellar.

BEET MATH

1 pound = 4 to 5 medium beets without greens
= 3 cups cubed beets
= 4 cups grated beets

1 pound greens = 1½ to 2 cups cooked

Dark red beets will stain countertops, hands, and wooden cutting boards, so take care when working with them. The stain is water-soluble, so you should be able to wash it out. White, golden, and candy-stripe beets do not stain.

Roasting will help the beets retain the best color and flavor. Beets are surprisingly good grilled, another dry-heat cooking method. Boiling isn't the best way of cooking beets because flavor and color are leached into the cooking water. Although you can find recipes that use uncooked beets, I recommend you taste a raw beet before you commit yourself to a recipe. I find the flavor of raw beets overwhelmed by a mineral tang.

Cooked beets with Skordalia (page 381) is a wonderful, and traditional, combination. Replace the apple with sliced roasted beets in Endive, Apple, and Walnut Salad (page 334) for a different take on a wonderful salad. Or add sliced roasted beets to the Endive and Goat Cheese Salad (page 335), another great combination.

Beet greens are as valuable as the beets themselves. They can be cooked any way you would cook Swiss chard (see pages 162 to 167).

TIMING

Steaming: 25 to 30 minutes for 2- to 3-inch beets; 10 to 12 minutes for ½-inch cubes
Boiling: 20 to 25 minutes for 2- to 3-inch whole beets
Sautéing: 4 to 8 minutes for grated beets
Roasting: 50 to 60 minutes for foil-wrapped beets at 350°F
Grilling: 15 to 20 minutes for ¼-inch slices

jeweled beet salad

The colors are as vibrant as the flavors in this salad of grated beets and ribbons of greens, dressed with a light citrus vinaigrette and crumbled goat cheese.

SERVES 6

4 medium-size beets with greens
¼ cup rice vinegar, plus more to taste
2 tablespoons chopped fresh chives
2 tablespoons chopped fresh mint
1 tablespoon fresh orange juice
¼ cup extra-virgin olive oil
　Salt and freshly ground black pepper
4 ounces soft fresh goat cheese, crumbled

1 Separate the beet greens from the roots. Discard any bruised or damaged leaves. Chop the stems into ¼-inch pieces and the leaves into ¼-inch ribbons. Peel the roots and grate with a box grater or food processor.

2 Combine the greens and grated roots in a steamer and steam over boiling water for about 5 minutes, until tender. Immediately plunge into cold water to stop the cooking. Drain well.

3 Whisk together the vinegar, chives, mint, and orange juice in a medium bowl. Whisk in the oil until it is fully incorporated. Season with salt and pepper. Add the greens and beets and toss to mix. Taste again and add more salt and pepper or vinegar if desired.

4 Crumble three quarters of the goat cheese over the salad and toss to mix. Garnish with the remaining goat cheese and serve.

roasted beet salad with greens and crispy shallots

When beets are roasted, their flavor is intensified. When you pair the sweet beets with the peppery greens, the mustardy dressing, and the crispy shallots, you get a salad of terrific flavor, textures, and colors. This knockout salad deserves a course all by itself.

If you happen to have grown beets of different colors (purple, golden, marbled), show them off here.

■ SERVES 4 ■

12 small beets (about 2 pounds), tops and roots trimmed to 1 inch

4–6 cups torn greens, such as arugula, escarole, endive, frisée, and watercress

½ cup Mustard Crème Fraîche (page 97)

½ cup Crispy Fried Shallots (page 422)

1 Preheat the oven to 400°F.

2 Wash the beets, but do not peel. Divide between two large sheets of heavy-duty aluminum foil and fold each to form a well-sealed packet. Roast the beets for 50 to 60 minutes, until the largest beet is easily pierced with a fork or metal skewer. Remove from the oven, open the packet, and let cool. When the beets are cool enough to handle, peel and slice.

3 On a large platter or individual salad plates, make a bed of the greens. Top with the beets. Drizzle on the dressing. (You can use a squeeze bottle for this to great effect, but the dressing will flow off a spoon in an even line if you are careful.) Garnish with the shallots and serve at once.

beet and new potato salad

Neon, lurid, garish — it's hard to find an exact description for this dazzlingly bright, magenta-colored salad of beets and potatoes, garnished with chopped hard-cooked eggs. The sweet beets are combined with new potatoes, sour cream, dill, and horseradish. Bed it on greens and serve with dark Russian rye or pumpernickel, and you have a lovely salad supper.

■ SERVES 4–6 ■

12 small beets (about 2 pounds), tops and roots trimmed to 1 inch

1½ pounds new potatoes, scrubbed and quartered if large

2 tablespoons extra-virgin olive oil

1 tablespoon cider vinegar

Salt and freshly ground black pepper

1 cup sour cream (regular or reduced fat) or yogurt

2 tablespoons chopped fresh dill

2 scallions, chopped

1 teaspoon prepared horseradish, or to taste

1 hard-cooked egg, chopped (optional)

1 Preheat the oven to 400°F.

2 Wash the beets, but do not peel. Divide among three large sheets of aluminum foil. Wrap to form well-sealed packets. Roast for 50 to 60 minutes, until the largest beet is easily pierced with a fork or metal skewer. Remove from the oven, open the packets, and let cool.

3 Meanwhile, boil the potatoes in salted water to cover in a medium saucepan until just tender, about 25 minutes. Drain well and transfer to a large bowl. Add the oil and vinegar. Toss to mix. Season to taste with the salt and pepper and set aside.

4 When the beets are cool enough to handle, slip off the skin and cut into wedges to match the size of the potato pieces. Add to the potatoes.

5 Mix together the sour cream, dill, scallions, and horseradish. Add to the potatoes and beets and toss to mix. Taste and adjust the seasonings. The salad should sit for at least 30 minutes before serving. If you like, you can hold it in the refrigerator for up to 1 day.

6 Before serving, garnish with the chopped egg, if desired.

borscht

"Everything I do, I do on the principle of Russian borscht. You can throw everything into it — beets, carrots, cabbage, onions, everything you want. What's important is the result, the taste of the borscht." So wrote Yevgeny Yevtushenko, the Russian poet. Me, I just stick to beets, a little onion, some potato for texture. This is a classic Jewish-style borscht.

SERVES 4–5

6 medium-size beets, tops and roots trimmed to 1 inch
1 onion, diced
2 russet potatoes, peeled and diced
3 cups vegetable or chicken broth (see page 8 or 9)
2 tablespoons chopped fresh dill, plus additional for garnish
2 tablespoons fresh lemon juice, or to taste
Salt and freshly ground black pepper
Sour cream or plain yogurt, to garnish

note If you like, chop the greens and steam until tender, 3 to 5 minutes. Stir into the broth along with the beets.

1 Preheat the oven to 400°F.

2 Wash the beets, but do not peel. Divide the beets between two large sheets of heavy-duty aluminum foil and fold each to form a well-sealed packet. Roast for 50 to 60 minutes, until the largest beet is easily pierced with a fork or a metal skewer. Remove from the oven, open the packets, and let cool. When the beets are cool enough to handle, peel and cut into shoestrings.

3 Meanwhile, combine the onion, potatoes, broth, and dill in a medium saucepan. Bring to a boil, then reduce the heat and simmer until the potatoes are completely tender, about 20 minutes. Cool briefly.

4 Mash the potatoes into the broth. Stir in the beets. Season with lemon juice, salt, and pepper.

5 Serve hot or chilled, garnishing each bowl with a dollop of sour cream and a sprig of dill.

sautéed grated beets

Here's the simplest and fastest way I know to cook beets. I've made this by sautéing the beets in both butter and olive oil, but the butter tastes better by far, even though the olive oil is a healthier choice.

SERVES 4

4–5 medium-size beets

3 tablespoons butter

1–2 tablespoons fresh lemon or orange juice, plus more to taste

Salt and freshly ground black pepper

1 Peel and grate the beets using a food processor or box grater.

2 Melt the butter in a large skillet over medium heat. Add the beets and stir to coat with the butter. Add 1 tablespoon of the juice, cover, and simmer over low heat, stirring occasionally. Add another tablespoon of juice if the beets are sticking to the bottom of the pan. Cook until tender but not mushy, 7 to 10 minutes.

3 Remove the cover and season to taste with the salt and pepper and additional juice if desired. Serve hot.

roasted orange-butter beets

Simplicity is best when it comes to your garden-fresh produce. Roasting brings out the best flavor of beets. A touch of orange adds a little sweetness.

SERVES 4

4–6 medium-size beets, tops and roots trimmed to 1 inch
1 tablespoon butter
1 tablespoon orange juice concentrate
Salt and freshly ground black pepper

1 Preheat the oven to 400°F.

2 Wash the beets, but do not peel. Divide between two sheets of heavy-duty aluminum foil and wrap each to form a well-sealed packet. Roast for 50 to 60 minutes, or until the largest beet is easily pierced with a fork or metal skewer. Remove from the oven, open the packets, and let cool. When the beets are cool enough to handle, peel and cut into slices or thin wedges.

3 Melt the butter in a large skillet. Add the orange juice concentrate and stir until well blended. Add the beets and toss until hot. Season with salt and pepper. Serve hot.

CULTIVAR TASTING NOTES

Beets are a strongly flavored vegetable, and people tend to love them or hate them. The familiar red-purple varieties have the strongest flavor. Most people would be hard-pressed to distinguish flavor differences among the white, golden, and Chioggia (red and white) beets, except to say they are milder in flavor than the red-purple ones.

"I HAVE A GARDENER'S PHILOSOPHY about everything I do," Roger Doiron tells me. "Gardeners don't put a seed in the ground and expect tomatoes the next day. And I don't expect Kitchen Gardeners International to be an instant success. But I do think the message of Kitchen Gardeners — that it is important to celebrate and promote homegrown foods and a more self-sustainable lifestyle — is something that many people can embrace."

Doiron is an environmentalist — and a food lover. He grew up in Maine, where small food gardens were a common backyard feature. Then he moved to Europe to work for Friends of the Earth. He married a Belgian woman and became closely acquainted with a lifestyle where everyone gardens, the way Americans used to do. And he was exposed to very, very good food.

Through his work with Friends of the Earth, Doiron became aware of the dangers of genetically modified food crops and the numerous health and environmental problems associated with the globalization of our food supply: "Being a food lover, I saw the potential for getting people motivated to work on the big environmental issues via food.

"There are problems with, for example, Vermonters eating apples from New Zealand. What I want to do is work on the relocalization of food, as opposed to the globalization of food."

The place to start, reasons Doiron, is in the backyard, in the kitchen garden, where people all over the planet grow their own food: "You don't always have to focus on the bad things. You can emphasize the positive. You can have a global perspective that in the end serves the people and the planet. In the summer, I don't want to eat hot-house-grown tomatoes from the Netherlands. But I would be happy to be in touch with Dutch people about their wonderful ways of cooking, say, potatoes and kale. We can import and export know-how on how to grow and cook our own foods."

Still a seedling, the Kitchen Gardeners International seems to have sprouted on fertile ground. "The response to our launch has been very encouraging," says Doiron. "We now have more than one thousand people from thirty countries subscribed to our e-mail newsletter, from Alabama to Albania." Through its newsletter and other activities, KGI offers gardeners and food lovers a connection to a multicultural world of kitchen gardening. Its plans include new activities for bringing kitchen gardeners together, such as an annual celebration called Kitchen Garden Day, online discussion forums, and the organization of a biannual international gathering.

"It's good for the environment to grow and eat your own organic produce and it's good for your own health and happiness. A win-win situation."

pickled beets

We've all seen — and ignored — pickled beets on salad bars, but they are worthy of attention when prepared well. Roasting the beets before pickling them in a sweet-sour syrup intensifies the beet flavor in a very pleasing way. If you like, save the brine for pickling and dyeing hard-cooked eggs.

▪ SERVES 6–8 ▪

4–6 medium-size beets, tops and roots trimmed to 1 inch
1 cup apple cider vinegar
1 cup water
½ cup sugar
1 piece ginger (2 inches long), peeled and sliced
2 garlic cloves, sliced
½ teaspoon salt
Freshly ground black pepper

1 Preheat the oven to 400°F.

2 Wash the beets, but do not peel. Divide between two large sheets of heavy-duty aluminum foil and wrap to form two well-sealed packets. Roast for 50 to 60 minutes, until the largest beet can be pierced easily with a fork. Remove from the oven, open the packets, and let cool.

3 Meanwhile, combine the vinegar, water, sugar, ginger, garlic, and salt in a nonreactive medium-size saucepan. Simmer over low heat for about 10 minutes, or until syrupy. Pour the syrup into a large bowl and let cool.

An old Ukrainian proverb warns, "A tale that begins with a beet will end with the devil."

4 Peel the beets, then cut into thin wedges or slices. Add the beets to the syrup and season generously with pepper. Stir gently to coat the beets with the syrup. Cover and marinate overnight in the refrigerator.

5 Before serving, remove the ginger and garlic slices and bring to room temperature.

BEET FACTS & FICTIONS

BEETS HAVE BEEN AROUND for more than 2 millennia, and for most of that time, they've been considered a valuable food source, prized for the green leafy tops, that grows wild throughout the Mediterranean region. The Greeks were said to offer beet greens to the god Apollo on a silver platter at the temple of Delphi. The Romans collected beet greens for food and medicine.

The cultivation of beets took hold throughout Europe, and beets were especially important in the northern and eastern parts of the continent, where the stored roots kept families fed during long winter freezes. The bulbous root was a result of 17th-century breeding efforts.

Russian healers claimed beets could cure tuberculosis, scurvy, and toothache, while Russian peasants believed it worked as an insecticide. Some Russian women used beet pigment to rouge their cheeks and keep away mosquitoes.

During Napoleonic times, beets took on a new role. In 1812, France, while locked in war with England, was shut off from overseas sugar imports. Napoleon issued a challenge to French scientists to come up with a new way to produce the sweet stuff, and they did. They turned to the forgotten work of a French botanist, who 200 years earlier had derived a sticky, sweet syrup from beets. Sugar from beets became a very important food commodity.

Today most of the beet crop in the United States is grown for animal fodder or sugar processing. What's grown for human consumption as a vegetable could be fit on only 8,000 acres of land in all of the United States. More acreage is devoted to turnips (11,500) and radishes (14,600). About two thirds of the beet crop ends up in cans and jars, a process that isn't likely to gain the beet any new fans. Indeed in 1977, American farmers processed about 2 pounds of beets for every American; by the 1990s that figure was down to below seven tenths of a pound.

A Popular Vegetable with Many Cousins

BROCCOLI HAS BECOME such a garden staple it is hard to imagine that only 50 years ago it was rarely found outside of Italian or Chinese gardens. Today one can grow a whole garden filled with broccoli and related vegetables, such as broccoli rabe, broccoflower, and Chinese broccoli. They aren't really all broccoli plants, but they extend the season for this nutrient-rich green vegetable.

Broccoli rabe is a sprouting broccoli. It has a sharper flavor than broccoli. It is cooked like a hearty green. Broccoflower, also known as Romanesco broccoli, is actually a cauliflower. You'll find them in seed catalogs under broccoli or cauliflower, so look in both places. The heads are lime green with pointed, spiraled pinnacles. In the garden and in the kitchen, treat these like cauliflower. Chinese broccoli, also known as Chinese kale and gai lan, is quite similar to broccoli rabe, but sweeter in flavor. It is terrific stir-fried.

GROWING Broccoli does best in nitrogen-rich soil in full sun with moderate and even watering. Some broccoli varieties do best planted early in the season. Other varieties should be planted in summer for harvest in fall or early winter. In general, broccoli does best in cooler weather with adequate water.

SOWING Start plants indoors 6 to 8 weeks before the last frost for a summer crop. Sow outdoors in early summer for a fall crop. Broccoli rabe is grown much the same as broccoli.

CULTIVATING Fertilize every 3 to 4 weeks.

HARVESTING Harvest broccoli when the head is dark green and fully formed but the buds are tightly closed. Harvest by cutting the head from the stalk with a knife. Every few days, harvest the side shoots to extend the harvest. Harvest broccoli rabe, which forms loose sprouting shoots, when young, at least before the buds open. The stems tend to become woody, so younger plants are more tender. But once the stems become woody, the leaves still may be good to eat.

BROCCOLI MATH

1 large head with stalk = ¾ to 1 pound
1 pound broccoli = 5 to 6 cups florets and sliced stems
1 pound broccoli rabe = 6 to 8 cups sliced stems and leaves

I can't emphasize enough the importance of giving homegrown broccoli a quick salt-water bath to coax the perfectly disguised cabbage worms out of their hiding places. Every time I have skipped this step, I have been punished by finding dead worms in the broccoli. Needless to say, most people find dead worms in their vegetables incredibly yucky.

If your broccoli is fresh and grown under optimal conditions, trimming away the outer layer from the stalks isn't needed. If your broccoli has been sitting forgotten in the refrigerator, or if it was grown under hot, dry conditions, peeling might be a good idea.

Broccoli does not forgive overcooking. Cooked broccoli should be bright green, with no trace of olive color.

Broccoli rabe has great flavor. Some people find it too bitter, but it is not terribly bitter when the plant is grown without stress and has been recently harvested. With adequate watering and reasonably cool temperatures, this green is quite mild and docile; even with overgrowing it will retain its flavor, although the larger stems will become too woody to chew. Any recipe that works for kale will work for broccoli rabe.

BROCCOLI NUTRITION NOTES

Broccoli is one of the superheroes in terms of nutrition. A ½-cup serving of cooked broccoli provides plenty of vitamins A and C, as well as folic acid, calcium, and iron — all for only 22 calories.

TIMING

Blanching: 3 to 6 minutes
Boiling: 4 to 6 minutes
Steaming: 4 to 7 minutes
Stir-frying or sautéing: 4 to 5 minutes

sesame broccoli noodle salad

Because broccoli has become a year-round supermarket item of higher than average quality, we think of using broccoli in all kinds of cold-weather dishes. But for northerners like myself, broccoli is a summer vegetable — perfect for using in dishes that are quickly made and served at room temperature — like this one.

Salad

SERVES 4

- 1 pound fresh Chinese noodles or ¾ pound angel-hair pasta
- 1 tablespoon dark sesame oil
- 1 pound broccoli (1 large head), stem peeled and diced and florets broken into small pieces (about 6 cups)
- 1 cup julienned baby carrots or 1 red bell pepper, julienned
- 2 tablespoons sesame seeds, toasted

Sweet Soy Dressing

- 2 tablespoons rice vinegar
- 2 tablespoons hoisin sauce
- 2 tablespoons soy sauce
- 1 tablespoons sherry or Chinese rice wine
- 1 tablespoon chopped fresh cilantro (optional)
- 2 garlic cloves, minced
- 1 teaspoon minced fresh ginger
- 2 tablespoons dark sesame oil

1 To make the salad, cook the noodles in a large pot of boiling salted water until just done. Drain and rinse well to cool. Transfer the noodles to a large salad bowl and toss with the sesame oil.

2 Steam the broccoli over boiling water until tender, about 4 minutes. Drain, plunge into cold water to stop the cooking, and drain again.

3 Add the broccoli and carrots to the noodles and toss again.

4 To make the dressing, combine the vinegar, hoisin sauce, soy sauce, sherry, cilantro, if using, garlic, and ginger in a small bowl. Whisk in the sesame oil until well combined.

5 Pour the dressing over the noodles and vegetables and toss. Sprinkle the sesame seeds over the salad and serve.

barley broccoli salad

Looking for a change of pace from pasta salads? Look no further. Its nutty flavor makes barley the perfect grain to complement broccoli in a salad.

SERVES 4–6

1 cup pearl barley

3 cups water

½ teaspoon salt

¾ pound broccoli (1 large head), stems peeled and diced and florets broken into small pieces (about 6 cups)

2 scallions, chopped

1 carrot, diced

¾ cup Black & Green Olive Vinaigrette (page 94)

1 Combine the barley, water, and salt in a large saucepan. Bring to a boil, cover, reduce the heat, and simmer until all the water is absorbed, about 30 minutes. Spoon into a large bowl and let cool, stirring every once in a while. (You can speed up the cooling by rinsing under cold water and draining well.)

2 Bring a large pot of salted water to a boil. Add the broccoli and boil just until tender, about 4 minutes. Drain, plunge into cold water to stop the cooking, and drain again.

3 Transfer the barley to a large bowl. Add the broccoli, scallions, and carrot and toss well. Pour in the vinaigrette and toss well. Serve at room temperature.

sautéed broccoli

Steamed broccoli served with a squeeze of lemon and a sprinkling of salt and pepper is a fine thing, a pure and healthful meditation on green. But broccoli slicked with a flavorful dressing of olive oil and garlic is a sensual delight. The blanching is necessary to tame the wild broccoli; skip the blanching and the flavor is sharper and the texture woody.

SERVES 4–6

3 heads broccoli (2–3½ pounds), trimmed and cut into long spears

3 tablespoons extra-virgin olive oil

2 garlic cloves, finely minced

2 tablespoons chopped fresh parsley

Salt and freshly ground black pepper

1 Bring a large pot of salted water to a boil. Add the broccoli and boil until just tender, about 4 minutes. Drain and plunge into cold water to stop the cooking process.

2 In a large skillet, heat the oil over medium heat. Add the garlic and sauté until fragrant and pale gold, about 1 minute. Add the broccoli and parsley and sauté just until the broccoli is heated through, about 3 minutes. Season with the salt and pepper and serve at once.

According to the *Guinness Book of World Records*, the largest broccoli ever seen was a 35-pounder grown in Palmer, Alaska, by John and Mary Evans in 1993.

bowties 'n' broccoli

There are few dishes as simple and fast as this one, and fewer still more delicious and satisfying. The broccoli cooks in the same pot as the pasta while the garlic is sautéed in olive oil. Toss it all together with a sprinkling of Parmesan, a handful of herbs, and a fistful of olives, and dinner is done. This dish is also terrific with broccoli rabe — but reduce the cooking time by a minute or two.

■ SERVES 4–5 ■

1 pound bowtie pasta

1½–2 large heads broccoli (1½ pounds), stalks sliced crosswise, florets broken into small pieces (about 9 cups)

⅓ cup extra-virgin olive oil

1 tablespoon minced garlic

½ teaspoon crushed red pepper flakes

¼ cup chopped fresh parsley

1 tablespoon chopped fresh mint

1 cup pitted cured black olives

1 cup freshly grated Parmesan, plus more for serving

Salt and freshly ground black pepper

1 Bring a large pot of salted water to a boil.

2 When the water begins to boil, add the pasta and cook, stirring occasionally, for 5 minutes. Add the broccoli stems and continue cooking for 2 minutes. Add the florets and cook until the pasta and broccoli are tender, about 5 minutes longer. Reserve ½ cup of the cooking water and drain the pasta and broccoli. Return the pasta and broccoli to the pot.

3 While the pasta is cooking, heat the olive oil in the medium skillet over medium-low heat. Add the garlic and red pepper and sauté until the garlic is fragrant and pale gold, about 3 minutes. Stir in the parsley and mint. Remove from the heat.

4 Pour the oil mixture into the pasta and broccoli and toss to mix. Add the olives and Parmesan and season with salt and pepper. Add as much of the reserved cooking water as needed if the pasta seems dry.

5 Transfer to a warm serving bowl and serve immediately, passing the additional cheese at the table.

sautéed broccoli rabe

Broccoli rabe cooks more quickly than broccoli and doesn't require blanching before sautéing. It is somewhat more bitter than broccoli, which is good in a hearty green.

SERVES 4

2 tablespoons extra-virgin olive oil
10 cups (1–1½ pounds) chopped broccoli rabe
2 garlic cloves, minced
Salt and freshly ground black pepper

1 Heat the oil in a large skillet over medium-high heat. Add the broccoli rabe and garlic and stir until the broccoli rabe wilts and is coated with oil, about 1 minute. Season with salt and pepper

2 Cover and steam until the leaves are wilted and the stems are tender, 3 to 4 minutes. Serve hot.

chicken and broccoli in mornay sauce

If you ask most kids their favorite way to eat broccoli, chances are they will tell you they like it with cheese sauce. Broccoli and cheese is a perfect combination, so why not enjoy it as a one-dish dinner with chicken?

■ SERVES 4 ■

3 large heads (1½ pounds) broccoli, stems sliced and florets broken into small pieces (12 cups)

1 cup unbleached all-purpose flour

3 tablespoons butter

2 tablespoons extra-virgin olive oil

1–1½ pounds boneless, skinless chicken breast cutlets

Salt and freshly ground black pepper

2 garlic cloves, minced

1 cup chicken broth (page 9)

1 cup milk

¾ cup grated Gruyère cheese

1 Bring a large pot of water to a boil. Add the broccoli and blanch for 3 minutes. Drain and immediately plunge into cold water to stop the cooking. Drain well. Transfer the broccoli to a clean towel and pat dry.

2 Put ¾ cup of the flour in a shallow bowl. Preheat the oven to 350°F. Grease a 9- by 13-inch baking dish with butter.

3 Heat 2 tablespoons of the butter and the olive oil in a large skillet over medium-high heat. Season the chicken with the salt and pepper. Dredge the chicken in the flour and add to the skillet in a single layer. Sauté the chicken on both sides until browned, about 4 minutes per side. Remove the skillet from the heat and transfer the chicken to a bowl to keep warm while you prepare the sauce.

4 Return the skillet to medium heat. Add the remaining 1 table-spoon butter and the garlic. Sprinkle in the remaining ¼ cup flour and whisk until smooth. Stir in the broth and milk and bring to a boil. Remove from the heat and stir in ½ cup of the cheese. Taste and add more salt and pepper if desired.

5 To assemble the casserole, arrange the broccoli in the baking dish. Pour half the sauce over the broccoli. Arrange the chicken on top. Cover with the remaining sauce. Sprinkle the remaining ¼ cup cheese over all.

6 Bake for 30 minutes, until bubbling and browned.

7 Serve hot.

chinese beef and broccoli

The trick to a successful stir-fry is, of course, to have everything chopped and ready to go before you start cooking. With this stir-fry, you can do the prep work hours in advance (when the kitchen is still cool), including blanching the broccoli and marinating the meat. Then you can quickly cook dinner in less time than it takes to cook the rice. Perfect for a busy summer day. You can substitute Chinese broccoli or broccoli rabe for the regular broccoli, but skip the blanching step.

SERVES 4

1 pound beef, preferably flank steak or top sirloin roast, cut into matchsticks

3 tablespoons oyster sauce

3 tablespoons soy sauce

2 tablespoons Chinese rice wine or dry sherry

1 tablespoon sugar

2 teaspoons dark sesame oil

½ teaspoon freshly ground black pepper

2 large heads broccoli (2 pounds), stems sliced and florets roughly chopped (12 cups)

⅓ cup chicken broth (see page 9)

1 tablespoon cornstarch

3 tablespoons peanut or canola oil

1 tablespoon minced fresh ginger

1 tablespoon finely minced garlic

Hot cooked white rice

1 Combine the beef, oyster sauce, 2 tablespoons of the soy sauce, 1 tablespoon of the wine, sugar, sesame oil, and pepper in a medium bowl and set aside to marinate.

2 Bring a large pot of water to a boil. Add the broccoli and blanch for 3 minutes, until the broccoli is barely tender and bright green. Drain, plunge into cold water to stop the cooking, and set aside to drain.

3 To make the sauce, combine the broth, remaining 1 tablespoon soy sauce, remaining 1 tablespoon wine, and cornstarch. Whisk until thoroughly combined.

4 Heat a large wok or skillet over high heat. Add 1 tablespoon of the oil and heat until very hot. Add the half the beef and marinade and stir-fry, stirring constantly, until well browned, about 4 minutes. Use a heatproof rubber spatula to scrape the beef into a medium bowl and keep warm. Return the wok to high heat. Repeat with another 1 tablespoon of the oil and the remaining beef and marinade. Transfer the beef and marinade to the bowl and wipe out the wok.

5 Heat the remaining 1 tablespoon oil over high heat until very hot. Add the broccoli and stir-fry, stirring constantly, until heated through, about 3 minutes. Push the broccoli to the sides of the pan and add the ginger and garlic. Cook until fragrant, about 45 seconds. Toss with the broccoli.

6 Return the beef to the wok. Whisk the sauce and pour into the wok. Cook, stirring constantly, until the sauce is thickened and evenly coats the beef and broccoli, about 1 minute.

7 Serve immediately with the hot rice.

WHAT'S IN A NAME?

The name "broccoli" came from the Latin *bracchium*, which means strong arm or branch. Broccoli was commonly eaten by the Romans in the second century, but it wasn't until Catherine de' Medici introduced it to France in 1533 that broccoli spread beyond Italy. It was variously called Calabrese and Italian asparagus and sprout colli-flower.

Think Pickles

I WAS HOPING TO LEARN the art of pickling at my grandmother's knee. "You just put the cucumbers in a crock with salt water," she told me dismissively. At this point in her life, she was free from the demands of keeping house and she had no intention of donning an apron ever again.

"How much salt?" I persisted.

"Enough salt so it's just before you gag," she said, and resumed her crossword puzzle.

My grandmother, a woman of iron will, who could remove casseroles from the oven with her bare hands, who could knit a sweater and read a book at the same time, could apparently drink highly concentrated brines of salt water without gagging. My first batch of pickles — obviously not enough salt — created rotten cucumbers. I had much to learn.

Pickling is an ancient art, seemingly as old as cucumbers. Cleopatra, ruler of Egypt, believed they contributed to health and beauty. Olives were pickled by the Greeks and Romans; the Russians pickled beets; the Koreans made kimchi. Queen Elizabeth I of England developed a passion for pickles, as did Presidents George Washington, Thomas Jefferson, and John Adams. Troops under Julius Caesar and Napoleon relished the thought of having crunchy pickles at mealtime, and during World War II, the United States government earmarked 40 percent of pickle production for the Armed Forces.

As a gardener, it is nearly impossible to look upon cucumbers as just an addition to salads. This is one harvest that is impossible to stay on top of — unless you think pickles.

GROWING Cucumbers are hot-weather plants that like to climb. They require full sun, lots of water, and fertile soil.

SOWING Sow indoors 3 weeks before the last frost or sow outdoors after the last frost and the soil has warmed to about 70°F.

CULTIVATING Provide a trellis for this vine crop, and your cucumbers will be cleaner, straighter, and less inclined to rot.

HARVESTING If you keep the vines picked, the harvest season will be extended; the vines will continue to produce flowers and new fruit. Small cucumbers are tastier, crispier, and less seedy, which is another reason to keep the fruits picked. Cucumbers like to hide behind the foliage, so check under the leaves.

CUCUMBER MATH

1 pound fresh cucumbers = 4 cups sliced or cubed

During the cucumber season, I make cucumber salads almost daily. The cucumbers may appear alone or with tomatoes later in the season. The salad may be dressed with a combination of yogurt and garlic (the Greek salad *tzatziki*) or with an oil and vinegar dressing, with herbs that complement the main dish (cilantro with Mexican meals; oregano or basil with Italian meals; dill, tarragon, mint, chervil, scallions any time). If you have the time, salt the cucumbers (about 1 teaspoon salt per 4 cups sliced cucumbers) and let them drain for 30 minutes before mixing with the dressing to get rid of excess moisture. If the cucumbers are seedy, slice them in half lengthwise and remove the seeds with a teaspoon before slicing. As for peeling cucumbers, it just isn't needed with most homegrown cucumbers because they won't be waxed. However, some people prefer to peel slicing cucumbers, such as Marketmores. The choice is yours.

All cucumbers can be pickled. Pickling cucumbers are generally preferred because of their thin skin and small size. Asian and Middle Eastern cucumbers can be pickled when sliced. American slicing cucumbers can be pickled as slices, but it isn't my favorite use for them — they tend to be too seedy.

tzatziki

What makes this cucumber salad special is Greek-style yogurt — thick, tangy, delicious. It isn't always easy to find — but sour cream makes a reasonable substitute. This is the perfect dish to accompany any grilled foods, but especially grilled vegetables, such as eggplant, and grilled lamb. Stuff the grilled food into pita pockets and top with tzatziki for a delicious main course.

■ SERVES 6–8 ■

6 cups quartered and thinly sliced cucumbers (peeled and seeded if desired)

1 teaspoon salt, or more as needed

2 cups Greek yogurt or sour cream

2 garlic cloves, minced

Freshly ground black pepper

1 Combine the cucumbers and 1 teaspoon of the salt in a colander and toss to mix. Let drain for 30 to 60 minutes. Transfer the cucumbers to a clean kitchen towel and pat dry.

2 Combine the cucumbers, yogurt, and garlic in a large bowl. Season generously with the pepper and more salt, if desired.

3 Set aside at room temperature to allow the flavors to develop for at least 30 minutes before serving.

COOL AS A CUCUMBER

In the 1600s physicians treated fever victims by having them lie in a bed of sliced cucumbers, hence the expression "cool as a cucumber." As for eating cucumbers, French scholar Louis Lémery, in *Treatise of All Sorts of Foods* (1702), recommends cucumbers only for "young Persons of a hot and bilious Constitutions."

raita

When Indian food is on the menu, a cooling raita is a must. This relish brings sanity to the palate when fire is on the tongue.

■ SERVES 4–6 ■

6 cups coarsely grated or finely chopped cucumbers (peeled and seeded if desired)

2 teaspoons salt

1 cup plain yogurt

2 tablespoons chopped fresh mint

¼ teaspoon ground cumin

1 Combine the cucumber and salt in a colander and toss to mix. Let drain for 30 to 60 minutes. Transfer the cucumbers to a clean kitchen towel and pat dry.

2 Combine the yogurt, mint, and cumin in a small bowl.

3 Transfer the cucumbers to a salad bowl. Pour the yogurt mixture over the cucumbers and toss gently.

4 Set aside at room temperature to allow the flavors to develop for at least 30 minutes before serving.

TYPES OF CUCUMBERS

American Slicing Cucumbers The familiar cucumber most Americans grew up eating. Dark green skins and crisp, white flesh. Many people feel that of all the cucumbers, these have the least flavor because they have been bred to produce fruits that ship well, rather than taste best. Marketmore is a common American slicing cucumber variety.

American Pickling Cucumbers Sometimes called Kirby cucumbers, Kirby is only one common cultivar. Pickling cucumbers are small, thin skinned, and uniform. Pickling cucumbers tend to be earlier than other cucumbers.

Asian Cucumbers These are long, thin-skinned cucumbers that range in flavor from slightly bitter to slightly sweet. Trellises help to keep the cucumbers straight. They can be used in any recipe calling for a slicing cucumber.

Middle Eastern Cucumbers These are thin skinned, lightly ridged, slim, and fairly straight, at least when grown on trellises. The flesh is crunchy, juicy, and slightly green in color. These resemble the hothouse or "English" cucumbers commonly found in supermarkets. They can be used in any recipe calling for a slicing cucumber.

Continuing on the theme of cucumbers in a creamy sauce, here is a favorite salad of the American South. Interestingly, this same recipe is a Finnish favorite, known in Finland as kurkusalaatti. *By any name, it is addictively delicious.*

SERVES 4–6

8 cups very thinly sliced cucumbers (peeled and seeded if desired)

2 teaspoon salt

1 cup sour cream (nonfat sour cream is acceptable)

3 tablespoons white vinegar

3 tablespoons chopped fresh dill

1 teaspoon sugar

Freshly ground black pepper

1 Combine the cucumbers and salt in a colander and toss to coat. Set aside to drain for 30 to 60 minutes. Transfer the cucumbers to a clean kitchen towel and pat dry.

2 Mix together the sour cream, vinegar, dill, sugar, and black pepper in a small bowl.

3 Combine the cucumbers and sour cream dressing in a medium bowl. Toss gently to coat the cucumbers with the dressing.

4 Serve immediately. The salad can be held for up to 4 hours in the refrigerator. Stir well before serving.

A Good Idea

"He has been eight years upon a project for extracting sunbeams out of cucumbers, which were to be put in phials hermetically sealed, and let out to warm the air in raw inclement summers."

—Jonathan Swift,
Gulliver's Travels

japanese pickles

More like marinated cucumbers than pickles, these delicate, subtly flavored cucumbers are wonderful to serve with grilled foods. I try to keep a batch going in the refrigerator through most of the summer.

SERVES 6

½ cup rice vinegar

2 teaspoons sugar

1 teaspoon salt

6 cups very thinly sliced cucumbers (peeled if desired)

1 mild sweet onion, thinly sliced

1 red or green fresh chile, such as a jalapeño, seeded and finely sliced

1 Combine the vinegar, sugar, and salt in a small saucepan or microwave container and heat just enough to completely dissolve the sugar. Let cool to room temperature.

2 Combine the cucumbers, onion, and chile with the vinegar mixture and toss gently. The cucumbers will seem dry, but the salt will draw out moisture from the cucumbers to create more brine.

3 Cover and refrigerate for at least 30 minutes before serving. The cucumbers can be stored for up to a week in the refrigerator.

Don't forget how lovely it can be to enjoy a light lunch or afternoon snack of iced tea and cucumber sandwiches on a shady porch on a sunny afternoon. The classic cucumber sandwich is made with crustless white bread and fresh creamery butter. Thinly sliced whole wheat bread — with or without crusts — herbed cream cheese (page 204), and thinly sliced cucumbers is another winning combination.

cucumber-cashew salad

For nights when the menu is Asian, a creamy cucumber salad won't do. Turn to these cool crisp cucumbers, paired with salty sweet cashews and a mild tamari dressing. Salted roasted peanuts can replace the cashews.

■ SERVES 4 ■

2 pounds cucumbers (3 large), halved (peeled and seeded if necessary), and sliced

1 cup roasted salted cashews

3 scallions, trimmed, or 6 stems garlic chives, finely chopped

3 tablespoons rice vinegar

1 tablespoon mirin

1 tablespoon tamari

1 teaspoon sugar

1 teaspoon minced fresh or pickled (sushi) ginger

2 tablespoons dark sesame oil

Salt and freshly ground black pepper

1 Combine the cucumbers, cashews, and scallions in a salad bowl.

2 Whisk together the vinegar, mirin, tamari, sugar, and ginger in a separate small bowl. Whisk in the oil. Pour over the salad and toss gently.

3 Season with salt and pepper. Serve immediately.

quick crock pickles

I make these pickles several times during the season. If I don't have enough cucumbers to fill a jar, I'll add other vegetables, such as cauliflower or carrots, and they also pickle nicely. If I don't have enough pickling cucumbers, I throw in 4-inch chunks of Middle Eastern cucumbers (which are thin skinned like pickling cucumbers), and they make a fine pickle also.

■ **MAKES 1 GALLON** ■

8 cups water

1 cup distilled white vinegar

¼ cup pickling salt

6 pounds pickling cucumbers

6 dill heads or 12 young dill shoots

8 garlic cloves, peeled

1 Combine the water with the vinegar and salt in a sterilized 1-gallon-or-larger container. Mix well, until the salt has dissolved.

2 Slice ¹⁄₁₆ inch off the blossom end of each cucumber. Add the dill, garlic, and cucumbers, in order, to the brine solution. Make sure the cucumbers are completely submerged in the brine.

3 Cover the container with a zippered bag filled with water to exclude the air. Set the jar where the temperature will remain at about 68°F.

4 Check the jar daily, and remove any scum that forms on the surface. (If air is completely excluded, the scum will not form.)

5 The pickles will be ready in 2 to 3 days, although full flavor will not be reached for another 4 to 6 weeks. If your kitchen is reasonably cool, you can leave these pickles out for up to 2 weeks. If the brine starts to become cloudy, refrigerate immediately to prevent spoiling. The flavor of the dill and garlic will continue to develop. The pickles will keep for up to 3 months in the refrigerator.

Freezer pickles taste fresher than canned pickles. In this recipe, the flavorings are the same as a traditional bread-and-butter pickle, but the flavor is fresh and bright — more like a marinated cucumber than a true pickle. The recipe is designed to be multiplied if you have more cucumbers than you know what to do with. These pickles make a terrific addition to cheese sandwiches.

MAKES 1 QUART

4 cups very thinly sliced cucumbers
1 onion, very thinly sliced
2 teaspoons salt
1¼ cups white vinegar
½ cup sugar
½ teaspoon ground turmeric
¼ teaspoon celery seeds
¼ teaspoon freshly ground black pepper
⅛ teaspoon dry mustard

1 Combine the cucumbers, onion, and salt in a colander. Let stand for at least 2 hours.

2 Meanwhile, combine the vinegar and sugar in a small saucepan over low heat and stir until the sugar is dissolved. Stir in the turmeric, celery seeds, black pepper, and mustard. Let cool to room temperature.

3 Pack the cucumbers into freezer containers, leaving at least 1 inch headspace. Pour in the brine. The brine will not cover the cucumbers. Mix well. Then freeze.

4 Defrost in the refrigerator for at least 8 hours before serving.

"It has been a common saying of physicians in England, that a cucumber should be well sliced, and dressed with pepper and vinegar, and then thrown out, as good for nothing."

—Samuel Johnson,
Boswell: *The Journal of a Tour to the Hebrides with Samuel Johnson*

THE ANCIENT SUMERIANS, who are credited with the earliest human civilization, farmed in the Fertile Crescent (the valleys of the Tigris and Euphrates rivers) in 3500 BC. What we know about them was preserved in the *Gilgamesh*, a Sumerian cuneiform that is the first known written legend and tells of a great flood in which man was saved by building an ark. In the *Gilgamesh*, it is mentioned that Sumerian foods included wild cucumbers. The cucumber is believed to be native to the great Indian center of plant origins, which lies between the northern part of the Bay of Bengal and the Himalayas. The cucumber has never been found wild anywhere, but species closely related to it have been found wild in that region of India.

From there the cucumber spread widely. The cucumber was mentioned in the Bible and was being grown in North Africa, Italy, Greece, Asia Minor, and other areas at the beginning of the Christian era. The Roman emperor Tiberius demanded cucumbers daily, which required farmers to use artificial methods of growing the hot-weather crop, including transporting plants around in wheelbarrows to catch the sun's rays. Charlemagne had cucumbers growing in his gardens in ninth-century France. They were known in England in the early 1300s, but the art of growing them was apparently lost there as a result of a long period of war and turmoil. Cucumbers were reintroduced into England from the Continent some 250 years later.

Columbus planted cucumbers in Haiti in 1494, and possibly on other islands. Explorers who touched Virginia in 1584 mentioned cucumbers. Presumably the Natives' knowledge of cucumbers had spread after its introduction by Spaniards far to the south. Cucumbers were grown in Virginia in 1609 and in Massachusetts in 1629.

Today, cucumbers are found all over the world. There are several distinctly different types of cucumber — from tiny little gherkins to 2-foot-long English greenhouse varieties — and all were known at least 400 years ago.

"I WASN'T GOING TO MAKE CUCUMBER PICKLES this year, since my eldest child, the big pickle eater, has been away at college, and we've got dozens of jars left over from last year. But I still put in a few cucumber plants, and now I can't give away all the cucumbers . . ."

Linda Ziedrich is the author of *The Joy of Pickling* (Harvard Common Press, 1998). Her book contains "200 flavor-packed recipes of all kinds of produce from garden to market," and after years of experimenting, Ziedrich sometimes feels like she has had enough pickles. But there is always something new to try, and this keeps Ziedrich going:

"Last Christmas my husband gave me a wonderful new stoneware pickle pot from Germany, with weights made to fit and a trough to hold water; the water creates a seal that keeps out the wrong microbes. It's like the Chinese pickle pot illustrated in my book. So of course I have to pickle cucumbers in my beautiful pot, and if they don't all get eaten, I'll can a few jars . . . We've been pickling a lot of beans for the past month or so, and I'll certainly pickle peppers and eggplant this year."

How did this passion for pickling begin? "When we lived near Boston," explains Ziedrich, "my husband pickled beans and cucumbers, but since our vegetable plot was just an eight-by-ten-foot piece of a community garden, we didn't have much really fine raw material. I got interested in pickling only after we moved to a house in the Santa Cruz Mountains with a big backyard.

There I grew and pickled some beans, and from the long-neglected fruit trees in the yard I made great batches of pickled pears and plums — that is, pears and plums in syrup flavored with spices and vinegar. But I really didn't think of this as pickling. It was only after my eldest son fell in love with cucumber pickles, which I never ate myself, that I found a new interest. I balked at the price of store pickles and the additives on the label. So I started both planting and pickling cucumbers.

"Pickling cukes in vinegar was easy, but my interest and taste buds really perked when I started brining the cucumbers — that is, fermenting them, in the style of Eastern Europe and Jewish-American delis." These pickles are known as kosher dills.

I asked Ziedrich if she had any surprises when she researched her book. Her first surprise, she recalls, is that "pickles are such an important part of cuisines all over the world. . . .

"As I worked on the book," says Ziedrich, "I learned more surprising things. I learned that societies and individuals within them differ enormously in their tastes in pickles. I learned that tastes in pickles have changed over time in general, but that a lot of people still love the old types. I learned that some really weird pickles have been popular at various times and in various places — like pickled walnuts, green walnuts in their husks that are brined till they blacken and then pickled in sweetened, spiced vinegar. I understand that those are still popular in England."

As a former experimental pickler myself, I know that experimentation can lead to the accumulation of a lot of pickles. I asked Ziedrich what she does with all her pickles.

"My family ate quite a lot of pickles for a few years. Unfortunately, no one in the immediate family much liked sweet cucumber pickles, so those went to extended family members or to the compost. If I didn't like a pickle, though, I'd always tinker with the recipe until at least I didn't dislike it. Then I'd try it on someone who really liked pickles of its type."

Ziedrich finds plenty of occasions to serve pickles: "I serve pickles with sandwiches for lunch, pickles as appetizers before dinner, pickles as salads, pickles as table sauces — chutneys and salsas, for example. I use pickles in the kitchen, too: I put pickled eggplant cubes and sliced pickled garlic or shallots in salad; I use *tuong* (hot red chiles ground with vinegar and garlic) and my ketchuplike tomato-pepper sauce in all sorts of dishes."

I ask Ziedrich if she has any advice for people who are just starting to learn how to make pickles. She tells people that fruits and vegetables are not worth preserving if they are not fresh and tasty. "If they've never done canning and are afraid to try, I tell them not to bother, but to make small quantities at first and to store the pickles in the refrigerator. If they are experienced canners who haven't done pickling, I tell them not to put their cucumber pickles in a boiling-water bath, which could make them mushy. The low-temperature pasteur-ization method is definitely preferable." (With this method, you pack the vegetables and liquid into hot jars, seal the jars with hot lids, and place the jars in water heated to 120 to 140°F. Then you add hot water to cover the jars by at least 1 inch and heat the water to 180°F and keep the water at that temperature for at least 30 minutes. You need an accurate thermometer. You also need to pay close attention because even heating the water to 185°F will soften the texture of the pickles.)

"I recommend canning to anyone who is comfortable with the process and whose family eats a lot of pickles of the type in question. But if you don't know whether you'll like a certain type of pickle, or if it's not something you expect to eat often or in large quantity, why not start with a single jar and store it in the refrigerator? People also need to consider that canning can affect quality. A boiling-water bath certainly doesn't hurt the quality of dilly beans, but when you heat brined cucumbers, you're killing off microbes that many people find helpful for digestion, and you're probably also reducing the levels of some vitamins."

And is there one pickle Ziedrich can't live without? "I can't say that I have one favorite pickle," she says. "Dilly beans are perhaps most useful to me, because every child who visits here loves them, so if I can't get kids to eat fresh vegetables, I can always feed them pickled beans. I rarely eat dilly beans myself, because usually the kids start eating them as soon as I open the jar, so they are all gone by the time I sit down at the table."

You'll Never Have Too Many Once You Try Roasting Them

LIKE ALL GARDENERS, I was often faced with a glut of fresh snap beans, or green beans. Even with staggered plantings, the harvest seems to happen all at once. The first planting is delayed because of cold weather; then a spot of hot weather enables the second planting to catch up to the first one. The result: instant overabundance.

All that changed once I started roasting snap beans.

The process couldn't be simpler: Slick the beans with a little oil and roast in a hot oven for about 15 minutes. Sprinkle with coarse salt and enjoy. The beans aren't lovely, but they are so tasty, they disappear on the way to the table. And because the beans lose volume as they roast, it turns out that it takes 2 pounds to make enough for four people. That is a lot of beans. So bring on the harvest.

GROWING Beans are warm-weather plants. Don't sow before the soil warms up, and give them full sun, moderately good soil, and plenty of water once the plants have flowered. Bush beans can be planted in beds. Pole beans need the support of a trellis or tepee. Plant groups of four to six beans around each pole with 16 inches between groups.

SOWING Sow when the soil temperature reaches 60°F. Make several plantings 10 days apart for a continual harvest throughout the summer.

CULTIVATING Water lightly and regularly from germination to flowering, then increase the amount of water through harvest. Avoid over-head watering, which wets the leaves and pro-motes diseases, such as bean rust. Fertilize young bean plants with an organic fertilizer, such as fish emulsion, every 2 weeks, then once every 3 to 4 weeks when the plant is full size.

HARVESTING Snap beans are harvested when "green," or young, when the beans inside the pod are small and tender and the pods are thin. Beans that are harvested too late will be tough and stringy. At peak times, this means picking at least every other day. Pole beans have a longer harvest season than bush beans and pro-duce more pods. Pods can be left on the poles to continue to mature into shell beans.

TIMING

Blanching: 2 to 3 minutes
Boiling: 3 to 4 minutes
Steaming: 3 to 5 minutes
Sautéing or stir-frying: 4 to 7 minutes
Roasting: 15 minutes at 450°F
Grilling: 8 to 10 minutes
Braising: 20 minutes

When cooking snap beans, consider the diameter of the pod. The smaller the diameter, the briefer the cooking. So test your beans and remove them from the heat when they have reached a stage of tenderness that appeals to you. Tender filet beans should be lightly steamed, then dressed with a vinaigrette. Stir-frying and sautéing are also fine for tender beans. Medium-size beans are excellent for roasting and grilling. Braising is best for over-grown beans. Wax beans require less cooking than green beans. Flat or Romano beans tend to be tougher and require more cooking.

There's a handy little gadget called a bean frencher. It shreds snap beans into narrow strips. The process goes fairly quickly, but it is done bean by bean. The job almost requires a shaded porch on a lazy afternoon and a glass of lemonade. If you have overgrown beans, the frencher will make the beans tender for sautéing and stir-frying. Also, frenching purple beans makes them more accept-able for adding raw to a salad, which is the only way to enjoy the color of these beans, since they turn green when cooked.

Recipes often require "trimming" the beans. To do this, slice off the narrow tips on each end of the pod.

SNAP BEAN NUTRITION NOTES

Low-calorie green beans (just 44 calories in a whole cup) are loaded with nutrients. They are an excellent source of vitamins K and A and fiber. Plus, green beans are a very good source of vitamin C, riboflavin, potassium, iron, manganese, folate, magnesium, and thiamin and are a good source of phosphorus, calcium, niacin, vitamin B_6, copper, protein, and zinc.

SNAP BEAN MATH

1 pound = about 100 beans
1 pound = 4 cups chopped

green bean salad with sesame-soy vinaigrette

Who can forget his first taste of three bean salad? The amazing thing is that it still can be found — in all its canned glory — on salad bars. I think it is getting sweeter. This salad is the antidote — salty, savory, fresh.

■ SERVES 6 ■

5 tablespoons soy sauce

¼ cup rice vinegar

2 tablespoons Chinese rice wine or dry sherry

1 tablespoon tahini

2 garlic cloves, minced

¼ cup dark sesame oil

2 pounds green beans, trimmed

½ cup flaked almonds

3 tablespoons sesame seeds

1 Bring a large pot of salted water to a boil.

2 While the water heats, prepare the vinaigrette. Combine the soy sauce, vinegar, rice wine, tahini, and garlic in a large bowl. Whisk in the oil until completely emulsified.

3 When the water boils, add the beans and blanch until barely tender, about 3 minutes. Drain well. Add the beans to the vinaigrette while still warm.

4 Mix in the almonds and sesame seeds. Serve warm or at room temperature.

roasted green beans

There is no better way to prepare green beans. Roasting tames the grassy undertones in green beans and enhances their sweetness. These green beans cannot be made too often.

SERVES 4

2 pounds green beans, trimmed
2 tablespoons extra-virgin olive oil
Coarse-grained sea salt or kosher salt

1 Preheat the oven to 450°F. Lightly grease a large sheet pan or shallow roasting pan with oil.

2 Arrange the green beans in a single, uncrowded layer on the prepared pan. Drizzle the oil over the beans and roll the beans until they are evenly coated.

3 Roast for about 15 minutes, or until the beans are well browned, shaking the pan occasionally for even cooking.

4 Transfer the beans to a shallow serving bowl or platter and sprinkle with the salt. Serve immediately.

sautéed green beans with garlic and tomato

Often the second planting of green or wax beans ripens with tomatoes. This is a delicious way to prepare the beans, bringing new life to what often becomes an overly familiar vegetable. This basic cooking method can be adapted to other flavorings for beans.

■ SERVES 4 ■

1 pound green or wax beans, trimmed
2 tablespoons extra-virgin olive oil
2 garlic cloves, minced
1 teaspoon finely chopped fresh oregano
2 plum tomatoes or 1 slicing tomato, diced
2 tablespoons fresh lemon juice or balsamic vinegar
Salt and freshly ground black pepper

1 Bring a medium pot of salted water to a boil. Add the beans and blanch until just barely tender, about 3 minutes. Drain well.

2 Heat the oil over medium heat in a large skillet. Add the garlic and cook until fragrant, about 1 minute. Add the beans, oregano, and tomatoes. Cook until the beans are heated through, about 3 minutes longer.

3 Season with lemon juice, salt, and pepper. Serve hot.

scalloped green beans

Could this dish be the original farmhouse casserole that inspired the insipid Thanksgiving green bean casserole of our youth — the one with the cream of mushroom soup and canned French-fried onion rings? I think it is possible, but this version is ten times better. The beans slow-cook to a tender-crisp perfection. The beans you use can be somewhat overmature (see Note)— which makes it perfect for the overambitious gardener.

SERVES 4

3 tablespoons butter

3 tablespoons unbleached all-purpose flour

1½ cups milk

1½ cups grated sharp Cheddar

2 pounds green or wax beans, trimmed and cut into 2-inch pieces (7 to 8 cups)

1 onion, halved and sliced

Salt and freshly ground black pepper

¼ cup dried bread crumbs, or ½ cup fresh

note The timing is perfect for slightly overgrown beans. Reduce the baking time if you are using young, immature beans, or a particularly tender variety of beans, such as Dragon's Tongue. Wax beans are generally more tender and cook faster than green beans.

1 Preheat the oven to 350°F. Grease a 9- by 13-inch baking dish with butter.

2 Melt the butter in a medium saucepan over medium heat. Stir in the flour with a wooden spoon to make a smooth paste. Stir in the milk and bring to a boil. Reduce the heat and stir in the cheese. Cook, stirring constantly, until the cheese is melted and the sauce is smooth, about 3 minutes.

3 Layer the beans and onion in the baking dish, generously sprinkling with the salt and pepper as you layer. Cover with the cheese sauce. Sprinkle the bread crumbs over the dish.

4 Bake for 60 minutes.

5 Serve hot.

pan-roasted green beans with warm soy vinaigrette

By sautéing the green beans in small batches in a hot skillet, you get a result that is similar to roasting in the oven. These beans are crispy and very flavorful.

SERVES 4

3 tablespoons soy sauce

1 tablespoon Chinese rice wine or dry sherry

1 tablespoon rice vinegar

1 teaspoon dark sesame oil

Freshly ground black pepper

1 tablespoon peanut or canola oil

1 pound green beans, trimmed

2 garlic cloves, minced

1 teaspoon minced fresh ginger

1 tablespoon sesame seeds

1 Preheat the oven to 200°F. Place a serving platter in the oven to keep warm.

2 To prepare the vinaigrette, whisk together the soy sauce, rice wine, vinegar, sesame oil, and black pepper to taste in a small bowl.

3 Heat a large cast-iron skillet over high heat. Add the canola oil, swirl to coat the bottom of the pan, and continue heating until shimmering, about 30 seconds. Add about one third of the green beans in a single layer to the skillet and cook until tender, turning occasionally with tongs or a spatula, 4 to 7 minutes, depending on the thickness of the beans and how tender you want them. Transfer the beans to the platter in the oven to keep warm. Continue cooking the beans in batches until all the beans are cooked.

4 Return the skillet to the stove and reduce the heat to medium. Add the garlic and ginger and sauté until fragrant, about 30 seconds. Add the vinaigrette and heat through, about 30 seconds.

5 Pour the warm vinaigrette over the beans, sprinkle with the sesame seeds, and serve immediately.

chicken curry
with green beans

My family can never get enough curry, so I try to accommodate their desires as much as possible. This version, with green beans, is a summertime standard. But it is equally good made with peas, asparagus, broccoli, or cauliflower.

■ SERVES 4–5 ■

1 pound green beans, trimmed and cut into-2 inch lengths

3 tablespoons canola oil

1 medium onion, thinly sliced

2 garlic cloves, minced

1 jalapeño, seeded and minced

2 tablespoons minced fresh ginger

2 tablespoons curry powder

1 pound boneless, skinless chicken breasts, cut into ½-inch strips

1½ cups fresh or canned diced tomatoes

1 can (14 ounces) unsweetened coconut milk

¼ cup chopped fresh cilantro

3 tablespoons chopped fresh basil

Salt and freshly ground black pepper

Cayenne

Hot cooked basmati rice, to serve

1 Blanch the green beans in a large pot of boiling salted water until just tender, about 3 minutes. Drain and set aside.

2 Heat the oil over medium-high heat in a large heavy-bottomed saucepan or Dutch oven. Add the onion and sauté until fragrant, about 2 minutes. Reduce the heat to medium and add the garlic, jalapeño, ginger, and curry powder. Sauté until the onion is tender and the spices are fragrant, stirring frequently, 2 to 3 minutes longer.

3 Add the chicken and sauté, stirring frequently, until the chicken is cooked through, about 5 minutes. Add the tomatoes, coconut milk, and green beans. Bring to a boil, then reduce the heat to a simmer. Add the cilantro and basil. Season to taste with the salt and pepper. Add the cayenne to taste, starting with just a pinch and adding more, depending on how hot you enjoy your curries. Simmer for 10 minutes.

4 Serve hot over a bed of rice.

SNAP BEAN CULTIVAR TASTING NOTES

Pole beans are generally regarded as sweeter and more flavorful than bush beans. **Blue Lake** is a standard green pole bean that tastes just like a green bean should. **Fin de Bagnol** is an excellent heirloom filet bean with intense flavor. It grows as a bush bean. Wax beans are generally milder (blander) in flavor than green beans. **Dragon's Tongue** beans are one of the best-tasting raw beans we have ever grown. The beans are a flat, Italian-type yellow bean with purple streaks. The purple disappears when the beans are cooked.

dry-cooked green beans

My favorite Chinese restaurant served a dish by this name, and I thought it was possibly the best single dish I had ever eaten. When I researched the recipe, I found that the green beans were generally deep-fried in this classic preparation. Well, of course, everything tastes better fried, but who wants to eat that way? I tried making the dish by roasting the green beans, which is an alternative "dry"-heat method, and the results were excellent. Maybe dry-roasted green beans aren't classic, but they are delicious — and good for you.

SERVES 4

Meat and Marinade

½ pound ground pork

2 teaspoons soy sauce

1 tablespoon black bean sauce

1 tablespoon Chinese rice wine or sherry

1 teaspoon Chinese chili paste with garlic

½ teaspoon dark sesame oil

Sauce

2 tablespoons soy sauce

1 tablespoon Chinese rice wine or sherry

1 tablespoon water

1 teaspoon sugar

Green Beans

2 pounds green beans, trimmed

4 tablespoons peanut oil

2 teaspoons minced ginger

2 garlic cloves, minced

Hot cooked rice

1 Preheat the oven to 450°F. Generously grease a large sheet pan or shallow roasting pan with oil.

2 Combine the pork, soy sauce, bean sauce, wine, chili paste, and sesame oil in a medium bowl. Mix well and set aside.

3 Mix the soy sauce, wine, water, and sugar in a bowl or glass measuring cup. Set aside.

4 Combine the beans and 3 tablespoons of the oil in a large bowl and toss to coat the beans with the oil. Arrange the beans in a single layer on the prepared pan. Place the pan on the lowest rack in the oven and roast until the beans are barely browned and tender, 12 to 15 minutes.

5 Heat the remaining 1 tablespoon oil in a wok over high heat. Add the pork and marinade and stir-fry until the meat browns, about 5 minutes. Push the meat to the sides of the wok and add the ginger and garlic. Stir-fry until fragrant, about 30 seconds. Add the beans and sauce and stir together to coat the beans with the sauce. Stir-fry for 1 minute to allow the flavors to blend. Serve hot over rice.

dilly beans

Canning dilly beans may be a chore in the hot summer, but we are always glad to have some for snacking on once summer has faded to a memory. Before my youngest son was born, jars of pickles tended to accumulate from year to year. Not anymore. I could probably can cases of these and still not have enough. The recipe is designed to be multiplied by however many beans you happen to have on hand.

MAKES 1 PINT

1 cup white vinegar

½ cup water

1 garlic clove

1 dill head or 4-inch sprig of fresh dill

1 teaspoon pickling salt

2 cups green beans, trimmed to 4 inches in length

1 Bring the vinegar and water to a boil in a nonreactive saucepan.

2 Meanwhile, pack each clean, hot canning jar with the garlic, dill, and salt. Pack in the green beans, leaving ½ inch headspace.

3 Pour the hot brine over the beans, leaving ½ inch headspace. Seal.

4 Process in a boiling-water bath for 10 minutes (see pages 475 to 477). Cool undisturbed for 12 hours. Store in a cool, dry place. Or omit the canning step and leave in the refrigerator. Do not open the jars for 6 weeks to allow the flavors to develop.

THE ORIGINAL *Phaseolus vulgarius* was a native of Central America that was domesticated more than 5,000 years ago and widely grown in North and South America. By the time the Spanish arrived in the New World in the 1600s, there were numerous different varieties of beans growing.

In its dried form, *Phaseolus vulgaris* includes haricot beans, kidney beans, cannellini beans, navy beans, black beans, and pinto beans. In its young, tender form, when the pods are still edible, beans are variously known as snap beans, string beans, and green beans. This grouping also includes wax beans, purple snap beans, filet beans (or French beans or haricots verts), and flat beans (or Italian flat beans, Roma beans, or Romano beans). Modern breeding practices have mostly eliminated the tough, fibrous strings, but a fresh bean will break with an audible "snap," hence the preferred name.

Easy, Delicious, Beautiful

I WASN'T ALWAYS A BIG FAN of Swiss chard. In fact, I stopped allocating space for it in my garden, since I had left it unharvested too many times. Then, some years back, Johnny's Selected Seeds catalog featured Bright Lights Swiss chard on its cover. One look at those neon pinks and yellows and, well, how could I resist?

It wasn't until I started experimenting with a baked Swiss chard gratin that I understood the error of my ways. What I learned is that Swiss chard needs more cooking time than I would have thought. With longer cooking times, chard's flavor is coaxed to reveal itself, and the texture becomes unctuous and silky.

Chard is a long-season green. In northern gardens, it can be planted in late spring and will continue to grow until it frosts. Harvest just the outer leaves to keep the plant going for a long season. In warmer areas, chard is often grown and harvested throughout the winter months.

GROWING Swiss chard is a very accommodating green: It can tolerate light frosts in spring and fall, tolerates light shade, and is moderate in its requirements for moisture and nutrients.

SOWING Sow outdoors after the last frost.

CULTIVATING Provide even watering.

HARVESTING Harvest the whole plant, leaving 1 inch of stem above the soil, and another plant will grow from the crown to provide a second harvest. Or cut only the outer stalks from several plants for a continuous harvest throughout the summer.

CHARD MATH
1 pound Swiss chard = 6 to 8 stems with leaves
= 15 cups chopped

Chard is closely related to beets. Ruby chard is almost indistinguishable from beet greens; hence, the recipes are interchangeable. Baby Swiss chard can be added to salads, but I think chard is best fully mature and cooked.

TIMING
Blanching: 3 to 4 minutes stems,
2 to 3 minutes leaves
Sautéing: 3 to 4 minutes stems,
2 to 3 minutes leaves
Braising: 35 to 40 minutes

swiss chard stracciatella

Comfort soup or tonic? The soup is a bit of both — it feels like a comfort soup going down, but it has to be very healthy with all those delicious greens. Stracciatella *means "little rags" in Italian; it is so named because the egg and cheese form little raglike shreds. My kids call it "Italian egg drop soup."*

■ **SERVES 4–6** ■

6 cups chicken broth, preferably homemade (page 9)

3 garlic cloves, minced

1 pound (6–8 stems with leaves) ruby, green, or rainbow chard, very thinly sliced (see Note)

2 tablespoons freshly grated Parmesan, plus more for serving

2 large eggs, beaten

Salt and freshly ground black pepper

note You can substitute escarole or Belgian endive for the chard in this recipe.

1 Combine the broth and garlic in a large saucepan and bring to a boil over medium-high heat. Add the chard, cover, reduce the heat to medium, and cook until the chard is tender, about 8 minutes.

2 Stir in the Parmesan and simmer for 1 minute.

3 Beat the eggs in a small bowl. Bring the soup to a boil. With a fork, gradually stir the eggs into the soup. Cook briefly, stirring constantly with a fork until threads appear, less than 1 minute. Season to taste with the salt and pepper.

4 Serve immediately, passing additional cheese at the table.

braised chard

Here is a simple way to enjoy chard.

2 pounds (12–16 stems with leaves) ruby, green, or rainbow chard, leaves cut into 1-inch ribbons and stems diced

¼ cup extra-virgin olive oil

¼ cup vegetable or chicken broth (page 8 or 9) or water

1 onion, diced

3 garlic cloves, minced

Salt and freshly ground black pepper

1 Combine the chard, oil, broth, onion, and garlic in a large Dutch oven or large wide saucepan. Season with salt and pepper. Cover and bring to a boil.

2 Reduce the heat and cook over medium heat until the chard is completely tender, about 35 minutes. Taste and adjust the seasoning. Serve hot.

CHARD FACTS & FICTION

SWISS CHARD WAS CULTIVATED as a leaf vegetable in Greece by around 400 BC. Varieties were developed with widened stems, which were used as a vegetable similar to asparagus. It was not until the late 16th century that large-root beets branched off from this leaf vegetable.

Ruby-colored chard was once grown exclusively to be eaten at Christmas in the south of France and constituted the highlight of the Christmas Eve meal. Only the stems, having a flavor said to be reminiscent of artichoke hearts, were eaten. Swiss chard is a popular vegetable in Provence and is grown abundantly in the districts around the Rhône Valley because it can withstand cold weather and is harvested up until frost. Where the Swiss fit into all this is not known.

swiss chard gratin

My love affair with Swiss chard began with this simple, classic preparation.

SERVES 6

2 pounds (12–16 stems with leaves) ruby, green, or rainbow chard, stems sliced and leaves cut into 1-inch ribbons

4 tablespoons butter

1 onion, halved and sliced

¼ cup unbleached all-purpose flour

2 cups milk

1 cup grated Gruyère

Salt and freshly ground black pepper

¼ cup dried bread crumbs

WHAT'S IN A NAME?

Swiss chard or chard is actually a beet. Botanists distinguish among three major types of beets: *Beta vulgaris* ssp. includes the familiar beet we eat in borscht as well as the sugar beet; *Beta vulgaris* ssp. Maritime is the wild sea-beet, which may be the original beet; and *Beta vulgaris* ssp. *cicla* is Swiss chard, possibly the oldest of the cultivated beets. Chard is also variously known as white beet, strawberry spinach, seakale beet, leaf beet, Sicilian beet, spinach beet, Chilean beet, Roman kale, perpetual spinach, and silverbeet.

1 Bring a large pot of salted water to a boil. Add the chard stems and cook for 2 minutes. Add the leaves and continue to cook for another minute. Drain well.

2 Preheat the oven to 350°F. Grease a 1½-quart casserole or 9- by 13-inch baking dish with butter.

3 Melt the butter over medium heat in a medium saucepan. Add the onion and sauté until soft, about 3 minutes. Whisk in the flour to form a paste. Whisk in the milk and bring to a boil. Reduce the heat and stir in the cheese. Season with salt and pepper and remove from the heat. Fold in the chard.

4 Transfer the chard mixture to the prepared casserole dish. Sprinkle the bread crumbs on top.

5 Bake for 25 to 35 minutes, until the sauce is bubbling and the top is browned. Serve hot.

braised chard pizza

Garlic-scented ricotta cheese makes a bed for silken Swiss chard in this lovely green-and-white pizza.

SERVES 6

1 recipe Basic Pizza Dough (page 12; follow the instructions in step 1 below while the dough is rising)

2 pounds (12–16 stems with leaves) ruby, green, or rainbow chard, leaves cut into 1-inch ribbons and stems diced

⅓ cup extra-virgin olive oil

¼ cup water

1 onion, diced

Salt and freshly ground black pepper, plus more to taste

3 garlic cloves, minced

1 tablespoon fresh oregano leaves or 1 teaspoon dried

1 pound ricotta

1 cup freshly grated Parmesan

1 While the pizza dough is rising, braise the chard. Combine the chard, oil, water, and onion in a large Dutch oven or a large wide saucepan. Season with salt and pepper. Cover and cook over medium heat until the chard is completely tender, 30 to 45 minutes. Drain well (but reserve the cooking liquid for flavoring stocks or soups or for cooking grains).

2 Preheat the oven to 500°F.

3 Stir the garlic and oregano into the ricotta and season to taste with more salt and pepper. With the dough spread over pizza or baking pans as instructed, spread half the ricotta over each. Spoon the chard on top of the ricotta. Top with the Parmesan.

4 Bake for 12 to 15 minutes, until the crusts are golden and the Parmesan is melted.

5 Slice and serve warm.

chard and ravioli

A magic formula: Take two big bunches of chard from the garden. Combine with pantry and freezer staples. The result — much greater than the sum of its parts — is an incredibly delicious, healthful one-dish vegetarian meal. It doesn't get much better or much easier than this. This is a family favorite.

■ SERVES 4 ■

2 pounds (12–16 stems with leaves) red, green, or rainbow chard, leaves cut into 1-inch ribbons and stems diced

2 tablespoons extra-virgin olive oil

2 garlic cloves, minced

1 shallot, minced

Pinch of crushed red pepper flakes

Salt and freshly ground black pepper

1 package (30 ounces) frozen cheese-filled ravioli

½ cup freshly grated Parmesan

1 Bring a large pot of salted water to a boil. Add the chard stems and boil for 2 minutes. Add the leaves and continue to boil until just wilted, about 30 seconds. Remove the vegetables with tongs or a slotted spoon and drain well.

2 Bring the water back to a boil.

3 Meanwhile, heat the oil in a large skillet over medium-high heat. Add the garlic, shallot, and red pepper and sauté until fragrant, about 1 minute. Add the chard and continue to sauté until heated through, about 3 minutes. Season with salt and pepper.

4 Add the ravioli to the boiling water and simmer (do not boil) until the ravioli are all cooked through and rise to the surface of the water, about 5 minutes. Drain well.

5 In a large serving bowl or platter, combine the ravioli and chard and toss together. Sprinkle with half the Parmesan and toss again. Sprinkle the remaining Parmesan on top and serve.

penne with chard and sausage

"Not at all yucky" was my son's comment the first time I served this. He would prefer his pasta free of vegetables, but makes the occasional exception, especially if there is sausage in the mix. I considered his words high praise at the time. Personally, I love the combination of pasta and greens.

SERVES 4–5

2 tablespoons extra-virgin olive oil

1 pound sweet or hot Italian sausage, removed from its casings and crumbled

1½ pounds (9–12 stems with leaves) ruby, green, or rainbow chard, thinly sliced

3 garlic cloves, minced

1½ cups diced fresh or canned tomatoes

1 cup chicken broth (page 9)

3 tablespoons chopped fresh basil

1 tablespoon chopped fresh mint

1 pound penne or other similar short pasta

Salt and freshly ground black pepper

Freshly grated Parmesan, to serve

1 Heat the oil in a large heavy saucepan or Dutch oven over medium-high heat. Add the sausage and sauté until brown, 8 to 10 minutes. Add the Swiss chard and garlic and sauté until the chard is wilted and the garlic is fragrant, about 3 minutes. Add the tomatoes, broth, basil, and mint. Reduce the heat and simmer while you cook the pasta.

2 Bring a large pot of salted water to a boil. Add the pasta and cook until al dente; drain well. Transfer to a warmed serving bowl.

3 Season the pasta sauce with salt and pepper. Add the sauce to the pasta and toss well. Serve immediately, passing the Parmesan at the table.

Nature's Blank Palette

A FEW YEARS AGO, I WAS ASKED to work on the 25th anniversary edition of *The Classic Zucchini Cookbook*. The book, originally published in the 1970s, contained some laughably dated recipes. I eliminated recipes calling for cream of mushroom soup, Jell-O, and any number of ground beef–zucchini casseroles and developed some 100 new recipes. I've never had more fun in the kitchen — and I am still not tired of zucchini.

You can do anything with summer squash! Its delicate (some would say bland) flavor makes it unusually adaptable. Looking for something Italian? Add zucchini to your favorite pasta recipe. Want to go Mexican? Sauté some zucchini and season with chili powder and lime juice. Hungering for Chinese? Stir-fry summer squash with some Chinese cabbage. Need a dessert, a bread, a muffin? Look no further than the ever-prolific zucchini, the plant that just won't quit.

And, by the way, if you are tired of reading about the New England myth that explains why New Englanders have to lock their cars in September (to keep them from being filled with zucchini), don't assume this is just another urban legend. It happened to me on my birthday one year. I am still plotting my revenge.

SOW & REAP

GROWING As long as you can provide warm temperatures and plenty of water, summer squash will do well. It does best in full sun and in fertile soil. Two summer squash plants will provide sufficient squash to satisfy a "typical" family of four. More plants is an embarrassment.

SOWING Sow seeds indoors 3 to 4 weeks before the last frost if you want to get a jump on the season. Or sow outdoors when the soil temperature reaches 70°F. Succession planting will extend the harvest.

CULTIVATING Provide water. In rich soil, no additional fertilizing is needed.

HARVESTING Great squash requires frequent harvesting of small fruits — when they are 4 to 5 inches long. Small squash has the best flavor and the fewest seeds. Harvesting often will prolong the period of harvest, though the yields will start to decline with most varieties after about a month or so. Be sure to check under the foliage for fruits that may be hiding.

SUMMER SQUASH MATH

Baby squash = 2 to 4 inches long, less than 6 ounces
Small squash = 4 to 6 inches long, 7 to 11 ounces
Medium squash = 8 to 10 inches long, 12 to 16 ounces
Large squash = anything above 1 pound
1 pound squash = 4 cups sliced or diced or julienned
= 3½ cups grated (or 1¾ cups after salting and draining)

KITCHEN NOTES

Summer squash is at its best when it is briefly cooked. It can be served plain or with just butter or herbs to emphasize its delicate flavor. Or it can be combined with bold flavors to make a more exciting dish. Squash cooked by dry-heat methods — frying, grilling, roasting, and sautéing — usually has more flavor than squash cooked by steaming or boiling.

To prepare summer squash, wash it thoroughly. Trim off the blossom and stem ends. Then slice, chop, or grate as the recipe suggests.

To coax the most flavor out of summer squash, it is a good idea to drain it first to concentrate the flavors. Slice or grate the squash and toss with 2 teaspoons salt. Then set it aside for about 30 minutes. The squash will lose about one quarter of its volume as excess moisture is released from its cells. Wring the squash dry in a clean kitchen towel or squeeze by hand. The squash is now ready to cook with. A less effective method that can be used with grated squash is to simply wring it dry in a clean kitchen towel.

Unless you are preparing squash to masquerade as apple, don't peel the squash, as this is where most of the nutrition, fiber, and flavor lie. Dessert and bread recipes that use grated squash really taste best with overgrown squash. Young squash may add a bitter "green" flavor to a cake or bread.

TIMING

Blanching: 1 to 2 minutes
Deep-frying: 2 to 3 minutes at 365°F (batter dipped)
Sautéing or stir-frying: 4 to 5 minutes
Grilling: 4 to 5 minutes per side
Roasting: 15 minutes at 450°F

zucchini-potato frittata

Frittatas are simple to make, amazingly versatile in what can be tossed in with them and how they can be served. The ingredients here — summer squash, potatoes, Canadian bacon, Cheddar, and eggs — make a good combination for breakfast, brunch, lunch, or dinner, served warm or at room temperature. If you like, call it a tortilla as they do in Spain, and serve it at room temperature with drinks.

■ SERVES 4–6 ■

1 medium zucchini or yellow summer squash, sliced
Salt
4–5 tablespoons extra-virgin olive oil, or more as needed
1½ pounds waxy potatoes, thinly sliced
1 large onion, halved and thinly sliced
¼ pound smoked Canadian bacon or ham, diced
6 eggs
Freshly ground black pepper
1 cup grated Cheddar

1 Combine the zucchini and 1 teaspoon salt in a colander and toss well. Set aside to drain for 30 minutes.

2 Heat 3 tablespoons of the oil over medium-high heat in a large, well-seasoned cast-iron skillet or ovenproof nonstick skillet. Add the potatoes and onion, reduce the heat to medium-low, and cook, flipping and stirring occasionally, until the potatoes are soft, about 20 minutes. Increase the heat to medium-high and continue cooking, tossing occasionally, until the potatoes are brown, about 5 minutes. Remove the potatoes with a slotted spoon but keep the skillet on the burner.

3 Transfer the zucchini to a clean kitchen towel and pat dry. Add the zucchini and Canadian bacon to the skillet and sauté over medium-high heat, until the zucchini is just tender, about 4 minutes. Remove the zucchini and Canadian bacon with a slotted spoon. Keep the skillet over the heat.

4 Beat the eggs and pepper to taste in a medium bowl until well blended. Fold in the potatoes, zucchini and Canadian bacon, and cheese.

5 Preheat the oven to 350°F. Add 1 to 2 tablespoons of the remaining oil to the skillet as needed to lightly coat the bottom. Pour in the egg mixture, reduce the heat to medium-low, and cook without stirring until the bottom is set, about 10 minutes.

6 Transfer the skillet to the oven and bake until the top is set, 5 to 15 minutes, checking every 5 minutes.

7 Place a serving plate on top of the skillet and carefully invert. The frittata should fall out of the pan. Cut into wedges and serve.

zucchini cheese squares

My kids love these "zucchini pillows." The texture is softer than a bread and denser than a soufflé, with just the trace of crunch from the onions. It makes a great side dish, especially on a picnic, where the squares can be eaten out of hand. You can use slightly overgrown zucchini here.

SERVES 6–8

3 cups grated zucchini

2 teaspoons salt

1½ cups unbleached all-purpose flour

1 tablespoon baking powder

1 onion, diced

2 cups grated Cheddar

2 teaspoons fresh thyme leaves

1 teaspoon freshly ground black pepper or lemon pepper

½ cup canola oil

3 large eggs, beaten

1 Combine the zucchini and salt in a colander and toss to mix. Set aside to drain for 30 minutes. Squeeze out the excess water.

2 Preheat the oven to 350°F. Grease a 7- by 11-inch baking dish with butter.

3 Stir together the flour and baking powder in a medium bowl. Add the onion, zucchini, cheese, thyme, and pepper. Mix well with a fork, breaking up any clumps of zucchini. Whisk together the oil and eggs in a small bowl. Pour into the zucchini mixture and mix well. Spread evenly in the baking dish.

4 Bake for about 35 minutes, until golden.

5 Let cool on a wire rack for 5 minutes. Cut into squares and serve warm or at room temperature.

ALL OF THE SUMMER SQUASH have tender, edible skins and flesh that range from mild and nutty to buttery or cucumber-like. Although there are differences in flavor among summer squash varieties grown side by side under optimal conditions, most people find the differences hard to discern. Add, say, lots of rain, and the flavor differences almost disappear. Therefore, most summer squash recipes are interchangeable. But the shapes and appearance of summer squash vary quite a bit, so this should be a consideration when choosing which varieties to grow.

Cocozelle An heirloom type of zucchini from Italy, these zucchini have raised ribs or stripes. The flavor is superior when the vegetable is young.

Crookneck Yellow Squash and Yellow Summer Squash
The crook is being bred out of yellow summer squash, as are the warts that give the skin a bumpy appearance. Most yellow summer squash are straight and smooth skinned, but the older, bumpy skin varieties may have better flavor. Zephyr looks like a smooth-skinned yellow crookneck half dipped in green paint. A favorite among growers for its good keeping qualities while still on the vine, it has excellent flavor and texture.

Middle Eastern Summer Squash These summer squash are typically rounder than most zucchini and pale green in color. They may be called Lebanese, Egyptian, Cousa, Kuta, or Magda squash. Use for any zucchini recipe. They are good for stuffing.

Pattypan Squash With shapes like flying saucers, these scalloped squash are best when small, 2 to 3 inches in diameter. The interesting shapes make them particularly appealing for slicing and grilling, roasting, or sautéing. They are also wonderful stuffed. Pattypans come in colors ranging from cream to green. These squash may go under the name of scallopini or cymling.

Round Zucchini These may be called globe zucchini or apple squash. Ronde de Nice is an heirloom cultivar that is highly regarded. Pick round zucchini when they are small. They are excellent stuffed.

Zucchetta Rampicante These are also known as Italian trombone squash or Tromboncino squash. The fruit, which are borne on vigorously growing vines, are pale green and trombone shaped. The vines should be supported on trellises and the squash are best when 12 to 15 inches long. This squash is virtually seedless and stands up well to cooking.

Zucchini The classic zucchini is a dark green cylinder with mild flavor. Golden zucchini are increasingly common. Costata Romanesco is an heirloom cultivar that has very good flavor.

summer squash pizza

There comes a time in all gardeners' lives when we find ourselves sneaking zucchini or summer squash into every dish we cook — pizza, pasta, pancakes — nothing escapes. Salting and sautéing the squash first ensures that the final dish will not be watery. In the case of this simple pizza variation, the squash is a delicate and delicious addition.

■ SERVES 6 ■

1 recipe Basic Pizza Dough (page 12; follow the instructions in step 1 below while the dough is rising)

2 medium yellow summer squash or zucchini (or one of each), quartered and sliced

2 teaspoons salt

2 tablespoons extra-virgin olive oil

3–4 garlic cloves, minced

2 tablespoons chopped fresh basil

2 cups well-seasoned tomato sauce

3 cups grated mozzarella

1 While the dough is rising according to the recipe instructions, combine the squash and salt in a colander and set aside to drain for at least 30 minutes. Transfer the squash to a large clean cloth towel and pat dry.

2 Heat the oil in a large skillet over medium-high heat. Add the squash and sauté until it begins to soften, about 2 minutes. Add the garlic and continue to sauté until the garlic is fragrant, about 1 minute. Remove from the heat and stir in the basil.

3 Preheat the oven to 500°F and place an oven rack on the lowest shelf.

4 You will be baking these pizzas one at a time, so it is most time-efficient to assemble them one at a time as well. With the dough spread over the pizza pans or baking sheets according to the recipe instructions, spread 1 cup of the sauce over one. Scatter 1½ cups of the mozzarella over the sauce. Scatter half the squash over the cheese.

6 Bake the pizza for 10 to 12 minutes on the bottom oven rack, until the crust is golden. Meanwhile, assemble the second pizza. Bake the second pizza when the first pizza is done.

7 Serve both pizzas while still warm.

SQUASH BLOSSOMS

SQUASH PLANTS BEAR male and female blossoms. The stem of the female flower eventually begins to swell. This swelling is the squash forming in its initial growth stage. The dried female blossom often must be plucked from the end of the mature vegetable. Male blossoms, having long since met their responsibilities in the pollination process, simply fall off and decay.

When first blooming, the squash may produce only male blossoms. These may all fall off. But don't be disappointed; this is a common occurrence. Have faith that the female blossoms will appear. It is the female blossom that produces squash, so pick only surplus male blossoms for cooking.

The male blossom, easily identified by a long, slender stem, can be used to make several different types of dishes. Most elegantly, they can be dipped in a tempura batter and fried (see pages 38–39). Or, picked while still in the budding stage, the blossoms can be lighted sautéed in butter. Stuffing possibilities are limited only by your imagination. The blossoms can be sliced into strips and added to omelets, pastas, soups, and salads.

To prepare blossoms for cooking, clean a blossom by carefully opening a couple of the petals. Remove the stamens, if present. Trim the stem to about ½ inch in length. Gently dip or rinse the blossom in cool water to remove any dirt or insects. Allow to dry on paper towels. Refrigerate until you are ready to cook. Squash blossoms are highly perishable.

pasta with
summer squash and shrimp

Family getting tired of zucchini? Combine it with shrimp, North Americans' favorite seafood, and make everyone happy. With saffron and wine in the sauce, this version is particularly luxurious. Enjoy the rest of the wine with dinner.

■ SERVES 4–6 ■

2 medium-sized zucchini, quartered and sliced

2 medium-sized yellow summer squash, quartered and sliced

2 teaspoons salt

½ cup dry white wine

¼ teaspoon crushed saffron threads

3 tablespoons extra-virgin olive oil

1 red bell pepper, cut into ¼-inch strips

3 large ripe tomatoes, seeded and diced

2 garlic cloves, minced

Salt and freshly ground black pepper

1¼ pounds shrimp, shelled and deveined

¼ cup chopped fresh basil

1 pound shells, penne, or other medium-size pasta shape

1 Combine the zucchini, summer squash, and salt in a colander. Toss to mix and set aside to drain for 30 minutes. Transfer to a clean dish towel and wring dry.

2 Fill a large pot with salted water for the pasta and bring to a boil. Combine the wine and saffron in a small bowl and set aside.

3 Heat the oil in a large skillet over medium-high heat. Add the red pepper, zucchini, and summer squash and sauté until the squash begin to soften, 3 to 4 minutes. Stir in the tomatoes, garlic, and wine mixture. Simmer for 5 minutes. Add the shrimp and continue to simmer until the shrimp are pink and cooked through, about 5 minutes. Remove from the heat and stir in the basil. Season with salt and pepper.

4 When the pasta water comes to a boil, add the pasta and cook until al dente, according to the package directions. Reserve ½ cup of the pasta cooking water and drain the pasta.

5 Add the pasta to the shrimp mixture and toss together until the pasta is well coated with the sauce. Add as much of the reserved pasta liquid as needed to moisten the pasta. Serve immediately.

chile-lime chicken sautéed with zucchini

It is an unfortunate twist of fate that the garden is often at its most prolific at the very time when the kitchen is hottest and the least desirable place to be. There's no slaving over a hot stove for this quick one-dish supper. The fresh vegetables and piquant flavors may be just the thing to perk up faded appetites. Chipotles en adobo — or smoke-dried jalapeños in adobo sauce — provide the spark. These chiles are canned and found with Mexican foods in most supermarkets.

SERVES 4–6

4 medium zucchini or yellow summer squash (or a mixture), halved and sliced

Salt

1 pound skinless, boneless chicken breasts, cut into thin strips

Juice of 1 large lime or 2 medium ones, (3 to 4 tablespoons)

2–4 teaspoons minced chipotle chile en adobo

Salt and freshly ground black pepper

4 tablespoons extra-virgin olive oil

1 green bell pepper, julienned

1 red bell pepper, julienned

2 ripe tomatoes, seeded and diced

4 scallions, white and tender green parts only, sliced

¼ cup chopped fresh cilantro

1 garlic clove, minced

Warmed flour or corn tortillas or hot cooked rice, for serving

Sour cream, for serving

1 lime, cut into wedges, for serving

1 Combine the squash and 2 teaspoons salt in a colander. Toss to mix and set aside to drain for 30 minutes.

2 While the squash drains, combine the chicken and lime juice in a nonreactive bowl. Mix in the chipotle chile, adding more or less depending on how hot you want the dish to be. Set aside while you prepare the remaining vegetables.

3 Heat 2 tablespoons of the oil in a large skillet over medium-high heat. Add the chicken and marinade and sauté until the chicken is tender and no longer pink, about 4 minutes. Remove the chicken and juice from the skillet, set aside, and keep warm.

4 Blot the squash with a clean kitchen towel. Return the skillet to medium-high heat, add the remaining 2 tablespoons of the oil, and heat for about 1 minute. Add the summer squash and red and green bell peppers. Sauté until the squash is crisp-tender, 3 to 5 minutes.

5 Return the chicken to the skillet. Add the tomatoes, scallions, cilantro, and garlic and cook until the tomatoes are heated through, about 5 minutes. Season with salt and pepper. Taste and adjust the seasonings.

6 Serve hot, passing the warm tortillas, sour cream, and lime wedges at the table. Or, spoon the rice onto a serving platter or individual plates. Spoon the chicken mixture on top of the rice. Pass the sour cream and lime wedges at the table.

zucchini-cheddar breakfast biscuits

The zucchini pretty much disappears in these smoky good biscuits, especially if you use golden zucchini or yellow summer squash. I call these "breakfast biscuits" because the flavor brings to mind a certain ubiquitous breakfast sandwich, but they make a fine accompaniment for a dinner of soup and salad.

◼ MAKES 24 BISCUITS ◼

2 cups shredded zucchini or yellow summer squash

1 teaspoon salt

4 ounces high-quality bacon, preferably applewood smoked

3 cups unbleached-all-purpose flour

1 tablespoon baking powder

2 teaspoons baking soda

½ teaspoon freshly ground black pepper

4 tablespoons cold unsalted butter, cut up

1 cup grated Cheddar

¾ cup buttermilk

1 Combine the zucchini and salt in a colander and set aside to drain for 30 minutes. Squeeze out any excess moisture and place in a small mixing bowl. You should have about ½ cup zucchini.

2 Cook the bacon in a large skillet over medium heat until crisp, about 10 minutes, stirring occasionally. Remove with a slotted spoon and set aside on paper towels to drain. Chop fine and set aside.

3 Preheat the oven to 400°F.

4 Sift the flour, baking powder, baking soda, and pepper into a large bowl. Cut in the butter until the mixture resembles coarse crumbs. Add the cheese, bacon, and zucchini and toss with a fork to mix well. Stir in the buttermilk to form a stiff dough.

5 Transfer the dough to a lightly floured board and knead briefly until smooth. Pat out or roll out until about 1 inch thick. Stamp out biscuits with a 3-inch round cutter and place on a baking sheet about 1 inch apart.

6 Bake the biscuits for 15 minutes, until golden.

7 Serve the biscuits hot out of the oven.

WHAT TO DO WITH OVERGROWN ZUCCHINI

Zapple it! If you peel an overgrown zucchini and cook it in lemon juice until tender, then sweeten it with sugar and apple pie spices, the result is a filling that tastes just like apple pie. Imagine the possibilities . . .

zapple muffins

First day of school is "muffin morning" at my son's school. Parents are invited to stay for the first hour of school, have coffee and muffins, and meet other parents — not to mention ease the transition for the new kids. Even those who know my predilection for sticking zucchini into "everything" assume there are apples — in addition to the zucchini — in these muffins. This tastes best with overgrown squash; young squash will add a bitter flavor.

■ MAKES 18 MUFFINS ■

Zapplesauce

- 4 cups peeled, seeded, and diced zucchini or summer squash
- ⅓ cup fresh lemon juice
- ½ cup packed light brown sugar
- 2 teaspoons ground cinnamon
- ¼ teaspoon ground nutmeg

Muffin Batter

- 3 cups unbleached all-purpose flour
- 1 tablespoon baking powder
- 1 teaspoon baking soda
- 1 teaspoon salt
- ¼ teaspoon ground nutmeg
- ½ cup butter, softened
- 1 cup sugar
- 2 large eggs
- ¼ cup buttermilk

1 To make the zapplesauce, combine the zucchini and lemon juice in a nonreactive saucepan. Bring to a boil over medium-high heat. Reduce the heat and simmer until tender, about 10 minutes. Add the brown sugar, the cinnamon, and the nutmeg. Simmer, stirring occasionally, for 20 minutes, until slightly thickened. Let cool to room temperature.

2 Preheat the oven to 350°F. Grease 18 regular-size muffin cups with butter.

3 Sift together the flour, baking powder, baking soda, salt, and nutmeg in a large bowl.

4 Beat together the butter and sugar in another large mixing bowl. Add the eggs, one at a time, beating after each addition. Beat in the flour mixture, alternating with the buttermilk, until smooth. Stir in the zapplesauce just until evenly distributed.

5 Divide the batter among the prepared muffin cups. The batter will be stiff; an ice-cream scoop does a great job of distributing it.

6 Bake the muffins for 25 to 30 minutes, until they have risen and a knife inserted in the center of one comes out clean.

7 Turn the muffins out of the pan to cool on a wire rack.

zapple pie

In the tradition of the great Ritz Cracker mock apple pie comes the mock apple pie made with overgrown zucchini. It turns out that if you peel zucchini and cook it in lemon juice, then sweeten it with sugar and apple pie spices, you get a pie that could fool all but the most discerning palates. My kids love this pie. It works best with older, overgrown squash. Young fresh squash will have a trace of bitterness that advertises the pie's vegetable origins.

SERVES 6–8

Pastry for a 9-inch double-crust pie (page 10)

6 cups peeled, quartered, cored, and thinly sliced zucchini or summer squash

½ cup fresh lemon juice

¾ cup firmly packed light or dark brown sugar

1½ teaspoons ground cinnamon

¼ teaspoon ground ginger

¼ teaspoon freshly ground nutmeg

2 tablespoons instant tapioca

1 tablespoon granulated sugar

1 Prepare the pie dough according to the recipe directions and refrigerate.

2 Combine the zucchini and lemon juice in a medium saucepan. Bring to a boil, reduce the heat, and simmer until the zucchini is tender, about 10 minutes, stirring occasionally for even cooking. Add the brown sugar, cinnamon, ginger, and nutmeg and simmer for 5 minutes longer.

3 Remove the zucchini from the heat. Stir in the tapioca and let stand for 15 minutes.

4 Preheat the oven to 425°F with a rack in the lower third of the oven.

5 Spoon the zucchini mixture into the pastry. Moisten the edge of the bottom crust with water. Fold the dough circle in half, lift off the work surface, place the pastry across the center of the filled pie, and unfold. Trim the edge ½ inch larger than the pie plate and tuck the overhang under the edge of the bottom crust. Crimp the edges with a fork or make a fluted pattern with your fingers. Make several decorative slits in the top crust to allow steam to escape.

6 Bake the pie in the lower third of the oven for 20 minutes. Reduce the heat to 350°F and continue to bake for 30 minutes. Sprinkle the top of the pie with the granulated sugar and continue to bake for 10 to 15 minutes longer, until the crust is golden and the juices are bubbly.

7 Cool the pie on a rack. Serve warm or at room temperature.

dark chocolate–zucchini bundt cake

The zucchini barely makes an appearance in this rich moist chocolaty cake. It requires no frosting, but a dusting of confectioners' sugar gives it a finished look.

■ SERVES 12–16 ■

2¼ cups unbleached all-purpose flour
¾ cup unsweetened cocoa powder
2 teaspoons baking powder
1 teaspoon baking soda
1 teaspoon salt
½ teaspoon ground cinnamon
2 cups lightly packed brown sugar
½ cup butter, at room temperature
2 large eggs
3 ounces baking chocolate, melted and cooled
1 teaspoon pure vanilla extract
½ cup coffee
3 cups grated zucchini or summer squash
Confectioners' sugar, for dusting

1 Preheat the oven to 350°F. Grease a 10-inch fluted tube pan with butter.

2 Sift the flour, cocoa, baking powder, baking soda, salt, and cinnamon into a medium bowl.

3 Beat together the brown sugar and butter in a large mixing bowl. Add the eggs, one at a time, beating well after each addition. Beat in the melted chocolate and vanilla. Add the flour mixture, alternating with the coffee, and beat until smooth. Fold in the zucchini. Scrape the batter into the prepared pan.

4 Bake for 50 minutes, until a skewer inserted in the cake comes out smooth.

5 Cool the cake in the pan on a rack for 10 minutes. Invert onto the wire rack, remove the pan, and leave on the rack to cool completely. Dust with confectioners' sugar right before serving.

ANNUAL HERBS

Herbs are an essential part of every kitchen garden. Some are perennial plants; they will come back year after year (page 92). Others are annuals and must be replanted each year. Some of the annuals, like dill, are quite willing to self-sow each year. The question then becomes how willing you are to allow the "volunteers" to flourish in odd places throughout the garden.

Basil This is the herb that tops most people's list of favorite herbs. It is essential to many dishes from the Mediterranean and Southeastern Asia. I usually set out a few plants that were started indoors and then sow a larger patch from seed. Basil is easy to grow. When the seedlings are 2 inches high, pinch out the growing tips so the plants will be bushy. Continue to harvest by pinching off the tips, and don't let flowers develop. The plants will last until the first frost.

Basil is best preserved by making pesto (page 6). Pesto freezes very well.

Cilantro Also known as fresh coriander and Chinese parsley, cilantro is necessary for many Tex-Mex and Southeast Asian dishes. People tend to love this pungent herb or hate it — the haters claim that cilantro tastes like soap. The leaves are rather similar to flat-leaf parsley, but they are more tender in texture and more aromatic. It is best to sow directly outdoors, with repeat sowings every 3 weeks for a continuous warm-weather supply. Cilantro will self-sow.

Dill Dill's buttery flavor goes well with most garden vegetables and is the essential flavoring in many pickles. It does well directly seeded in the spring and is very likely to self-sow in future years.

Parsley Parsley is a biennial that is most commonly grown as an annual. It is one of the slowest seeds to germinate; it doesn't hurt to soak the seeds for 24 hours before sowing. Parsley can be curly-leaved or flat-leaved.

WHEN ED BEHR DECIDES TO investigate a subject, you can be sure he will look at the subject from every angle — and in great depth. So when Ed asked this question in his newsletter, "What creates the best vegetable?" I couldn't help but be intrigued.

Behr is the editor and founder of *The Art of Eating*, a quarterly newsletter devoted to exploring the best food and wine — what they are, how they are produced, and where to find them (the farms, markets, shops, restaurants). In his own words, "More often than not, the best food and wine are traditional, created when people had more time and when food was more central to happiness than it is today. I look for the logic of geography, methods, and culture that makes good food good — that gives character and the finest flavor."

Behr visits passionate growers to understand why some raw materials are so much better than others. He also seeks out the most accomplished artisans to understand their methods. Behr believes that on the farm and in workshops and kitchens, what is treated least usually tastes best:

"The best vegetables are in most cases the very freshest, not stored at all but cooked as soon as possible after they are picked. The best olive oil is wholly unrefined. The best hams are patiently dry-cured. The most delicate fresh cheese is made on the farm with raw milk, and the curd is hand-ladled into molds, so it is broken as little as possible. The most flavorful honey is not only unheated but still in the cells of the comb, sealed by the bees under wax."

Behr calls gardening his "favorite recreation of the year." Because he lives in northern Vermont, he uses cloches and cold frames to extend the season. His garden is a modest 60 feet by 75 feet — all hand-dug "out of a sense of pleasure," he says.

But if there is pleasure in gardening, there is also a deeper understanding of how food is supposed to taste that can be gained only by direct experience: "I almost think that food writers are crippled in their writing if they don't garden. If they live in New York and have some European travel, they are still missing some deep understanding of the connection between food and land."

Behr explains, "How a vegetable is grown affects flavor. Every year some things do well and others don't. Vegetables taste different early in the season, in the middle, and late in the season. The most interesting thing to me is how the taste gets to be the way it is. Of course, respectful cooking techniques are a part of it."

Early in the season, Behr grows a lot of lettuce. He likes a romaine type known as Reuben. Tennis Ball and Tom Thumb are velvety Bibb lettuces he grows. He doesn't grow buttercrunch and says, "If you want crunch, why not be honest and just raise iceberg?"

Oakleaf is another old variety he likes, but don't mention mesclun seed mixes to Behr; he shudders at the thought of them: "I don't understand why people use those [seed mixes]. They are messy in the garden and my experience is that they are annoying. An odd choice of vegetables. They don't seem happy together. I'm more focused on history. It bothers me that people are basically making fake mixes of what is a mix of wild greens. They take a beautiful concept and tart it up."

Behr's most favorite vegetable? "I really, really love zucchini. I grow them to a twelve- or fifteen-inch size. I grate it, salt it, and drain it for thirty to forty-five minutes. Then I squeeze out the moisture and sauté it in butter or olive oil. Then I use it in a zucchini omelet or a baked pudding." He prefers Cocozelle and Romanesco Costata, older varieties that he calls slightly more tender. He notes that these varieties have a high proportion of foliage to vine and speculates that this higher proportion somehow makes a tastier variety, in the same way that tomatoes from indeterminant vines are tastier than ones from determinant vines.

And about tomatoes? "Early varieties just don't have enough time to accumulate flavor. It's a concept that just won't work," he says.

He is equally opinonated about beans. Fin de Bagnol is an old French variety that he grows, noting that trimming isn't necessary if beans are harvested young. And, he says, "some wax beans are better than others, but none are as good as green beans."

When Behr decided to investigate for his newsletter what makes vegetables taste good, he visited several market gardeners, including Elliot Coleman, author of *The New Organic Grower* (Chelsea Green, 1995). Coleman and his wife, Barbara Damrosch, who is also well known as an author and gardener, live on the coast of Maine at Four Seasons Farm. Their farm and gardening practices emphasize producing a year-round harvest, even in their harsh climate, through the use of season extenders, such as greenhouses and Reemay cloth. Also, they have completely built up their soil with manure, mulches, and compost, since they couldn't rely on the stony soil of the Maine coast. Behr also visited Tom Chino, in California, whose fame derives from the fact that Alice Waters buys vegetables from Chino for her legendary restaurant, Chez Panisse.

Behr concludes that it is the combination of environment (soil and climate), vegetable variety, and methods of cultivation that makes a vegetable superior. And, he notes, when you add in factors like freshness and ripeness, then only a small market grower or home gardener is likely to ever produce superior vegetables.

The Art of Eating has appeared four times a year since the first eight-page letter of 1986. There is no advertising. Each issue is now 32 pages long, handsomely printed, and illustrated with photographs in black and white. There are typically several recipes, notes on resources, book reviews, and addresses of exceptional open-air markets, bakers, cheesemakers, cheese shops, wineries, olive-oil mills, charcutiers, chocolatiers, or restaurants (from haute cuisine to simple and local).

mid- to late summer

ARTICHOKES

CELERY & CELERY ROOT

CHILES & PEPPERS   CORN

EGGPLANT   FENNEL

OKRA   SHELL BEANS

SWEET POTATOES

TOMATOES

NOW BEGINS THE SEASON of the continual harvest. Vegetables are ripening fast and furiously. Summer squash and cucumbers must be picked almost daily. Dinners become much simpler. The heat discourages cooking, but who could improve on a meal made of a loaf of French bread and a salad of tomatoes and fresh mozzarella? When the corn ripens, nothing is more appealing than a meal of sweet corn, barely steamed, slathered in butter and seasoned lightly with sea salt. The garden requires little of us, but yields and yields and yields.

Noble Vegetables

ARTICHOKES POSE UNIQUE PROBLEMS for both the gardener and the cook. For the gardener, the problem is setting aside space for a fairly large plant (about 4 feet in all directions), only to harvest a handful of flower buds. This is in addition to the necessity of tricking the artichoke plant into thinking it is growing in a hospitable climate, if you don't happen to live in California. For the cook, the problem is ruthlessly trimming away about two thirds of the vegetable to get to the tender heart. Not to mention the problem of protecting your hands from the prickly leaves and keeping the artichokes from turning black as you work.

So, it should go without saying that the artichoke is a challenging plant. But, oh, the rewards. The artichoke, a member of the thistle family, produces jagged, gray-green leaves and showy fat flower buds. Should you forget to harvest the buds, they open into spectacular blue-purple flowers. But why would anyone forget? This vegetable is one of the tastiest in the plant kingdom. All it requires is steam (and butter) to create a feast fit for royalty. But should you go further, into the realm of braising or stuffing, you will be rewarded with the admiration of all your peers.

I don't grow artichokes myself. In my mountaintop garden, I have to fool tomatoes into thinking it is warm enough to grow — forget about tricking artichokes into thinking they are annuals and ready to make buds. I do admire those who have the patience for this vegetable, and I never pass up the opportunity to enjoy the fruits of someone else's labors.

GROWING The artichoke is a perennial or biennial in warm climates; in cold climates it is grown as an annual. Where winter temperatures never go below 14°F (USDA Zones 8 to 11), artichokes can be grown as perennials, producing buds in the second year in late summer and fall. They will continue to produce buds for 3 to 5 years. In warm, dry climates, such as the southwestern United States, buds may form all year long but will be of highest quality in the spring. In colder climates (Zones 7 to 4), artichokes will grow as an annual, provided they are given at least 250 continuous hours (10½ days) between 35° and 50°F. This is usually done in a cold frame, with the frame open during the day for cooling and closed at night for frost protection.

SOWING Sow indoors in late winter to early spring, about 10 weeks before the last frost. In cold climates, after giving the seedlings the prescribed cold treatment, set the plants 2 to 4 feet apart in beds after the soil temperature is above 60°F.

CULTIVATING Artichokes require plenty of water throughout the season and are heavy feeders, doing best in rich soil and fed once a month with compost tea or an organic fertilizer, such as fish emulsion.

HARVESTING The flower buds of the artichoke plant are harvested. They are ready when the bud is firm, tight, and an even green color. As it begins to open, the bud becomes less tender, so don't hesitate to harvest. The buds mature from the top of the plant down, with the terminal (and often largest) bud ready before the smaller lateral buds. Using a sharp knife, cut through the stem about 4 inches below the bud.

The size of the artichoke depends on where it is grown on the plant. The terminal bud will be the largest, while "baby" artichokes grow out of the side bracts. The size dictates how it is best prepared. Large and medium artichokes are good for steaming. Medium are best for braising and stuffing. Small artichokes can be grilled, roasted, fried, sautéed, or braised and should be picked young, before they have developed a choke.

Artichokes that will be steamed require less trimming than artichokes that will be braised or stuffed. To trim an artichoke for steaming, slice off the top quarter of the artichoke (the top two rows of leaves). Use kitchen shears to remove the sharp tips from the remaining leaves. Cut the stems so the plants will stand upright.

To prepare an artichoke for braising, first prepare a large bowl of acidulated water (1 tablespoon of lemon juice per cup of water). Snap off the tough outer leaves until you reach the tender inner yellow leaves. Trim around the base of the artichoke and down the stem. Slice in half and trim away the fuzzy choke as well as the purple-tipped leaves at the center of the artichoke. Alternatively, you can snap off the tough outer leaves, trim the base, then cut off the top half of the leaves and scoop out the choke. Be ruthless about trimming away the tough leaves. There is nothing appealing about ending up with a mouthful of unchewable fiber.

The same enzyme that discolors artichokes as soon as they are cut will react to aluminum cookware and utensils, so be sure to use nonreactive cookware with artichokes.

TIMING
Steaming: 20 to 40 minutes
Braising: 15 to 30 minutes (for quarters)
Grilling: 10 minutes for steamed, trimmed halves
Roasting: 20 minutes for steamed hearts at 425°F

braised artichokes

The work is in the trimming of the artichoke; the actual cooking is quick and easy. If your only experience with fresh artichokes is steaming them, this is an excellent recipe to try next.

SERVES 4

6 large, 8 medium, or 12 small artichokes

3 tablespoons butter or extra-virgin olive oil

2 garlic cloves, minced, or 1 shallot, minced

1 tablespoon minced fresh herbs (tarragon, chervil, basil, thyme, summer savory, alone or in any combination) (optional)

1 cup vegetable or chicken broth (page 8 or 9)

½ cup dry white wine

Salt and freshly ground black pepper

1 If you are using large or medium-size artichokes, trim away the tough outer leaves, peel the stems, cut into quarters, and remove the choke. If you are using small artichokes, simply peel off the tough outer leaves and cut into halves.

2 Melt the butter in a large deep skillet over medium heat. Add the garlic and sauté until the garlic turns pale gold, about 3 minutes. Add the artichokes and sauté, turning the artichokes until they are well coated with the butter, for 5 minutes. Add the herbs, if using, broth, and wine. Bring to a boil, cover, reduce the heat, and simmer until tender, stirring occasionally, 15 to 30 minutes.

3 Transfer the artichokes to a serving dish with a slotted spoon. Raise the heat under the remaining braising liquid and cook until the sauce is slightly thickened and syrupy, 1 to 2 minutes. Season to taste with the salt and pepper, pour over the artichokes, and serve.

YOU CAN'T REALLY THINK about the history of the artichoke plant without glancing toward the cardoon, from which the artichoke plant arose. The cardoon, a native of the Mediterranean region, has a flower head and an appearance midway between the artichoke and the thistle, their common ancestor. According to Elizabethan folklore, the artichoke was created when a beautiful woman angered the gods and was turned into a thistle.

Both the ancient Greeks and Romans regarded the cardoon as a great delicacy. At some point, the artichoke was developed — the edible flower bud of a thistle in the sunflower family. It was called in Arabic *al kharshuf*. Brought to Spain by the Moors, it became *alcahofa*. In the 9th or 10th century, the Italians changed the name to *carciofa*. Ancient physicians prescribed artichokes to enhance the flailing libidos of men and as a remedy for a variety of physical ailments.

Catherine de' Medici, perhaps the most famous of vegetable lovers, was married to King Henry II of France when she was only fourteen. She introduced many vegetables to the French court, including the artichoke, which was thought to be an aphrodisiac. King Henry, who was considerably older than his child bride, is said to have consumed a great deal of artichokes.

The German poet Goethe was not so enamored of artichokes. Traveling through Italy from 1786 to 1788, he observed that "the peasants eat thistles."

French settlers in Louisiana introduced the artichoke to the New World in the mid-1800s. In the late 19th century, Spanish immigrants began planting California's first commercial artichoke fields, south of San Francisco. In Castroville, California, the artichoke capital of the United States, Marilyn Monroe was named the first Artichoke Queen in 1948.

clam and artichoke stew

Serve with French bread for dipping into the briny juices and plenty of napkins for mopping up after this rustic stew.

SERVES 4

2 lemons

6 large, 8 medium, or 12 baby artichokes

2 tablespoons extra-virgin olive oil

1 leek, trimmed and sliced

1 carrot, finely diced

1 celery stalk, finely diced

2 garlic cloves, minced

¼ cup chopped fresh parsley, plus more for garnish

3 cups seeded, diced tomatoes

¾ cup white wine

1 bottle (8 ounces) clam juice

2 tablespoons chopped fresh oregano

Salt and freshly ground black pepper

4 pounds Manila, mahogany, or littleneck clams, scrubbed

1 Fill a large bowl with cold water. Juice 1½ lemons and combine the juice with the water.

2 If you are using large or medium-size artichokes, trim away the tough outer leaves, peel the stems, cut into quarters, and remove the choke. If you are using small artichokes, simply peel off the tough outer leaves and cut into halves. As you trim each artichoke, rub the cut sides with the remaining lemon half. Drop them into the bowl of lemon water and make sure that all are submerged.

3 Heat the oil over medium-high heat in a large Dutch oven. Add the leek, carrot, celery, garlic, and parsley and sauté until limp, about 3 minutes. Add the tomatoes, wine, clam juice, and oregano. Season to taste with the salt and pepper. Bring to a boil.

4 Drain the artichokes and stir into the tomato mixture. Cover, reduce the heat, and simmer until the artichokes are tender, 20 to 30 minutes.

5 Add the clams, cover, increase the heat, and steam until the clam shells are open, about 10 minutes. Discard any clams that do not open.

6 Ladle into bowls and serve hot, garnished with the parsley.

THE INEDIBLE CHOKE

Despite the fact that you harvest only the flower bud of the artichoke plant, there is still much that is inedible. The bracts, or leaves, on the exterior of the bud are inedible because they are too tough and fibrous. The fuzzy choke and the purple-tipped tiny leaves that surround the choke are likewise inedible. Only the meaty heart and stem and the bottom portion of the inner leaves are edible.

Stuffing artichokes with a tasty blend of cheese and crumbs, then braising adds extra layers of flavor.

SERVES 4

Stuffing

2 cups (4 ounces) fine fresh bread crumbs

3 sun-dried tomato halves

3 garlic cloves

1 strip lemon zest, 2 inches long

Leaves from 2 sprigs parsley

Leaves from 1 sprig oregano, basil, thyme, or mint

2 tablespoons extra-virgin olive oil

½ cup freshly grated Parmesan

Salt and freshly ground black pepper

Artichokes

4 large artichokes

2 lemons, halved

1½ cups vegetable or chicken broth (page 8 or 9)

½ cup dry white wine

2 tablespoons extra-virgin olive oil

Salt and freshly ground black pepper

2 tablespoons butter

1 To make the stuffing, preheat oven to 350°F. Spread out the bread crumbs in a shallow baking pan and bake until pale golden, about 10 minutes. Cool the crumbs completely.

2 Combine the sun-dried tomatoes, garlic, lemon zest, parsley, and herb in a food processor and process until well chopped. Add the crumbs, Parmesan, and salt and pepper, drizzle in the oil, and pulse briefly until well mixed.

3 To trim the artichokes, fill a large bowl with cold water. Juice 1½ of the lemons and add the lemon juice to the water. Use the remaining lemon half to rub the cut surfaces of the artichoke. Cut off artichoke stems and discard. Cut off the top ½ inch of one artichoke and remove the tough outer leaves. Trim the base of the artichoke. Separate the leaves slightly with your thumbs and pull out purple leaves from center and enough yellow leaves to expose fuzzy choke. Scoop out choke with melon-ball cutter, then squeeze some lemon juice into cavity. Place the trimmed artichoke in the water. Trim the remaining artichokes in same manner.

4 To stuff, spoon about 2 tablespoons stuffing into the cavity of each artichoke and, starting with bottom leaves and spreading the leaves open as much as possible without breaking them, spoon a rounded ½ teaspoon stuffing inside each leaf.

5 To cook artichokes, combine the broth, wine, and oil in a large saucepan. Season with salt and pepper. Add the artichokes so they are standing upright. Cover and bring to a boil. Reduce the heat and simmer until the leaves are tender, about 50 minutes. Transfer the artichokes with tongs to four soup plates.

6 Bring the cooking liquid to a boil. Whisk in the butter and cook until slightly thickened. Pour over the artichokes and serve.

artichoke and tomato casserole

The artichokes are first steamed, then baked in a casserole with tomatoes, pesto, and Parmesan cheese. Serve it as a vegetarian main course with bread and salad, or as a side dish.

■ SERVES 4–6 ■

6 large, 8 medium, or 12 baby artichokes
4 tablespoons best-quality olive oil
2 leeks, white and tender green parts, trimmed and sliced
1 red bell pepper, diced
4 garlic cloves, minced
Salt and freshly ground black pepper
½ cup pesto (page 6)
2 large ripe tomatoes, peeled, seeded, and diced
½ cup freshly grated Parmesan
2 tablespoons dried bread crumbs

1 If you are using large or medium-size artichokes, trim away the tough outer leaves, peel the stems, cut into quarters, and remove the choke. If you are using small artichokes, simply peel off the tough outer leaves and cut into halves.

2 Steam the artichokes over boiling water until tender, 20 to 40 minutes.

3 Heat 3 tablespoons of the oil in a large skillet over medium-high heat. Add the leeks, bell pepper, and garlic and sauté until just tender, about 4 minutes. Add the artichokes and sauté to coat with the oil, about 1 minute. Season generously with salt and pepper.

4 Preheat the oven to 350°F. Lightly grease a 2-quart shallow baking dish or gratin dish with oil.

5 Spread half the sautéed vegetables in the baking dish. Dot with ¼ cup of the pesto and top with half the tomatoes and half the cheese. Repeat the layer. Sprinkle with the bread crumbs and drizzle the remaining 1 tablespoon oil on top.

6 Bake for about 45 minutes, until most of the liquid released by the tomatoes evaporates and the bread crumbs are golden. Serve immediately.

ARTICHOKES AND HEALTH

Although touted as an aphrodisiac, artichokes have other proven virtues. They are low in calories — only 60 calories for one medium-sized cooked artichoke. The artichoke is a natural diuretic, and it is said to be a digestive aid. Some studies suggest that fresh artichokes help control blood sugar levels and lower cholesterol. Artichokes are also a good source of fiber, potassium, and magnesium.

No Thriving with Neglect

IT ISN'T THAT CELERY IS SO DIFFICULT TO GROW —
it's just that it absolutely requires nutrient-rich soil and plenty
of moisture. Some plants, when they don't get what they need,
produce smaller fruits or a reduced yield. But the celery plant is
the yield, and if it doesn't get what it needs, it becomes bitter,
fibrous, and woody.

Celery root, also called celeriac, knob celery, and turnip-rooted
celery, is a close relative of celery and is a little less fussy to grow.
Whereas celery is grown for its stems (also called ribs), celery root
is grown for its rounded root. Its flavor is quite similar to that of
celery, but somewhat nuttier.

Celery and celery root are both enjoyed raw or cooked. The
most famous celery root preparation is the French salad *céleri en
rémoulade,* a celery root slaw with a mustardy dressing. Celery root
makes a fine addition to soups and stews and is wonderful roasted
— like most root vegetables. Finely chopped celery stems and
leaves are used as aromatics in many soups and stews. Braising is
a wonderful way to cook celery, and so is stir-frying. Celery is, of
course, delightful raw — essential to the texture of tuna salad and
the perfect vehicle for dips. Without celery, we would have no
Waldorf salad, no ants on a log, and no celery soda.

GROWING Celery and celery root are long-season plants that need very rich soil and plenty of water throughout the growing season.

SOWING Sow indoors about 10 weeks before the last frost. Germination is tricky. Sow the seeds on a potting mixture rich with organic matter and lightly cover with potting mix. Don't cover heavily because the seeds need light to germinate. Keep the soil between 65° and 75°F. Transplant into individual pots as soon as the plants have two true leaves. The plants can be transplanted to the garden when they have four or five leaves and the day temperatures are consistently about 55°F and night temperatures are above 40°F. Warming the soil with plastic mulch is a good idea, as is keeping the plants warm under a floating row cover. Set the plants 8 inches apart.

CULTIVATING Side-dress with fish emulsion during the growing season and provide it with lots of water.

HARVESTING Begin harvesting the outer stalks of the plants whenever you like. Harvest whole plants by cutting them at the soil line. This, too, can be done when the plants are at any size. Cover to keep plants going if a light frost is threatened, but harvest before a hard freeze. Celery will keep in the refrigerator for a couple of weeks, or longer in a root cellar.

The flavor of celery is strongest in the outer stalks and mildest in the interior, or "heart." Many people reserve the heart for serving raw and cook with the outer, more strongly flavored ribs.

Celery is an aromatic vegetable. Combined with onion, carrots, and parsley, it is often sautéed in olive oil to form the flavor foundation of a soup, stew, or sauce. When cooked alone, in a braised or stir-fried dish, celery becomes sweet and is softened.

To prepare celery for cooking, wash and dry the individual ribs. Trim off the bottoms and tops. If you have difficulty biting into a stalk without coming away with strings, you would do best to peel the outside of the stalk to remove the strings. The dark leaves at the top of the bunch can be saved in plastic bags in the refrigerator and used as you would use parsley.

Celery root is always peeled before it is used and often is cooked before it is eaten. It can be cooked in any way you cook root vegetables, which to my mind means it is best roasted.

CELERY MATH
1 pound celery = 4 cups chopped, diced, sliced, or julienned ribs

TIMING
Sautéing or stir-frying: 5 minutes
Braising: 25 minutes
Roasting: 20 to 25 minutes at 425°F (celery root)

celery stuffed with herbed cheese

The recipe makes about 1 cup of herbed cheese, enough to stuff one or two bunches of celery. But you can also use it as a dip for other vegetables or as a spread for cucumber sandwiches.

SERVES 6–12

Herbed Cheese

1	garlic clove, peeled
8	large basil leaves
2	tablespoons dill leaves
2	tablespoons parsley leaves
8–12	chive stems
2	tablespoons summer savory, oregano, mint, thyme, or sage leaves
8	ounces Neufchâtel cream cheese, at room temperature
1	tablespoon fresh lemon juice
	Salt and freshly ground black pepper

1–2 bunches celery, trimmed and cut into 4-inch lengths

1 Combine the garlic, basil, dill, parsley, chives, and summer savory in a food processor and process until finely chopped. Scrape down the sides of the bowl and add the cream cheese, lemon juice, and salt and pepper. Process until well blended. Taste and adjust the seasoning.

2 Transfer to a bowl, cover, and refrigerate for at least 1 hour, to blend the flavors.

3 Spread on the celery sticks and serve.

MY BUNCH IS YOUR STALK

Celery language can be confusing. What Easterners call a bunch (basically the whole, trimmed plant), Midwesterners call a stalk. To an Easterner, a stalk is a single stem, also called a rib.

celery root rémoulade

A classic French salad, think of this as an upscale coleslaw. The texture is the same; the flavors creamy and tangy. The hard-cooked egg adds richness to the salad, but it is not essential.

SERVES 4–6

About 1 pound celery root
Juice of 1 lemon
⅓ cup mayonnaise
⅓ cup sour cream
¼ cup chopped fresh parsley
2 tablespoons chopped cornichons
1 tablespoon capers
1 hard-cooked egg, finely diced (optional)
Salt and freshly ground black pepper

1 Peel the celery root(s) and cut into quarters. Shred in a food processor or with the coarse side of a box grater.

2 Immediately transfer the celery root to a medium bowl and toss with the lemon juice to prevent discoloring.

3 Add the mayonnaise, sour cream, parsley, cornichons, capers, and egg, if using. With a large rubber spatula, mix well. Add salt and pepper to taste.

4 Chill for at least 1 hour in the refrigerator before serving, to allow the flavors to blend.

roasted celery root & carrots with blue cheese dressing

In my opinion, most vegetables taste better roasted. So why not carrot and celery (root) sticks? Carrots and celery with blue cheese dip is a traditional accompaniment for Buffalo chicken wings. This fork version is the perfect match for any spicy chicken dish.

■ SERVES 4 ■

2 pounds celery root (2 medium), peeled and cut into ¼-inch by 2-inch sticks

1 pound carrots (4 large), cut into ¼-inch by 2-inch sticks

2 tablespoons canola oil

Salt and freshly ground black pepper

1 cup Blue Cheese Dressing (page 99)

1 Preheat the oven to 425°F. Lightly grease a large sheet pan (preferred) or shallow roasting pan with oil.

2 Combine the celery root sticks, carrot sticks, and oil in a large bowl. Season with salt and pepper. Toss to coat the vegetables with the oil. Transfer the vegetables to the prepared pan and arrange in a single layer.

3 Roast for 25 to 30 minutes, until the vegetables are tender when pierced with a fork, stirring or shaking the pan occasionally for even cooking.

4 Serve the vegetables hot, passing the dressing on the side.

braised celery

Braising is truly the best way to cook celery. It is a gentle method that coaxes the best flavor from this rather bland vegetable.

SERVES 4

2 tablespoons extra-virgin olive oil

1 bunch celery, ends trimmed and stalks cut into 2-inch lengths

2 shallots, minced

1 cup vegetable or chicken broth (page 8 or 9)

Salt and freshly ground black pepper

1 teaspoon fresh lemon juice

1 tablespoon butter

1 Heat the oil over medium heat in a large skillet. Add the celery and shallots and cook until slightly softened and fragrant, about 5 minutes.

2 Add the broth, season with salt and pepper, lower the heat, cover, and gently cook until the celery is completely tender, about 20 minutes.

3 Remove the celery with a slotted spoon and transfer to a serving platter. Add the lemon juice and butter to the skillet. Increase the heat and cook until the remaining liquid thickens to a syrupy consistency, 1 to 2 minutes. Spoon over the celery and serve.

THE BENEFIT OF CELERY

Celery has been used as a cure for ailments as various as colds, flu, indigestion, arthritis, gout, "dropsy," insomnia, nervousness, and cancer. The Chinese prescribe celery seed for those with high blood pressure. A tea made of 1 to 2 teaspoons of crushed seeds per cup of boiling water, steeped for 10 to 20 minutes, is said to be a mild relaxant.

sweet and sour celery

Braising is the best way to cook celery, but the vegetable is still bland. Perk up the flavor by braising in a sweet and sour liquid. Serve this room-temperature dish as an appetizer or side dish.

■ SERVES 4 ■

1 bunch celery

3 tablespoons extra-virgin olive oil

2 shallots, minced

½ cup vegetable or chicken broth (page 8 or 9)

2 tablespoons fresh lemon juice

2 tablespoons raisins

1 tablespoon brown sugar

Salt and freshly ground black pepper

1 Mince the celery leaves and set aside. Trim the celery, discarding any tough portions from the top and bottom of each stalk. Peel the outside of the outer stalks to remove any stringy fibers. Cut the stalks into 2-inch lengths. You should have about 4 cups.

2 Heat the oil in a large saucepan over medium heat. Add the shallot and sauté until fragrant, about 2 minutes. Add the celery and sauté until slightly softened, about 3 minutes.

3 Add the broth, lemon juice, raisins, brown sugar, and salt and pepper. Bring to a boil over high heat. Reduce the heat, cover, and simmer, turning once, until the celery is tender, about 20 minutes.

4 Remove the cover, increase the heat, and boil until the liquid in the pan reduces to a syrupy glaze, 2 to 3 minutes. Stir in the celery leaves, adjust the seasoning to taste, and serve immediate or at room temperature.

CELERY FIRST CAME TO KALAMAZOO via a Scotsman named Taylor who brought the seeds from his homeland. Celery remained a garden plant until 1866, when a couple of Dutch farmers, Cornelius De Bruin and John De Kam, began growing celery as a crop. Within 5 years, celery, grown as a major commercial crop, was being shipped via rail from Kalamazoo. By 1874, large bunches of celery were sold on the Michigan Central Railroad to travelers, who were apparently enticed by this regional specialty. By the 1880s, there were more than 350 celery farmers in Michigan and more than 4,000 acres planted in celery.

Celery found its way into various products, including salad dressings, mustard, celery pepper, canned celery, celery pickles, and, most famously, celery soda. Kalamazoo soda fountains featured celery phosphate, crème de celery, and mugs of hot ox celery. The drugstores also sold Farnum's Famous Kalamazoo Celery and Pepsin Chewing Gum, Kalamazoo Celery Pepsin Bitters and Celery, and, from the Kalamazoo Soap Company, Celery Tar Soap.

Samuel Dunkley, a celery shipper with a sideline of various celery products, marketed Celerytone, a sexual stimulant. The advertisements claimed "The beneficial effect of the peculiar properties of celery upon the nervous and sexual system is wonderful and unequaled."

In the kitchens of the Chinese-American restaurants of my youth, Chinese vegetables were scarce and celery filled in as a substitute. In this version of a classic stir-fry of chicken and mushrooms, celery provides the crunch. It is delicious — authentic or not.

SERVES 4

Chicken and Marinade

1 pound boneless, skinless chicken breasts, cut into thin strips

2 tablespoons soy sauce

1 tablespoon Chinese rice wine or dry sherry

1 teaspoon dark sesame oil

1 tablespoon cornstarch

Sauce

½ cup chicken broth (see page 9)

2 tablespoons soy sauce

2 tablespoons rice wine

2 teaspoons sugar

1 tablespoon cornstarch

Vegetables

4 tablespoons peanut or canola oil

4 cups sliced fresh mushrooms

4 cups diagonally sliced celery

4 cups diagonally sliced bok choy

½ cup sliced canned water chestnuts

1 scallion, white and tender green parts, minced

1 piece ginger, 1 inch long, minced

2 garlic cloves, minced

Hot cooked white rice

1 Combine the chicken with the soy sauce, wine, sesame oil, and cornstarch and mix to combine. Set aside to marinate for at least 15 minutes.

2 To make the sauce, combine the broth, soy sauce, rice wine, sugar, and cornstarch. Set aside.

3 Heat a large wok or skillet over high heat. Add 2 tablespoons of the oil and let heat. Add the chicken and marinade and stir-fry until the chicken changes color and is mostly cooked, about 4 minutes. Add the mushrooms and continue to stir-fry until the mushrooms are tender and have given up their juice, about 5 minutes. Use a heatproof rubber spatula to scrape the chicken mixture into a bowl, and keep warm.

4 With the wok on high heat, add the remaining 2 tablespoons oil. When the oil is hot, add the celery and bok choy and stir-fry until tender, about 4 minutes. Add the water chestnuts and stir-fry to heat through, about 1 minute.

5 Push the vegetables to the sides of the wok and add the scallion, ginger, and garlic. Fry for about 30 seconds, until fragrant, then mix into the vegetables.

6 Return the chicken and mushroom mixture to the wok and stir-fry to mix well, about 1 minute. Add the sauce and continue to stir-fry until the sauce thickens and coats the vegetables, about 1 minute. Serve immediately over the hot rice.

MAKE MINE CELERY

When eating a corned beef or pastrami sandwich in a Jewish deli in New York City, the drink of choice is Dr. Brown's Cel-Ray, a "celery soda with other natural flavors." It has been manufactured by the Canada Dry Bottling Co. of New York since 1869, and its main flavor ingredient is an extract of celery seed. What does it taste like? Some people say it tastes like ginger ale mixed with celery, others that it tastes like slightly sweetened celery. Its following is devoted, but small.

F THERE IS ONE THING YOU CAN COUNT ON when it comes to gardening with children, it is that kids like to dig in dirt. When my kids were little, I found that they were happiest with a corner of the garden where they could dig roadways and tunnels and run their trucks.

I thought perhaps the kid–dirt connection had to do with the fact that my kids were both boys, but it turns out to be the impression of teacher-naturalist Rebecca Byard also. A preschool teacher in Cambridge, Massachusetts, during the school year and a camp counselor at Massachusetts Audubon Society's Drumlin Farm in Lincoln, Massachusetts, during the summer, Byard spends plenty of time with little kids in dirt:

"My kids this year are really into dirt. They just love to dig. I am thinking of building a worm-composting bin in the classroom. It will solve our composting problem and give their worms a good home. These kids need to learn more about worms. They are always digging them up, then trying to make homes for them in the sandbox. Doesn't work for the worms."

Byard spent her early years in Ithaca, New York, where her father always tended a vegetable garden. "I remember the garden being really big, but actually I think it was pretty small. I don't remember ever helping but I do remember keeping my dad company and being really curious about the plants. I remember we had sunflowers and they were huge and beautiful," she says.

At Oberlin College, in Ohio, Byard majored in biology and environmental studies. Meanwhile, she was also a head cook at her dining co-op, where the emphasis was on using local foods. "One summer I came back to school early to can peaches and tomatoes for the dining co-ops. The Oberlin Student Cooperative Association paid six or so workers to can for three weeks with the intent that the canned food would be distributed to the co-ops during the winter when there wasn't so much local food. Someone did the math and found that it would be cheaper to hire students to can local organic food than buying the canned organic equivalent in the winter. We got to visit the orchards and farms and purchase the 'seconds' of the peaches and tomatoes by the crate. The first week we did peaches. Imagine blanching, peeling, cutting, and canning peaches for eight hours a day. At first it smelled really good and we snacked as we went. We ate peach smoothies, peach cobbler, peach this and that, but by the end of the week we were so sick of peaches that just the smell of them was a bit sickening. Canning tomatoes and making and canning salsa were more fun because of all the other ingredients in salsa. The whole experience was really a positive one and I learned a lot about canning in general."

These days, Byard lives in an apartment in Somerville, Massachusetts, and gardens in a tiny strip of a backyard. "The garden is only about two feet by eight feet, but we cram in a lot of things — peas, beans, lettuce, squash. Plus we have tomatoes, peppers, and herbs in pots." Farming at Drumlin in the summer gets Byard out of the city and into the country, just as it does for the campers.

"This past summer I worked with six- and seven-year-olds at the camp," she says. "At that age kids can begin to get familiar with the basic idea of gardening. You put a seed in the ground and give it water and sun and it grows. They can learn how to take care of plants, what kinds of stuff you can grow. And then we eat it.

"After we did chores, we usually did some sort of garden craft, and then the kids would pick whatever vegetables were ready for harvest. And we'd always pick some edible flowers — nasturtiums or Johnny jump-ups. We'd take it all inside, wash it, cut it up, and make a big salad. The kids really loved the salad. They'd say things like, 'This is the best salad I've ever had.'"

At Drumlin Farm, weeding was generally a well-enjoyed chore: "We weeded corn that was a lot taller than the kids. They loved it. They liked to see the clear progress they were making. And they liked getting into the dirt, getting dirty."

Back to the dirt, again: "You know, when you garden with kids, you can tie it in with just about anything. You can teach them about dirt ecology, about nutrition, sustainability, birds, bugs. It's all there."

Some Like 'em Hot

PASSIONS RUN DEEP when it comes to growing and cooking with chiles. To the uninitiated, chiles are aromatic vegetables, flavor accents. But to the initiated, those who subscribe to *Chile* magazine or are members of the Transcendental Capsaicinophilic Society, a self-described cult dedicated to the worship of chiles and hot foods, chiles are more than a vegetable: They are a lifestyle.

I was once asked to judge a chile-cooking contest. I was the only cooking professional on the judging panel; the others were simply hotheads. The hotter the food, the higher the score. A brilliant chocolate cake, nuanced with herbal, floral chile flavors, scored high in my book, low in everyone else's. An unspeakably vile cayenne beer that grabbed me by the back of the throat and turned me upside down . . . that received the winning score.

Clearly, there is no agreement among cooks as to what one should or should not do with a chile. Fortunately, such a wide range of seeds is available that there is a chile to suit every palate. Bell peppers, those widely popular vegetables, are simply another variety of chiles, albeit without the heat. Much of my cooking is with bell peppers, because they are so sweet and flavorful, so readily adaptable as a vegetable or flavor accent, so good roasted, grilled, or sautéed. Chiles, of course, have their uses. We all need a little heat in our lives, even — or especially — us Northerners.

SOW & REAP

GROWING Chiles are warm-weather plants. They do best in slightly acidic soil with even watering until the fruit sets; after the fruit has set, they do better in slightly dry conditions. They require full sun.

SOWING Sow indoors 8 weeks before the last frost. Transplant seedlings when the temperature is consistently warm. Set the plants about 1 foot apart. A teaspoon of sulfur or a book of matches placed in each planting hole will give the transplants a boost.

CULTIVATING Give heat with floating row covers and mulch. Keep the soil evenly moist. About 6 weeks before the first frost, prune back the top branches and flowers. The plant strength will go to existing chiles, not new growth, and the remaining chiles will mature faster.

HARVESTING Begin harvesting chiles when green. The more green fruits you harvest, the more the plant will continue to set fruit. Red fruits are sweetest. They are also generally hottest. As with tomatoes, just before the first freeze you can pull up the entire plant and hang it upside down in a dry, airy location, such as a garage. Green chiles will ripen right on the plant.

CHILE MATH
1 pound fresh chiles = 3½ cups diced or julienned

KITCHEN NOTES

The seeds and inner membranes are where the most heat is found in chiles. Whether to scrape this part of the vegetable away depends on how much heat you want. With bell peppers, the membranes and seeds should be removed.

Capsaicin is the enzyme found in chiles that is responsible for the heat. It is an oil-soluble compound, meaning water will just spread it, not dilute it. When seeding chiles, take care to wear gloves and to avoid touching your face with your hands. Thoroughly wash your hands, cutting board, and utensils under running water with plenty of soap.

If you are uncertain as to how hot your chile is, you can taste it or you can take an educated guess based on its appearance. Generally speaking, the smaller and thinner the pepper, the hotter it will be. This rule of thumb applies to different types of chiles but also to chiles of the same kind. Mild chiles include bell peppers, cherry peppers, Hungarian hot wax, Italian frying peppers, and poblanos. Jalapeño is considered medium-hot. Serrano and cayennes are hotter. Hotter still is the habanero.

Roasting directions are given on page 19.

TIMING
Sautéing or stir-frying: 3 to 5 minutes
Roasting: 10 to 20 minutes (whole)
Grilling: 10 to 20 minutes (whole)
Braising: 10 to 15 minutes

marinated roasted peppers

When I put out an appetizer of cheese and crackers, I like to set out a bowl of these peppers for people to spoon on top of the crackers. If there are any leftovers, I find any number of uses for them. Nothing beats these peppers as a relish for grilled cheese sandwiches and turkey sandwiches. The peppers can add punch to pasta salads and potato salads. They can top bruschetta (page 301), crostini, and pizza. They can add distinction to sautéed zucchini, steamed green beans, and hash browns. They can . . . well, you get the idea.

SERVES 6–8

6 bell peppers of any color, preferably some that are red or yellow

2 tablespoons extra-virgin olive oil

1 tablespoon fresh lemon juice

2 tablespoons chopped fresh basil

Salt and freshly ground black pepper

1 Preheat the broiler. Lightly grease a baking sheet with oil.

2 Place the peppers on the prepared baking sheet with space between each one. Broil 4 inches from the heat until charred all over, turning several times. This will take 10 to 20 minutes. The peppers may not cook at the same rate.

3 As the peppers become charred, place them in a covered bowl, plastic bag, or paper bag. Seal and allow the peppers to steam for at least 10 minutes to loosen the skins.

4 Slit the peppers over a medium bowl to catch the juice that runs from them. Scrape or peel the skins and discard. Scrape and discard the seeds and membranes. Cut the peppers into matchsticks. Add to the pepper juices in the bowl.

5 Add the oil, lemon juice, basil, and salt and pepper to taste. Allow to stand for at least 30 minutes before serving. The peppers will keep for 7 to 10 days in the refrigerator. Serve at room temperature.

smothered pork chops

With the green and red peppers providing the flavor, this simple dish is fast and easy to make. It is equally good made with chicken instead of pork. Serve with rice or a crusty French bread to mop up the delicious pan juices.

SERVES 6

2 tablespoons extra-virgin olive oil

4 bell peppers of various colors, cut into thin strips

2 onions, halved and cut into slivers

1 fresh chile, seeded and cut into thin strips (optional)

3 garlic cloves, minced

6 pork chops, cut 1 inch thick

Salt and freshly ground black pepper

1 tablespoon sherry vinegar

1 Heat the oil in a large skillet over medium heat. Add the bell peppers, onions, chile, if using, and garlic and sauté until softened, about 8 minutes. Remove from the pan and set aside.

2 Reheat the same skillet over high heat. Add the pork chops and season with the salt and pepper. Sear on both sides, about 4 minutes per side. Spoon the pepper mixture over the pork chops, reduce the heat to medium, and let the pork cook until tender, no longer pink, and the juices run clear, about 30 minutes.

3 Drizzle in the vinegar and serve, spooning the pepper mixture and pan juices over each chop.

pickled mixed peppers

You can multiply this recipe by however many peppers you wish to pickle. I find more uses for pickled sweet peppers than for pickled hot peppers. Pickled sweet peppers are terrific in grilled cheese sandwiches or tucked into a baguette spread with goat cheese. A pita pocket stuffed with slices of grilled or broiled eggplant, pickled peppers, and feta cheese is another wonderful combination.

MAKES 1 QUART

1½ cups white vinegar
1 tablespoon sugar
1 teaspoon salt
4 cups sliced mixed sweet peppers
Boiling water

1 Heat the vinegar, sugar, and salt to just boiling in a nonreactive saucepan.

2 Pack the peppers into a hot, sterilized quart jar. Fill with the hot brine. Top off the jar with the boiling water, leaving ½ inch headspace. Seal with a canning lid.

3 Let cool and refrigerate for several months or process in a boiling-water bath (pages 475-477) for 5 minutes. Store in a cool, dry place for up to a year.

roasted bell pepper fettuccine

A sauce made with roasted red peppers is worthy of the effort of making homemade pasta. Best of all, it is a sauce of utter simplicity and ease of effort. If you have a food processor and a pasta roller (admittedly a specialty gadget, but worth owning, especially if you have kids who like to "help" in the kitchen), homemade pasta takes relatively little time and effort. If you don't own the necessary gadgets, then buy fresh pasta. Part of the charm of this dish is that fresh pasta does an excellent job of absorbing the flavor of the sauce.

SERVES 6

- 6 medium red bell peppers, roasted (page 15)
- ¼ cup extra-virgin olive oil
- 2 garlic cloves, minced
- 1¾ pounds fresh fettuccine
- 10 basil leaves, torn
  Salt and freshly ground black pepper
  Freshly grated Parmesan, to serve

1 Begin heating a large pot of salted water for the pasta.

2 Cut slits in the peppers and drain briefly into a small bowl to catch the juices. Scrape or peel the skins and discard. Scrape and discard the seeds and membranes. Cut the peppers into matchsticks.

3 Heat the oil over medium heat in a very large skillet or Dutch oven. Add the garlic and peppers and sauté until fragrant, about 2 minutes. Reduce the heat to low.

4 Cook the pasta until just barely al dente. Reserve about 1 cup of the pasta cooking water. Drain the pasta.

5 Add the pasta to the peppers along with ½ cup of the pasta cooking water. Toss to mix. Add the remaining ½ cup only if the pasta seems dry. Add the basil, and salt and pepper to taste, and toss again. Serve immediately, passing the cheese at the table.

pasta ribbons with peppers

Who doesn't find the bright colors and sweet flavors of bell peppers appealing? This pasta dish takes advantage of peppers' good looks and outstanding flavor — all whipped together in the time it takes to bring the pasta water to a boil.

■ SERVES 4 ■

1 onion, quartered
1 celery stalk, roughly chopped
1 carrot, roughly chopped
2 garlic cloves
3 tablespoons extra-virgin olive oil
½ cup finely diced prosciutto
6 red, green, yellow, or purple bell peppers, cut into thin strips
¼ cup chopped fresh basil
Salt and freshly ground black pepper
1 pound fresh fettuccine, cut into 4-inch pieces
1 cup freshly grated Parmesan

1 Combine the onion, celery, carrot, and garlic in a food processor and pulse until finely chopped.

2 Heat the oil in a large saucepan or Dutch oven over medium heat. Add the onion mixture and sauté until fragrant and softened, about 3 minutes. Add the prosciutto and sauté until crisp, about 5 minutes.

3 Stir in the bell peppers, cover, and cook for 10 minutes, until the peppers are soft. Stir in the basil and season generously with salt and pepper.

4 Cook the pasta in a large pot of salted boiling water until al dente. Drain, reserving ½ cup of the cooking water.

5 Add the pasta to the bell pepper sauce. Toss and add the reserved cooking water as needed to make the pasta moist.

6 Transfer the pasta and sauce to a serving dish or individual serving plates. Sprinkle with a few tablespoons of the cheese and serve, passing the remaining cheese at the table.

cheese-stuffed roasted peppers

Green peppers stuffed with rice or ground meat filling make a homey main dish like mom used to serve. Here the peppers are roasted first, then stuffed with smoked mozzarella and herbed croutons. The result is a tasty morsel, delicious as an appetizer or side dish.

■ SERVES 4–8 ■

4 red bell peppers, roasted and peeled (page 15)
½ pound smoked mozzarella, grated (about 2 cups)
2 cups Herbed Croutons (page 14)

1 Preheat the oven to 375°F. Spray a 9- by 13-inch baking dish with nonstick cooking spray.

2 Cut the roasted peppers in half, scrape out seeds and membranes, and lay them flat on a work surface, skin-side down. Spread ½ cup cheese on each pepper half. Sprinkle ¼ cup croutons on top. Wrap the peppers around the filling and skewer closed with toothpicks. Unless the peppers are unusually large, you will not be able to completely enclose the filling, and the toothpicks will hold them only partially closed. Transfer to the baking dish.

3 Bake until the cheese has melted, 15 to 20 minutes.

4 Remove the toothpicks before serving. Serve hot.

kung pao chicken

I worked my way through college, part of the time doing prep work at a Chinese restaurant run by a nuclear physicist whose postdoc had ended. He introduced me to this dish, and I have loved it ever since. This isn't Mr. Wong's Kung Pao Chicken, but it's close.

■ SERVES 4 ■

Chicken and Marinade

1 pound boneless skinless chicken breasts, cut into 1-inch pieces

1 tablespoon Chinese rice wine or dry sherry

1 tablespoon soy sauce

1 teaspoon chili paste with garlic

1 teaspoon sugar

Sauce

¼ cup chicken broth (page 9)

2 tablespoons rice wine or dry sherry

2 tablespoons hoisin sauce

2 tablespoons soy sauce

2 teaspoons dark sesame oil

4 garlic cloves, minced

2 teaspoons cornstarch

1 tablespoon water

Vegetables

3 tablespoons peanut or canola oil

2 red bell peppers, cubed

2 green bell peppers, cubed

2 fresh red or green hot chiles, seeded (optional) and diced

1 cup sliced water chestnuts

4 scallions, white and tender greens, sliced

½ cup roasted unsalted peanuts

Hot cooked white rice, for serving

1 Combine the chicken, rice wine, soy sauce, chili paste, and sugar in a medium bowl. Set aside to marinate for about 30 minutes.

2 To make the sauce, combine the broth, wine, hoisin, soy sauce, sesame oil, and garlic in a small bowl and set aside. Dissolve the cornstarch in the water in another bowl and set aside.

3 Heat a large wok over high heat. Add 1½ tablespoons of the oil and swirl to coat the sides of the pan. Add the chicken and marinade and stir-fry for 4 to 6 minutes, until the chicken pieces are tender and no longer pink. Use a heatproof rubber spatula to scrape the chicken and sauce out of the wok into a medium bowl and keep warm.

4 Heat the remaining 1½ tablespoons oil in the wok, still over high heat. Add the red and green bell peppers and the chiles and stir-fry until the peppers have softened, 3 to 4 minutes. Add the water chestnuts and scallions and stir-fry for 1 minute.

5 Return the chicken to the wok and stir-fry for 1 minute to heat through. Add the broth mixture and bring to a boil. Add the cornstarch solution and cook, stirring, until the sauce boils and thickens. Add the peanuts and toss to coat.

6 Serve hot over the rice.

PRESERVING CHILES

YOU DON'T NEED TO RUSH to dry chiles or preserve them. Chiles can keep for months in a basket on the counter. For long-term storage, though, the oldest, easiest, and most common way to preserve chiles is to dry them.

The thinner the walls of the chile, the better they will air-dry. Simply string them and allow to dry in a sunny location. Jalapeños and poblanos are difficult to air-dry well because they are thick walled. For those chiles, use a food dehydrator. Simply place them whole or cut in half in a single layer on the racks and follow the instructions for your model.

You can also freeze chiles. Chop them, spread out in a single layer on a baking sheet, and freeze. Once frozen, store in resealable plastic bags and use as needed.

chile con queso

Poblano chiles are large, mildly hot chiles with a distinctively fruity flavor. If you don't have poblanos for this recipe, you can substitute other chiles; just don't use a whole pound of wickedly hot ones, or few will be able to enjoy the dip.

■ SERVES 4–8 ■

2 tablespoons extra-virgin olive oil

1 onion, very thinly sliced

4 large poblano chiles, or about 1 pound mixed chiles, roasted and peeled

1 cup grated Monterey Jack

1 cup grated Cheddar

¼ cup sour cream

Salt

Chopped fresh cilantro, to garnish (optional)

12 small (6-inch) flour tortillas, heated, or tortilla chips

1 Preheat the oven to 300°F and place a heatproof serving bowl in the oven.

2 Heat the oil in a medium skillet over medium heat. Add the onion and sauté gently until softened but not browned, about 10 minutes. Slice the chiles and add to the skillet. Sauté until heated through, about 3 minutes.

3 Add the cheeses by the handful and stir until melted, about 3 minutes. Stir in the sour cream and season with the salt to taste.

4 Remove the serving bowl from the oven. Transfer the cheese mixture to it and sprinkle with cilantro, if using. Serve with the tortillas or chips.

pickled chiles

Multiply this recipe by however many peppers you wish to pickle. Remember that a little pickled pepper goes a long way. Try sprinkling them on top of nachos before they go into the oven, or add sparingly to sandwiches or quesadillas. You will need sterilized pint canning jars. One jar will keep in the refrigerator for several months. If you are making more than one jar, plan to process in a hot-water bath.

MAKES 1 PINT

1 cup white distilled or cider vinegar
½ cup water
1 tablespoon sugar
1 garlic clove
½ teaspoon mustard seeds
½ teaspoon pickling salt
2 cups sliced fresh chiles, seeded if desired

1 Heat the vinegar, water, and sugar to just boiling in a nonreactive saucepan.

2 Fill a hot, sterilized pint jar with the garlic, mustard seeds, salt, and chiles, in that order. Fill with the hot brine, leaving ½ inch headspace. Seal with a canning lid.

3 Let cool and refrigerate for several months, or process in a boiling-water bath (pages 475–477) for 5 minutes. Store in a cool, dry place for up to a year.

CHILES IN HISTORY

Wild chiles made their first appearance around 7000 BC in Mexico. They were cultivated by 3500 BC. The first European to "discover" chiles was Christopher Columbus, who was looking for an alternative to black pepper, which is why he called the pods he found *pimiento*, after the Spanish word for black pepper. The Spaniards and Portuguese spread chiles to India and Southeast Asia, where chiles were readily adapted into cuisines that already valued highly spiced foods. Chiles also spread throughout Europe and the Middle East.

hot pepper–basil jelly

If you have a stock of homemade hot pepper jelly in the cupboard, you are never without the basis for a quick potluck offering or appetizer. A quick stop at the store for crackers or a baguette and some Cheddar or Brie and you have the fixings for an appetizer that can be thrown together at the very last minute. The hot peppers you use are entirely up to you — but do cut back on the amount you use if your chiles are habaneros or other mouth-searing varieties.

MAKES 7 OR 8 HALF-PINT JARS

5 cups chopped sweet bell peppers (all one color or an assortment of colors)

Approximately 1 cup chopped and seeded chiles

Leaves from 2 large sprigs basil

2½ cups cider vinegar

6½ cups sugar

2 packages (3 ounces each) liquid pectin

1 Combine the bell peppers, chiles, and basil in a food processor and process until finely minced. Transfer to a tall, nonreactive saucepan. Add the vinegar and bring to a boil. Reduce the heat and simmer for 5 minutes.

2 Stir the sugar into the pepper mixture and bring to a full rolling boil over high heat. The mixture should be boiling so furiously that you cannot stir it down. It will take 10 to 15 minutes to reach this point.

QUELLING THE BURN

When the chile burn is more than you can bear, try eating bread, pasta, potatoes, or a banana. Since capsaicin is an oil, it won't mix with water. But any oil-absorbing food will help stop the burning.

3 Add the pectin and boil for 1 full minute.

4 Ladle the hot jelly into sterilized half-pint canning jars with two-piece canning lids, leaving ¼ inch headspace. Wipe the rims of the jars with a clean cloth. Place the lids in position and tighten the screwbands. Process in a boiling-water bath (pages 475–477) for 5 minutes. Store in a cool, dry place for up to a year.

MAKING CHILE RISTRAS

IN THE SAME WAY that garlic is traditionally braided and hung to dry, so are strings of chiles. The chile string is called a ristra. There are several different ways one can assemble the ristra. Indeed, there are professional ristra makers in New Mexico and other parts of the Southwest who can assemble full, beautiful ristras in wreaths, crosses, and other shapes.

The simplest method is to use a large needle threaded with string. Push the needle through the base of the stems, pushing the chiles up tightly against each other. This produces a thin ristra, but it promotes better air circulation. Other methods of stringing ristras can be found at www.fiery-foods.com. Dry your ristras in a location where the air circulates freely. A sunny window works well.

An Ancient Plant of Many Uses

NO WONDER CORN IS ONE OF THE "THREE SISTERS" in Native American food lore (along with beans and squash). Sweet corn is best enjoyed fresh, as a vegetable. Field corn makes high-quality animal feed. Flint corn is hard and grown to be ground into cornmeal. Popcorn may be popped into a snack. Corn husks can be used as a wrapping for tamales or any food that you'd like to steam over a grill, or they can be made into dolls. Cobs can be simmered to make a broth or they can be added to hot coals to give grilled foods extra smoke flavor. They can be used as insulation. Corn silk can be brewed to make a tea.

Sweet corn, grown as a vegetable, is the quintessential and most ephemeral of summer flavors. It represents more of a challenge for the gardener than the cook. The gardener must not only perform all the usual gardening chores of soil preparation, cultivation, and performance of vigilance against all manner of insects and diseases, the gardener must also protect against wily critters (raccoons, deer, and woodchucks) to finally harvest the corn at its peak of perfection (and not one minute too late). The cook need do nothing more than start a fire in the grill or boil a pot of water. If the corn is really sweet and tender, it is delicious raw. It is strictly kudos to the gardener who grows the delicious ear, and kudos to the cook who knows when to step back and let the plain vegetable be served unadorned.

GROWING Sweet corn requires a warm site in full sun and grows best in very rich, well-drained, slightly acid soil.

SOWING Sow outdoors 1 week after the last frost. (The old rule of thumb is to sow when the leaves of the white oak are as big as a squirrel's ear.) Sow seeds 1 inch deep and 8 inches apart. To ensure good pollination, plant each variety in blocks of four short rows, rather than single rows. Sow every 2 weeks for staggered harvest. Figure you will get 10 to 20 ears of corn for every 10 feet of row.

CULTIVATING Corn requires plenty of fertilizer and water to grow well. Water regularly and fertilize every 2 weeks with fish emulsion. Keep the weeds down.

HARVESTING As a rule of thumb, corn matures 17 to 24 days after the first silk strands appear. The husk will be green, the silks dry-brown, and the kernels full size, and yellow or white to the tip of the ear. You can also judge maturity by using a thumbnail to puncture a kernel. If the liquid is clear, the corn is immature; if it is milky, the corn is ready; and if there is no sap, you're too late. Cover immature ears checked by this method with paper bags to prevent insect or bird damage. Experienced gardeners can feel the outside of the husk and tell when the cob has filled out.

Corn should be harvested in the cool temperatures of early morning, when its sugar content is highest. For the best quality, plunge the just harvested ears into ice water or put them on ice for a short time. Then store in the refrigerator until you are ready to cook them.

Although nothing beats simply steamed, grilled, or roasted corn-on-the-cob, there are times when you will want to remove the kernels from the cobs. The easiest way to do this is to husk the corn, then cut the ear in half horizontally. Stand the cobs on the cut sides and remove the kernels by slicing down with a sharp knife. Kernels will go flying, so be prepared. If you are making a soup or sauce or other "wet" preparation, scrape the cobs with the dull side of a knife to extract the delicious "milk" from the cobs. To extract even more milk, grate the kernels off the cobs with a box grater. This is a very messy technique, requiring clothing and wall protection, but well worth it flavorwise.

Corn kernels are surprisingly versatile. A cup or so of raw kernels makes a fine addition to salads and salsas. Corn kernels can be tossed into vegetable soups, sautés of mixed vegetables, and stir-fries. They go surprisingly well in pasta sauces.

TIMING
Blanching: 3 minutes
Steaming: 4 to 10 minutes on the cob; 4 minutes for kernels
Sautéing or stir-frying: 3 to 5 minutes for kernels
Grilling: 15 to 20 minutes on the cob
Roasting: 20 to 30 minutes at 500°F on the cob in husks; 15 minutes at 500°F on the cob with husks removed

CORN MATH
1 ear of corn = ½ to 1 cup kernels
1 pound = 5 to 6 ears

corn and
sweet potato chowder

Freshness is everything when it comes to most corn dishes, and corn chowder is no exception. In this version the sweet potatoes highlight the sweetness of the corn and add a beautiful contrasting color. The same method will work with the traditional onion replacing the leek and the traditional white potatoes replacing the sweet potatoes — but you will lose a little flavor and a lot of striking color.

SERVES 6–8

8 ears corn, husked and silked

6 cups vegetable or chicken broth (page 8 or 9)

2 tablespoons butter

1 leek, white and tender green parts, thinly sliced

1 garlic clove, minced

1 large sweet potato, peeled and diced

Salt

1½ cups half-and-half

1 tablespoon sugar, or to taste

Freshly ground black pepper

1 Strip the kernels from the corn and set aside. Combine the broth and corncobs in a large pot and bring to a boil. Reduce the heat and simmer for 30 minutes. Strain, discarding the cobs and reserving the broth. It should now be infused with corn flavor.

2 Melt the butter over medium heat in a large saucepan. Add the leek and sauté until softened, about 3 minutes. Add the garlic and sauté for another 2 minutes. Add the stock, corn kernels, sweet potatoes, and salt to taste. Bring to a boil, lower the heat, and simmer for 25 to 30 minutes, until the potatoes are tender.

3 Add the half-and-half and sugar. Season with the pepper. Taste and season with more salt, sugar, and pepper, if desired. Simmer for 5 minutes. Serve hot.

roasted corn-on-the-cob

For the best flavor, corn should be roasted in its husks, and it doesn't matter whether you do it in the oven or on the grill. Either way will give you the best roasted sweet corn. The downside of grilling is that it requires a grill. The downside of using the oven is that it is messy; you will have to sweep out the bottom of the oven the next day.

SERVES 4–8

8 ears fresh corn
Salt and freshly ground black pepper
Butter (optional)

1 Preheat the oven to 500°F or prepare a medium-hot fire.

2 Peel back the husks of the corn and remove the silks. Then fold back the husks, smoothing them into place. They will fit loosely, leaving the tips of the ears exposed.

3 Place the corn directly on the oven rack or grill rack and oven-roast for 20 to 30 minutes or grill for 15 to 20 minutes, until the corn is lightly browned, turning occasionally.

4 Remove the husks; it is a good idea to wear oven mitts and to work over a large bowl or newspaper to catch the crumbling husks.

5 Serve at once, passing salt, pepper, and butter at the table.

A BRIEF CORN HISTORY

ORN (*ZEA MAYS*) ORIGINATED AS A WILD GRASS, in Mexico or Central America. It is no longer found in the wild. There are conflicting theories about its origins, and its earliest ancestors may never be agreed upon. What is known is that the earliest domesticated corn dates back about 5,000 years and was about the size of a pencil eraser.

Some time around the year AD 800, corn was developed into a staple crop in North America by the Zuni tribe in what is today New Mexico and Arizona. They developed corn in six different hues: red, white, yellow, blue, speckled, and black. These cultivars were known as the six corn maidens, able to turn grass into corn by dancing.

By the time Columbus arrived in the New World, there were some 200 to 300 different breeds of corn grown, encompassing all the types of corn we know today: sweet, pop, flint, flour, and dent corn.

fresh corncakes

These corncakes are truly corny — and the secret is grating the corn to extract as much juice from the cobs as possible. This job is best done in the sink or outdoors, where you won't mind the spatters from this messy operation. These corncakes make a great casual supper or a fine weekend breakfast.

■ MAKES 4–6 SERVINGS (ABOUT 22 PANCAKES) ■

6 ears corn, husked

Milk

1¼ cups unbleached all-purpose flour

1 cup yellow stone-ground cornmeal

2 tablespoons sugar

1 tablespoon baking powder

1 teaspoon baking soda

1 teaspoon salt

2 large eggs, slightly beaten

3 tablespoons canola oil

Pure maple syrup, warmed

1 Grate the corn into a large bowl using a box grater. Transfer to a glass measure; you should have about 1⅓ cups. Add enough milk to make 2 cups.

2 Stir together the flour, cornmeal, sugar, baking powder, baking soda, and salt in a large bowl. Make a well in the center and add the eggs and oil. Stir well to combine.

3 Preheat the oven to 200°F. Place four to six plates in the oven to keep warm, if desired. Spray a well-seasoned cast-iron griddle or nonstick frying pan with nonstick cooking spray and heat over medium heat.

4 Pour the batter onto the griddle to make 4-inch pancakes. Cook until bubbles appear on the top of the pancakes and the bottoms are lightly browned, about 2 minutes. Turn and cook on the second side until golden, about 1 minute longer.

5 Keep the pancakes warm in the oven while you cook the rest of the batter. Serve at once, passing the maple syrup at the table.

POPCORN PRIMER

POPCORN IS GROWN JUST AS SWEET CORN IS GROWN; the trick is in the harvesting and drying so the kernels have just the right amount of dryness to avoid mold and spoilage but enough moisture so that steam will be produced to provide the "pop."

Harvest the popcorn ears before a hard frost, when the husks are dry and brown and the kernels are plump, well colored, and shiny. Remove the husks and spread out the ears or hang in mesh bags in a cool, well-ventilated space. Let the ears dry for about a month.

After a month of curing, the kernels can be taken off the ears and stored in airtight jars. There's no real mystery to removing the kernals. Simply grasp the ear firmly in both hands and twist until the kernels drop out. The kernels are sharply pointed, so protect your hands with gloves.

Before storing the kernels, test a batch of popcorn. If they pop nicely, store the kernels in airtight glass jars. If they pop weakly, continue drying, but test every few days. Pop homegrown popcorn just as you would store-bought. Heat a few tablespoons of oil in a deep pot. Sprinkle in enough kernels to coat the bottom and cover the pot. Pop the popcorn over medium heat. As soon as you hear the first kernel pop, shake the covered pot vigorously while the rest pop. Shaking prevents the kernels from burning, and the unpopped kernels stay on the bottom nearest the heat. If you're using a popcorn popper, follow the manufacturer's instructions.

When the popping stops, remove the pot from the heat, remove the lid, and let the steam escape. The popcorn is ready. Enjoy it plain, or add your favorite topping.

pan-roasted corn and shrimp salad

You'll need a good nonstick or well-seasoned skillet for this recipe. The corn is roasted in a dry pan and it leaves a residue, which is then deglazed with the vinaigrette.

■ SERVES 4 ■

Kernels from 6 ears corn
1 red or green bell pepper, diced
1 onion, diced
6 tablespoons extra-virgin olive oil
2 tablespoons sherry vinegar
2 tablespoons chopped fresh cilantro
1 tablespoon chopped fresh mint
Salt and freshly ground black pepper
1¼ pounds shrimp, shelled and deveined
8–12 cups torn fresh salad greens
2–4 tomatoes, diced

1 Heat a large skillet over high heat. Add the corn, bell pepper, and onion and roast until browned, 20 minutes, stirring and scraping the pan occasionally.

2 Turn off the heat and add the oil, vinegar, cilantro, mint, and salt and pepper to taste. Scrape up the browned bits from the pan and stir into the corn. Transfer the mixture to a bowl and return the skillet to the stove.

3 Heat the skillet over high heat. Add the shrimp and sauté until cooked through, 4 to 5 minutes.

4 To serve, arrange the greens on individual serving plates. Spoon the corn mixture over the greens. Spoon the tomatoes around the corn. Top with the shrimp and serve.

pasta with golden corn sauce

In the time it takes to heat the pasta water and cook the pasta, the sauce will be made. The most time-consuming part is stripping the kernels from the corn.

■ SERVES 4 ■

Kernels from 6 ears corn
1½ cups chicken broth (page 9)
Pinch of saffron threads
½ cup heavy cream
¼ pound smoked turkey or ham, cut into thin strips
1 cup halved or quartered cherry tomatoes
¼ cup chopped fresh basil
Salt and freshly ground black pepper
1 pound linguine or spaghetti

1 Bring a large pot of salted water to a boil for the pasta.

2 Combine the corn, chicken broth, and saffron in a medium saucepan. Bring to a boil and simmer until the corn is tender, about 1 minute.

3 Transfer the corn mixture to a blender or food processor, add the cream, and pulse to make a coarse purée. Return the mixture to the saucepan and add the turkey, tomatoes, and basil. Season with salt and pepper. Keep warm over low heat.

4 Cook the pasta to just al dente. Drain.

5 Combine the pasta with the sauce in a serving bowl, toss well, and serve immediately.

CORN SHOOTS

Baby corn shoots have intense corn flavor, are yellow in color, and surprisingly tender — not at all like the grasslike shoots in the garden. How are they grown? The method is simple. Grow the shoots in total darkness — indoors — for about 3 weeks. Prepare a seedbed in a box with a layer of moist, rich soil. Soak popcorn kernels in water to cover for 4 hours, lay them on the soil, and water once. Store the box in a closet or root cellar. Begin checking after 2 weeks, especially in warm weather. You must catch them when they are still young and tender.

"I FELL IN LOVE WITH CORN when I first came to America," explains Olwen Woodier, author of *Corn* (Storey Books, 2002). "I was living in New York City at the time, and we would go to East Hampton every weekend to visit my mother-in-law and escape the heat of the city. My husband always insisted on buying fresh corn from roadside farmstands and we had to cook it that very day. Silver Queen — that was the variety we loved best back then."

Growing up in the northwest of England, near the border with Wales, Woodier knew about corn — or maize, as they called it. It was something fed to cattle. She had her first taste of sweet corn when she was in Switzerland, but it was frozen, and not at all compelling. "It really wasn't until I came to the United States that I had fresh corn," she says. "And I loved it."

Woodier turned her passion for corn into a book of 140 corn recipes and gardening information. And she still isn't tired of the subject — or the taste — of fresh corn: "Strangely enough, I never tire of corn. And I love to try new varieties."

With 140 recipes at her fingertips, how does Woodier prefer to prepare corn? "At the beginning of the season, I like it just simply cooked, dropped in boiling water for a few minutes. Nothing more. Then after about of month of that, I start throwing it on the grill. I shuck it first, otherwise it's too messy. Then I roll it in a little herbed oil and grill it. The time really depends on whether you like it well done or not. I usually grill the ears for about ten minutes, turning it every two minutes or so. If I want it buttery, I foil-roast it. When you butter corn, you tend to use more than when you oil it — and I don't like the butter dripping into the grill, so I use the foil. I grill in foil for about fifteen minutes.

"Another thing I like to do is dry roast the kernels in a nonstick frying pan for a couple of minutes. It is like toasting nuts. You strip the kernels off the cob and toast them so they are still crunchy. Then I might add a little butter at the end.

"Or I might sauté the kernels with a little oil or butter and some pepper. I often add a handful of corn to a stir-fry. Sometimes we have too much corn to eat all in one sitting. So if I find myself with corn in the refrigerator, I will usually add it to muffin batter, or even cakes. Sometimes, I sauté the kernels with a little basil and toss them in an omelet or frittata. Of course, some of the new supersweet or sugar-enhanced varieties will hold up in the refrigerator for a few days."

Woodier makes it a point to seek out farmstands that offer varieties of corn she hasn't yet tasted. She thinks Silver Queen is still the gold (or silver) standard when it comes to good corn taste, but late-season Silver King is one of the few supersweet varieties that offer good corn flavor as well as long-lasting sweetness. Candy King and Kandy Korn are two other supersweet varieties she likes.

Among the bicolors, she likes a variety called Peaches & Cream.

Since moving to Virginia from upstate New York, Woodier is still working on building up her garden. Lately she has taken to growing more and more baby corn: "The trick with baby corn is figuring out when to harvest it. You have to harvest it as soon as the silks emerge. It's a little tricky. But it's worth it. Baby corn is grown from a dwarf variety. It doesn't take up much space and you don't have to separate varieties. I've tried Golden Midget and Baby. Baby corn is much better fresh than canned. Very tender. You should try it."

Next year I think I will.

corn risotto

There's corn in the broth in which the rice cooks and corn folded into the risotto at the end. Vegetarians can omit the smoked turkey.

■ SERVES 4 ■

1 cup water

Kernels from 3 ears corn

3½ cups vegetable or chicken broth (page 8 or 9)

½ cup dry white wine

2 teaspoons sugar

½ teaspoon ground turmeric

2 tablespoons extra-virgin olive oil

2 cups Arborio rice

1 red bell pepper, finely chopped

2 shallots, minced

¼ pound smoked turkey breast, diced

¼ cup chopped fresh basil

Salt and freshly ground black pepper

1 Bring the water to a boil in a small saucepan. Add the kernels from two ears of the corn, cover, and cook until quite tender, 2 to 3 minutes. Let cool slightly. Pour into a blender and purée.

2 Return the corn purée to the saucepan and add the chicken broth, wine, sugar, and turmeric. Heat to boiling, then reduce the heat and let the mixture simmer.

3 Heat the oil in a large skillet over medium heat. Add the rice, bell pepper, and shallots and sauté until the rice looks dry, 4 to 5 minutes.

4 Add 1 cup of the corn–broth mixture and cook over medium heat, stirring constantly, until the liquid is absorbed. Continue adding more of the mixture, 1 cup at a time, cooking and stirring after each addition. The liquid should be mostly absorbed before you add the next cup.

5 When all the broth has been added, remove from the heat. Stir in the turkey, the remaining corn, and the basil. Season with salt and pepper. Cover and let heat through for about 1 minute. Serve immediately.

BABY CORN

GROWING BABY CORN is an interesting new challenge for gardeners. Baby corn truly is immature corn, but there are seed choices that are specifically chosen for growing multiple ears. You can harvest immature corn from field corn, regular sweet corn, sugary enhanced, and supersweet corn varieties, and there won't be discernible differences in sweetness, since the ears are harvested before pollination and before sugar is stored in the kernels.

To get the greatest yield of baby corn, plant corn seed much closer together than usual; sow each seed about 4 inches apart in the row. Keep the row spacing to the normal 30 to 36 inches apart.

Whether you are harvesting immature lower ears on the regular cornstalk or immature ears from "baby corn" vari-eties, harvesting at the right time is tricky. You may need to harvest a sampling every day until you determine the best time to harvest. Remember that ears on the same stalk will not develop at the same rate. The ear will have just produced silks, but the ears will not be filled out. Baby corn ears are best harvested when they are 2 to 4 inches long and ⅓ to ⅔ inch in diameter.

Husking the ears is time-consuming and removing the silks near impossible. Fortunately, at this stage of immaturity, the silks are quite edible. Baby corn can be steamed or boiled for 5 to 10 minutes and served whole, to be eaten cobs and all. Test the corn before removing it from the heat. Baby corn can be stubbornly tough. If that's the case, keep cooking.

chicken with creamy
corn sauce

Here's a dinner that can be whipped together in under an hour and is as fine a dish as one could desire — a terrific combination of veggies and comfort. The plate will be lacking in color, so steamed green beans, sliced tomatoes, or another colorful vegetable is a must.

■ SERVES 4 ■

¾ cup unbleached all-purpose flour

2 tablespoons chopped fresh thyme, plus additional thyme leaves to garnish

Salt and freshly ground black pepper

4 boneless, skinless chicken breast halves

2 tablespoons extra-virgin olive oil

Kernels from 4 ears fresh corn

2 scallions, white and tender green parts, chopped

1 garlic clove, minced

3 tablespoons white wine

1½ cups chicken broth (page 9)

2 tablespoons heavy cream

Garlic Mashed Potatoes (page 440), to serve

1 Combine the flour, thyme, a generous pinch of salt, and a few grinds of pepper in a shallow bowl. Dredge the chicken in the flour, turning to coat on all sides.

2 Heat the oil in a large skillet over medium-high heat. Shake off any excess flour on the chicken and place the chicken in the skillet. Cook until well browned and cooked through, about 5 minutes per side. Transfer to a plate and keep warm.

3 Sauté the corn, scallions, and garlic in the skillet until the scallions are wilted, about 1 minute. Add the wine and deglaze the pan, stirring well and cooking until all the wine is evaporated. Add the broth and boil until reduced by about a third. Whisk in the cream. Season with more salt and pepper. Return the chicken to the pan just long enough to heat through, 1 to 2 minutes.

4 Serve the chicken and mashed potatoes on plates, spooning the corn sauce over both. Garnish with a sprinkling of thyme leaves.

CORN CHOICE

THERE ARE A HUGE NUMBER OF sweet corn varieties to choose from, including heirlooms and hybrids. There are yellow, white, and bicolor kernels, not to mention early, mid-season, and late-season varieties. Theoretically, a continuous harvest can be planned by planting early, mid-season, and late-season varieties or by making successive plantings of the same variety every 2 weeks or when the last planting has three or four leaves (corn sown in early spring will take longer because of cool temperatures). But if you want a continuous harvest, you have to devote a large amount of space to the corn, since you have to plant in blocks to ensure good pollination.

Heirloom corn is a nonhybrid corn. You can save the seeds from year to year. It has good old-fashioned corn flavor, but the sugars in the kernel begin to convert to starch as soon as it is harvested. Normal sugary (abbreviated SU) is the sweet corn home gardeners have been growing for years. It has a "sugary (SU) gene" that makes its kernels sweet and creamy, but the sugars convert to starches after harvest quite quickly.

Sugary enhanced hybrids (abbreviated SE) combine the best qualities of the sweet and supersweet types of corn. They're tender, creamy-textured, and superb for eating. Once harvested they will keep their sweet flavor for a day or so in the refrigerator.

Supersweet hybrids (abbreviated Sh2) contain the shrunken -2 gene and have a higher sugar content than standard SU varieties. Their kernels have a tough-skinned rather than a creamy texture.

The surprise is that some of the newly developed supersweet varieties of corn are a little too sweet, and somewhat lacking in corn flavor.

Made for the Grill

NO VEGETABLE TAKES SO WELL to the grill as eggplant. It is the only garden vegetable that can absorb a marinade and provide that extra burst of flavor. Grilled eggplant steaks can form the centerpiece of a vegetarian meal. You can use it as the main ingredient in a sandwich — stuff it into a pita pocket and serve it with a Santorini Salad (page 319) or Tzatziki (page 136), or layer it with fresh mozzarella and sliced tomatoes on toasted whole wheat spread with pesto (page 6). Or layer grilled eggplant slices with goat cheese in foccacia and grill it under a weight to make panini. Grilled eggplant slices can form a layer in lasagna, replace fried eggplant in eggplant Parmesan, or top a pizza. A classic Middle Eastern appetizer is made by spreading grilled eggplant slices with yogurt that has been flavored with plenty of minced garlic and mint. The possibilities are endless.

On the other hand, no other garden vegetable is quite so difficult to get right on the grill. Slice it too thin and it will char. Slice it too thick and it will dry out and become leathery before it is done. Brush it with oil too soon and the oil will disappear. Here's the secret: Slice the eggplant ⅜ inch thick, brush with oil just before you place it on the grill, and grill over a hot fire. You will be rewarded with perfectly grilled eggplant, slightly crusty on the outside, moist and flavorful on the inside.

GROWING Eggplant likes constant heat throughout its growing season. It needs plenty of water, full sun, and protection from bugs, which will delight in feasting on it.

SOWING Start plants indoors about 8 weeks before the first frost and be sure to harden the plants off before transplanting to the garden. Transplant to the garden when the soil temperature is at least 70°F, the daytime temperature is consistently above 70°F, and the nighttime temperature is consistently above 60°F.

CULTIVATING Floating row covers and mulch to provide steady heat and bug protection are a good idea.

HARVESTING Once the fruits are half size, you can begin to harvest them. Frequent harvesting will stimulate more fruit production.

EGGPLANT MATH

Eggplants vary widely in size.
1 large eggplant = 1½ to 2 pounds
1 pound = 12 to 16 slices
= 6 cups cubes
= 5 cups diced

Many recipes call for salting eggplant before cooking to draw out the bitterness. But freshly harvested eggplant is not bitter, so this step is usually not necessary. However, if you are planning to sauté or broil eggplant, salting will draw out excess water and the eggplant will cook without steaming. To salt, lay the slices, salted-side down, on paper towels and let drain for 20 minutes. Then sprinkle with salt, turn over, and drain for 20 minutes on the second side.

Peeling is generally optional, but I find the skins tough and bitter. In general, the long, tapered Oriental eggplants have sweeter, thinner skins than the purple globe types. White eggplants often have tough skins.

When roasting or grilling a whole eggplant, as for Baba Ghanoush (page 244), it is very important to prick the eggplant in several places to allow steam to escape. Cleaning up an exploded eggplant is no fun at all.

When roasting, grilling, or broiling eggplant, slice the eggplant about ⅜ inch thick. Brush one side of the slices with oil just before cooking. Brush the other just before turning. The ideal cooked slices will be well browned and slightly crusty on the outside and moist inside.

TIMING

Sautéing or stir-frying: 5 to 10 minutes (cubes)
Frying: 10 to 14 minutes (slices)
Broiling: 10 to 14 minutes (slices)
Grilling: 10 to 14 minutes (slices); 30 to 50 minutes (whole)
Roasting: 20 to 25 minutes (slices) at 400°F; 30 to 40 minutes (whole) at 400°F

baba ghanoush

The best baba ghanoush starts with eggplant grilled over a wood fire. Then the eggplant is drained to remove any bitter juices, which greatly improves the flavor and texture of the finished dish. Finally, the dip must be well beaten (a food processor helps) to achieve a creamy consistency. Don't forget to pierce the eggplant in several places before grilling — there's a good chance it will explode if you do not.

SERVES 6

2 pounds eggplant (1 large or 2 medium)

¼ cup packed flat-leaf parsley leaves

2 garlic cloves

3 tablespoons fresh lemon juice, plus more to taste

2 tablespoons tahini (sesame paste)

2 tablespoons extra-virgin olive oil

1 teaspoon salt, plus more to taste

Freshly ground black pepper

Flatbread or sesame crackers, to serve

1 Soak a handful of wood chips in water to cover for a few hours before you are ready to grill.

2 Prepare a medium-low fire in the grill. When the grill is ready, put the soaked wood chips directly on top of the lit charcoal. If you are using a gas grill, place the soaked chips in a perforated disposable metal pan and set the pan directly on the burner. Or use the chip holder that comes with many gas grill models.

3 Prick the eggplant with a fork in several places on all sides. Place on the grill, cover with the lid, and grill, turning occasionally, until the eggplant is completely soft and collapsed, 30 to 50 minutes.

4 Place the eggplant in a colander, slice open with a knife, and allow to drain and cool for about 30 minutes.

5 Combine the parsley and garlic in a food processor and process until finely chopped. Remove the eggplant flesh from the skin and add the flesh to the food processor along with the lemon juice, tahini, oil, a generous pinch of salt, and a few grinds of pepper. Process until fairly smooth. Taste and adjust the seasonings, adding more salt, pepper, or lemon juice as needed.

6 Cover and let stand for at least 30 minutes to allow the flavors to blend. Serve at room temperature with flatbreads or sesame crackers for scooping up the dip.

EGGPLANT HISTORY

The first eggplants grown in North America were white and looked something like eggs, hence the name. In Europe, eggplant is known as *aubergine*. Its origins are probably Indian, though the first written record of eggplant was in China during the fifth century. Eggplant made its way from India to Europe through the Middle East via Arab traders. It is one of the most popular vegetables throughout Asia and the Mediterranean.

soy-sesame grilled eggplant

When you are looking for a make-ahead vegetable dish that can be served at room temperature, consider the eggplant. In this case, slices of eggplant are grilled or broiled, then combined with a spicy marinade featuring soy sauce and Chinese chili paste with garlic. It's not the most beautiful dish in the world, but a scattering of sesame seeds brightens the dark colors of soy and eggplant. The flavor is intense and delicious.

Three pounds of eggplant is about two large globe eggplants. This dish works well with any variety of eggplant. If the eggplant is long and curved, like some varieties are, it may be more convenient to slice the eggplant horizontally. The point is to make the slices about ⅜ inch thick for even cooking and big enough not to fall through the grates of the grill.

■ SERVES 4–6 ■

Eggplant

3 pounds eggplant (about 2 large or medium), peeled and sliced lengthwise ⅜ inch thick

4 tablespoons peanut oil

Marinade

5 tablespoons soy sauce

2 tablespoons dark sesame oil

2 tablespoons mirin, Chinese rice wine, or sake

1 tablespoon rice vinegar

1 tablespoon chili paste with garlic

1 tablespoon sugar

2 garlic cloves, minced

3 scallions, whites and tender greens, finely chopped

Garnish

2 tablespoons sesame seeds

1 Prepare a medium-hot fire in the grill or preheat the broiler.

2 Brush the eggplant with oil on one side. Grill the eggplant, oiled-side down, until browned, 5 to 7 minutes. Or broil the eggplant oiled-side up until brown, 5 to 7 minutes. Brush the second side with oil, turn, and continue to grill or broil for 5 to 7 minutes, until tender and browned. The eggplant should be slightly crusty on the outside but soft and moist inside.

3 Slice the eggplant into bite-size pieces and transfer to a medium bowl.

4 Combine the soy sauce, sesame oil, mirin, vinegar, chili paste, sugar, garlic, and scallions in a small bowl. Mix well. Pour over the eggplant and toss to mix.

5 Let stand at least 30 minutes to allow the eggplant to absorb the flavors of the marinade. You can hold this dish in the refrigerator for up to 3 days. Just before serving, sprinkle with the sesame seeds and serve warm or cold.

grilled eggplant salad

The great thing about this salad is that it can be made in advance. So, with a little planning, you can grill the eggplant whenever the grill is going, and serve the salad at a later date.

SERVES 4–6

2 large eggplants, about 3 pounds, peeled and sliced ⅜ inch thick

Extra-virgin olive oil

½ red onion, minced

½ cup finely chopped fresh parsley

1 large garlic clove, minced

2 tablespoons finely chopped fresh mint

Juice of 1 lemon (3 tablespoons), or to taste

Salt and freshly ground black pepper

1 Prepare a medium-hot fire in the grill.

2 Brush the eggplant slices with oil on one side just as you place them on the grill. Grill the eggplant until brown on the first side, 5 to 7 minutes. Brush with oil on the second side, turn over, and continue grilling until tender, 5 to 7 minutes longer. Transfer to a cutting board and chop.

3 Combine the eggplant, onion, parsley, garlic, and mint in a large salad bowl and toss to mix. Add the lemon juice and season generously with salt and pepper.

4 Cover and let stand for 2 hours or refrigerate for up to 2 days. Taste and adjust the seasoning. Serve at room temperature or chilled.

caponata

Caponata is a traditional sweet-and-sour mixture of vegetables from Sicily. It can be served on an antipasto platter or as a side dish or relish.

SERVES 4–6

1 large eggplant (1½–2 pounds), peeled and diced
1 onion, diced
2 tablespoons extra-virgin olive oil
2 tomatoes, diced
1 celery rib, diced
½ cup chopped green olives
2 tablespoons chopped fresh parsley
2 tablespoons chopped fresh basil
2 tablespoons red wine vinegar, or to taste
2 teaspoons capers
1 teaspoon sugar, or to taste
Salt and freshly ground black pepper

1 Preheat the oven to 400°F. Lightly grease a large sheet pan (preferred) or shallow baking pan with oil.

2 Mound the eggplant and onion on the prepared pan. Drizzle the oil over them and toss gently to coat. Arrange in a single layer.

3 Roast for 20 to 25 minutes, stirring occasionally, until the eggplant is tender.

4 Transfer the eggplant to a large bowl. Add the tomatoes, celery, olives, parsley, basil, vinegar, and capers. Sprinkle with the sugar and season with salt and pepper. Toss gently to mix. Taste and adjust the seasoning.

5 Let sit for at least 30 minutes to allow the flavors to develop. The caponata can be made a few days in advance and stored in the refrigerator in an airtight container. Serve at room temperature.

A grilled or broiled slice of eggplant is delicious on its own, but you can also use it as a basic building block for a sandwich or as a topping for pizza.

1 medium eggplant (about 1 pound), peeled and sliced ⅜ inch thick

1 tablespoon salt

⅓ cup Classic Vinaigrette (page 90), Herb Vinaigrette (page 91), Miso Vinaigrette (page 95), or your favorite bottled Italian-style salad dressing

1 Sprinkle the eggplant slices with the salt and let drain in a colander for 30 minutes. Rinse well and pat dry. Transfer the eggplant to a shallow baking dish and pour the vinaigrette over it. Let stand for at least 15 minutes to absorb the marinade.

2 Prepare a medium-hot fire in a grill or preheat a broiler.

3 Grill or broil the eggplant, turning occasionally, until tender and grill-marked, 10 to 14 minutes. The eggplant should be slightly crusty on the outside but still moist and soft inside. Serve hot.

S O DECLARED MY BROTHER IN 2004. My brother, normally an even-tempered guy, has declared war on "critters" in his garden: "There always seems to be something munching in the garden. But I'm not sharing this year."

His solution? Solarize the soil under a layer of black plastic mulch. "It gets so hot under the plastic, you kill all the weed seeds, insects, nematodes, viruses, what have you," he says.

My brother, Joe Chesman, lives and gardens in Alabama, on the Gulf Coast. He has been gardening in the same spot for 6 years.

"My soil is getting better every year. I have a compost pit. I throw in all the leaves, grass cuttings, weeds. In this hot weather, you wouldn't believe how fast it turns into compost. Besides compost, I add lime periodically — everyone does down here. And I do use a little chemical fertilizer. Nutrients just don't stay in this soil. They leach right through it. I have raised beds. That helps some."

But isn't solarizing the soil a little extreme? "We've had four mild winters in a row, so the insect problem is getting worse. Besides, they [area gardening consultants] recommend it every 5 to 6 years. So that's what I did this year for my big garden. I have a small plot that I'll solarize next year. This year I still had my tomatoes, my sweet peppers, cucumbers, bush beans. Usually I just do sugar snaps and English peas in the small garden."

So, I ask, will the soil be healthy and the critters kept at bay with solarizing?

"Well," he admits, "it's not just insects that give me trouble. I've got skunks, possums, squirrels, birds. This year, I lost a lot of my oranges to possums. And the plums disappear. I'm not sure just what is getting those. They leave no evidence behind. But the fruit trees are at risk. I harvested my first figs this year. No papaws yet . . ."

Papaws, also known as custard apples, were growing wild in the Carolinas when the first European settlers arrived. The fruits are eaten out of their skins with spoons, and the flesh has the texture of custard with a flavor that is a blend of apple, banana, and strawberry. Joe planted papaws his first year in Alabama and has yet to harvest any.

Our conversation turns to oranges, and Joe starts to get excited about the heavy crop of satsumas he expects to harvest at Thanksgiving time, but I steer the conversation back to his failures. There's a bit of sibling rivalry between us and hearing about his successes isn't as rewarding as it should be.

I ask him what is different about gardening in the South, compared to upstate New York, where we grew up, and Colorado, where he lived most of his adult life. "You get a long growing season," he reflects. "But that means there's plenty of time for drought, or too much rain. There's always some challenge — weather, disease . . . " His voice trails off.

"There's a lot of critters that will help you harvest, but none that will help you grow it."

eggplant lasagna

Eggplant adds a meaty quality to this vegetarian lasagna, which is a very popular item at potlucks and buffet dinners. It is also a good way to introduce reluctant children to eggplant. You don't have to tell them what they are eating until they have cleaned their plates.

SERVES 6–9

⅓ cup extra-virgin olive oil

4 garlic cloves, minced

2 teaspoons chopped fresh rosemary

2 teaspoons chopped fresh thyme

Salt and freshly ground black pepper

2 large eggplants (about 3 pounds), peeled and sliced lengthwise ⅜ inch thick

1 pound (about 2 cups) ricotta cheese

1 egg, slightly beaten

2 tablespoons chopped fresh basil

3 cups shredded mozzarella

1 cup freshly grated Parmesan

4 cups well-seasoned tomato sauce

12 no-cook lasagna noodles

1 Preheat the oven to 425°F. Lightly grease two large sheet pans (preferred) or shallow roasting pans with oil.

2 Combine the oil, garlic, rosemary, thyme, and salt and pepper to taste in a small bowl. Mix well. Brush the eggplant slices on one side with the seasoned oil and set the slices, oiled-side down, on the prepared pans. Roast in the oven for 15 to 20 minutes, until browned on the bottom. Brush the second side with oil, turn the slices over, rotate the pans from top to bottom and side to side, and continue roasting for another 15 to 20 minutes, until browned on the second side. Remove the pans from the oven and reduce the oven temperature to 350°F.

3 Combine the ricotta, egg, and basil in a medium bowl and mix well. Combine the mozzarella and Parmesan in a second bowl and toss to mix.

4 To assemble the lasagna, spread about 1 cup of the sauce in a 9-inch by 13-inch baking dish. Place three lasagna noodles over the sauce. The noodles should not touch or overlap. Spread 1 cup of the sauce over the noodles. Arrange a layer of one third of the eggplant over the sauce. Spread one third of the ricotta mixture evenly over the eggplant. Sprinkle a fourth of the mozzarella and Parmesan cheeses on top. Repeat the layer twice. Top with the remaining three lasagna noodles. Spread the remaining sauce on top. Sprinkle with the remaining mozzarella and Parmesan. Cover with foil.

5 Bake the lasagna for 30 minutes. Remove the foil and bake for another 10 to 15 minutes, until hot and bubbly.

6 Let the lasagna stand for 5 minutes before cutting into serving pieces. Serve warm or hot.

The lasagna can be assembled and held for up to 8 hours in the refrigerator. Add 15 minutes to the baking time if it is cold when placed in the oven. Or the lasagna can be baked in advance and frozen for up to a month. Bake it still frozen and covered with foil, adding 30 minutes to the baking time.

eggplant pizza

Rather than scatter a few pieces of sautéed, broiled, or roasted eggplant on top of a pizza topped with tomato sauce and cheese, I make a sauce of eggplant, onion, green pepper, and mushrooms. This pizza is rich in flavor and very satisfying.

SERVES 4–6

Basic Pizza Dough (page 12; while the dough is rising, follow the instructions in steps 1 and 2)

3 tablespoons extra-virgin olive oil

1 large eggplant (1½ to 2 pounds), peeled and diced

1 onion, diced

1 green bell pepper, diced

2 cups sliced white mushrooms

3 cups finely chopped seeded ripe tomatoes

4 garlic cloves, minced, plus more to taste

¼ cup chopped fresh basil

2 tablespoons chopped fresh oregano

Salt and freshly ground black pepper

2 cups grated mozzarella

½ cup freshly grated Parmesan

1 While the pizza dough rises according to the recipe instructions, prepare the sauce. Heat the oil in a large skillet over medium-high heat. Add the eggplant, onion, green pepper, and mushrooms (the skillet will be quite full). Sauté, stirring frequently and carefully, until the eggplant is completely tender and the mushrooms have given up their juice, about 15 minutes.

2 Stir in the tomatoes, garlic, basil, and oregano. Season with salt and pepper. Simmer for 10 minutes. Taste and add more garlic and salt and pepper, if desired.

3 With the dough now stretched over the pans and the oven pre-heated to 500°F according to the recipe instructions, spoon half the sauce over each pizza with a slotted spoon. Top each with half of the mozzarella and half of the Parmesan.

4 Bake the pizzas side by side on the bottom rack of your oven for 12 to 15 minutes, until the crust is browned and the cheese is melting and bubbling. If the two pizzas do not fit side by side, bake the pizzas on two racks, switching the pizzas midway through the baking process. Serve hot.

EGGPLANT CULTIVARS

Eggplant is so bland that differences in flavor among the cultivars are very, very subtle. It is probably the case that growing conditions have more impact than cultivar. But eggplant is a tropical beauty of a plant. If you have the right growing conditions, then consider growing an orchard of these dazzlers. Indeed, the first eggplants grown in this country were grown as ornamentals. Because the eggplant, like the tomato, is a member of the deadly nightshade family, people were reluctant to eat it.

Eggplants, which are technically berries, range in color from purple to white, with lavender, rose, and green in between; they may also be solid or striped. The shapes may be long and tapered, round, or pear-shaped. The flowers are usually showy and purple. The plants are about the same size as pepper plants, which makes them an attractive 2- to 3-foot bush in the garden.

lamb-stuffed eggplant

The flavors are classically Mediterranean in this combination of eggplant, lamb, and feta.

SERVES 4

1 zucchini, diced

Salt

4 small or 2 medium eggplants

3 tablespoons extra-virgin olive oil

1 pound ground lamb

1 onion, diced

1 cup crumbled feta (about ⅓ pound)

2 tablespoons chopped fresh oregano

2 tablespoons chopped fresh parsley

1 tablespoon minced lemon zest

Freshly ground black pepper

Topping

1 cup yogurt

½ cup lightly packed mint leaves

1 Toss the zucchini with 1 teaspoon salt and set aside in a colander to drain for 30 minutes.

2 Preheat the oven to 425°F.

3 Cut the eggplant in halves lengthwise. Score the eggplant flesh with diagonal cuts about ½ inch apart in both directions. Run the knife all the way around each eggplant half, about ¼ inch from the skin. Brush the eggplants with 2 tablespoons of the oil and place cut sides up on a baking sheet. Season with salt. Bake until lightly browned and barely tender, 15 to 25 minutes. The timing will depend on the size of the eggplants; it is better to err on the side of overcooking than undercooking.

4 While the eggplants bake, heat the remaining 1 tablespoon oil in a large skillet over medium-high heat. Add the lamb and onion and cook the meat is browned, about 8 minutes.

5 Pat dry the zucchini with paper towels. Add to the skillet and sauté until barely tender, about 3 minutes. Remove the skillet from the heat and stir in the feta, oregano, and parsley.

6 When the eggplants have baked, scoop out the flesh and transfer to a cutting board. Chop the flesh and stir into the lamb mixture. Taste the mixture and season generously with salt and pepper. Spoon into the eggplant shells and return the shells to the baking sheet.

7 Bake for about 20 minutes, until the filling is hot and bubbly and the eggplant shells are completely tender. Serve hot.

A Vegetable That Deserves More Attention

FENNEL, FLORENCE FENNEL, anise, anise bulb — its names are many. Fennel doesn't enjoy the popularity here that it does in Italy. But give it time. Once more people have tasted it, they will be clamoring for it.

Raw fennel is surprising juicy and refreshing. It has a licorice flavor, but it is mild and not overwhelming (as licorice candy can be). You might think that you won't like fennel because you don't like licorice and you hate black jelly beans. I know I was mistaken that same way. Instead, compare fennel to celery, though it is juicier, less stringy, and more flavorful that celery. A small bowl of raw fennel set out with bowls of olives makes a fine appetizer. It is served with fruit and cheese as a dessert in Italy. Fennel, like celery, has very few calories, making it an ideal snack.

Cooked fennel is surprisingly sweet, and the licorice flavor is even more subdued. The texture softens with cooking, but it does not become stringy as celery does. Fennel is just as good raw in a salad as it is roasted and served simply, or added as an accent to a pasta sauce or soup.

GROWING Fennel is relatively easy to grow. It requires full sun and light but steady water.

SOWING Sow indoors about 1 month before the last frost.

CULTIVATING Keep the soil evenly moist. Mulch around the base of the plant to keep the bulb blanched and tender.

HARVESTING Harvest the entire plant when the bulb is about 4 inches across and firm to the touch.

FENNEL MATH
1 pound = 3 cups chopped or sliced

Fennel is an odd-looking plant. It has a white, bulbous base from which green stalks arise. The stalks sport feathery, dark green fronds. The bulb is what is eaten, the stalks are trimmed away (a few may be added to broth), and the feathery fronds are used as an herb or garnish for dishes in which the bulb is featured.

To prepare fennel for cooking, slice off the root end. Then slice off the stalks, leaving the bulb, which is layered. Remove all tough or blemished layers from the bulb, usually the outermost layers. Cut the bulb in half and remove the core. Then slice or cut into wedges, as required by the recipe. Save a few fronds for a garnish.

Fennel is delicious raw, but can be sautéed, braised, baked, grilled, or roasted. Roasting brings out the most flavor. For a grown-up take on macaroni and cheese, slice a couple of fennel bulbs and sauté them with garlic in the butter you use to make the cheese sauce.

TIMING
Sautéing or stir-frying: 4 minutes
Braising: 20 minutes
Grilling: 10 to 12 minutes
Roasting: 15 minutes at 425°F

fennel, apple, and pecan salad

People don't often expect raw fennel in salads, so this salad always generates comments at a potluck. The salad looks lovely if you leave the slices large, but I like small pieces so each fork brings up both pieces of apple and fennel at the same time.

SERVES 6

⅓ cup buttermilk

1 shallot, minced

2 tablespoons extra-virgin olive oil

2 tablespoons white balsamic vinegar

Salt and freshly ground black pepper

2 fennel bulbs (about 2 pounds), trimmed, cut into quarters, and thinly sliced

2 large apples, quartered, cored, and thinly sliced

1 cup pecans, toasted

Chopped fennel fronds, to garnish

1 To make the dressing, whisk together the buttermilk, shallot, oil, vinegar, and salt and pepper to taste in a small bowl.

2 Combine the fennel, apples, and pecans in a large bowl. Toss to mix. Pour in the dressing. Taste and adjust the seasonings. Garnish with the fennel fronds and serve.

fennel, orange, and olive salad

It is the contrasts of sweet and salty, crunchy and soft that make this salad such a delight.

SERVES 4

2 fennel bulbs (about 2 pounds), trimmed, cut into quarters, and thinly sliced

2 oranges, peeled, halved, and thinly sliced

1 cup pitted black olives, such as Kalamata

¼ red onion, thinly sliced

5 tablespoons extra-virgin olive oil

3 tablespoons fresh lemon juice

1 tablespoon orange juice, preferably freshly squeezed

Salt and freshly ground black pepper

Chopped fennel fronds, to garnish

1 Combine the fennel, oranges, olives, and onion in a large bowl. Toss to mix.

2 Whisk together the oil, lemon juice, and orange juice in another large bowl. Pour over the salad. Season with salt and pepper. Let stand for at least 30 minutes to allow the flavors to develop.

3 Garnish with the fennel fronds and serve.

fennel gratinée

I can't think of any vegetable that isn't delicious when prepared this way. You can even make this dish in advance and reheat in the oven before running it under the broiler to brown the top.

SERVES 4

2 tablespoons extra-virgin olive oil

4 fennel bulbs, trimmed and sliced

2 tablespoons butter

2 tablespoons unbleached all-purpose flour

1 cup milk

1 cup freshly grated Parmesan

Salt

Freshly grated nutmeg

A GLOWING REPORT

In 1824, the American consul in Florence sent fennel seeds to Thomas Jefferson at Monticello, along with this glowing report:

"The Fennel is beyond, every other vegetable, Delicious. It greatly resembles in appearance the largest size of Sellery, perfectly white, and there is no vegetable equals it in flavour. It is eaten at Dessert crude and with, or without Dry Salt, indeed I preferred it to every other vegetable, or to any fruit . . ."

1 Heat the oil in a medium saucepan over medium-high heat. Sauté the fennel until slightly softened, 4 to 5 minutes. Transfer the fennel to a 1½-quart gratin or baking dish and then cover to keep warm.

2 Preheat the broiler.

3 Melt the butter over medium heat in the same saucepan. Whisk in the flour and cook until the mixture is fragrant, about 2 minutes. Whisk in the milk and cook until smooth, stirring frequently. Add ½ cup of the Parmesan and season to taste with salt and nutmeg.

4 Pour the white sauce over the fennel. Top with the remaining ½ cup Parmesan.

5 Place the dish under the broiler and broil until the top is browned and bubbling, 3 to 4 minutes. Serve hot.

braised monkfish with fennel

Monkfish may not be the "poor man's lobster" as it has been described, but it is a sweet and mild fish, perfect for combining with sweet and mild fennel. This is a dish that demands a loaf of crusty French bread for sopping up the delicious pan juices.

SERVES 4

2–3 tablespoons extra-virgin olive oil
2 pounds monkfish fillets, trimmed and cut into 3-inch pieces
Salt and freshly ground black pepper, plus more to taste
2 fennel bulbs, trimmed and sliced
1 leek, thinly sliced, or 1 red bell pepper, cut into thin strips
4 garlic cloves, minced
½ cup dry white wine
1 can (15 ounces) diced tomatoes (do not drain)
½ teaspoon saffron threads, crumbled

1 Heat 2 tablespoons of the oil in a large skillet over medium-high heat. Season the fish with a generous pinch of salt and a few grinds of pepper, add in a single layer to the skillet, and sear on both sides until lightly colored, 2 to 3 minutes per side. Transfer the fish to a plate and keep warm. Repeat with remaining fish, if necessary.

2 Add the remaining tablespoon oil if necessary to coat the bottom of the pan. Add the fennel, leek, and garlic to the skillet and sauté until the vegetables soften, 4 to 5 minutes. Add the wine, tomatoes with their juice, saffron, and salt and pepper to taste. Place the fish in the skillet, cover, reduce the heat to low, and braise until the fish is tender and flakes easily with a fork, about 10 minutes.

3 Remove the fish and vegetables to a warmed serving platter. Bring the braising liquid to a boil and boil for a few minutes to reduce it. Spoon over the fish and serve.

Fennel's sweet flavor appears twice — in the vegetable and in the seasoning for the Italian sausage. Nonetheless, the effect is subtle and delicious. The sliced Florence fennel adds a nice crunch to the dish.

■ SERVES 4–6 ■

2–3 tablespoons extra-virgin olive oil

1 pound sweet or hot Italian sausage, removed from its casings

2 fennel bulbs, trimmed, quartered, and sliced, with 1 tablespoon fronds reserved

1 small onion, diced

1 can (28 ounces) Italian plum tomatoes with purée

¼ cup red wine

2 large garlic cloves, minced

Salt and freshly ground black pepper

1 pound ziti or other short pasta

Parmesan, for serving

1 Heat 2 tablespoons of the oil in a large saucepan over medium-high heat. Add the sausage and sauté, crumbling and breaking the meat up with a spoon, until meat has lost its pink color, about 8 minutes. Remove from the saucepan with a slotted spoon and drain on a plate lined with paper towels.

2 Add the additional tablespoon oil to the pan if it is dry. Add the fennel and onion and sauté until the fennel is tender-crisp, about 4 minutes. Return the sausage to the pan. Add the tomatoes, wine, garlic, and salt and pepper to taste. Reduce the heat to low and simmer while you prepare the pasta.

3 Bring a large pot of salted water to a boil. Add the pasta and cook until al dente. Remove about ½ cup of the pasta cooking water. Drain well.

4 Add the pasta to the sauce and mix well. Add as much of the reserved cooking water as needed if the pasta seems dry.

5 Transfer the pasta and sauce to a large serving bowl. Garnish with the reserved fennel fronds and serve, passing the Parmesan at the table.

FENNEL'S RELATIVES

Florence fennel, *Foeniculum vulgare* var. *azoricum,* is a biennial that is grown for its bulbs, which are actually not bulbs at all, but thickened leaf stems. It is very closely related to common, bronze, or wild fennel *(Foeniculum vulgare* var. *dulce),* which is grown and used as an herb. Common fennel is the variety from which the oval, greenish brown fennel seeds come. The seeds are used in both sweet and savory foods, such as fresh Italian sausage, as well as to flavor many liqueurs.

Common fennel can grow up 3 to 5 feet tall (Florence fennel will only grow up to 2 feet tall) and is extremely attractive to all manner of beneficial insects and butterflies. It also readily crosses with dill and is said to inhibit the growth of other members of the Umbelliferae family, especially carrots.

The seeds are used medicinally in teas to calm colicky babies and stimulate milk production in nursing mothers. The foliage is said to repel witches, if they are a problem for you.

The Garden Beauty Queen

IF THE APPEARANCE OF YOUR GARDEN is as important to you as the vegetables it produces, then okra should be included in your plan — whether or not you garden in the South. A close relative of the hibiscus, the plant produces showy yellow or rose flowers, and the pods grow upright like so many little torches. It is a spectacular-looking plant.

The objection many people have to okra is its texture — when cut, the pods exude a gelatinous (some say slimy) liquid. As always, it is the gardeners who have the advantage here. The younger the pods are when picked, the less slippery is the liquid inside the pods.

The one place the gardeners do not have the advantage is in the actual act of harvesting. Wearing long sleeves is a must — the leaves give many people a rash.

SOW & REAP

GROWING This warm-weather crop requires warm soil and full sun. Warm the soil with black plastic 3 to 4 weeks before transplanting or planting.

SOWING In colder climates, start plants indoors 4 to 6 weeks before the last frost date and set out plants 1 foot apart. In warm climates, sow directly.

CULTIVATING Water plants regularly and fertilize once a month with fish emulsion.

HARVESTING Pick when the pods are about 2 inches long and harvest daily to encourage the plants to keep producing pods.

OKRA MATH

1 pound okra = 8 cups whole
= 4 cups sliced

KITCHEN NOTES

When the harvest comes on, think Indian, Caribbean, African, and, of course, deep South. Vinegar and acidic vegetables, such as tomatoes, cut through the slippery liquid the pods exude. Okra adapts well to strong seasonings and is perfect in a stew, where it contributes a silken body to the cooking liquid. Pickling okra becomes almost inevitable, unless you can give some away. It is great to be able to pull out a jar of pickled okra to accompany a wintry couscous or curry.

TIMING

Sautéing: 5 to 10 minutes
Deep-frying: 3 minutes in oil heated to 365°F
Braising: 25 minutes
Roasting: 15 minutes at 425°F
Grilling: 8 to 10 minutes

sautéed okra with tomatoes

Okra and tomatoes are a classic combination — and this simple dish shows how right the two vegetables are for each other.

SERVES 4

2 tablespoons extra-virgin olive oil
1 pound okra, stems removed and pods sliced (4 cups)
1½ cups diced fresh or canned tomatoes
¼ cup chopped fresh basil
Salt and freshly ground black pepper

1 Heat the oil in a large saucepan over medium-high heat. Add the okra and sauté until the okra is tender and bright green, 3 to 4 minutes.

2 Stir in the tomatoes and simmer until the tomatoes are slightly broken down and heated through, 3 to 4 minutes. Stir in the basil and season with salt and pepper. Serve immediately.

WHAT'S IN A NAME?

Okra has more names than most vegetables. It has two Latin names: *Abelmoschus esculentus* and *Hibiscus esculentus*. It is also know as lady's fingers, gombo, gumbo, quingombo, okro, ochro, quiabo. In Spanish okra is *quibombo;* the French words are *gombo, bamia,* and *bamya;* in Hindi it is *bhindi;* and in the eastern Mediterranean and Arab countries, it is *bamies.*

The word *okra* probably derives from one of the Niger-Congo group of languages (the name for okra in the Twi language is *nkuruma*). The term *okra* was in use in English by the late 18th century.

oven-fried okra

Everything is better fried, but no one thinks it's a very good idea to make a steady diet of frying. Oven frying allows you to get similar results — without the mess of frying and without consuming a great deal of oil. The crumbs absorb the okra juices, taming the texture and making this an acceptable way to serve a troublesome vegetable, even to those who claim to hate okra.

■ SERVES 4 ■

2 tablespoons canola or peanut oil

1 pound okra, stems removed and pods sliced ¼ inch thick (4 cups)

½ cup dried bread crumbs

½ teaspoon salt

½ teaspoon dried thyme

½ teaspoon freshly ground black pepper

1 Preheat the oven to 425°F. Pour the oil onto a baking sheet and spread for an even coating.

2 Combine the okra, bread crumbs, salt, thyme, and pepper in a medium bowl. Toss until well coated. With a slotted spoon, transfer the okra to the baking sheet, shaking off the excess crumbs.

3 Bake for about 15 minutes, or until the okra is well browned and tender, turning once. Serve hot.

curried okra

Okra, known as bhindi *in Hindi, is quite common in India. Here's a typical way it is prepared. In India, where curry powder is not sold, garam masala is a spice blend. Although it can be made of different spices, it is rare to find choices in blends here. It will typically contain black pepper, cinnamon, cloves, coriander, cumin, cardamom, fennel, mace, and/or nutmeg. Look for garam masala wherever Indian foods or gourmet spices are sold.*

SERVES 4

3 tablespoons canola oil

1 teaspoon cumin seeds

2 onions, halved and thinly sliced

2 garlic clove, minced

2 teaspoons curry powder

1 pound okra, trimmed and sliced ½ inch thick (4 cups)

1 cup seeded and diced tomatoes

2 teaspoons garam masala

Salt and freshly ground black pepper

Cayenne

1 Heat the oil in a medium saucepan over medium heat. Add the cumin seeds and toast for about 10 seconds. Add the onions, garlic, and curry powder and sauté slowly until the onions are soft and golden, about 10 minutes.

2 Add the okra, tomatoes, and garam masala. Season with salt, pepper, and cayenne. Cover and cook over medium heat for about 20 minutes, until the okra is tender, stirring occasionally. Uncover and cook for 5 minutes longer.

3 Taste and adjust the seasoning. Serve hot.

Cajun spicing enlivens a combination of sausage and okra. The stew can be made in under an hour. It is terrific served on rice or with French bread.

SERVES 4

3 tablespoons extra-virgin olive oil

1 onion, diced

2 celery stalks, diced

1 green bell pepper, diced

1 chile of your choice, seeded and diced

3 garlic cloves, minced

1 pound Italian hot sausage, removed from its casings and crumbled

1 pound okra, trimmed and sliced

2 cups diced and seeded tomatoes

¼ cup chicken broth (page 9)

¼ cup chopped fresh parsley

2 tablespoons chopped fresh thyme

2 bay leaves

Salt and freshly ground black pepper

Cayenne or Louisiana-style hot sauce

1 Heat the oil over medium-high heat in a large skillet or saucepan. Add the onion, celery, bell pepper, chile, and garlic and sauté until the vegetables are slightly softened, about 3 minutes. Add the sausage and sauté until browned, about 8 minutes. Add the okra and sauté until coated with oil, about 3 minutes.

2 Stir in the tomatoes, broth, parsley, thyme, and bay leaves. Season with salt, pepper, and cayenne. Cover, reduce the heat, and simmer for 20 minutes, until the okra is tender, stirring occasionally.

3 Remove the bay leaves. Taste and adjust the seasoning. Serve hot.

gumbo

A specialty born of the Creole cooking of New Orleans, gumbo is a thick, stewlike soup, most often made with shellfish and sausage. It always begins with a dark roux, a well-cooked paste of flour and oil, which thickens the stew and adds a silky texture, as well as a deep, rich background flavor. This dish is a reason in itself to grow okra.

SERVES 6–8

1 tablespoon extra-virgin olive oil

1 onion, diced

1 green bell pepper, diced

2 celery stalks, thinly sliced

2 jalapeño chiles, seeded (optional) and diced

4 garlic cloves, minced

6 cups chicken broth (page 9)

1 pound okra, stems removed and pods sliced (4 cups)

1 pound andouille or other spicy smoked sausage, sliced

1½ cups seeded and diced tomatoes

¼ cup chopped fresh parsley

2 bay leaves

2 tablespoons fresh thyme leaves

½ teaspoon freshly ground black pepper, or to taste

½ teaspoon white pepper, or to taste

½ teaspoon cayenne, or to taste

Salt

¼ cup canola oil

¼ cup unbleached all-purpose flour

1 pound shrimp, shelled and deveined

Hot cooked rice

Filé powder

Louisiana-style hot sauce

OKRA HISTORY

Okra, a tropical plant, probably originated somewhere around Ethiopia, and was cultivated by the ancient Egyptians by the 12th century BC. Its cultivation spread throughout North Africa and the Middle East. Okra came to the Caribbean and the U.S. in the 1700s, probably brought by slaves from West Africa. In Louisiana, the Creoles learned from slaves the use of okra to thicken soups, and it is now an essential ingredient in the dish that is called gumbo.

1 Heat the olive oil in a large soup pot. Add the onion, bell pepper, celery, chiles, and garlic and sauté until the onion is limp, about 4 minutes.

2 Add the broth, okra, sausage, tomatoes, parsley, bay leaves, thyme, black pepper, white pepper, and cayenne. Season with salt. Bring to a boil, then simmer for about 30 minutes.

3 Meanwhile, in a large skillet, combine the canola oil and flour, stirring with a wooden spoon to make a smooth paste. Cook over medium-low heat until the paste is a rich brown, stirring frequently, for close to 30 minutes. Do not let the mixture burn. If it does, you must throw it out and start over again. This is the darkened roux that gives gumbo its characteristic flavor and color.

4 Carefully stir the roux into the gumbo, protecting your arms from hot spatters. Add the shrimp. Taste and adjust the seasonings. Simmer for another 15 minutes, until the shrimp are pink and firm.

5 Remove the bay leaves. Taste and adjust the seasoning. To serve, ladle the gumbo over rice in large soup bowls. Pass the filé powder and hot sauce at the table.

WHAT IS FILÉ POWDER?

Filé powder is used to thicken and flavor gumbo. It is made from the ground dried leaves of the sassafras tree. Cajun cooks adapted it from the Choctaw Indians of Louisiana as they adapted their rustic French cooking to bayou country. Today it can be found wherever there is an extensive choice of spices. It is stirred in after the dish has been removed from the heat and contributes a woodsy flavor.

They Weren't All Created Equal

MANY PEOPLE WILL TELL YOU that they don't care for shell beans. I used to say so myself. It turns out, I was mistaking my aversion to the frozen lima beans I was served as a child for all fresh shell beans. What a mistake!

Shell beans are the seeds of legumes that are harvested when still green. Regardless of variety, they share some cooking characteristics. But the flavors vary widely. It was fresh fava beans that changed my mind about all shell beans. Then I tasted green soybeans (edamame) and I fell in love.

I would make a habit of eating shell beans on a regular basis, if only the fresh shell bean season was not so brief.

And therein lies the whole problem of shell beans. Too many of us ate our first shell bean as an overcooked, underseasoned, once frozen lima. It is time to denounce frozen limas once and for all.

GROWING Shell beans are grown just as green beans are, but they are left to grow in the pod beyond the green bean stage. They are warm-weather plants, grown as bush beans or pole beans. Don't sow before the soil warms up, and give them full sun, moderately good soil, and plenty of water once the plants have flowered. Bush beans can be planted in beds. Pole beans need the support of a trellis or tepee. Plant groups of four to six beans around each pole with 16 inches between groups.

SOWING Sow when the soil temperature reaches 60°F. Make several plantings 10 days apart for a continual harvest throughout the summer.

CULTIVATING Water lightly and regularly from germination to flowering, then increase the amount of water through harvest. Avoid over-head watering, which wets the leaves and pro-motes diseases, such as bean rust. Fertilize young bean plants with an organic fertilizer, such as fish emulsion, every 2 weeks, then once every 3 to 4 weeks when the plants are full size.

HARVESTING Shell beans are harvested when they are fully mature but not yet beginning to dry. The pods will be fully colored and somewhat tough. They should feel lumpy, indicating that the seeds within are fully developed.

TIMING
Steaming: 5 to 35 minutes
Boiling: 5 to 25 minutes
Braising: 5 to 30 minutes

SHELL BEAN MATH
1 pound of beans in the pod = 2 to 2½ cups shelled beans

Shell beans will mature all at once, so unless you staggered the planting, you will have an abundance on your hands. You can store the beans in their pods in plastic bags in the refrigerator for just a few days. Once shelled, they will only keep for a day in the refrigerator. You can simmer most shell beans until just tender and keep them in their cooking liquid for a few days before adding them to a recipe. Soybeans boiled in their pods will keep for a few days in a plastic bag in the refrigerator.

There are more flavor differences among various types of shell beans than there are among types of green or snap beans, so it is worth trying a good selection.

All shell beans benefit from cooking in seasoned water. In addition to salt, flavor the cooking water with a diced onion, garlic, and herbs. Steaming shell beans works, but the skins tend to shrivel and you can't impart flavor.

To cook fava beans, shell them first. Cover with lightly salted water in a saucepan and bring to a boil. Boil for 5 to 10 minutes, until tender. Drain into a colander and run under cold water. Use a sharp knife to slice open the translucent skin of each bean and pop or squeeze the bean out of its skin.

Edamame are best boiled in their pods. They are very difficult to shell unless they are cooked first.

NUTRITION NOTES
All shell beans are good for you, being a particularly good source of B vitamins, protein, and fiber — but edamame is a superstar, nutrition-wise.

Edamame, or soybeans, are a rich source of isoflavones, compounds that may help to reduce cholesterol, fight cancer, and strengthen bones. They are also an excellent source of protein, fiber, and B vitamins. It is the only vegetable that contains all nine essential amino acids. This makes edamame a complete protein source, similar to meat and eggs.

edamame

If you've never tasted green soybeans boiled in the pod and then sprinkled with coarse salt, you will not believe how good they taste. You may even have bought the beans with good intentions, as I have done, then left them to rot in the vegetable drawer of your refrigerator. But just try them once; I guarantee that you will become a believer.

SERVES 4 OR 5 AS A SNACK OR APPETIZER

1 pound green soybeans in shell
1 tablespoon coarse sea salt

1 Rinse the soybean pods. Bring a large pot of water to a boil.

2 Add the soybeans still in the pods and boil for about 5 minutes, until the beans are tender and no longer taste raw. Drain well.

3 Place the beans in a serving bowl. Toss with the salt. Serve at room temperature, providing a bowl for the discarded pods. To eat, pop open a pod and bring the pod to your lips. Holding the pod at both ends, press the outside seam of the bean against your lips. Nibble the beans out of the pods, getting a little salt with them as you lick your lips. Or place a whole pod in your mouth and let your teeth squeeze the beans out of the pod, then discard the pod.

curry-spiced edamame

As good as salted edamame are, one can get tired of them. Here's a variation that will make your lips sing.

SERVES 4 OR 5 AS A SNACK OR APPETIZER

1 pound green soybeans in shell
1 tablespoon coarse sea salt
1 teaspoon curry powder
1 teaspoon garlic powder
¼ teaspoon ground cayenne

1 Rinse the soybean pods. Bring a large pot of water to a boil.

2 Add the soybeans still in the pods and boil for about 5 minutes, until the beans are tender and no longer taste raw. Drain well.

3 In a serving bowl, combine the salt, curry powder, garlic powder, and cayenne and mix well. Add the beans. Toss with the spice mixture. Serve at room temperature, providing a bowl for the discarded pods. To eat, pop open a pod, bring the pod to your lips, and nibble the beans out of the pods, getting a little spice with it as you lick your lips. Or place a whole pod in your mouth and let your teeth squeeze the beans out of the pod, then discard the pod.

Chili-Spiced Edamame Variation
Replace the curry-spice mixture with 1 tablespoon salt, 1 teaspoon chili powder, 1 teaspoon garlic powder, ½ teaspoon ground cumin, and ½ teaspoon cayenne.

rice and edamame salad

Anyone who suffered through the misguided brown rice and soybean loaves of the Diet for a Small Planet *days of the early '70s would be forgiven for looking askance at this recipe. But fear not, it is healthy, but delicious also. Such a high-protein, high-fiber main-dish salad makes great eating after a long hot day of gardening chores — or swimming.*

■ SERVES 4–6 ■

3 pounds green soybeans in the shell
2 cups white or brown rice, cooked and cooled
1 cup bean sprouts
1 carrot, grated
4 scallions, chopped
2 tablespoons chopped fresh cilantro

Dressing

5 tablespoons tamari
3 tablespoons rice wine vinegar
1 tablespoon mirin
1 tablespoon sugar
1 piece (1 inch long) fresh ginger, peeled and minced
1 garlic clove, minced
2 tablespoons dark sesame oil

1 Bring a large pot of water to a boil. Add the soybeans and cook until a test bean is tender, about 5 minutes. Drain, let cool, then shell. You should have about 3 cups.

2 Combine the rice with the soybeans, bean sprouts, carrot, scallions, and cilantro in a large salad bowl.

3 Combine the tamari, vinegar, mirin, sugar, ginger, and garlic in a small bowl. Whisk in the oil.

4 Pour the dressing over the salad and toss lightly. Serve at once.

sautéed shell beans with thyme

Thyme is my favorite seasoning for shell beans. The balsamic vinegar brings out the natural sweetness in the beans. This simple dish is a wonderful way to enjoy fresh shell beans.

SERVES 4

2 pounds fresh shell beans in the pods
2 tablespoons extra-virgin olive oil
1 shallot, minced
2 garlic cloves, minced
2 teaspoons chopped fresh thyme
1 teaspoon balsamic vinegar
Salt and freshly ground black pepper

1 Shell the beans. You should have 2 to 2½ cups. Place the beans in a medium saucepan and cover with lightly salted water. Cover the pot and bring to a boil over high heat. Reduce the heat and boil gently until the beans are completely tender: 8 to 10 minutes for small beans, 15 minutes for medium-size beans, and 20 to 30 minutes for large beans. Drain, reserving the cooking liquid.

2 Heat the oil in a large skillet. Add the shallot and garlic and sauté until the shallot is limp, about 2 minutes. Add the drained beans and thyme and toss to coat with the oil. Add ⅓ to ½ cup of the reserved cooking liquid and the vinegar and bring to a boil.

3 Remove from the heat and season to taste with the salt and pepper. Serve hot.

"EVERYBODY GARDENS IN ALASKA," garden writer Jeff Lowenfels tells me. But not everybody thinks as creatively or originally as Lowenfels, the originator of the remarkably successful Plant a Row for the Hungry program.

"I was in Washington, D.C., walking with my hands in my pockets, and it was cold, like ten below zero. I had just eaten at this very fancy restaurant and I was heading back to my very nice hotel and my nice warm bed when a man approached me. He asked if I would give him some money so he could get something to eat. I'd read the signs that said not to give money to panhandlers because it just encourages them, and I knew there were plenty of services available to homeless people. So I shook my head and kept walking. The guy walked along beside me and said, 'I really am homeless and I really am hungry. You can come with me and watch me eat!' But I kept on walking, even though I had coins in my pocket.

"The incident bothered me for the rest of the week. I felt really bad. And on the flight home to Anchorage, I came up with idea of suggesting to the readers of my column that everybody should plant an extra row in the garden for the hungry. It guess it was a way to assuage my guilt. I called my idea 'Plant a Row for Bean's.'" Bean's Café is a soup kitchen in Anchorage that feeds hundreds of hungry Alaskans every day.

The idea took off. Then, in 1995, the Garden Writers Association of America held its annual convention in Anchorage, and Lowenfels pitched the idea of the garden writers taking his idea and making it into a national program. The idea was to have every member of the Garden Writers Association of America write or talk about planting a row for the hungry sometime during the month of April. And they did. Since then millions of pounds of food have been donated to food banks and soup kitchens directly from small-scale gardeners as a result of Lowenthal's simple idea:

"It's just a natural. There's a certain time in the spring and everyone goes out and buys their six-packs of plants and plants them. Then everything is ready for harvest at the same time. Gardeners always have extra, and they like to share." He is proud that his program takes place throughout the country with no help from the government.

Lowenfels is no stranger to the concept of sharing. He quips that his garden is shared with the moose that roam freely in his yard. He has learned to hide his vegetables among perennial flowers and to grow in hanging baskets. "Anywhere to fool the moose," he explains.

He is also keen to sharing his gardening information through his column in the *Anchorage Daily News*. Lowenfels writes the longest running gardening column in America — it has been running for 29 years. He is currently writing a book about manipulating the science behind organic gardening to increase soil productivity.

As for Plant a Row for the Hungry, it has been written about by garden writers all over the country and even included in the book *Chicken Soup for the Gardener's Soul*.

If you would like to participate, here's what you can do:

1. Plant an extra row in your garden, no matter its size.

2. Plant vegetables and fruits that travel and keep well. Broccoli, cabbage, carrots, peas, green beans, tomatoes, sweet peppers, eggplants, summer squash (including zucchini), winter squash, onions, beets, apples, and pears are all good candidates. Herbs are also welcome.

3. Harvest and thoroughly clean the produce.

4. Contact your local food bank, soup kitchen, church, social agency, or Salvation Army to donate the fresh produce.

Fava beans are particularly delicious prepared in this simple way. But if you are using them, remember that they probably need to be skinned after they are blanched. Test a bean by slitting open the skin and squeezing out a bean. If a brilliant green bean pops out of a rubbery translucent skin, then skin them all. If, on the other hand, the skin is barely perceptible and resists your best efforts to remove it, don't bother.

SERVES 4

2 pounds fresh shell beans in the pods

2 tablespoons extra-virgin olive oil

2 shallots or 2 garlic cloves, minced

¼ cup vegetable or chicken broth (page 8 or 9), or 2 tablespoons white wine and 2 tablespoons water

2 tablespoons chopped fresh herbs (basil, oregano, thyme, parsley, alone or in any combination)

Salt and freshly ground black pepper

1 Shell the beans. You should have 2 to 2½ cups. Place the beans in a medium saucepan and cover with lightly salted water. Cover the pot and bring to a boil over high heat. Reduce the heat and boil gently until the beans are barely tender: 5 to 25 minutes. Drain.

2 Heat the oil in a medium saucepan over medium heat. Add the shallots and sauté until limp, about 2 minutes. Add the beans, broth, and herbs. Season with salt and pepper. Simmer, covered, until the beans are completely tender, about 5 minutes. Serve hot.

WHAT'S IN A NAME?

Edamame is a soybean, harvested at the shell bean stage when the beans are still green and succulent. The word *edamame* means "beans on branches" in Japanese because the beans grow in clusters on bushes.

simple succotash

The secret to a great succotash is to infuse fresh shell beans with great flavor, which you can never do with frozen beans. Then fold in the sweetest, crispest corn you can find and barely cook it. The result is a dish rich in flavor and texture contrasts — nothing at all like the dish you get when you work with frozen vegetables. This dish has the potential to eliminate the phrase "sufferin' succotash" from our vocabulary.

SERVES 4–6

1 cup freshly shelled beans (such as cranberry beans, green soybeans, or lima)

1 small onion, finely chopped

1 cup water

3 tablespoons dry white wine

1 tablespoon butter

1 tablespoon chopped fresh thyme

Salt and freshly ground black pepper

Kernels stripped from 6 ears corn

1 Combine the beans, onion, water, wine, butter, and thyme in a medium saucepan. Bring to a boil, cover, reduce the heat, and simmer until the beans are tender, 10 to 25 minutes. Doneness will depend on the variety of bean; beans should be completely cooked through and tender.

2 Stir in the corn and cook until just barely heated through, about 2 minutes. Taste and season with salt and pepper. Serve immediately.

Shrimp and shell beans make a fine combination, but feel free to substitute other quicker-cooking vegetables, including green beans. Peas are terrific, too, but if the peas are fresh, then you'll have to use canned tomatoes. I have especially enjoyed this made with green soybeans (boiled in the pods for 5 to 10 minutes, then shelled).

SERVES 4

2 pounds shell beans in the pod, shelled (about 2 cups)
1 tablespoon fresh thyme leaves or 1 teaspoon dried
1 teaspoon salt, plus more to taste
¼ teaspoon freshly ground black pepper, plus more to taste
⅓ cup extra-virgin olive oil
1 onion, minced
1 carrot, minced
1 celery stalk, minced
4 garlic cloves, minced
1½ pounds shrimp, shelled and deveined
3 tablespoons vegetable or chicken broth (page 8 or 9)
2 tablespoons dry sherry
2 large tomatoes or 4 plum tomatoes, diced (about 2 cups)
2 tablespoons minced fresh parsley
Hot cooked rice
Salt and pepper

1 Combine the beans, thyme, 1 teaspoon salt, ¼ teaspoon pepper, and water to cover in a small saucepan. Bring to a boil, then reduce the heat, cover, and simmer until the beans are tender, 10 to 30 minutes. Set aside.

2 In a large skillet or Dutch oven, heat the olive oil over medium heat. Add the onion, carrot, celery, and garlic and sauté until fragrant, about 2 minutes. Add the shrimp and sauté until the shrimp are firm and pink, about 5 minutes.

3 Drain the beans.

4 Stir the beans, broth, sherry, tomatoes, and parsley into the shrimp and cook for another 2 minutes. Season with salt and pepper. Serve over hot rice.

Cranberry Beans These beans are called horticultural beans and shell-outs in various parts of the United States. In Italy they are called borlotti beans. Tongues of fire is a very closely related bean. The flavor is mild, and some would describe it as similar to that of a chestnut. This is an excellent choice for succotash.

Black-Eyed Peas These are also known as black-eyed suzies, black-eyed beans, Southern peas, lady peas, cream peas, brown-eyed peas, and crowder peas. These beans are very closely related to mung beans and probably originated in China. They came to the United States through the African slave trade and are most popular in the South. This is the traditional bean to use in hopping John.

Edamame Edamame, also called butterbeans and green soybeans, are particularly tasty. The butterbean name is actually quite apt; they are buttery and rich tasting. If you have bad memories of dried soybeans tasting like dirty socks, put that taste sensation away. Fresh edamame tastes nothing like that nasty flavor.

Fava Beans The robust, earthy flavor of these beans makes them a perfect match for peppery olive oil, strongly flavored herbs, and full-flavored cheeses. The simplest way to enjoy them is to boil them until tender, then toss with quality olive oil, fresh lemon juice, and garlic. Fava beans are also known as broad beans, horse beans, and Windsor beans. This is an ancient bean, dating back to the Bronze Age.

Lima Beans Limas have a buttery flavor, which makes them a match for serving simply with butter and salt and pepper. There are two distinctively different varieties: large limas (*Phaseolus limensis*) and small limas (*Phaseolus lunatus*). Small limas, also known as butter beans and baby limas, are thinner skinned and less starchy than large limas. They are also more heat- and humidity resistant. Both types of limas originated in Peru.

A Real Headliner

VEGETABLES DON'T USUALLY MAKE headline news, but the sweet potato grabbed the media spotlight when the Center for Science in the Public Interest ranked the sweet potato as the single most nutritious vegetable in the world. They urged people to forget about those marshmallow-topped holiday casseroles and to start giving the sweet potato its proper place in everyday diets.

One baked sweet potato contains only 140 calories, yet provides twice the recommended daily allowance of vitamin A and almost half the needed vitamin C. It is an excellent source of calcium, iron, and thiamin. Sweet potatoes are low in sodium and a good source of fiber — with the skin, a sweet potato has more fiber than a bowl of oatmeal. In a report on a 2-year research study on diet and cancer by the National Academy of Sciences, sweet potatoes were cited as one of the top four cancer-fighting foods. With endorsements like these, it is easy to see why sweet potatoes are attracting our attention.

Have you had your sweet potato today?

GROWING Sweet potatoes need a long growing season, but there are some 90-day varieties that can be grown even in the North. Most varieties are ready to harvest 3 to 4 months after planting. None withstands frost damage. The soil should be fertile, slightly acidic (pH 5.6 to 6.5), very loose, and raised in hills or ridges to give the roots room to swell and expand.

SOWING Sow rooted cuttings in loose, fertile soil 2 weeks after the last average frost date. Most people start their own rooted cuttings, or slips, from store-bought sweet potatoes. But northern growers may want to look specifically for Centennial, Georgia Jet, and Vardaman, which are ready for harvest in 90 days.

CULTIVATING Avoid fertilizing healthy plants; too much nitrogen will reduce the yield and produce long, thin roots. Sweet potatoes require full sun and small amounts of watering.

HARVESTING To harvest, cut back the vines and lift the roots from the ground with a garden fork, taking care to avoid piercing the skins. Wash and enjoy them within the next month or so, or cure them for long-term storage. To cure sweet potatoes, let them sit in the sun for a day, then move them to a shady area that remains above 80°F for 7 to 10 days. If properly cured, the sweet potatoes will store well for about 6 months in a root cellar or similar cool, humid environment.

Like Irish potatoes, raw sweet potato flesh will discolor if exposed to the air for too long. So if you want to slice the potatoes awhile before cooking, it is a good idea to hold them in a pan of cold water until you are ready to cook. Then drain the potatoes and pat dry with a clean kitchen towel.

Whenever a recipe calls for cooked or mashed sweet potatoes, bake them for best flavor. Using a microwave may be faster, but flavor is sacrificed. Sweet potatoes can be baked for 1 hour at 400°F. Remove and let stand for 5 to 10 minutes. The skins will peel off easily. Pack into a dry measuring cup with a fork.

Grilled sweet potatoes are delicious but tricky. Slice them about ⅜ inch thick so they will cook through. Grill over a low or medium fire; if they start to char, move the slices to the cooler regions of the grill.

TIMING
Steaming: 10 to 12 minutes for cubes
Boiling: 5 to 10 minutes for cubes
Baking: 45 to 60 minutes for whole potatoes at 350°F
Roasting: 15 minutes for diced sweet potatoes at 500°F
Grilling: 10 to 15 minutes sliced ⅜ inch thick
Braising: 35 minutes for slices

SWEET POTATO MATH
1 pound sweet potatoes = 2⅓ cups diced
= 3 cups sliced
= 4 cups grated
1 large sweet potato = 2 cups sliced
= 1½ cups cubed
= 2½ to 3 cups grated
1 large sweet potato (baked) = 1 cup mashed

roasted sweet potato salad with sesame-lime vinaigrette

Were sweet potatoes developed just for the moment they were married to a sesame-lime dressing? The combination of flavors — sweet, salty, sour — and textures — soft and crunchy — is in perfect harmony in this salad. This is a terrific salad that holds up well at a picnic or on a buffet table. If you like, bed it in a nest of sharp-tasting greens to add yet another level of flavor and texture.

SERVES 4–6

2 pounds sweet potatoes, peeled and diced

2 tablespoons canola oil

Salt and freshly ground black pepper

1 red bell pepper, diced

4 scallions, white and tender green parts, sliced on the diagonal, or 1 sweet onion, halved and sliced

3 tablespoons chopped fresh cilantro, plus more to taste

Sesame-Lime Vinaigrette

1 piece ginger, 1 inch long, peeled and sliced

1 garlic clove

¼ cup fresh lime juice, plus more to taste

3 tablespoons canola oil

1 tablespoon dark sesame oil

1 tablespoon fish sauce

1 teaspoon sugar

Salt and freshly ground black pepper

note Tossing a salad with two rubber spatulas is a good way to handle fragile ingredients, such as roasted sweet potatoes.

1 Preheat the oven to 500°F. Lightly grease a large sheet pan (preferred) or a large shallow roasting pan with oil.

2 Combine the sweet potatoes, oil, and salt and pepper to taste in a large bowl. Toss to coat. Arrange the sweet potatoes in a single layer in the prepared pan. Do not crowd the potatoes, or the final texture will be too mushy.

3 Roast in the lower third of the oven for about 15 minutes, until the potatoes are tender, stirring or shaking the pan once for even cooking.

4 While the potatoes roast, make the dressing. Combine the ginger and garlic in a blender and finely chop. Add the lime juice, canola oil, sesame oil, fish sauce, and sugar and process until well mixed. Season with salt and pepper.

5 Combine the roasted potatoes, red pepper, scallions, and cilantro in a large salad bowl. Toss gently to mix. Pour in the dressing and toss gently until fully mixed. Taste and add salt, pepper, lime juice, or cilantro as needed. Serve warm or at room temperature.

SWEET POTATO CULTIVARS

Which one makes the best baked potato? What's a good choice for a muffin? Here's a run-down on the varieties and their cooking properties.

Jersey, Hanna, and Golden Sweet are yellow-fleshed, fairly dry, and not overly sweet. These are a good choice to use for whipped potatoes, purées, and soufflés.

Garnet, Jewel, Centennial, Beauregard, Hernandez, and Darby are moist types, suited for all kinds of cooking and baking. Of these, Garnet is a favorite for its rich flavor.

Nancy Hall, a popular yellow sweet potato, is also delicious baked.

seasoned sweet potato oven fries

Restaurants are now serving sweet potato fries, and most people who dare to try them love them. But why bother with deep-frying when you can oven-fry? Just be sure to roast them in a very hot oven, and use a large pan. If you want to make more, it is better to roast in batches than to crowd the pan. The spices add just the right panache to the sweet potato flavor, making a ketchup or mustard sauce irrelevant.

■ SERVES 2–4 ■

4 medium sweet potatoes

2 tablespoons canola oil

1 teaspoon garlic salt

½ teaspoon ground cumin

½ teaspoon salt, or more to taste

¼ teaspoon ground chipotle chile (or substitute another ground chile)

¼ teaspoon freshly ground black pepper

⅛ teaspoon ground allspice

Coarse sea salt (optional)

1 Preheat the oven to 500°F. Lightly grease a large sheet pan (preferred) or shallow roasting pan with oil.

2 Peel the potatoes and cut each into sticks about ¼-inch thick. Combine the oil, garlic salt, cumin, salt, ground chipotle, black pepper, and allspice in a large bowl and mix well. Add the potatoes and toss to coat. Arrange the potatoes in a single layer on the prepared pan.

3 Place the baking sheet on a rack in the lower third of the oven. Roast for about 20 to 30 minutes, until the potatoes are well browned and crisp, turning once or twice, and shaking the pan for even cooking. (The timing will depend on how crowded the pan is.)

4 Briefly drain on paper towels to blot excess oil. Taste and sprinkle with salt, if using. Serve hot.

WHAT'S IN A NAME?

Sweet potatoes were discovered in the New World and were known by the Taino Indians as *batata*. The name came to be translated into the Spanish *patata*, the French *patate*, and the English *potato*. When it came to give the new plant a scientific name, Carolus Linnaeus, the 18th-century Swedish botanist who created the widely adopted system of plant classification, called the new vegetable *Ipomoea batata* from the Greek *ips* ("worm") and *homoios* (which means like). Apparently he thought the twining vines that grow underground look like worms.

miso-glazed sweet potatoes

A tombstone in Japan bears the inscription, "The Grave of Professor Sweet Potatoes," commemorating the life work of Kon-yo Aoki, who died in 1771, the George Washington Carver of sweet potatoes in Japan. He introduced sweet potatoes to his country as food for the poor, figuring that sweet potatoes were twice as nutritious as rice, acre for acre. Today, sweet potatoes are still popular in Japan. Miso is, of course, a basic flavoring ingredient in Japan. Made from fermented soy and a grain, it comes in many colors and flavors. Miso lasts forever in the refrigerator. It is found wherever Japanese foods and health foods are sold.

SERVES 4–6

2 tablespoons canola oil

2 tablespoons mirin

1 tablespoon tamari

1 tablespoon yellow or red miso

2 teaspoons pickled (sushi) ginger, minced

3 pounds sweet potatoes, peeled and diced

Salt and freshly ground black pepper

1 Preheat the oven to 475°F. Lightly grease a large sheet pan (preferred) or shallow roasting pan with oil.

2 Combine the oil, mirin, tamari, and miso in a large bowl. Whisk to combine. Stir in the ginger. Add the sweet potatoes and toss with a rubber spatula to coat well. Transfer the potatoes to the prepared pan.

3 Roast for 15 to 20 minutes, stirring occasionally, until the sweet potatoes are tender.

4 Season generously with salt and pepper and serve hot.

best-ever mashed sweet potatoes

Hats off to the tireless testers at Cook's Illustrated, *who developed this method of braising sweet potatoes in butter to produce potatoes that are rich and flavorful with perfect texture. Quite simply, there is no better way to make mashed sweet potatoes, and the method is as easy as it is exquisite. The potatoes taste best if you use cream, but milk is just fine to use if you don't want to indulge in the cream.*

SERVES 4

4 tablespoons butter

2 tablespoons light cream, heavy cream, or whole milk

1 tablespoon pure maple syrup, or more as needed

1 teaspoon salt, or more as needed

2 pounds sweet potatoes, peeled, quartered lengthwise, and thinly sliced

Freshly ground black pepper

The sweet potato shares a name with the white potato, but that's about all. The sweet potato is a member of the morning glory family. A true root vegetable, the sweet potato plant forms roots, which store food and swell to form the spuds. The white potato, by contrast, forms tubers along underground stems.

1 Combine the butter, cream, syrup, salt, and sweet potatoes in a saucepan. Cover and cook over low heat, stirring occasionally, until the potatoes are quite tender and fall apart as you stir, about 35 minutes.

2 Remove the pan from the heat and mash the potatoes with a potato masher. Whip with a whisk or spoon. Season with pepper, taste, and adjust the seasoning. Transfer to a serving dish and serve hot.

sweet potato pie with praline topping

Here's a real American combination — both sweet potatoes and pecans are indigenous to the Americas. This is a great choice at holiday time for those who can't choose between the sweet potato (or pumpkin) pie and the pecan pie.

SERVES 6–8

Unbaked pastry for a single-crust 9- or 10-inch pie (page 10)

2 cups cooked mashed sweet potatoes (about 2 medium sweet potatoes)

⅓ cup light brown sugar

3 tablespoons bourbon or dark rum

1 teaspoon ground cinnamon

½ teaspoon ground ginger

½ teaspoon salt

¼ teaspoon freshly grated nutmeg

2 large eggs

1½ cups (12 ounces) evaporated milk

Topping

¼ cup butter

½ cup dark brown sugar

1 tablespoon milk

1 teaspoon pure vanilla extract

⅓ cup whole pecans

1 Preheat the oven to 425°F.

2 Line a 9- or 10-inch pie pan with the prepared pastry, trimming and fluting the edges according to the recipe instructions. Place in the refrigerator for at least 30 minutes.

3 Combine the sweet potatoes, brown sugar, rum, cinnamon, ginger, salt, and nutmeg in a large bowl and beat until smooth. Beat in the eggs and evaporated milk. Pour into the pie shell.

4 Place the pie on the lower third of the oven and bake for 10 minutes. Reduce the heat to 350°F and continue baking for 25 minutes.

5 To make the topping, melt the butter in a small skillet over medium heat. Add the sugar and stir until melted. Cook, without stirring, for 3 minutes. Remove from the heat and beat in the milk and vanilla. Stir in the pecans. Spoon the topping evenly over the pie. Increase the heat to 375°F and continue baking for another 10 minutes, until the pie is mostly set. (It will continue to cook after it is removed from the oven.)

6 Cool the pie on a rack for about 30 minutes before serving warm, or chill and then serve.

SWEET POTATOES EVERYWHERE

In the United States, when food scientists need to manufacture a sweetener or a thickener, they are likely to turn to corn, our staple crop. Elsewhere, food scientists turn to the sweet potato. In Peru, sweet potatoes are made into starch, flour, bread, and chips. In the Philippines, they are made into ketchup, jam, juice, powdered soup, and ice cream. In Japan, sweet potatoes are made into sweet caramels and toffees, syrup, four kinds of noodles, and a type of liquor.

coconut–sweet potato pie

For those who fear piecrust, here's a crust that is pressed into the pan. It is a rich combination of pastry and coconut. There is also coconut and coconut milk in the filling.

■ SERVES 6 ■

Crust

1⅓ cups unbleached all-purpose flour
2 tablespoons granulated sugar
½ teaspoon salt
6 tablespoons butter, cut into pieces
¼ cup sweetened flaked coconut
1 large egg yolk
2 tablespoons cold water

Filling

2 cups cooked mashed sweet potatoes
2 large eggs
1¼ cups low-fat or regular coconut milk
⅓ cup sugar
1 teaspoon pure vanilla extract
1 teaspoon ground cinnamon
½ teaspoon ground ginger
½ teaspoon salt
¼ cup sweetened flaked coconut

1 Preheat the oven to 425°F.

2 To make the crust, combine the flour, sugar, and salt in a food processor and pulse to mix. Add the butter and pulse until the mixture resembles coarse crumbs. Pulse in the coconut. With the motor running, add the egg yolk and water and process until the mixture forms a ball.

3 Pat the dough into a 9-inch pie pan. Make a fluted rim at the top edge of the crust.

4 To make the filling, combine the sweet potatoes, eggs, coconut milk, sugar, vanilla, cinnamon, ginger, and salt in a food processor and process until smooth. Pour into the crust. Sprinkle the coconut over the top.

5 Bake for 10 minutes. Lower the heat to 300°F and continue to bake for 50 minutes, until the filling is firm and set. Serve warm or cooled.

SWEET POTATO HOUSEPLANTS

Sweet potatoes are so versatile, they even make attractive houseplants. Just place a sweet potato in a jar of water with the narrow end down. Put the jar in a warm dark place and keep the jar filled with water. New roots will start to grow, and in about 10 days the stem will start to grow. As soon as the stem emerges, put the jar in a sunny window. As the vine grows, it can be left to trail or trained to climb. The sweet potato will provide the plant with food for quite a while. But to keep the plant alive indefinitely, add plant food to the water or replant in potting soil.

The Stars of Summer

WHAT FOOD LOVER DOESN'T LOOK FORWARD to summer as tomato season? Though summer also means perfumed melons, pungent pesto, and honey-sweet fresh corn, no summer flavor beats that first ripe red tomato, eaten out of hand like an apple, salt shaker in the other hand, juices running down the chin. Even gardeners who have nothing more than a square foot of sunshine on an urban balcony are more likely to grow tomatoes than any other vegetables. With the resurgence and availability of seeds and seedlings of heirloom tomatoes, tomato flavor has never been better.

GROWING Tomatoes are a heat-loving crop that do best in light, fertile soil with moderate to heavy watering during growth and less watering during harvest. Indeterminant tomato plants should be supported with trellises or stakes.

SOWING Sow indoors 6 to 7 weeks before the last frost. Transplant to the garden when all danger of frost is past. Successive transplanting into larger pots creates stronger seedlings. Harden off before transplanting to the garden. Dig a 6-inch hole and plant deep enough so only about 4 inches of the plant will be above the soil. Clip off any leaves that will be buried.

CULTIVATING Brush the plants lightly with your hand twice a day to promote stronger plants. Fertilize every 2 to 3 weeks with compost tea or fish emulsion. Mulch well. Prune suckers to direct growth to the main stem. When the plant reaches the top of the support, begin pruning back the tops.

HARVESTING The best tomatoes are harvested when the skin of the tomato yields slightly to pressure. If you must harvest unripe tomatoes to spare them from frost, pull the whole plant by the roots and hang it in a frost-free shed, porch, or cold attic. Or harvest the tomatoes by the branch, leaving the tomatoes still attached to the plant. Arrange the tomatoes in a single layer upon layers of newspaper in a cold, unheated room. Check the tomatoes for ripening often. You should continue to have fresh tomatoes from your garden for another 4 weeks or so.

For most recipes, washing, coring, then slicing or cutting the tomatoes into chunks is all the preparation that is required. Peeling isn't necessary if you are going to use the tomatoes raw in salads or salsas. In cooked dishes, you may or may not notice the skins. To peel tomatoes, drop them into a pot of boiling water for 15 to 30 seconds. Use a slotted spoon to transfer them to a bowl of ice water and let cool for about 1 minute. Then remove the skin with a pairing knife.

To seed a tomato, cut it in half horizontally. Then gently squeeze each half to release the seeds. Don't worry if a few seeds remain.

If you freeze tomatoes, tomato sauces, or salsas, defrost the frozen product in a colander set over a bowl to collect the excess liquid. Return back to the dish as much liquid as needed and discard the rest (or add to soups and broths).

TIMING

Sautéing: 5 to 10 minutes
Broiling: about 10 minutes
Roasting: 2 hours at 350°F for plum tomato halves, 20 minutes at 425°F for cherry tomatoes
Grilling: 6 to 8 minutes for slices, 5 minutes for cherry tomatoes

TOMATO MATH

1 pound fresh tomatoes = 3 cups sliced
= 1¾ cups diced

fresh salsa

It's not the recipe that makes a great salsa, it's using the best-tasting vine-ripened tomatoes and tasting and adjusting to get the right balance of sweet, hot, and savory flavors. Chop the tomatoes by hand. The other ingredients can be chopped by hand or in a food processor. The chile you choose will contribute the heat; I leave it up to you to choose your favorite variety. When in doubt, jalapeño is usually a good choice.

MAKES 2 CUPS

2 cups seeded and finely chopped tomatoes

¼ cup finely chopped scallions, white and tender green parts

¼ cup finely chopped fresh chile, such as jalapeño (seeded if desired)

¼ cup finely chopped green or red bell pepper

2 tablespoons finely chopped fresh cilantro

1–2 tablespoons fresh lime juice

Salt and freshly ground black pepper

Sugar (optional)

1 Mix together the tomatoes, scallions, chile, bell pepper, cilantro, 1 tablespoon of the lime juice, and the salt and pepper.

2 Let sit for 15 to 30 minutes. Taste and adjust the seasonings, adding sugar to taste, if using, and more lime juice, and salt and pepper, if desired.

tomato bruschetta

Bruschetta (pronounced broo-SKET-tah) in its simplest form is simply toasted bread, which is often rubbed with garlic and drizzled with olive oil. It was originally developed as a way to serve slightly stale, or day-old, bread. When bruschetta is topped with tomatoes or other garden vegetables, it becomes a meal in itself — or at least an appetizer.

SERVES 4–6

2–3 large tomatoes, diced

4 large basil leaves, sliced into ribbons

Salt and freshly ground black pepper

12 slices French or Italian country-style bread, sliced about ⅓ inch thick

3–4 garlic cloves, halved and slightly crushed

¼–⅓ cup olive oil

Shaved Parmesan or crumbled goat cheese (optional)

Pepper Bruschetta Variation
Replace the tomatoes with Marinated Roasted Peppers (page 216) and prepare as above.

1 Prepare a medium fire in a charcoal or gas grill, or preheat the broiler.

2 Combine the tomatoes and basil in a medium bowl. Season with salt and pepper and set aside.

3 Toast the bread over the fire or under a broiler until very lightly colored but still soft. Rub one side of each slice with the garlic.

4 Drizzle each slice with 1 to 1½ teaspoons oil. Using a slotted spoon, top each slice with a spoonful of tomatoes.

5 Serve as is, or top each slice with a little cheese.

tomato-mozzarella salad

We live down the road from a pair of tomato growers, which is more unusual than it sounds, considering we live in a tiny mountaintop town. Mia and Freeman Allen, at Mountainyard Farm, grow their tomatoes in greenhouses and have the earliest tomatoes in these parts. I don't know if I could get through the summer without those fresh, local tomatoes, since my first tomato harvest may be as late as mid-August and my first frost can be as early as late August. This salad, with or without the mozzarella, shows up regularly at any potluck Mia attends. Because it is such a simple combination of ingredients, this is the time to use your very best olive oil and very best vinegar.

■ SERVES 4–6 ■

3 large juicy ripe tomatoes, sliced
8 ounces fresh mozzarella, sliced
8 large basil leaves, torn
½ red or sweet onion, thinly sliced
2 tablespoons extra-virgin olive oil
1 tablespoon best-quality sherry, balsamic, or red wine vinegar
Sea salt and coarsely ground black pepper

Fan the tomatoes and mozzarella in alternating slices on a platter. Sprinkle the basil and onion on top. Drizzle with the oil, then the vinegar. Season generously with salt and pepper and serve.

TOMATO CULTIVAR TASTING NOTES

Now that many heirloom tomato varieties are regularly available at many farmers' markets, it is possible to conduct a cultivar tasting at home, selecting a number of tomatoes and comparing one to another. But a word of caution: I conducted a tasting one year with tomatoes gathered at a farmers' market. Most of the tomatoes tasted waterlogged and bland. The weather had been rainy and cool, and these tomatoes were not at full flavor. Green Zebra, Brandywine, and Purple Cherokee were standouts. The rest were disappointing, pointing to the importance of soil, soil, soil — and climate.

everyday
tomato-cucumber salad

This salad makes an appearance at our table almost every night during the height of the tomato season. It can be varied to suit most main courses, and it is always welcome. If the mood is Mediterranean, then the herb may be oregano, basil, mint, or a combination of all three. If the mood is Mexican or Southeast Asian, the herb may be cilantro. If the cucumbers are more plentiful than the tomatoes, they might dominate the salad, or vice versa — there are no hard-and-fast rules.

SERVES 4

3–4 cups diced tomatoes or halved cherry tomatoes

3–4 cups diced cucumbers (peeled and seeded, if desired)

2 scallions, white and tender green parts, chopped, or ¼ red or Vidalia onion, sliced

Salt and freshly ground black pepper

3 tablespoons extra-virgin olive oil

1 tablespoon red or white wine vinegar, sherry vinegar, balsamic vinegar, herbal vinegar, or freshly squeezed lemon juice

¼ cup chopped fresh herbs (basil, chervil, cilantro, lovage, mint, oregano, parsley, summer savory, alone or in combination)

1 Combine the tomatoes, cucumbers, and scallions in a salad bowl. Season generously with salt and pepper.

2 Add the oil and vinegar and toss gently. Add the herbs and toss again. Let stand for at least 10 minutes before serving.

tomato–shell bean salad with goat cheese

Crunchy croutons and smooth goat cheese, sweet tomatoes, bitter greens, and unctuous olive oil — this salad has it all. It makes a wonderful main course for three, but can be stretched to serve six as a first course. If you don't have the exact ingredients called for in the recipe, use what you have on hand.

■ SERVES 3–6 ■

1–2 cups fresh shelled beans, preferably favas (1–2 pounds in the pod)

6 tablespoons extra-virgin olive oil

2 garlic cloves, halved

3 cups bread cubes (about 4 slices)

Salt and freshly ground black pepper

6 cups cherry tomatoes (a mixture of colors is recommended), halved

3 scallions, white and tender green parts, finely chopped

1 tablespoon red wine or sherry vinegar

3 cups mixed greens

8 ounces soft goat cheese, crumbled (optional)

Chopped basil leaves, for garnishing

1 Blanch fresh favas in boiling water for about 1 minute. Lift out, drop into cold water to cool, then drain. Peel the beans by pinching the skin and popping out the beans.

2 Cook the beans in plenty of boiling salted water until just tender, 5 to 15 minutes. The timing will depend on the size and freshness of the beans, so start testing after 5 minutes. Drain, plunge into cold water to stop the cooking, and drain again.

3 Warm 4 tablespoons of the oil and the garlic in a large skillet over medium heat for 5 minutes. Do not allow the garlic to brown. Remove the garlic with a slotted spoon and discard.

4 Increase the heat under the skillet to medium-high. Add the bread cubes, sprinkle with salt and pepper, and sauté until golden on all sides, stirring frequently, about 5 minutes. Remove from the skillet with a slotted spoon and transfer to paper towels to blot up excess oil and let cool.

5 Add the beans to the skillet and sauté until flavored with the garlic oil and warm, about 2 minutes.

6 Combine the tomatoes, beans, and scallions in a large bowl. Drizzle the remaining 2 tablespoons olive oil and the vinegar over the tomato mixture and season with more salt and pepper. Toss gently. Continue with the recipe or cover and hold for up to 1 hour.

7 Just before serving, arrange the greens on a serving platter. Mix the croutons into the tomatoes. Spoon the tomato mixture over the greens. Dot with the crumbled goat cheese, if using, and garnish with the basil. Serve at once.

Variations

Instead of fava beans or other shell beans, you can substitute green beans or zucchini. Green beans should be cut into 1-inch lengths and blanched for about 4 minutes. Zucchini and summer squash do not require blanching before they are sautéed, but salting and draining for 30 minutes is a good idea. Fresh sliced mozzarella cheese can replace the goat cheese.

OVEN-DRIED TOMATOES

Y OU DON'T HAVE TO LIVE IN THE ARID SOUTHWEST to make dried tomatoes. Although a dehydrator will yield the best results, you can dry tomatoes in a regular oven. Plum tomatoes will give the best results.

To prepare the tomatoes for drying, wash and dry them. Cut them in half and scoop out the seeds and cores. Pat the interior dry with paper towels.

Preheat the oven to 150°F. If your oven has an upper broiler element, turn it off. Place the tomatoes, cut-side up, on wire racks on baking sheets. Place in the oven. Close the door and bake for 30 minutes.

Open the oven door to let out the moisture. Leave it propped open and continue drying for 6 to 8 hours, or until the tomatoes are pliable and slightly leathery.

Condition the tomatoes by transferring them to a wicker basket and leaving the basket in a dry and airy place for 10 days. Stir the tomatoes at least once a day.

After the tomatoes are dried, they should be pasteurized to ensure that any insect eggs and spoilage organisms are destroyed. You can pasteurize in the oven or in a stand-alone freezer (the freeze compartment of a refrigerator is not cold enough). In the oven, arrange the dried tomatoes in a shallow layer on trays and bake for 10 to 15 minutes at 175°F. Let cool, then transfer to storage containers. To use the freezer, place the tomatoes in freezer bags and leave at 0°F for 2 to 4 days.

Store in an airtight container at room temperature and use as needed.

broiled tomatoes

When you tire of fresh sliced tomatoes, broiling the tomatoes brings out new flavors without much effort.

4 medium-large ripe but firm tomatoes, cut in half horizontally
Salt and freshly ground black pepper
⅓ cup dried bread crumbs
¼ cup finely chopped fresh parsley or basil
2 garlic cloves, finely chopped
Extra-virgin olive oil

1 Preheat the broiler.

2 Arrange the tomatoes cut-side up on a baking sheet. Sprinkle with salt and pepper. Drizzle with the oil.

3 Broil for 5 to 8 minutes, or until the tomatoes are very hot and the surfaces look a little shriveled.

4 Meanwhile, combine the bread crumbs, parsley, and garlic in a small bowl. Sprinkle the mixture over the broiled tomatoes. Drizzle with a little olive oil.

5 Return to the broiler and broil for 2 to 3 minutes longer, until the crumbs are golden. Serve hot.

sautéed cherry tomatoes

This is a simple side dish, but truly great tasting. If you grow cherry tomatoes in a rainbow of colors, so much the better.

SERVES 4

2 tablespoons extra-virgin olive oil

4 cups cherry tomato halves, stems removed

2 garlic cloves, minced

2 tablespoons chopped fresh herbs (basil, cilantro, chervil, mint, oregano, parsley, sage, tarragon, thyme, alone or in any combination)

Salt and freshly ground black pepper

1 Heat the oil in a large skillet over medium-high heat. Add the tomatoes and sauté until the tomatoes are heated through, about 3 minutes.

2 Add the garlic and sauté until fragrant, 30 to 60 seconds. Remove from the heat and season with the herbs and salt and pepper to taste. Serve immediately.

TOMATOES AND HEALTH

Oddly enough, cooked tomatoes pack more nutrition power than raw tomatoes. That's because cooked tomatoes offer a more concentrated source of lycopene, a cancer-fighting antioxidant. Lycopene, which is also responsible for making tomatoes red, has been shown to reduce the risk of prostate cancer; it may also protect again cervical cancer. Raw or cooked, tomatoes also offer a good dose of vitamins A and C.

baked tomatoes
with goat cheese

I often find myself with a glut of cherry tomatoes, meanwhile waiting patiently (or not) for the large heirlooms to ripen. When we are weary of tomato salads, it's time to start cooking the cherries.

SERVES 4

4 cups cherry (or any small) tomatoes, halved
2 tablespoons extra-virgin olive oil
    Salt and freshly ground black pepper
2 garlic cloves or 1 shallot
    Leaves from 1 sprig fresh basil
1 slice whole wheat or white sandwich bread
4 ounces goat cheese

1 Preheat the oven to 400°F.

2 Arrange the tomatoes in a single layer in a 1-quart gratin dish or baking dish. Drizzle the olive oil over the tomatoes. Sprinkle with salt and pepper.

3 Bake the tomatoes for 15 minutes, until they begin to be juicy.

4 Meanwhile, mince the garlic and basil in a food processor. Tear the bread into pieces and add to the food processor. Process until you have fine crumbs. Alternatively, the garlic and basil can be minced by hand and the bread grated to form crumbs. Mix together.

5 Remove the tomatoes from the oven. Crumble the goat cheese over the tomatoes. Sprinkle the seasoned crumbs over the goat cheese. Return to the oven and bake for about 5 minutes, until the cheese is melted and crumbs are golden. Serve hot.

THE MEXICAN HUSK TOMATO is small and round. It is most commonly green, like an unripe tomato, and its interior has pulp and seeds like a tomato. It is a native of Peru, was a staple in pre-Columbian cooking, and is a member of the nightshade family. And therein its resemblance to tomatoes comes to an end.

The tomatillo, more closely related to the Cape gooseberry than the tomato, is covered with a parchmentlike skin that peels off easily. The fruit, which can be used raw or cooked, has flavors of green apple and lemon, with herbal, tart undertones. It can be used raw or cooked. Cooking tempers the intensity of the flavor. The pulp is high in a pectin-like substance that acts as a natural thickener. Sauces made with tomatillos tend to thicken slightly upon refrigeration.

Tomatillos keep for several weeks in the refrigerator.

To prepare tomatillos for cooking, remove the paper husks and rinse off the sticky residue on the skins. Finely diced or puréed raw tomatillos add a fresh, tangy, citruslike flavor and are often used in Mexican table sauces.

Blanched for 5 minutes, the flavor of the tomatillo is surprisingly mellow. Roasting under a broiler or over an open gas burner or grilling tomatillos brings out more flavor. Dry roasting produces an earthy, nutty flavor. Place the tomatillos in a heavy skillet (preferably cast-iron). Turn heat to low. Roast for 20 to 30 minutes, turning occasionally, letting each side take on a rich, burnished golden color before turning.

Sometimes tomatillos are fairly mild and sweet; other times they will be mouth-puckeringly tart. A recipe made with tomatillos will require tasting and adjusting with sugar if the flavor is too tart.

pasta with fresh tomatoes and wilted greens

Fresh juicy tomatoes, barely cooked greens, deeply aromatic basil — this is one of the best dishes of summer. If you grow tomatoes in assorted colors and sizes, use them here, big and small. Cherry tomatoes can be halved; bigger tomatoes should be chopped. I grow a second crop of arugula in a partially shaded spot in the garden, just to have for tomato season. If you don't have arugula, watercress or spinach will work.

SERVES 4–6

- 6 cups chopped ripe tomatoes
- 1 cup cured pitted black olives, such as niçoise or Kalamata
- ⅓ cup basil leaves, cut into thin strips
- ⅓ cup extra-virgin olive oil
- 2–4 garlic cloves, minced
- Salt and freshly ground black pepper
- 6 ounces arugula, coarse stems removed and leaves roughly chopped (about 8 cups)
- 1 pound rotini, shells, penne, or other pasta
- Freshly grated Parmesan, for serving

1 In a large serving bowl, combine the tomatoes, olives, basil, oil, garlic, and salt and pepper to taste. Toss gently to mix. Cover the bowl with plastic wrap and leave for 4 hours or up to all day if more convenient. Do not refrigerate.

2 Bring a large pot of salted water to a boil. Place a large colander in the sink and put the arugula in it.

3 Cook the pasta in the boiling water following the package directions. Drain the pasta over the arugula in the colander so the hot water wilts the arugula.

4 Add the hot pasta and arugula to the tomato mixture and toss gently. Serve at once, passing the Parmesan at the table.

tomato pesto tarts

The secret to using fresh tomatoes in a pizza or tart is to salt the sliced tomatoes and let the salt draw out the excess water for about 30 minutes. Then pat dry with paper towels.

SERVES 4–6

2 pounds tomatoes, cored and sliced ¼ inch thick

1 teaspoon salt (approximately)

2 unbaked 9-inch or 10-inch homemade (page 10) or store-bought (see Note) pastry rounds

1 large egg, lightly beaten

½ cup freshly grated Parmesan

½ cup pesto (page 6)

½ cup grated mozzarella

Refrigerated piecrust is easy to use in this recipe and yields wonderful results. The piecrusts are sold in 15-ounce boxes in the refrigerated section of the supermarket. Each box holds two 10-inch rounds of pastry, all ready to be fit into a pan, filled, and baked.

1 Cover a large work surface with a double layer of paper towels. Arrange the tomatoes in a single layer on the towels. Sprinkle evenly with the salt. Let stand for 30 minutes.

2 Preheat the oven to 375°F. Line a large baking sheet with foil.

3 Place the pastry round on the baking sheet.

4 Brush the pastry with the beaten egg, leaving a 2-inch border around the edges. Sprinkle ¼ cup of the Parmesan over each pastry. Spread ¼ cup of the pesto over the Parmesan on each pastry.

5 Place a double layer of paper towels over the tomatoes and press firmly to dry. Arrange the tomatoes on top of the pesto in overlapping circles. Sprinkle the mozzarella over the tomatoes. Fold the dough up to partially cover the filling and crimp to finish the edges.

6 Bake for 25 to 35 minutes, or until golden.

7 Let stand for 5 minutes. Cut into wedges and serve warm.

mussels in tomato-fennel broth

Many people who grow fennel find it hard to come up with enough different ways to serve it. It is an odd little aromatic vegetable, strongly reminiscent of licorice, and it pairs beautifully with tomatoes. If you don't have fennel, substitute a couple of celery stalks and throw a tablespoon of fennel seeds or a couple of bay leaves into the broth. The flavor will be different but still pleasing. Serve this with plenty of crusty French bread for sopping up the broth.

SERVES 4

4 pounds mussels in their shells
2 tablespoons extra-virgin olive oil
1 fennel bulb, trimmed and sliced
1 leek, trimmed and sliced
1 carrot, diced
4 garlic cloves, minced
1½ cups white wine
4 cups seeded and chopped fresh tomatoes
Salt and freshly ground black pepper
¼ cup chopped fresh fennel leaves or parsley

1 Wash the mussels in cold water, pulling off any beard hanging from the shells. Discard any mussels that do not close if tapped on a counter. Also discard those with broken shells. Set the cleaned mussels aside.

2 In a large pan over medium heat, heat the olive oil. Add the fennel, leek, carrot, and garlic. Sauté until fragrant, about 3 minutes.

3 Increase the heat, add the white wine and tomatoes, and simmer for 10 minutes, to allow the flavors to blend. Season with salt and pepper.

4 Add the mussels. Cover the pan and steam for about 5 minutes. Check to see if the mussels have opened. If not, cover and let cook for a minute or two more, until all the shells are open. When most of the shells are open, remove from the heat and discard any mussels that have not opened.

5 Ladle the broth and mussels into bowls, sprinkle with fennel leaves, and serve.

THE PERFECT SANDWICH

As the tomato season rolls in, I challenge myself to find the perfect tomato sandwich. One year I think nothing tops buttered homemade wheat bread and tomato, with salt and lots of pepper. The next year, I swoon regularly over sandwiches made with foccacia, pesto, prosciutto, and tomatoes. I can never decide. Here are some of the best:

Tomato Sandwich Every once in a while, it is worth splurging on fresh European-style butter. When tomatoes are ripe, this is the time. Sea salt and freshly ground black pepper are a must. The best bread will vary with the mood.

BLT Nothing beats this classic. The mayonnaise must be Hellman's or Best Foods. Miracle Whip is a travesty.

Roast Beef and Tomato with Mustard Crème Fraîche (page 97). Rye bread is terrific here.

Tomato-Anchovy Sandwich Best on grilled bread lightly brushed with olive oil. Add a slice of grilled onion. This feels like a plowman's lunch. Go weed the garden afterward.

Tomato-Pesto Sandwich Ripe, sliced tomatoes, freshly made pesto (page 6), and good Italian or French bread. A slice of provolone does no harm.

Grilled Vermont Cheddar and Tomato Sandwich A hometown favorite, on rye or whole wheat. I like a slice of onion.

Tomato-Avocado Sandwich Mash the avacado onto whole wheat. Top with sliced tomatoes and crumbled goat cheese.

Tomato-Aioli Sandwich Rich, garlicky, homemade aioli (page 380) and tomatoes. Make this one open-face, on slices of lightly toasted French bread.

chicken breast niçoise

Here's a quick, stovetop dish for a hot summer night. Serve with a salad, or perhaps steamed green beans, and French bread for mopping up the sauce.

SERVES 4

2 tablespoons extra-virgin olive oil
4 large boneless, skinless chicken breast halves
  Salt and freshly ground black pepper
1 large onion, sliced
4 garlic cloves, minced
4 cups seeded and diced tomatoes
1 cup cured pitted black olives, such as niçoise or Kalamata
½ cup chicken broth (page 9)
½ cup dry white wine
1 tablespoon dried herbes de Provence (page 7)

1 Heat the oil in a large skillet over medium-high heat. Add the chicken breasts, season with a pinch of salt and a few grinds of pepper, and cook until well browned on the bottom, about 4 minutes. Turn the breasts over, season the second side, and cook until well browned, 3 to 4 minutes. Remove the chicken from the skillet and set aside to keep warm.

2 Sauté the onion in the skillet until soft, about 2 minutes. Add the garlic and sauté until fragrant, about 30 seconds. Add the tomatoes, olives, broth, wine, and herbs. Cook until the tomatoes are broken down and the sauce is somewhat thickened, about 10 minutes. Taste and adjust the seasoning.

3 Return the chicken to the skillet, reduce the heat, and continue cooking until the chicken is heated through and no longer pink in the middle, about 5 minutes. Serve hot.

basic tomato sauce

When tomatoes are ripening fast and furiously, you need a good pasta sauce. This one has great flavor, but it takes surprisingly little time because the excess water is drained away, rather than cooked away. It is also a sauce that can be frozen or canned for future enjoyment. The sauce can be used in many ways, including as a topping for pizza and pasta.

MAKES 4 CUPS

6 pounds plum tomatoes, coarsely chopped (about 16 cups)
1 tablespoon salt, or more as needed
2 onions, diced
4 garlic cloves, minced
½ cup fresh basil leaves
¼ cup extra-virgin olive oil
½ teaspoon granulated sugar
Freshly ground black pepper

1 Cook the tomatoes with 1 tablespoon salt over medium heat for 10 minutes, stirring frequently.

2 Transfer to a colander and drain for 1 hour.

3 Return the tomatoes to the saucepan and add the onions, garlic, basil, oil, and sugar. Cover and simmer for 40 minutes, stirring occasionally.

4 Run the sauce through a food mill. Discard the seeds and skins. Return to the saucepan and boil until it reduces by about a third and has a good thickness. Season with salt and pepper. Serve hot.

I F YOU CAN GROW ONLY ONE TYPE OF TOMATO this year, grow Pink Brandywine. That's the advice of Lawrence Davis-Hollander, who knows tomatoes. The director of the Eastern Native Seed Conservancy, Davis-Hollander is the man responsible for conserving the seeds of more than 200 food plants every year, 90 of them tomatoes.

"I'd tell people to grow Pink Brandywine," he says, "because, first, it is the most accessible of the heirloom varieties. But what's not to like? It's rich, meaty, obviously a good tomato.

"Food tastes are subjective," explains Davis-Hollander. "Maybe it doesn't have the flavor nuances of some of the other tomatoes. But no one would disagree about Pink Brandywine; it's almost universally liked. And it's perfect for a backyard grower."

The conservancy is a small nonprofit organization (Davis-Hollander, a garden manager, and one summer intern) whose mission is to "promote and foster the essential connection between people and useful plants, especially heirloom food plants, through education, seed conservation, and the advocacy of genetic diversity." This means they seek out, plant, and preserve all kinds of rare seeds, mostly food plants — vegetables, grains, and fruits, such as tomatoes.

Typically these are old varieties — heirlooms. The plants may have cultural or historical significance. Many were once grown by Native Americans or have some connection with American history. Some of the plants are rare or endangered. The Heirloom Tomato Diversity Field Project brings together farmers, culinary professionals, food purveyors, and the public to highlight the qualities of heirloom tomatoes. Annually they grow dozens of varieties in all sizes and colors, including wild, historic, American, and European types. And all this culminates in the Epicurean Tomato Fete, a festival that brings together gardeners and chefs.

Davis-Hollander's personal favorite tomatoes include Livingston's Beauty, Aunt Ruby's German Green, Lambert's General Grant (also known as Dr. Neal), Magnus, Winsall (Wins All), Indian Moon, Eva Purple Ball, Cardinal, and Ponderosa Pink. He looks for flavor in his tomatoes, so he chooses heirloom and historic varieties. Heirloom tomatoes, he notes, tend to ripen in September and "like a little pampering."

For backyard growers, he recommends staking and tying the plants with cotton rags. There's something appealing, he says, about the look of a tomato staked that way: "You know, whose underwear is that?"

chipotle salsa

When tomatoes are coming in fast and furious, consider making a cooked salsa that you can process in a boiling-water bath. Chipotle chiles, smoke-dried jalapeños, add a lick of fire to this otherwise simple salsa.

MAKES 4 PINTS

24 cups quartered ripe tomatoes
8 garlic cloves, peeled and left whole
2 cups white distilled vinegar
4 chipotle chiles
2 onions, finely minced
1 cup finely minced fresh green chiles
1 cup finely minced sweet bell pepper
Salt

1 Combine the tomatoes, garlic, vinegar, and chipotles in a large nonreactive saucepan. Bring to a boil, reduce the heat, and simmer until the tomatoes are very soft, stirring occasionally, about 45 minutes.

2 Process the tomato mixture through a food mill, discarding the seeds and skins.

3 Return the strained mixture to the saucepan and add the onions, fresh chiles, and bell pepper. Simmer until the salsa has reduced to a nice thick sauce, about 1 hour. Season to taste with the salt.

4 Ladle the hot salsa into clean hot pint jars, leaving ¼ inch headspace. Seal. Process in a boiling-water bath (pages 475–477) for 15 minutes. Let cool undisturbed for 12 hours. Store in a cool, dry place for up to a year.

FROM MID- TO LATE SUMMER, there are always vegetables ready to be harvested. Many of the early summer vegetables, such as zucchini and cucumber, continue to bear fruit, as long as they weren't coaxed into production too early. The wise gardener is also harvesting a second crop of green beans, having had the foresight to stagger the plantings. This is the perfect time to cook wonderful feasts of vegetables — mixing and matching freely.

santorini salad

A traditional vegetable and feta salad, dressed with olive oil and fresh lemon juice, Santorini Salad sparkles with fresh flavors. Add a crusty loaf of bread, a well-chilled white wine, and perhaps some grilled shrimp, and you will have a very fine summer meal.

SERVES 4

2 teaspoons finely minced lemon zest

3 tablespoons fresh lemon juice

1 sweet onion, halved and thinly sliced

¼ cup extra-virgin olive oil

1 tablespoon chopped fresh oregano

Salt and freshly ground black pepper

2 large tomatoes, diced

1 cucumber (peeled and seeded if desired), diced

1 green bell pepper, diced

1 red bell pepper, diced

1 cup fresh cooked or canned or frozen and defrosted artichoke hearts

1 cup Kalamata olives

6–8 ounces feta, crumbled

1 Combine the zest, juice, onion, olive oil, and oregano in a medium bowl. Season with salt and pepper. Toss well and let stand at room temperature for about 10 minutes.

2 Combine the tomatoes, cucumber, green and red bell peppers, artichokes, and olives in a large bowl. Add the onion mixture and toss well. Add the cheese and toss again.

3 Serve immediately.

tomato-vegetable soup

As summer turns slowly to fall, soup begins to be an option. With a topping of pesto, this tomato-vegetable soup has all the flavors of summer.

SERVES 4–6

8 cups chopped tomatoes

5 cups vegetable or chicken broth (page 8 or 9)

1–2 leeks or 1 large onion

1–2 carrots

½ pound shell beans in pods (1 cup shelled) or 1 cup chopped green beans

2 tablespoons extra-virgin olive oil

2 tablespoons chopped fresh oregano leaves

1 tablespoon chopped fresh thyme leaves

3 garlic cloves, minced

Salt and freshly ground black pepper

Kernels from 2 ears corn

½ cup small soup pasta (optional)

Sugar (optional)

Pesto (page 6)

1 Combine the tomatoes and 2 cups of the broth in a medium saucepan. Bring to a boil, reduce the heat, and simmer until the tomatoes are completely tender, about 30 minutes.

2 Meanwhile, thinly slice the leeks and carrots. Shell the beans.

3 Pass the tomatoes through a food mill to remove skins and seeds.

4 Heat the oil in a large saucepan over medium-high heat. Add the leeks and carrots and sauté until the leeks are soft, about 4 minutes. Add the shell beans, remaining 3 cups broth, tomato purée, oregano, thyme, garlic, and salt and pepper to taste. Bring to a boil, then reduce the heat and simmer until the beans are completely tender, 20 to 30 minutes.

5 Add the corn kernels and soup pasta, if using. Continue to simmer until the pasta is cooked through, about 10 minutes.

6 Taste and adjust the seasoning. If the flavors do not seem balanced, consider adding sugar, ½ teaspoon at a time, as well as more salt and pepper. To serve, ladle the soup into individual bowls. Top each with a spoonful of pesto and serve.

vegetable antipasto

A platter of marinated and cooked vegetables makes a fine summer meal with a selection of cheese and fresh Italian bread.

SERVES 8

Braised Artichokes (made with olive oil, not butter) (page 194), at room temperature

Marinated Roasted Peppers (page 216)

Caponata (page 249)

Roasted Green Beans (page 149)

Brine-cured black or green olives

Arrange the various vegetables and olives on a large serving platter or a series of platters and serve at room temperature.

ratatouille

In the perfect ratatouille, the flavors are blended, yet each vegetable remains distinct. The vegetables are neither mushy nor undercooked. To do this properly, sauté each vegetable separately in a large skillet and then combine them in a saucepan just long enough to blend the flavors. Chopped fresh basil, or a little thyme or oregano, makes a fine addition.

■ SERVES 6–8 ■

7 tablespoons extra-virgin olive oil
1 medium eggplant, peeled and diced
   Salt and freshly ground black pepper
1 onion, diced
1 small green bell pepper, diced
1 small red bell pepper, diced
2 small zucchini, diced
2 small yellow summer squash, diced
2 ripe tomatoes, seeded and diced
4 garlic cloves, minced
1 can (8 ounces) unseasoned tomato sauce or tomato purée

1 Heat 3 tablespoons of the oil in a large skillet over medium-high heat. Add the eggplant and season with salt and pepper. Sauté until browned, juicy, and cooked through, 10 to 12 minutes. Transfer to a medium saucepan with a slotted spoon.

2 Return the skillet to medium-high heat and add 2 more tablespoons of the oil. Sauté the onion and bell peppers in the oil until tender-crisp, 3 to 5 minutes. Transfer to the saucepan with a slotted spoon.

3 Return the skillet to medium-high heat and add the remaining 2 tablespoons oil. Add the zucchini and summer squash and season with salt and pepper to taste. Sauté until tender-crisp, 3 to 5 minutes. Transfer to the saucepan and add the tomatoes, garlic, and tomato sauce.

4 Simmer the ratatouille for 15 minutes over medium heat.

5 Taste and adjust the seasoning. The flavor will improve if the ratatouille sits at room temperature for 1 to 2 hours. Serve at room temperature, or reheat and serve warm.

wheat berry tabouli

Chewy wheat berries replace the traditional bulgur in this summery salad.

SERVES 6–8

1 cup wheat berries

4 cups water

3 cups quartered and thinly sliced cucumbers (peeling and seeding optional)

2 cups parsley leaves, snipped or pulled from the stems

2–3 ripe tomatoes, diced

½ Vidalia or other sweet onion, diced

¼ cup chopped fresh mint leaves

3 tablespoons extra-virgin olive oil

¼ cup fresh lemon juice

Salt and freshly ground black pepper

1 Combine the wheat berries and water in a medium saucepan. Bring to a boil, reduce the heat, cover, and cook until tender, about 1½ hours. (You can reduce the cooking time to 50 to 60 minutes by soaking the berries overnight before cooking.) When the berries are tender, drain off any excess water. Allow to cool.

2 Combine the cooked wheat berries with the cucumbers, parsley, tomatoes, onion, and mint in a large salad bowl. Toss to mix. Add the oil and toss again. Add the lemon juice and salt and pepper to taste and toss again. Taste and adjust the seasoning.

3 Let stand for at least 30 minutes before serving.

summer vegetable bread pudding

Think of a savory bread pudding as a frittata made with bread cubes instead of potatoes. It makes a fine brunch dish and is terrific to take along to a picnic. This is the rare vegetable dish that is better on the second day. It looks best if baked in a springform pan and served in wedges, but feel free to substitute a 13- by 9-inch baking dish and reduce the baking time by about 10 minutes.

■ SERVES 8–12 ■

- 1 large tomato, diced
- 1 medium zucchini or yellow summer squash, quartered and sliced
- 2 teaspoons salt
- 5 large eggs
- 3½ cups milk
- 12 cups dried bread cubes
- 2 tablespoons butter
- 2 tablespoons extra-virgin olive oil
- 2 celery stalks, thinly sliced
- 1 leek, white and tender green parts only, trimmed and thinly sliced
- 1 red bell pepper, diced
- 1 carrot, grated
- ½ pound fontina, Cheddar, or Swiss cheese, grated (about 2 cups, packed)
- 2 sprigs fresh sage, finely chopped
- 2 sprigs fresh thyme, finely chopped
- ½ teaspoon grated lemon zest
  Freshly ground black pepper

1 Combine the tomato and zucchini with the salt in a colander and set aside to drain for at least 30 minutes.

2 Preheat the oven to 350°F. Lightly grease a 9-inch or 10-inch springform pan with butter.

3 In a large bowl, whisk together the eggs and milk. Add the bread cubes and let soak while you cook the vegetables.

4 Melt the butter with the oil in a large skillet over medium heat. Add the celery, leek, and bell pepper and sauté until softened, about 3 minutes. Add the zucchini, tomato, and carrot and sauté until all the vegetables are tender, about 3 minutes longer.

5 Add the vegetables, cheese, sage, thyme, and lemon zest to the bread cube mixture and gently toss. Season generously with the pepper and mix well.

6 Pack the mixture in the prepared pan. Place the pan on a baking sheet and bake for 55 to 65 minutes, until the top is crusty brown and a knife inserted in the middle comes out clean. If the pudding begins to look dark before it's finished, cover with foil.

7 Let cool before serving. If you want the pudding to serve in firm slices, cool overnight in the refrigerator and reheat or serve at room temperature.

pasta with grilled summer vegetables and goat cheese

Goat cheese makes an instant creamy sauce when tossed with hot pasta, but if you aren't a fan, you can substitute ricotta cheese. And if your garden grows with a different assortment of vegetables, why, try those instead. This is a recipe for an easy, lazy, delicious summer meal. Make sure you add good bread and a bottle of wine.

SERVES 4–6

1 small yellow summer squash, diced

1 small zucchini, diced

1 red bell pepper, diced

1 fennel bulb, cored and diced, or 1 cup green beans cut in 1-inch lengths

2 tablespoons extra-virgin olive oil

Salt and freshly ground black pepper

1 pound rotini or other short pasta

2 cups cherry tomatoes, halved

¼ cup loosely packed chopped fresh basil

2 garlic cloves, minced

6 ounces soft fresh goat cheese, crumbled

1 Prepare a medium-hot fire in the grill with a lightly oiled vegetable grill rack in place.

2 Begin heating a large pot of salted water for the pasta.

3 Combine the summer squash, zucchini, bell pepper, and fennel in a large bowl. Add the olive oil and salt and pepper to taste, and toss to coat.

4 Grill the vegetables, tossing frequently until tender and lightly charred, about 5 minutes. Set aside and keep warm.

5 Add the pasta to the boiling water and cook until just al dente. Reserve 1 cup of the cooking water and drain.

6 Return the pasta to the pot. Add the tomatoes, basil, garlic, and goat cheese. Pour in half the reserved cooking water and toss to form a creamy sauce. Add more water if necessary. Season generously with salt and pepper.

7 Transfer the pasta and sauce to a serving bowl. Top with the grilled vegetables and toss lightly. Serve at once.

summer seafood stew

This dish takes less than an hour to throw together, once you have harvested the vegetables and bought the seafood. Nothing more than a loaf or two of crusty French bread, a green salad, and a crisp white wine is needed to accompany the stew. The vegetables and the seafood can be varied, depending on what is appealing, but the corn is highly recommended for its sweetness.

■ SERVES 6–8 ■

1 onion, quartered

1 small carrot, chopped

1 celery stalk, chopped

1 cup fresh parsley leaves

4 garlic cloves

3 tablespoons extra-virgin olive oil

1 red or green bell pepper, diced

3–4 tomatoes, seeded and chopped

2 cups vegetable or chicken broth (page 8 or 9) or fish broth

¼ teaspoon saffron threads

Salt and freshly ground black pepper

24 hard-shell clams or mussels (about 2 pounds)

1 pound squid, cut into rings, or 1 pound whitefish, such as halibut, cod, snapper, sea bass, cut into chunks

1 cup green beans in 1-inch pieces

1 pound shrimp, shelled and deveined

1 medium-size zucchini or yellow summer squash, quartered and sliced

Kernels stripped from 1 to 2 ears corn

1 Process the onion, carrot, celery, parsley, and garlic in a food processor until finely chopped.

2 Heat the oil in a large saucepan or Dutch oven over medium-high heat. Sauté the finely chopped vegetables in the oil until fragrant, 3 to 5 minutes. Add the bell pepper and sauté until fragrant, 3 to 5 minutes.

3 Add the tomatoes, broth, saffron, and salt and pepper to taste. Bring to a boil, then reduce the heat and simmer for 10 minutes.

4 Add the clams, squid, and green beans to the broth, cover, and simmer for another 10 minutes. Add the shrimp, zucchini, and corn. Cover and cook until the shrimp are firm and all the clams are open, 5 to 10 minutes.

5 Taste and adjust the seasoning. Discard any clams that have not opened. Serve at once.

fall into winter

BELGIAN ENDIVES

BRUSSELS SPROUTS   CABBAGE

CARROTS   CAULIFLOWER

GARLIC   JERUSALEM ARTICHOKES

KALE LEEKS   ONIONS PARSNIPS

POTATOES   RUTABAGAS

WINTER SQUASH & PUMPKINS

FALL ARRIVES with the first hard frost. Frost may appear first as a whisper on a cool September morning. We notice a touch of black on the cucumber leaves high on the trellis. The basil patch is gone (anyone with any experience living up North will have harvested and made it all into pesto for the freezer).

Sometimes there will be a week or two of these light frosts. If the tomato plants have enough foliage to protect the tomatoes, we might ignore the weatherman's warnings — or we might faithfully cover the tomato patch with colorful sheets, blankets, and tarps every night. We keep an eye on the calendar and an ear to the weather reports. We know that a full moon during a patch of clear skies means the killing frost will arrive — as early as late August, as late as mid-October. But come it will.

There is much to be done. Onions will be pulled so the tops will die back and dry. Carrots and other long-keeping root crops can be left in the ground under a heavy layer of mulch, or perhaps pulled and layered in a bin with straw or sawdust. Winter squash needs to cure in a dry spot for a few weeks. Garden debris must be removed from the garden and composted.

There have been years when I left most of the garden cleanup for the following spring, but not since I started planting garlic. Now the cleanup and the planting for next year take place in one long fall weekend. Putting the garden to bed with a new crop already planted is the most optimistic chore I can imagine on a drear fall day.

The Basement Harvest

ANY FOOD PLANT that will grow in a dark basement in the middle of a northern winter must be held in the highest regard. Belgian endives may be the best — and laziest — way to extend the harvest season.

I love the story of how Belgian endives came into being. It seems that a Belgian farmer was growing witloof chicory for its root, which was used as a coffee substitute in Europe. He threw some of these roots into the soft soil in the corner of a dark shed and forgot them. Three weeks later, he found that tight blanched heads had grown. The result has been systematically cultivated ever since. Belgians call their endive "White Gold."

Belgian endive, also known as witloof chicory or French endive (pronounced ahn-deev), is a biennial plant. You grow it from seed in the garden through the usual growing season, but here's the difference: You don't harvest the leaves. Instead, just before the ground freezes, you take the plant indoors, pack it in a flowerpot, and leave it in the dark. In 3 to 4 weeks, the harvest will be ready. It's a little bit like magic.

GROWING This green is grown like a root crop. It needs fertile, loose soil and a 4-month growing season.

SOWING Sow in early spring for a fall harvest of roots.

CULTIVATING Space Belgian endive plants about 9 inches apart. Keep well watered and well weeded.

HARVESTING Carefully dig up the roots. Cut off any side roots. Then cut off the leafy tops to within 1 inch of the crowns, and shorten each root to a length of about 8 inches.

Store the roots in a perforated plastic bag in the refrigerator, and remove a few at a time for forcing.

To force, pack the roots upright in a deep flowerpot or wooden box filled with well-drained garden soil, sand, or new or used potting soil. Water thoroughly. Then cover the crowns of the plants with about 8 inches of dry sand, soil, or sawdust.

Leave the box in the basement or some other dark spot where the temperature is in the low 60s. Check every few days to make sure the mix around the roots is moist. In 3 or 4 weeks, tips of leafy heads will begin to peek through the top layer. Cut the head from the roots and compost the roots. There's only one harvest (of a "chicon") from a root.

Belgian endive has a bracing bitterness and a juicy texture. Cooking mellows the bitterness. Sliced raw, it wakes up a bland lettuce salad and provides a pleasing contrast to sweet fall fruits, such as apples and pears. It also makes a wonderful foil for earthy goat cheese. The spear-shaped leaves can be filled with a dab of goat cheese or boursin cheese and topped with a sprinkling of nuts to make a very attractive appetizer. Other possible toppings are cream cheese spreads and blue cheese dressing. Arrange in a starburst pattern.

The cut leaves brown quickly, so cut just before adding to a salad. Unless you want to keep the head intact, remove the core at the base of the leaves. When you want to prepare Belgian endive halves, trim the root end to leave just a 1/4-inch base, then slice horizontally.

TIMING
Braising: 25 to 40 minutes
Grilling: 8 to 14 minutes
Roasting: 20 to 25 minutes at 450°F

BELGIAN ENDIVE MATH
1 chicon = 2 cups sliced

endive, apple, and walnut salad

The combination of sweet-tart apples, pungent blue cheese dressing, and tangy greens is a winner. The salad is arranged, rather than tossed together, so give some thought to the platter you will use.

■ SERVES 4 ■

8 Belgian endives, halved, cored, and separated into leaves
1 cup Blue Cheese Dressing (page 99)
2 red apples, quartered, cored, and sliced
1 cup walnuts, toasted

Arrange the greens on a large platter with the tips of the leaves pointing out. Spoon the dressing on the greens. Arrange the apple slices on the dressed greens and sprinkle the walnuts over all. Serve at once.

endive and goat cheese salad

Simply wonderful is the only way to describe this salad — when it is made with top-quality ingredients. Every flavor counts, so use only the best.

SERVES 4–6

6 Belgian endives, cored

4 ounces soft fresh goat cheese, at room temperature

6–8 cups torn mixed greens (including some radicchio if possible)

3–4 tablespoons extra-virgin olive oil

1½–2 tablespoons fresh lemon juice

Coarse sea salt

1 Separate the endives into individual leaves and select the 12 largest leaves. Spread the leaves with the goat cheese.

2 Slice the remaining leaves into 1-inch strips and combine with the other greens on a large platter. Toss gently. Lightly dress the salad with the oil, lemon juice, and salt to taste and toss carefully.

3 Arrange the leaves with the goat cheese in a sunburst pattern on top of the greens and serve.

grilled belgian endives

Is the grill still out? Here's an accompaniment for what may be the last grilled meal of the season.

SERVES 4

4–8 Belgian endives
Extra-virgin olive oil
Coarse sea salt
Balsamic vinegar

1 Prepare a medium-hot fire in the grill.

2 Trim the root ends but leave at least ¼ inch of root. Slice the endives in half lengthwise. Brush with the oil.

3 Grill the endives until tender and lightly grill-marked, 4 to 7 minutes per side.

4 Arrange on a platter, sprinkle with the salt, and drizzle with a little balsamic vinegar. Serve hot.

braised belgian endives

Braising mellows the bitterness of Belgian endive and renders the texture silken.

SERVES 4

2 tablespoons extra-virgin olive oil

4 Belgian endives, ends trimmed and halved lengthwise

½ cup chicken broth (page 9)

Salt and freshly ground black pepper

2 teaspoons fresh lemon juice or white wine vinegar

1 tablespoon butter

1 Heat the oil over medium heat in a large skillet. Add the endives and cook until browned, turning once or twice, about 10 minutes.

2 Add the broth and season with salt and pepper. Lower the heat, cover, and gently cook until the endives are completely tender, about 15 minutes.

3 Transfer the endives to a heated serving platter. Add the lemon juice and butter to the skillet. Increase the heat and cook until the remaining liquid thickens to a syrupy consistency, 1 to 2 minutes. Spoon over the endives and serve.

crispy roasted endives

It seems that everyone likes a vegetable with a crumb topping. The crumbs beautifully complement the mild bitterness of the greens. The dish holds up well on a buffet and can be made ahead and reheated in the oven.

SERVES 6–8

About ¼ cup extra-virgin olive oil
8 Belgian endives, halved lengthwise
Salt and freshly ground black pepper
2 shallots, minced
2 garlic cloves, minced
½ red bell pepper, minced
¼ cup finely chopped prosciutto or ham
1½ cups fresh bread crumbs

1 Preheat the oven to 450°F. Use some of the oil to lightly grease a baking dish large enough to hold the endives in a single layer.

2 Arrange the endives in a single layer in the prepared baking dish and brush with some of the oil. Sprinkle generously with salt and pepper. Roast for 20 to 25 minutes, until tender and lightly brown. Remove the baking dish from the oven and preheat the broiler.

3 Meanwhile, heat 2 tablespoons of the oil in a large sauté pan. Add the shallots, garlic, bell pepper, and prosciutto and sauté until softened and fragrant, about 5 minutes. Stir in the bread crumbs and sauté until lightly colored, another 2 minutes. Season to taste with salt and pepper.

4 Cover the endives with the crumb mixture. Drizzle with any remaining oil.

5 Place the baking dish under the broiler just long enough to crisp the top, 2 to 5 minutes. Watch carefully and don't let the crumbs burn. Serve warm.

F EVER A GARDEN PLANT caused confusion, it is endive. It is known in this country as either Belgian endive or witloof chicory. The French call it *chicorée éndive*. No wonder we are all confused. Even the Latin names don't help.

Chicory and endive are very closely related. Both belong to the genus *Cichorium. C. intybus* has several forms (curly-leaved and smooth-leaved) and colors (green, red, and blanched). The green-leaf type, known as chicory in the United States and England, is called *chicorée endive* by the French. Sugarloaf is a common garden variety; it forms a relatively large romaine-type green head. The blanched form is variously called witloof, witloof chicory, French endive, Belgian endive, or *chicorée à grosses racines*. The red form is commonly known as radicchio, although the French may call it *chicorée sauvage à rouge feuille*.

C. endivia, a very closely related plant, may be broad-leaved or curly-leaved. Broad-leaved types are known variously as endive, escarole, Batavia, and chicory. The French call this kind *chicorée escarole.* Curly-leaved types were once called curly endive but are now more likely to be called by their French name, frisée. I think that may be a step in the right direction away from all this confusion.

Love 'em or Leave 'em

DURING WORLD WAR II, my father was stationed in England. The only green vegetable he saw for three years was Brussels sprouts. When he came home from the war, he made one request: My mother was never to cook Brussels sprouts. So I was well into my 20s before I ever met one.

The meeting was not auspicious. Steam-table Brussels sprouts are best avoided, and I'll say no more on the subject, other than the fact that about 80 percent of the U.S. crop ends up frozen (and probably destined for steam tables).

Among gardeners and farmstand consumers who eat only fresh Brussels sprouts, passions tend to run deep: People either love these assertive little cabbages or don't care for them at all.

The sprouts grow on thick stalks that reach 2 to 3 feet tall, and they ripen from the bottom up. If you dislike the strong flavor of Brussels sprouts, try harvesting them when they are just tiny buds, less than an inch in diameter. If they are very tender, slice them in half and add them to salads. Or toss them into stir-fries and sautés. If you wait to harvest until the sprouts are fully mature, pair them with strong flavors, such as bacon and mustard.

Northern gardeners are especially fond of Brussels sprouts because they are one of the hardiest vegetables in the garden. They will survive fall frosts and early snowfalls, and the cold actually makes them taste better. As a season extender in cold climates, Brussels sprouts are a real winner.

SOW & REAP

GROWING A hardy member of the cabbage family, Brussels sprouts do best in fertile soil with even moisture. They do best in full sun, but will tolerate light shade. Work compost or well-rotted manure into the soil to ensure fertility

SOWING Brussels sprouts are a long-season crop, taking at least 100 days to reach maturity, so most gardeners will want to start seeds indoors or in a cold frame about a month before the last frost. If your growing season is at least 4 months long, you can sow seeds outdoors. In very warm regions, they can be sown from mid-October to Christmas for a spring crop.

CULTIVATING Brussels sprouts do best in cool, evenly moist soils, so mulching is important. Staking may be necessary in windy areas. About a month before you expect a hard freeze, pinch off the growing tip on the stem to direct all the plant's energy into maturing the remaining sprouts.

HARVESTING You can begin harvesting whenever some of the buds are firm and about 1 inch in diameter. Break off the leaf stem below the bud and either snap off or cut the bud. If the plant is still productive but the night temperatures are near 25°F, cut down the whole plant, strip off the leaves, and hang the plant in a root cellar. The sprouts will be good for another 3 weeks.

KITCHEN NOTES

Brussels sprouts grown under ideal conditions — enough water, not too much heat — will be sweet and mild. More often than not, Brussels sprouts will have an assertive, sharp mustardy flavor. This is a vegetable that can stand up to strong flavors. Brussels sprouts are well matched with smoked bacon, mustard, and cream.

Cook's Illustrated, a cooking magazine dedicated to exhaustively testing kitchen techniques to reveal what is genuinely helpful and what is not, has found that it is not necessary to cut an X into the bottom of each whole sprout to ensure even cooking. It is, however, a good idea to cook sprouts of the same size, so if your sprouts vary in size, cut them into halves or quarters to even out the size differences.

Brussels sprouts will keep several weeks in a cool place, but their flavor is best when they are freshly harvested. Keep them, unwashed, in a perforated plastic bag in the refrigerator.

TIMING
Blanching: 6 to 8 minutes
Steaming: 8 to 12 minutes
Sautéing or stir-frying: 3 to 6 minutes
Roasting: 15 minutes at 425°F

BRUSSELS SPROUT MATH
1 pound sprouts = 4 cups halved sprouts
= 3–3½ cups whole sprouts

brussels sprouts with buttermilk dressing

Sometimes a gentle coddling will bring out the best in a strongly flavored vegetable. Here Brussels sprouts are gently steamed, then enveloped in a creamy sauce. This salad holds up well on a buffet table and is a great option for serving Brussels sprouts at a holiday feast.

SERVES 4

1½ pounds Brussels sprouts, trimmed and halved (6 cups)
½ cup buttermilk
½ cup mayonnaise
2 tablespoons fresh lemon juice
2 tablespoons chopped fresh parsley
1 garlic clove, minced
Salt and freshly ground black pepper

1 Steam the Brussels sprouts over boiling water until tender but still crunchy, about 8 minutes. Immediately plunge into cold water to stop the cooking. Drain well.

2 Process the buttermilk, mayonnaise, lemon juice, parsley, and garlic in a blender until thoroughly mixed. Season with salt and pepper.

3 About 30 minutes before serving, pour the dressing over the Brussels sprouts and toss gently. Toss again before serving.

roasted brussels sprouts

What a surprise this recipe was! In earlier experiments, I had found Brussels sprouts not suited to grilling. So I wrote a whole book on roasting vegetables and never experimented with Brussels sprouts. Then someone mentioned enjoying roasted Brussels sprouts at a Christmas dinner. I had to try them for myself — and I loved them.

■ **SERVES 4** ■

2 tablespoons extra-virgin olive oil
1–1½ pounds Brussels sprouts, trimmed and halved (6 cups)
Coarse sea salt or kosher salt

1 Preheat the oven to 425°F. Lightly grease a baking pan with oil.

2 Drizzle the oil over the Brussels sprouts in a large bowl and toss gently to coat. Arrange the sprouts in a single, uncrowded layer on the prepared pan.

3 Roast for about 15 minutes, or until the sprouts are tender and lightly browned, shaking the pan occasionally for even cooking.

4 Transfer the sprouts to a serving bowl and sprinkle with salt. Serve immediately.

THE BRUSSELS SPROUT STORY

BRUSSELS SPROUTS ARE MEMBERS of the cabbage family, a close relative of cabbage. Indeed, you can get a cabbage plant to act like a Brussels sprout by lopping off the growing tip. The plant will then make a number of small heads. But why would you want to?

The origin of Brussels sprouts is unclear. Although it may be the case that the Romans did eat them, the first printed reference to them is found in a 1554 book by Dutch botanist Dodonaeus. The sprouts were common in the market gardens outside of Brussels in the 18th century, hence the name. Belgians claim that Brussels sprouts, when eaten at the beginning of a meal, can prevent intoxication. A typical Belgian dish pairs Brussels sprouts with chestnuts. Germans call them *Rosenkohl,* or "rose cabbages," a poetic allusion to their similarity to rosebuds.

Coastal climates with a steady supply of moisture are perfect for Brussels sprouts, which explains why they are so commonly grown in England, where production outstrips U.S. production.

Brussels sprouts are high in fiber and are a good source of vitamins A and C, potassium, and iron.

brussels sprouts sautéed with bacon

Everyone loves bacon, but will they love Brussels sprouts if they are paired with bacon? It's worth a try if you have someone you want to coax into eating Brussels sprouts. This classic recipe is a staple in many households.

SERVES 4

1–1½ pounds Brussels sprouts, trimmed (3–4 cups)
4 strips bacon (about 1 ounce), diced
1 shallot, diced
Freshly ground black pepper

1 Steam the Brussels sprouts over boiling water until tender, about 8 minutes.

2 Meanwhile, cook the bacon in a large skillet over medium heat until it begins to release its fat, about 3 minutes. Add the shallot and continue to sauté until the bacon is crisp, 2 to 3 minutes longer. Drain off all the fat.

3 Add the Brussels sprouts to the skillet and cook over medium heat, tossing the sprouts until they have taken on the flavor of the bacon left in the pan, about 2 minutes. Season to taste with pepper and serve hot.

holiday brussels sprouts with pecans and cranberries

It was the cranberries that made a convert of a lifelong Brussels sprout avoider at a recent dinner at my house. The sweetness tamed the bitterness of the Brussels sprouts, while the pecans added buttery crunch. It didn't hurt at all that the sprouts were steamed lightly and not boiled to death, as she remembered them from her childhood.

SERVES 6

1¼–1½ pounds Brussels sprouts (3½–4½ cups)
½ cup dried cranberries
2 tablespoons butter
1 cup pecan halves
2 shallots, minced

1 Steam the Brussels sprouts and cranberries over boiling water until the Brussels sprouts are tender but still crunchy, about 8 minutes. Immediately transfer to a serving dish.

2 While the Brussels sprouts and cranberries are steaming, melt the butter in a small skillet over medium heat. Add the pecans and shallots and sauté until the shallots are translucent and the pecans are fragrant, about 3 minutes.

3 Pour the butter and pecan mixture over the Brussels sprouts and cranberries, toss gently, and serve.

sweet & spicy brussels sprouts with pork

One theory of Brussels sprouts cookery is to match its strong flavors with strongly flavored ingredients, as in this sweet and spicy stir-fry. Adding the full 3 teaspoons of chili paste may be a little too much for timid palates, but we like it that way at my house. Fermented black beans are salted and fermented black soybeans. They add a subtle flavor to the stir-fry. You can find them wherever Chinese foods are sold, usually in small plastic packages, shelved with other dried foods. They aren't exactly optional, but you can omit them if you must.

SERVES 4

1 pound ground pork

3 tablespoons soy sauce

2 tablespoons rice wine or sherry

2–3 teaspoons Chinese chili paste with garlic

1 teaspoon sugar

2 tablespoons cornstarch

1 cup chicken broth (page 9)

3 tablespoons peanut or canola oil

1 teaspoon dark sesame oil

1½–2 pounds Brussels sprouts, trimmed and halved (6–8 cups)

1 onion, halved and sliced lengthwise

1 tablespoon minced fresh ginger

3 garlic cloves, minced

2 teaspoons Chinese fermented black beans, rinsed and chopped

2 tablespoons hoisin sauce

Hot cooked rice

1 Mix the pork with 2 tablespoons of the soy sauce, the rice wine, chili paste, and sugar. In a small bowl, dissolve the cornstarch in the chicken broth.

2 Heat 1 tablespoon of the peanut oil with the sesame oil in a large wok or deep skillet over high heat. Add the pork mixture and stir-fry, breaking up the meat, until it is browned and the juices run clear, about 5 minutes. Scrape the mixture out of the wok and keep warm in a medium bowl.

3 Heat the remaining 2 tablespoons oil in the wok. Add the Brussels sprouts, onion, and remaining 1 tablespoon soy sauce. Stir-fry until the Brussels sprouts are barely tender-crisp, about 4 minutes. Push the Brussels sprouts to the sides of the wok and add the ginger, garlic, and black beans to the center. Fry until fragrant, about 30 seconds, then stir into the Brussels sprouts.

4 Add the pork and hoisin sauce to the wok and stir-fry for 1 minute to heat through. Stir the chicken broth mixture and add to the wok. Stir-fry until the sauce thickens and coats the Brussels sprouts, about 2 minutes longer.

5 Serve hot over rice.

Speaks Many Languages

I HAVE A FRIEND who went to college in China during the Cultural Revolution. He claims that cabbage was the only vegetable he ate for years at a time. While I can't believe his claim is literally true, I do believe that for months at a time, he ate cabbage daily. It was as much a staple food for him as rice.

Could I survive such a diet? I think so. As long as I was able to prepare cabbage as it is done around the planet.

Cabbage is an amazingly versatile vegetable. It is wonderful raw and terrific cooked; it pickles beautifully into sauerkraut and kimchi. And where would a barbecue sandwich be without its topping of coleslaw? Cabbage can be harvested young as a salad green or allowed to mature into a long-keeping head. Its leaves can be stewed or stuffed, braised with cream, or boiled with corned beef.

It is a powerhouse of nutrition, offering fiber and generous doses of vitamins A, B, and C, as well as iron, calcium, and potassium. Furthermore, research suggests that cabbage and other members of the cabbage family (collards, broccoli, Brussels sprouts, cauliflower, kale, and kohlrabi) inhibit the development of breast, stomach, and colon cancer due to phytochemicals called indoles. These indoles tend to burn up the female hormone estrogen. Indoles also tend to ward off cell changes that lead to colon cancer.

In 1984, the Food and Agriculture Organization of the United Nations listed cabbage as one of the top 20 vegetables considered an important food source for sustaining the world population. Is it sustaining you?

GROWING Cabbage does best in fertile soil and full sun, especially in cooler climates. In warmer climates, it does best in full sun but it tolerates light midday shade.

SOWING Sow indoors 4 to 6 weeks before the last frost. If your growing season is long enough, you can sow directly outdoors 10 to 12 weeks before the first frost for a fall crop.

CULTIVATING Cabbages are heavy feeders, requiring plenty of water until heads are formed and plenty of fertilizer. Mulching reduces stress on the plants, so the heads are better formed and less likely to split. The roots are close to the surface and are easily damaged, so avoid using a hoe near the plants.

HARVESTING Early varieties do not store well and should be harvested anytime after the heads reach softball size and used quickly. Late-season heads can tolerate a few mild frosts. You can cut off the heads and any damaged leaves and store in a root cellar on shelves or wrapped in newspaper. Or you can pull up the plants, roots and all, and hang the plants in the root cellar.

CABBAGE MATH
1 small head green cabbage = 2 pounds, trimmed
1 medium head green cabbage = 3 pounds, trimmed
1 pound cabbage = 4 cups shredded

The younger the cabbage, the sweeter and milder the flavor. Your homegrown or recently harvested cabbages will have superior flavor to any head that has been left in a cooler or root cellar. Discard the tough, dark, outer leaves of cabbages.

Cabbage that is slowly sautéed will turn mild and sweet, but boiling (and especially over-boiling) brings out nasty sulfurous compounds that are best left unexplored. If you are making a classic dish, such as corned beef and cabbage, you are less likely to overcook the cabbage if you steam it in a little of the liquid in which you cooked the corned beef, rather than boiling it.

To serve cabbage raw, simply shred it and add it to salads; this is especially a good use for red cabbage. Any cabbage — green, red, savoy, or Chinese — can be shredded and marinated Japanese style, in a little vinegar with sugar and salt. Coleslaw has a million variations — sweet, vinegary, mustardy, fruity. You can add shredded carrots, raisins, apples, nuts, seeds, and herbs to any coleslaw with good results. Sometimes I make My Mother's Mustardy Slaw (page 356) and add chopped dill pickles and sunflower seeds.

Savoy cabbage leaves are more tender than green cabbage leaves and so are well suited to stuffing. Chinese cabbages are delicious both stir-fried and pickled.

TIMING
Steaming: 5 to 8 minutes
Sautéing or stir-frying: 4 to 5 minutes
Braising: 15 minutes

baked egg rolls

Are baked egg rolls as good as deep-fried egg rolls? Well, truthfully, no. But are they a worthy alternative? Oh, yes! These disappear quickly in my house, and I make them often because they don't involve the muss, fuss, and guilt of the deep-fried originals.

SERVES 6–10

½ pound shrimp, shelled and coarsely chopped
1 tablespoon soy sauce
1 tablespoon dry sherry
1 teaspoon minced fresh ginger
2 garlic cloves, minced
1 teaspoon cornstarch
Canola or peanut oil
1 small head cabbage, trimmed, cored, and finely shredded
1 carrot, finely shredded
1 cup bean sprouts
4 scallions, finely chopped
1 teaspoon dark sesame oil
1 teaspoon salt
Freshly ground black pepper
1 pound package egg roll skins (about 20)
1 egg white

1 Combine the shrimp, soy sauce, sherry, ginger, garlic, and cornstarch. Set aside to marinate for at least 10 minutes.

2 Heat a large wok over high heat. Add 2 tablespoons oil and heat until almost smoking. Add the shrimp and marinade and stir-fry until the shrimp are pink and firm, 4 to 5 minutes. Add the cabbage and carrot and stir-fry until limp, about 3 minutes. Stir in the bean sprouts, scallions, salt, sesame oil, and pepper to taste. Remove from the heat.

3 Preheat the oven to 400°F. Preheat a baking sheet in the oven.

4 Place an egg roll skin on a work surface with one corner pointing toward you. Place about ¼ cup of filling in the middle of the skin. Bring the corner of the skin closest to you up over the filling and tuck into a log shape. Bring in the two side corners, apply egg white to the last corner of skin, and finish rolling up the egg roll, sealing the roll closed. Continue until all the filling is used. Don't worry if the skins rip a little — because you aren't frying the rolls, it won't make any difference in the final product.

5 When all the egg rolls are made, remove the hot baking sheet from the oven and lightly brush with oil. Place the egg rolls on the baking sheet and brush each roll with more oil.

6 Bake for 20 to 25 minutes, until crispy and lightly browned. Serve hot.

A GUIDE TO CHINESE CABBAGE AND OTHER GREENS

THERE IS A WHOLE WORLD OF Chinese greens that should not be missed. Some are true cabbages, others are more closely related to other brassicas. All are worthy of space in the garden. The nomenclature is highly variable from one seed catalog and one gardening book to another. *Oriental Vegetables,* by Joy Larkcom, is widely regarded as the most authoritative book on the subject.

Bok Choy Also called pak choi and choy sun. These are greens with white to green stems and dark green leaves. The dwarf varieties are harvested as "baby" bok choy. The stems are juicy and tender, the leaves mildly cabbagey. These are excellent in stir-fries and soups.

Chinese Cabbage There are two types of Chinese cabbage: napa, which is shorter with wide, crinkly leaves, and michili, with narrower and smoother leaves. Both are more tender and sweeter than European cabbages. Unlike European cabbages, they are not good keepers (wrap in plastic and keep in the refrigerator for 1 to 2 weeks). They are best suited for use in salads and stir-fries.

Choy Sum Choy sum and other flowering Chinese greens or Chinese broccoli or Chinese kale all look very similar but they belong to different groups of plants. They all have fairly thick stems and tender leaves and flowers. The flavor is rather mustardy and may be bitter or mild. These plants are well suited to stir-fries and pickling.

Tatsoi Also called rosette bok choy. It is often the Asian green included in mesclun mixes. It is quite similar in flavor to bok choy, with juicy stems and cabbage-tasting leaves. It is somewhat tougher and stronger-flavored than bok choy.

I welcome fall weather with the return of main-course soups to the menu. This is one similar to a soup my mother used to make. The original, which came from our Russian-Jewish background, was made with a tough cut of beef (or gray meat, as we kids used to call it) simmered for hours, and my mother sweetened the tomato-based broth with, of all things, gingersnap cookies. I prefer my peppery version, scented with cumin.

SERVES 4–6

2–3 tablespoons olive or canola oil

1 pound sweet or hot Italian sausage, removed from its casings and crumbled

1 small head cabbage, quartered, cored, and thinly sliced

1 onion, halved and thinly sliced

1 can (28 ounces) diced tomatoes or 3½–4 cups diced fresh

6 cups chicken broth (page 9)

1 teaspoon ground cumin

Salt and freshly ground black pepper

Freshly ground white pepper (optional)

Vegetarian Tomato-Cabbage Soup Variation

Omit the sausage. Substitute a neutral-tasting vegetable broth for the chicken broth. If desired, add 1½ to 2 cups cooked chickpeas when you add the broth and tomatoes to make this a main-course soup.

1 Heat 2 tablespoons of the oil over medium heat in a large soup pot. Add the sausage and sauté until completely browned, about 10 minutes, breaking up the sausage with a spoon or spatula as you stir. Remove from the pot with a slotted spoon and set aside on a plate lined with paper towels.

2 If the soup pot is mostly dry, add the remaining 1 tablespoon oil. Add the cabbage and onion and sauté until golden, 8 to 10 minutes. Add the tomatoes, broth, and cumin. Return the sausage to the pot. Bring to a boil, then reduce the heat and simmer for about 1 hour, until the cabbage is completely tender and the flavors are well blended.

I prefer to use low-fat chicken or turkey sausage for this healthy soup.

3 Taste and season with salt, black pepper, and white pepper, being especially generous with the peppers. Serve hot.

M Y GREAT-GRANDMOTHER WAS FAMOUS FOR her pickles and sauerkraut. My mother told me that the attic was always filled with bubbling crocks, and she remembers apples in the sauerkraut. I wish I had gotten a tutorial — I've found making sauerkraut is tricky. Some people are always successful, some people rarely (I am successful about half the time).

After many failures, I've concluded that sauerkraut should always be made with fresh, recently harvested cabbage (older cabbage will not yield sufficient juices to make enough brine). Sanitation is crucial! Finally, you must provide temperatures that are 65°F or lower for good flavor. Higher temperatures will cause the fermentation to go more quickly, often resulting in flavors that can only be described as skunky.

Here is a simple recipe to try. I recommend starting on a small scale. This recipe should yield 2 quarts. You can add a couple of tablespoons of chopped garlic, dill seed, or juniper berries to the cabbage to vary the flavor.

5 pounds trimmed fresh green cabbage
3 tablespoons pickling salt

1. Quarter the cabbage and remove the central core. Thinly shred using a food processor (use a slicing, not a grating, blade), a kraut cutting board, or a knife.

2. Mix the cabbage and salt thoroughly in a large bowl or crock. Let stand for at least 2 hours, until the cabbage has softened and begun to release liquid.

3. Pack the sauerkraut into a 1-gallon crock or glass jar. As you pack, tamp the cabbage very firmly, using a potato masher or your hands. Weight the top of the sauerkraut with a food-grade plastic bag filled with water to exclude air from the top of the sauerkraut. Cover the container with a towel and place in a cool place.

4. Check the sauerkraut after 24 hours. The cabbage should be completely covered in brine. If necessary, make more brine by dissolving 1½ tablespoons pickling salt in 1 quart water. Pour in enough brine to keep the cabbage submerged. Then cover with the plastic bag and towel and return to the cool place.

5. Check the sauerkraut every few days and remove any scum that appears on the surface. If air is fully excluded, no scum will form. You should see little bubbles rising to the surface, indicating that fermentation is taking place. Start tasting the sauerkraut in 2 weeks. It will be fully fermented in 2 to 6 weeks, depending on the temperature. It will smell pickled.

6. Store fermented sauerkraut in the refrigerator for several months. For long-term storage at room temperature, process sauerkraut in pint jars for 20 minutes in a boiling-water bath (pages 475–477).

7. Taste the sauerkraut before serving. If it is too salty, rinse before serving. Do not rinse more than you will serve and consume at a single sitting.

chinese noodle soup with cabbage

When I was in college, I worked at a Chinese restaurant. There I learned, as I had always suspected, the best dishes were off the menu. Mr. Wong sometimes served steaming, gingery noodle soups in great big bowls. Nothing took the chill off an Ithaca winter so well. This soup is as close as I have come to the memory of those fantastic soups.

SERVES 4–6

8 cups chicken broth (page 9)

¼ cup soy sauce or to taste (see Note)

1 tablespoon Chinese rice wine or sherry

6–12 dried wood ear mushrooms, chopped if large

2 tablespoons minced fresh ginger

3 cloves garlic, minced

3 scallions, finely chopped

Salt and freshly ground black pepper

¾ pound Chinese egg noodles

1 tablespoon dark sesame oil

2 cups chopped cooked chicken (from making the broth) or 1 pound firm or silken tofu, cubed

4–6 cups chopped Chinese cabbage, bok choy, or other Chinese green, or a mix of cabbage and greens

1 carrot, julienned

Chinese chili paste with garlic (optional)

note The amount of soy sauce used assumes starting with an unsalted broth. If your soup base is salty, adjust the soy sauce accordingly.

1 Combine the broth, soy sauce, rice wine, mushrooms, ginger, garlic, and scallions in a large saucepan. Season with salt and pepper. Simmer for 25 minutes.

2 Meanwhile, bring a large pot of salted water to a boil. Add the noodles and sesame oil and cook until the noodles are just barely tender. Drain well and return the noodles to the pot to keep warm.

3 Add the chicken, cabbage, and carrots to the broth and simmer for another 10 minutes, until the carrots are tender.

4 To serve, place a nest of noodles in each bowl. Ladle the broth, vegetables, and chicken over the noodles and serve hot, passing the chili paste at the table for those who like a little spice in everything they eat.

CABBAGE HISTORY

THE ORIGINAL WILD CABBAGE, native of coastal regions of Europe, was more like kale than a heading cabbage. Though it is difficult to discover exactly when cabbage became a cultivated crop, botanists estimate from a few hundred to a few thousand years BC. There is plenty of evidence to suggest that the ancient Greeks and Romans ate cabbage.

Cato, an ancient Roman statesman, circa 200 BC, advised eating raw cabbage seasoned with vinegar before a banquet to avoid drunkenness, while raw cabbage supposedly kept ancient Egyptians sober. Not surprisingly, the standard treatment of the day for a nasty hangover was more cabbage.

At some time in the first century BC, the first heading cabbages appeared. The cultivation of cabbage spread throughout Europe during the Middle Ages, mostly as a food for peasants. Cabbage in the form of sauerkraut was quite commonplace. Nomadic Turks introduced pickled cabbage into Poland and Hungary during the 16th and 17th centuries. Red cabbage was first developed in the 16th century.

Today, cabbage is familiar in many different cuisines. Stuffed cabbage is a favorite throughout Eastern Europe and Turkey, while sliced cabbage is a familiar addition to stir-fries and soups throughout Asia. The Japanese serve pickled cabbage as an appetizer; Koreans get daily benefits from cabbage in the form of kimchi. Germany's national favorite is the long-cooking stew of sweet and sour red cabbage, whereas the French and Belgians prefer their savoy cabbage. The Irish enjoy cabbage with potatoes in colcannon. In Scandinavia and the United States, cabbage is most popularly eaten as coleslaw.

my mother's mustardy slaw

The best coleslaw is probably the one you grew up with. Frankly, I've tasted many a slaw in my days, and my favorite is still my mother's. In case you didn't get a chance to record your own mother's, here's mine. Food processors take all the work out of making coleslaws, and letting them stand for at least an hour before serving to blend the flavors is the key to an outstanding salad.

SERVES 4–6

4 cups grated green cabbage

2 carrots, grated

¼ cup minced onion

1 cup mayonnaise (substitute reduced-fat mayonnaise for part or all, if desired)

3 tablespoons yellow ballpark mustard

Salt and freshly ground black pepper

1 Combine the cabbage, carrots, and onion in a large bowl.

2 Combine the mayonnaise and mustard in a small bowl and mix. Spoon over the cabbage mixture and mix until well combined. Add the salt and pepper to taste.

3 Refrigerate for at least 1 hour, up to 8 hours, before serving.

MEET THE CABBAGE FAMILY

Cabbage is in the family of vegetables known as crucifers, a name derived from their cross-shaped flowers. All cabbages are crucifers, including broccoli, Brussels sprouts, cauliflower, kale, and collards.

There are three branches to the cabbage families. Stem cabbages include kohlrabi, Chinese cabbage, kale, and collards. Smooth-leaf and curled-leaf cabbage include savoy, red, white, and green head cabbages and Brussels sprouts. Inflorescent cabbages include broccoli and cauliflower.

creamy coleslaw

Some people prefer a sweeter coleslaw. This version is slightly sweet and low in fat.

SERVES 8

8 cups shredded green cabbage

3 carrots, shredded

¼ Vidalia or other sweet onion, finely chopped

1½ cups buttermilk

3 tablespoons cider vinegar

3 tablespoons sugar

3 tablespoons mayonnaise

½–¾ teaspoon celery seed

Salt and freshly ground black pepper

1 Combine the cabbage, carrots, and onion in a large mixing bowl.

2 Stir together the buttermilk, vinegar, sugar, mayonnaise, and celery seed in a smaller bowl until well blended. Pour the buttermilk mixture over the cabbage mixture and toss to combine. Season with salt and pepper. The salad will be dry, but the longer it stands, the wetter it will become.

3 Refrigerate for at least 1 hour, up to 8 hours, before serving.

red-cooked cabbage

Red cooking is a Chinese method of braising foods in soy sauce, which then take on a deep, dark, supposedly red color. I don't see the red myself, but I do love the method, and it gives food a rich, but not overly salty, flavor. Try it.

■ SERVES 6–8 ■

3 tablespoons canola or peanut oil

1 small head cabbage, thinly sliced (about 8 cups)

½ cup vegetable or chicken broth (page 8 or 9)

⅓ cup soy sauce

2 tablespoons rice vinegar

1 tablespoon dry sherry or Chinese rice wine

1 tablespoon dark sesame oil

1 teaspoon black peppercorns

1 teaspoon five-spice powder

1 Heat the canola oil in a large Dutch oven over medium-high heat. Add the cabbage and sauté until slightly wilted, about 5 minutes.

2 Stir in the remaining ingredients and mix well. Cover, reduce the heat to a simmer, and cook for about 20 minutes, stirring occasionally, until the cabbage is completely tender and very flavorful. Serve hot.

haluska

Comfort food was redefined the day I first sampled haluska, a simple Hungarian dish of noodles, cabbage, and sour cream. It ranks with colcannon (page 466) as simple food, restorative of the soul. If you make this dish with fat-free sour cream and eggless "egg" noodles, the dish is also good for you. Serve it as a main dish or side dish.

■ SERVES 6–10 ■

¼ cup butter

1 medium head cabbage, shredded or very finely sliced

1 large onion, halved and sliced

1 pound egg noodles

1 pound carton sour cream (fat-free or reduced-fat is fine)

Salt and freshly ground black pepper

1 Begin heating a large pot of salted water for the noodles.

2 Melt the butter in a large Dutch oven over medium heat. Add the cabbage and onion and sauté, stirring frequently, until the cabbage is limp and completely tender, about 10 minutes.

3 Cook the noodles in the boiling water until tender, 7 to 9 minutes, or according to the package directions. Drain well.

4 Add the noodles to the cabbage and mix well. Add the sour cream and stir until distributed throughout the dish. Season with salt and pepper. Serve immediately.

Who Knew They Were So Much Better Fresh?

HOMEGROWN CARROTS ARE A FLAVOR REVELATION. Who knew that supermarket carrots, stored for months and shipped from afar, were so inferior to homegrown carrots? Not I. Like most of us, I thought that supermarket carrots were a perfectly acceptable product. Then I started growing my own. Now I can barely stand an out-of-season carrot.

I could probably quadruple the size of my carrot patch and still not grow enough. So eager are my kids for fresh carrots that they start harvesting as soon as the tops are big enough for them to identify the plants as carrots. This wouldn't be so bad if the carrot patch needed thinning, but I usually plant pelleted seed because I find thinning such a difficult chore. (I find it hard to discard a healthy plant, even when necessary for the remaining ones.)

I usually plant two varieties of carrots — an early variety that is best for eating fresh and young and a later variety that can be stored. Fresh summer carrots are perfect as they are, so I rarely cook with them. Cooking is for storage carrots, when the flavor is less than perfection, hence the placement of this chapter with other fall crops.

Carrots will keep reasonably well in plastic bags in the refrigerator for a couple of months. Storage in a root cellar is ideal. Even without a root cellar, you can mimic root cellar conditions by layering carrots in damp sand or sawdust in a bin, box, or plastic bucket and storing in a cool basement. Trim off the greens, leaving about 1 inch of stem, before storing.

SOW & REAP

GROWING Carrots do best in rich, loose soil. Grown in heavy or stony soil, these root vegetables are likely to be stunted or misshapen. Carrots prefer full sun but will tolerate light shade.

SOWING Carrots need soil temperatures of about 75°F. Sow from early spring to midsummer.

CULTIVATING Carrots prefer their roots to be cool and their tops warm, so mulch the soil to keep it cool. Thin plants to allow at least 2 inches between plants. Keep weeded.

HARVESTING If your soil is loose, you should be able to pull the carrots out of the ground. If the roots snap off, loosen the soil first with a pitchfork. Clip off the foliage, leaving 1 inch of stem. Brush off any loose soil and store in plastic bags in the refrigerator or layered in moist sand or sawdust in a root cellar.

TIMING

Steaming: 5 to 7 minutes, sliced or diced
Blanching: 4 to 6 minutes, sliced or diced
Sautéing or stir-frying: 5 to 8 minutes, diced, sliced, or julienned
Grilling: About 10 minutes for whole baby, diced, or sliced carrots
Roasting: 20 to 30 minutes at 425°F for whole baby, diced, sliced, or julienned carrots

KITCHEN NOTES

Carrots are delectable raw or cooked by just about any known cooking method. As with most root vegetables, roasting is probably the best way to prepare carrots. Grilling is another excellent, if nontraditional, way to prepare carrots. Grilled baby carrots make a wonderful summer dish. Just slick the carrots with a little olive oil, place on the grill (use a vegetable grill rack to keep the carrots out of the fire), and grill, turning frequently until tender, about 10 minutes.

Most people prefer their carrots peeled, but a good scrubbing is all that is really required for young, fresh carrots.

CARROT NUTRITION NOTES

Those bright orange carrots are an excellent source of beta-carotene, an antioxidant that may help prevent heart disease and some kinds of cancer. Carrots are also an excellent source of vitamin A, which helps maintain good eyesight, fight infection, and support bone growth. Carrots also deliver fiber, minerals, and vitamins C and E.

CARROT MATH

1 pound carrots = 4 to 6 large carrots
= 3 cups sliced or diced
= 4 cups grated

creamy dilled carrot slaw

Low-fat buttermilk provides the dressing for this spectacular salad. If you have a food processor for grating the carrots, you can throw the slaw together in minutes to have a colorful, healthy garnish on any plate that needs a little dressing up.

■ SERVES 4 ■

1 pound carrots, grated
3 scallions, green and tender white parts, finely chopped
2 tablespoons finely chopped fresh dill
1 tablespoon extra-virgin olive oil
½ cup buttermilk
2 tablespoons fresh lemon juice, or to taste
Salt and freshly ground black pepper

1 Combine the carrots, scallions, and dill in a medium salad bowl. Add the oil and toss to coat. Add the buttermilk and lemon juice. Season to taste with salt and pepper.

2 Cover and let stand for at least 30 minutes, or up to 2 hours, to allow the flavors to develop.

3 Stir well and adjust the seasonings before serving.

chilled carrot soup with tarragon

"Tastes like carrot-flavored velvet" was my son's comment upon first tasting this soup. The texture is luxurious, and the flavor is unabashedly carrot. If you prefer, the soup can be served hot.

■ SERVES 4 ▶

2 tablespoons canola oil

1 onion, finely chopped

1 pound carrots, sliced

3 cups chicken broth (page 9)

½ cup white wine

¼ cup white rice

2 tablespoons chopped fresh tarragon, plus more for garnishing

Salt and freshly ground white pepper

Sugar (optional)

1 Heat the oil over medium-high heat in a large saucepan. Add the onion and sauté for 3 to 4 minutes until soft. Add the carrots, 2 cups of the broth, the wine, rice, and tarragon. Season to taste with the salt and pepper. Bring to a boil. Reduce the heat to a simmer, cover, and cook, stirring occasionally until the carrots are completely soft, about 45 minutes. Remove from the heat and cool briefly.

2 Purée the carrot mixture in a food processor or blender. Return to the pot. Add the remaining 1 cup broth. Taste and adjust the seasoning. A pinch of sugar may help bring the flavors together.

3 Chill before serving or reheat to serve hot. Garnish with sprigs of fresh tarragon.

maple-roasted carrots

■ SERVES 5 ■

1 pound carrots, cut into thin 3-inch spears
1 tablespoon canola oil
   Salt
1 tablespoon butter
2 tablespoons pure maple syrup
   Chopped fresh parsley or cilantro, for garnish

1 Preheat the oven to 425°F. Lightly grease with oil a baking sheet just large enough to hold the carrots in a single layer.

2 Put the carrots on the prepared baking sheet. Drizzle with the oil and toss to coat. Arrange in a single layer.

3 Roast for about 15 minutes. Meanwhile, melt the butter in the maple syrup on top of the stove or in a microwave.

4 Drizzle the maple syrup mixture over the carrots. With a metal spatula, turn the carrots over. Roast for another 5 to 10 minutes, until the carrots are lightly browned and easily pierced with a fork. Stir with the spatula to coat the carrots with the glaze on the bottom of the pan and transfer to a serving dish.

5 Garnish with the parsley. Serve hot.

CARROT COLOR

MY SISTERS WERE CALLED "CARROT-TOP" when they were growing up because of their bright red hair, which, of course, was really orange in color. It was suggested that my auburn hair was a result of not eating my carrots. Such nutritional wisdom aside, I note that had my sisters been born in ancient Egyptian, their nickname would never have arisen, since carrots in ancient times were purple. The Romans cultivated both the purple carrot and a white one. By the 16th century, carrots were grown in purple, white, yellow, green, red, black — almost any color but orange. This bothered the Dutch, who were noted horticulturalists (think tulips) and were ruled by the House of Orange. They crossbred red and yellow carrots to produced orange carrots, which became all the rage. Today purple carrots and yellow are gaining popularity. My sisters' hair remains red, which is to say orange. ■

WHEN OSCAR BARKER SAYS that he has been gardening almost his whole life, he isn't exaggerating. His first garden was in a vacant lot in Yonkers, New York, during World War II; his most recent garden is in a community garden plot in St. Petersburg, Florida. And in between there were years of gardening in upstate New York. Oscar Barker is 79 years young and going strong.

Barker likens the community garden to the "old-fashioned victory gardens." The garden is operated by the city, which has installed watering outlets for every plot and brings in yards of topsoil every year. The city charges $25 every six months for plots that are 5 feet wide by 30 feet long.

Because the soil is so sandy and so low in fertility, Barker adds store-bought composted cow manure and fertilizes regularly with a chemical 6-6-6 fertilizer. "We get enough out of the garden to take care of the two of us [Barker and his wife, Patricia]. We aren't saving any money," he says, "but we sure do eat well." Barker harvests fresh vegetables almost all year. It's only in the summer that his vegetable production shuts down.

Obviously, gardening in Florida is very different from gardening up north. Barker finds it "too darn hot" to spend much time outside in the summer, so he plants a cover crop of peanuts and sweet potatoes in late May and leaves the garden unattended: "You have to plant a cover crop.

That's one lesson I learned early on. The cover crop keeps weeds and crabgrass down. One year, I didn't plant anything and the crabgrass took over. It made such a dense mat it broke my spade. My son had to rescue me . . .

"In August, I start right in with the hot-weather crops: tomatoes, eggplant, green peppers, string beans. Then later some beets, carrots. Come November, we'll be eating tomatoes. I usually grow Celebrity. That's one variety that really works for me. And string beans — I get three or four or five pickings. A real treat is the beets. They get to be as big as softballs and as sweet as can be.

"The hardest thing to get used to was the idea that you have to water more frequently. I live about a mile from the garden, so it's no chore to get out there. I aim for every other day. And I fertilize every three weeks with a handful of 6-6-6. That's different from the way I used to garden."

Barker describes the garden as a "potpourri" of folks. One of his fellow gardeners is a retired contractor in his mid-80s, originally from Wisconsin. Another is from Cuba. There are many young couples who have plots, as well as a middle school teacher who has a class garden. Still, the majority of gardeners at this garden are retired men.

"You can always find a neighbor who will lend a hand with the watering if you need it. People will share tools. It's a real community here," he says.

chocolate chip carrot cake

Can't decide between chocolate cake and carrot cake? I have the solution: carrot cake with chocolate chips. It has come to my attention, however, that not everyone likes chocolate. Purists may omit the chips, though I can't imagine why they'd want to.

Cake

2½ cups unbleached all-purpose flour

1½ teaspoons baking powder

1 teaspoon baking soda

1½ teaspoons ground cinnamon

½ teaspoon freshly grated nutmeg

¼ teaspoon ground ginger

1 teaspoon salt

1 pound (6–7 medium) carrots

1 cup granulated sugar

1 cup packed light brown sugar

4 large eggs

1½ cups canola oil

½ teaspoon pure vanilla extract

½ teaspoon almond extract

1 cup chopped walnuts or flaked almonds, toasted

1 cup mini chocolate chips

Cream Cheese Frosting

8 ounces cream cheese, at room temperature

¼ cup butter, at room temperature

1 teaspoon pure vanilla extract

1½ cups confectioners' sugar

1 Preheat the oven to 350°F. Grease a 13- by 9-inch baking pan with oil or spray with nonstick cooking spray.

2 Combine the flour, baking powder, baking soda, cinnamon, nutmeg, ginger, and salt in a large bowl.

3 Shred the carrots in a food processor. Add the carrots to the flour mixture.

4 Fit the processor with a metal blade. Combine the white and brown sugars and eggs in the food processor and process to mix. With the motor running, add the oil and extracts through the feed tube in a steady stream. Process until well mixed and emulsified, about 30 seconds. Scrape into the bowl with the carrots and flour mixture. Stir by hand until well mixed. Fold in the nuts and chips. Scrape into the prepared baking pan.

5 Bake for 35 to 40 minutes, until a tester inserted in the center of the cake comes out clean. Cool in the pan on a rack.

6 To make the frosting, combine the cream cheese, butter, and vanilla in a food processor and process until blended. Scrape down the work bowl, add the confectioners' sugar, and process until smooth. Spread on the cooled cake.

CARROT FLAVOR

Fresh garden carrots taste better than supermarket carrots mainly because we haven't had the time to mishandle the storage. Freshness being equal, the best-tasting carrots are ones grown between 60° and 70°F with even moisture. Carrots grown at higher temperatures will have shorter roots, while those grown at lower temperatures will have longer ones. Too little moisture slows the growth, and the carrot is likely to be more fibrous and less sweet. As for the soil, a high sodium and calcium content, such as found in soil reclaimed from the sea in the Netherlands and in parts of California, may result in sweeter carrots.

carrot muffins

It gives me great pleasure to sneak vegetables into treats for kids. A cinnamon-and-sugar topping makes these irresistible.

MAKES ABOUT 16 MUFFINS

3 cups unbleached all-purpose flour
1 tablespoon baking powder
1 teaspoon baking soda
1 teaspoon ground cinnamon
1 teaspoon salt
¼ teaspoon ground nutmeg
½ cup butter, softened
1 cup sugar
2 large eggs
1½ cups firmly packed grated carrots
¼ cup pure maple syrup
¼ cup sour cream or yogurt
1 teaspoon pure vanilla extract

Topping

½ cup sugar
1½ teaspoons ground cinnamon
5 tablespoons butter, melted

1 Preheat the oven to 350°F. Grease 16 regular-size muffin cups.

2 Sift together the flour, baking powder, baking soda, cinnamon, salt, and nutmeg.

3 Cream together the butter and sugar in a large bowl. Add the eggs, one at a time, beating after each addition. Beat in the carrots, maple syrup, sour cream, and vanilla. Beat in the flour mixture until smooth.

4 Divide the batter among the prepared muffin cups. The batter will be stiff; an ice-cream scoop does a great job of distributing it.

5 Bake the muffins for 25 to 30 minutes, until they have risen and a knife inserted in the center of one comes out clean.

6 Let the muffins cool in the pan on a wire rack for a few minutes.

7 To make the topping, mix together the sugar and cinnamon in a shallow bowl. When the muffins are just cool enough to handle, one at a time dip the tops into the melted butter, then into the sugar and cinnamon mixture, covering the tops completely. Let cool before serving.

CULTIVAR TASTING NOTES

Babette is a true baby carrot, meant to be harvested young, sweet, and tender.

Beta Sweet has purple skin and an orange interior. It has been developed to be especially rich in beta-carotene and anthocyanin, also a health-promoting antioxidant.

Nantes are a longtime favorite of home gardeners because they are sweet, crisp, and full-flavored. You can identify a Nantes carrot by its blunt tip and sausagelike shape. There are many Nantes crosses available, including **Bolero, Napoli, Sweetness II, Nelson, Mokum,** and **Scarlet Nantes.**

Nelson is a dependable variety for early harvest. It is a mainstay of many summer gardens, including mine.

Parisian Rondo is a round French heirloom.

Scarlet Wonder is a brilliant red, but average-tasting.

Queen or Brat of the Garden?

IN SOME CUISINES, cauliflower is treated quite nobly, the queen of vegetables. On the other hand, garden writer Ed Smith (*The Vegetable Gardener's Bible,* Storey Books, 2000) says, "Cauliflower has long had a reputation for being a vegetable prima donna. It is the easiest of the cabbage family to stress, and when it stresses, it acts like a two-year-old and bolts."

It was Mark Twain who remarked, "Training is everything. The cauliflower is nothing but a cabbage with a college education." That extra training makes cauliflower a highly versatile member of the cabbage family. Cauliflower can be roasted, steamed, boiled, sautéed, braised, stewed, and eaten raw. It is a veritable workhouse of flavor, high in nutrition, low in calories. Why, it is even considered a potato substitute among the low-carb crowd.

But unless you are a gardener who believes in pampering your vegetables, you might consider this one vegetable worth paying someone else to grow. I do. I hate it in the garden, but I love it in the kitchen.

GROWING Sow and weep is more like it. Cauliflower does best when it is treated with great respect all the way through its growing season. It requires disease-free, fertile, neutral or slightly sweet soil, and even watering, and it gives its best yields in full sun.

SOWING Sow indoors about 1 month before the last frost date. Provide a germination temperature of 70°F and early growing temperatures of at least 60°F. Transplant seedlings when they are 4 to 5 weeks old. Older seedlings will experience transplant shock, which may cause them to become root-bound and to stop growing.

CULTIVATING Keep evenly watered throughout the growing season. Fertilize with compost tea. Blanch the growing heads, bending a few leaves over the head and securing with twine. So-called self-blanching types will yellow without blanching, despite what may be written in seed catalogs.

HARVESTING Cauliflower is ready for harvest when the head is tight and fairly regular; about 4 days after blanching in warm weather and within 10 days in cooler weather. Don't wait any longer, because the head is prone to rotting. To harvest, slice the head off the stem.

The purple cauliflower varieties retain their color best when steamed. Generally, the purple types fade to light lavender, but are still beautiful. Combining white and purple varieties in a dish is very attractive. Purple types are supposed to taste like a cross between broccoli and cauliflower, but I think the cauliflower flavor predominates. The new orange varieties (more yellow than orange in my experience) become slightly brighter orange when cooked.

To prepare cauliflower for cooking, remove the leaves and cut away the core. Cut or break apart the florets.

Cauliflower can be added raw to salads. Green, purple, orange, and white cauliflower make a terrific crudités platter. Or steam cauliflower and season with sea salt and/or butter, or sprinkle with toasted buttered bread crumbs or grated Parmesan.

TIMING
Steaming: 3 to 6 minutes
Blanching: 3 to 6 minutes
Roasting: 20 minutes at 450°F

CAULIFLOWER MATH
1 large head = 6 cups florets
1 pound cauliflower = 4 cups florets

marinated cauliflower

Any time you are looking for a make-ahead vegetable dish — whether it is for an appetizer, salad, or even side dish — I believe this marinated cauliflower can fit the bill. Serve it as an hors d'oeuvre, with toothpicks nearby for serving, or place it in a colorful bowl to pass as a salad or side dish. The cauliflower will keep for several days.

SERVES 6–8

2 heads cauliflower, broken into florets
½ cup extra-virgin olive oil
¼ cup red wine vinegar
¼ cup chopped fresh parsley
1 tablespoon chopped fresh oregano, tarragon, summer savory, or basil, or 1 teaspoon dried
1 garlic clove, minced
1 teaspoon salt
Freshly ground black pepper

1 Bring a large pot of salted water to a boil. Add the cauliflower and boil until just slightly softened, about 3 minutes. The cauliflower should be slightly crunchy. Drain well.

2 Combine the oil, vinegar, parsley, herbs, garlic, salt, and pepper to taste in a large bowl. Whisk to blend. Add the still-warm cauliflower and toss gently with a rubber spatula. Marinate for 8 hours or longer in the refrigerator.

3 Remove from the refrigerator and allow to warm to room temperature before serving.

garlic- & cheese-crumbed cauliflower

A large head of cauliflower should serve about four but, in fact, the creamy cauliflower combines so successfully with the garlic-flavored crumbs that it is hard to stop eating it. This dish may convince even the pickiest eaters that cauliflower is a delicacy. If you are serving vegetable lovers, double the recipe.

SERVES 2–4

1 large head cauliflower, broken into florets
¼ cup butter
2 garlic cloves, minced
2 tablespoons minced fresh parsley
1 cup fresh bread crumbs (see Note)
½ cup grated Gruyère
Salt and freshly ground black pepper

1 Bring a large pot of salted water to a boil. Add the cauliflower and boil until tender, about 6 minutes. Drain well.

2 Preheat the oven to 375°F. Grease a 1½-quart baking dish with butter.

3 Melt the butter in a small saucepan over medium heat. Add the garlic and parsley and simmer just until fragrant, about 2 minutes.

4 Toss together the bread crumbs, cheese, and salt and pepper to taste in a small bowl.

5 Arrange the cauliflower in the prepared baking dish. Top with the crumb mixture. Drizzle the butter and garlic mixture over the top. Bake for about 15 minutes, until the cauliflower is hot and the crumbs are golden. Serve hot.

note Two to three slices of whole wheat sandwich bread whirled in a food processor will make 1 cup of fresh bread crumbs, perfect for this dish.

roasted spiced cauliflower

You will be amazed at how tender cauliflower can become with just dry heat. These cauliflower bites can be served as a side dish, hors d'oeuvre, or snack. You just can't stop eating them.

SERVES 2–4

¼ cup canola oil
1 teaspoon garlic salt
1 teaspoon curry powder
1 teaspoon ground cumin
½ teaspoon ground cardamom
½ teaspoon ground ginger
¼ teaspoon cayenne
¼ teaspoon freshly ground black pepper
1 large head cauliflower (about 3 pounds), cut into florets
Kosher or coarse salt

1 Preheat the oven to 450°F. Lightly grease a large sheet pan (preferred) or large shallow roasting pan with oil.

2 Combine the oil with the garlic salt, curry powder, cumin, cardamom, ginger, cayenne, and black pepper in a large bowl. Mix well. Add the cauliflower and toss to coat. Spread the cauliflower on the prepared pan in a single layer.

3 Roast for about 20 minutes, stirring occasionally, until the florets are tender-crisp and browned.

4 To serve, mound the florets on a serving platter and sprinkle with the kosher salt to taste.

You can turn this side dish into a vegetarian main dish by adding 2 cups of cooked chick-peas. Or sauté strips of chicken with the onion and make it into a main dish. In any case, you will want to serve it with rice or nan, to soak up the delicious tomato-based curry sauce.

SERVES 4

2 tablespoons canola oil

1 large onion, halved and sliced

2 garlic cloves, minced

1 teaspoon minced fresh ginger

5 teaspoons curry powder

2 teaspoons garam masala (available wherever Indian spices are sold)

1 teaspoon cumin seeds

1 teaspoon fenugreek seeds

2 cups water

1 cup tomato purée

1 head cauliflower, broken into 1-inch florets

Salt and freshly ground black pepper

Cayenne

⅓ cup chopped fresh cilantro

1 Heat the oil over medium heat in a large, nonstick saucepan. Sauté the onion, garlic, ginger, curry powder, garam masala, cumin seeds, and fenugreek in the oil until the onion is soft, about 8 minutes. Do not let the spices scorch; lower the heat as needed.

2 Stir in the water, tomato purée, and cauliflower. Cover and simmer until the cauliflower is tender, about 20 minutes. Season with salt, pepper, and cayenne. Simmer for an additional 10 minutes to allow the flavors to blend.

3 Just before serving, stir in the cilantro. Taste and adjust the seasoning. Serve hot.

A vegetable tart at a brunch is a welcome change from quiche — more vegetables and no eggs to compete with the other egg dishes.

SERVES 4–8

1 head cauliflower, broken into florets

2 tablespoons extra-virgin olive oil

2 leeks, trimmed and sliced

1 teaspoon chopped fresh thyme leaves or
½ teaspoon dried

Salt and freshly ground black pepper

Unbaked pastry for two 10-inch tarts (page 10)

8 ounces fontina, Gruyère, or Comté cheese, grated
(about 2 cups)

1 Preheat the oven to 425°F. Set out a large baking sheet.

2 Steam the cauliflower over boiling water until tender, about 7 minutes.

3 Heat the oil in a large skillet. Add the leeks and thyme and sauté until tender, about 4 minutes. Season to taste with the salt and pepper.

4 Place one piece of pastry on the baking sheet. Unfold the pastry and pinch together any tears. Sprinkle one quarter of the cheese over the pastry, leaving a 2-inch border around the edge. Arrange half the cauliflower over the cheese and top with half the leek mixture. Sprinkle with another one quarter of the cheese. Fold the dough over to partially cover the filling and crimp to seal the edges. Repeat with the remaining pastry, cheese, cauliflower, and leek mixture.

5 Bake for 20 to 25 minutes, until the crust is golden.

6 Cut into wedges and serve warm or at room temperature.

pasta with cauliflower in a spicy tomato sauce

Two pots dirtied and a low-fat, high-flavor, vegetable-rich dinner is ready in just more than a half hour. That's my kind of dish.

SERVES 4

1 head cauliflower, broken into florets
2 tablespoons extra-virgin olive oil
1 onion, diced
2 garlic cloves, minced
4 anchovy fillets (optional)
1 teaspoon crushed red pepper flakes
1 can (28 ounces) diced tomatoes with juice
1 cup pitted cured black olives, such as Kalamata
1 tablespoon capers
  Salt and freshly ground black pepper
1 pound rotini or other short pasta
  Freshly grated Parmesan, for serving

1 Bring a large pot of salted water to a boil. Add the cauliflower and boil until just barely tender, about 3 minutes. Remove from the water and set aside. Return the water to a boil for the pasta.

2 Heat the oil in a large saucepan over medium heat. Gently sauté the onion, garlic, anchovy fillets, if using, and crushed red pepper flakes in the oil until the onion is tender, about 4 minutes, stirring constantly. Add the tomatoes, olives, capers, and cauliflower. Taste, then season with salt and pepper (the anchovies and olives may contribute all the salt needed). Simmer for about 15 minutes while you cook the pasta.

3 Cook the pasta in the boiling water until al dente. Drain well.

4 Serve the pasta with the sauce spooned over the top. Pass the Parmesan at the table.

Planting Hope Each Fall

PLANTING GARLIC EACH FALL is an act of hope that salves the soul as the days shorten and the weather turns colder and damper. As I put the garden to bed, I take heart in knowing that garlic, in neat little rows, will sprout as soon as the snow melts. For a few short weeks, I am ahead of the season and its endless chores.

Garlic is not really a fall crop. It is usually harvested midsummer, opening up space in the garden for another crop. But I think of it as a fall crop because there is no rush to use it before it goes bad or loses its flavor. After it has been harvested and cured for 2 weeks or so, I braid the stems and hang the braids from nails in the kitchen. Every time I need a fresh bulb, I cut it from the braid. The garlic keeps well for months. There are few savory dishes that aren't enhanced by the addition of the "stinking rose." Depending on whether the garlic is used raw or roasted, the flavor may be sharp and pungent or sweet and nutty.

There are other reasons to grow and eat garlic — if you believe in the wisdom of the ancients. Aristophanes wrote that garlic gave courage. Pliny wrote that it cured consumption. The prophet Muhammad said it eased pain. But of everything I've read, I think only this is absolutely true, "Garlick maketh a man wynke, drynke and stynke" (Thomas Nash, 16th-century poet).

GROWING Garlic does best in deep, well-drained fertile soil. It yields best in full sun but will tolerate light shade. Garlic is very adaptable. Select your largest cloves to save for planting each year; the garlic variety will adapt to your growing conditions.

SOWING In cooler climates, plant cloves about a month before the soil freezes. In warmer regions, plant in early winter. After planting, mulch with a thick layer of straw or leaves.

CULTIVATING Keep the soil cool and free from weeds with a generous layer of mulch. Interplanting with lettuce or beets helps keep the soil cooler. Some varieties produce flower buds; some do not. If yours does, snip off the stem and bud. These are called scapes and can be used as a scallion in stir-fries, though they are tougher and require more cooking.

HARVESTING Each leaf expressed above the ground is a bulb wrapper below. You want to harvest when about 60 percent of the plant is still green, so there are five or six wrappers still around each bulb. Then you have to cure the bulbs to develop the fine flavor. What tastes hot and fiery becomes mellow after about a month of curing. Curing also dries the bulbs, which allows for long-term storage.

To harvest, loosen the soil with a garden fork and pull out the bulbs. Brush any soil off the bulbs and spread them out on a screen that allows for air circulation. Keep them out of the rain and let them dry for about 2 weeks, until the skins are dry and the necks are tight. Remove the tops and store the bulbs in a cool, dry place — or leave the tops in place and braid the bulbs into ropes.

Garlic can taste nutty and mild, or it can be peppery and harsh. To tame the harsh flavor of garlic, place the cloves in a small heatproof bowl, pour in boiling water to cover, and let the cloves steep for a few minutes before using.

Toward the end of winter, the garlic you have stored may begin to sprout. The sprout is often bitter and hard to digest, so it is a good idea to cut the clove in two and remove the green sprout.

There are many opinions on how best to peel garlic. I prefer smashing the cloves with the flat side of a chef's blade. The paper peels easily apart from the cloves and the garlic is ready for mincing.

TIMING
Sautéing or stir-frying: 30 to 60 seconds (minced cloves)
Roasting: 20 minutes at 350°F (whole bulbs)

GARLIC MATH
1 medium clove = ½ teaspoon minced garlic

aioli

Le Grand Aioli is a tradition of Provençe in which people celebrate the garlic harvest. In many villages, it used to be celebrated as a big potluck, where the women of the village would make huge quantities of aioli, a garlic-flavored mayonnaise, and the men would bring whatever foodstuffs they typically had on hand — the fishermen brought fish, the farmers brought vegetables, and so on. Today, Le Grand Aioli is more likely to be a catered affair, with a traditional meal of salt cod (brandade de morue) *and baby potatoes, fresh vegetables, and plenty of wine.*

Aioli by another name would be "food of the gods" — it is that heavenly. It has been called "the triumph of the provençal kitchen." Whatever its origins, it is terrific as a dip for vegetables or seafood. We like it as a spread on French bread or a topping on raw or roasted vegetables. For the best results, select the freshest garlic and eggs you can find.

MAKES 2½ CUPS

8–10 garlic cloves, peeled
2 large egg yolks, at room temperature, lightly beaten
Juice of 1 lemon (3 tablespoons)
1 teaspoon Dijon mustard
1 cup extra-virgin olive oil
1 cup canola oil
Salt and freshly ground black pepper

Eating eggs that are not completely cooked poses the possibility of salmonella food poisoning. The risk is greater for pregnant women, the elderly and very young, and people with impaired immune systems. If you are concerned about salmonella, you can use pasteurized eggs.

1 Purée the garlic in a food processor fitted with a steel blade. Add the egg yolks, lemon juice, and mustard and process until smooth.

2 Combine the olive and canola oils in a small bowl. With the motor running, slowly pour in the oil in a steady stream. Continue processing until you have a thick, shiny sauce. Season with salt and pepper and store in the refrigerator until you are ready to use it. Remember, with the raw yolks, it is quite perishable, so do not store for more than 4 hours before serving (see Note).

Skordalia is a traditional Greek garlic sauce. Don't be deceived by the simplicity of the recipe — people swoon over this dip with its velvety texture and heavenly flavor. It is terrific as a topping for any cooked vegetable, especially beets, or as a spread on toasted pita bread.

MAKES ABOUT 2 CUPS

1½ pounds baking or russet potatoes (2–4 potatoes), peeled and cut into chunks

6 garlic cloves, minced

⅓ cup fresh lemon juice

½ cup extra-virgin olive oil

Salt

If you hate to get the smell of garlic on your fingers, you will probably prefer to use a garlic press. I find them annoying to clean, although a toothbrush is said to do a good job of clearing away the bits of garlic that cling.

Pressing releases more flavor than mincing because the press causes more breakdown of the cells, which releases more of the pungent compound that gives garlic its distinctive flavor. Mincing to a smooth paste (aided by a pinch of salt) is equally effective at releasing the flavor.

1 Put the potatoes in a small saucepan and cover with salted water. Bring to a boil and boil until completely tender, about 15 minutes. Drain well.

2 Transfer the potatoes to the bowl of a standing mixer. Add the garlic and lemon juice and mash. Beat over medium speed until the potatoes are smooth.

3 With the mixer at medium speed, very slowly pour in the oil until the mixture is velvety smooth and the oil has been fully incorporated.

4 Season with salt as needed. Serve at room temperature.

Just put the garden to bed, and now you are looking for a quick supper to make? In a well-stocked kitchen, this hearty, satisfying soup can be thrown together with little or no planning.

SERVES 4–6

4 cans (15 ounces each) cannellini (white kidney) beans, rinsed and drained

4 cups chicken broth (page 9)

6 garlic cloves, minced

2 teaspoons fresh thyme or 1 teaspoon dried

½ pound Italian sausage, casings removed

2 carrots, diced

Salt and freshly ground black pepper

1 Combine the beans, broth, garlic, and thyme in a large soup pot. Cover and bring to a boil. Simmer for 10 minutes.

2 Meanwhile, brown the sausage in a nonstick skillet, about 5 minutes. Remove from the skillet with a slotted spoon and place on paper towels to drain off any excess fat.

3 Process the soup in a blender until smooth. Return the soup to the pot. Add the browned sausage and the carrots. Simmer for 10 minutes. Skim off any foam that rises to the top.

4 Adjust the seasonings with salt pepper and additional thyme if desired. Serve hot.

"Three nickels will get you on the subway, but garlic will get you a seat."

—Yiddish wisdom from New York City

You can multiply this recipe to make as much as you need. Each head will yield about 1 heaping tablespoon of purée. A great way to serve roasted garlic is as an accompaniment for bread. Offer the roasted cloves in one small dish and a very high-quality extra-virgin olive oil in another dish. Diners can dip the bread in olive oil, then smear a clove of roasted garlic on the bread.

MAKES 1 HEAD

1 whole head garlic
1 teaspoon extra-virgin olive oil
1 tablespoon water

1 Preheat the oven to 375°F.

2 Remove the outer papery covering on the garlic. Slice off the top of the head so most of the cloves are exposed. Place on a square of aluminum foil for easy cleanup, or select the smallest baking dish you have. Drizzle the oil over the top of the cloves. Sprinkle with the water. Fold the aluminum foil over the bulb to enclose it or cover the baking dish with aluminum foil.

3 Roast for about 20 minutes, until the garlic is soft and lightly browned.

4 To serve, separate the head into individual cloves. Allow your diners to squeeze out the softened garlic as needed. Or squeeze out the cloves into a small serving dish.

Herbalists claim garlic is the most potent antibacterial agent on the planet. It is also a strong antifungal agent. It has been shown to lower cholesterol and hypertension, reduce the size of cancerous tumors, and enhance the immune system. It also soothes asthma. Have you had your garlic today?

When there's "nothing" in the house to cook, there's often the fixings for spaghetti aglio e olio.

SERVES 4–6

⅓ cup extra-virgin olive oil

4–8 cloves garlic, minced

4 anchovy fillets, minced (optional)

½–1 teaspoon crushed red pepper flakes (optional)

1 pound spaghetti

2 tablespoons chopped fresh parsley

Salt and freshly ground black pepper

1 Bring a large pot of a salted water to a boil for the pasta.

2 Meanwhile, heat the oil in a large skillet over medium heat. Add the garlic, anchovies, if using, and red pepper, if using, and simmer until fragrant, stirring to dissolve the anchovies, 1 to 2 minutes. Let the garlic color slightly and remove from the heat immediately if it begins to get dark.

3 Cook the pasta until just barely al dente. Drain briefly and add the pasta to the skillet with some water still clinging to the strands. Add the parsley. Toss to coat the pasta with the oil. Season with salt and pepper and serve hot.

According to legend, four grave robbers looting plague victims' corpses in Marseilles in 1772 were amazingly immune to the plague. Their secret was garlic-infused vinegar, which they ate, bathed in, anointed their clothes with, and soaked into rags through which they breathed. It became known as the Vinegar of the Four Thieves. The custom of protecting oneself with garlic-infused vinegar caught on during the plague, as did wearing strings of garlic around one's neck.

BRAIDING GARLIC IS EASY. Also, a braid of garlic is the perfect way to preserve the bulb and ensure that it gets proper air circulation. In the Middle Ages, braids of garlic were hung over the cribs of newborns to protect the babies from being kidnapped by fairies.

Braid the garlic while the leaves are still attached and pliable, within 2 weeks of harvesting. Peel off loose skins, taking all the dirt with them. Rinse off any plants that are still dirty. Once dry, the dirt will stain the garlic bulbs, so be meticulous. Leave the garlic to dry for a few days.

Take three large heads and place them on a table with the stems pointing toward you. Braid the leaves together once or twice, close to the garlic heads; braid tightly so that the leaves don't show in between. Add a fourth head of garlic above the center one; include its stem with any one of the others and braid a little more. Next, add two more heads, this time to the side. Include the stems with the others and keep braiding. Add one, then two, then one again until the braid is as long as you want. For the best appearance, keep the heads close together. (When I am doing this for myself, however, I braid loosely, to make it easier to break off the garlic heads as I use them; I don't care how it looks.) To finish, braid the remaining leaves together, tie with twine, and trim the ends. Hang to dry.

They Grow Like Weeds

I AM THINKING OF PLANTING A GARDEN of the giants: in one corner, Jerusalem artichokes; in the opposite corner, horse-radish. Comfrey goes in one corner and mint in the other. Which will reach the center first?

Jerusalem artichokes are oddities — in the kitchen and in the garden. The plants, which are in the sunflower family, are native to Peru and went to France with some Brazilian natives, members of the Topinambous tribe, who had been brought back to Europe by an expedition in 1613. The French called the Jerusalem artichoke *topinambour,* after the tribe who introduced them. The Jerusalem part of the name artichoke may be a corruption of the Italian for sunflower, which is *girasole.* The artichoke part is usually credited to Samuel de Champlain, who noted that Natives in Canada ate these roots and that the roots tasted like artichokes, which they do not. Because the names are so confusing, some people have chosen to call this vegetable sunchoke, referring back to their sunflower origins.

Once planted, the Jerusalem artichoke will spread via tubers left in the ground. They produce a lovely display of rangy yellow flowers each fall. The tubers, which are harvested after a few hard frosts, are sweet and nutty in flavor.

GROWING Like others in the sunflower family, Jerusalem artichokes require full sun. They taste best after a few hard frosts. Because they spread via underground tubers and are quite vigorous, it is generally recommended to plant these in a separate bed.

SOWING After the last frost, divide the tubers into sections so that each piece has two eyes. Dig a trench about 6 inches deep and sprinkle in a few inches of compost. Plant the tubers into the compost, spacing 12 to 18 inches apart. Cover and water well.

CULTIVATING Keep weeds under control and water when needed.

HARVESTING Best if harvested after a few hard frosts. After the plants have turned brown, cut back the stalks. Loosen the soil with a fork. Use a fork to sift through the soil and collect only as many tubers as you will use in a couple of weeks. Mulch the bed with a thick layer of straw or leaves to keep the ground from freezing and continue to harvest for several more weeks. What is left in the soil will sprout up in the spring as next year's crop.

Although the skins are thin and edible, the chokes must be scrubbed very, very well since the irregular shape traps dirt, so I think it is just as easy to pare them with a knife as it is to scrub thoroughly. Jerusalem artichokes can be grated into salads and are said to taste like Brazil nuts when eaten raw. We prefer Jerusalem artichokes oven roasted above any other preparation method.

TIMING
Sautéing: 5 to 8 minutes, sliced
Roasting: 15 minutes at 500°F, sliced

JERUSALEM ARTICHOKE MATH
1 pound chokes = 3 cups sliced

sautéed jerusalem artichokes

If you've never tried Jerusalem artichokes, this no-frills recipe will show you what you've missed.

SERVES 4

2 tablespoons extra-virgin olive oil

2 shallots, diced

1½ pounds Jerusalem artichokes, scrubbed and sliced ¼ inch thick (about 5 cups)

Salt and freshly ground black pepper

½ lemon

1 Heat the oil in a large skillet over medium-high heat. Add the shallots and Jerusalem artichokes and sauté until the Jerusalem artichokes are crispy on the outside and soft on the inside, 5 to 8 minutes.

2 Season to taste with the salt and pepper. Squeeze the lemon over the Jerusalem artichokes and serve hot.

THE DARLING OF THE LOW-CARB CROWD

ONCE INTRODUCED, the Jerusalem artichoke was quickly adopted in Europe, though John Goodyear, revising Gerard's *Herball* in 1621, wrote, "which way soever they be dressed and eaten, they stir and cause a filthy loathsome stinking wind within the body, thereby causing the belly to be pained and tormented."

Some people are more tormented than others, no doubt related to how their bodies deal with the inulin present in the tubers. Inulin is a carbohydrate, related to fructose, but largely indigestible. For this reason, while some experience digestive distress after eating Jerusalem artichokes, diabetics and those on low-carb diets are encouraged to think of Jerusalem artichokes as a potato substitute and given the go-ahead to enjoy it freely.

If you experience flatulence when eating Jerusalem artichokes, you can try parboiling the pieces until crisp-tender, 5 to 15 minutes depending on the size. Then roast or sauté, reducing the cooking time as needed.

These crispy tidbits taste like a cross between a true artichoke and a hash brown. The texture is decidedly potato-like, but the flavor is much sweeter and more like a vegetable than a starch. The lemon in the herb mixture brings out the artichoke notes.

SERVES 4

2 pounds Jerusalem artichokes

3 tablespoons extra-virgin olive oil

Leaves from 1 sprig basil

2 garlic cloves

Zest of ½ lemon (1 tablespoon)

Coarse or kosher salt

1 Preheat the oven to 500°F. Lightly grease a large sheet pan (preferred) or large shallow roasting pan with oil.

2 Scrub the Jerusalem artichokes well or peel them. Cut off the irregular knobs to make reasonably regular shapes. Cut the Jerusalem artichokes into 1-inch pieces. Combine the Jerusalem artichokes with the oil in a large bowl and toss to coat. Arrange in a single layer in the prepared pan.

3 Roast for about 15 minutes, shaking the pan occasionally for even cooking. While the artichokes roast, combine the basil, garlic, and lemon zest in a mini food processor or on your cutting board and finely chop.

4 Sprinkle the lemon-herb mixture over the artichokes and continue to roast for about 5 minutes. The artichokes should be well browned and tender, and the garlic should be fragrant but not burned.

5 Transfer the chokes to a serving bowl or platter. Sprinkle with salt and serve at once.

HE INTERNET IS A WONDERFUL THING, connecting people in ways that have never happened before. And reconnecting them. I have the Internet to thank for the phone call I got one day from my old college friend Rob Hutchins.

In college, both of us had jobs cooking in fraternity houses as way of earning money. We often compared recipes. Now we are comparing gardens. Rob called his a "chick magnet" a few years ago. He told me that women were always impressed when he presented them with a bouquet of flowers that he had clipped from his own garden. But the ultimate way to impress a woman, he said, was to cook a meal with fresh vegetables from the garden.

His most memorable meal? It was homemade noodles with a basil pesto and fresh tomatoes, grilled zucchini, and just-picked corn. And for dessert, blackberries from the 75-foot row that bordered the backyard. "I remember the meal very well," says Rob. "The woman wasn't as memorable. But that was a great meal."

Time passed. Two years, in fact.

When I called him recently, I asked if the garden was still a chick magnet. "Did I really say that?" he asked sheepishly. "Well, if I did, I guess it's true. Because I'm married now — to a woman who gardens. Ani and I have a lot in common."

"So gardening is a successful dating strategy?" I asked.

"Well, I wouldn't rely on it totally. You need a few other strategies as well."

In Ani's case, he wooed her with great meals and flowers: wisteria, roses, and voodoo lilies.

"Voodoo lilies — very impressive flower," Rob explained. "They have tiger-spotted leaves and huge blossoms from March to May. The flowers are these long, deep purple, phallic-looking waxy flowers. They are pollinated by flies, so they exude a foul smell like rotting meat to attract them. I don't think they exactly won her heart, but maybe her mind. Ani brought them to school where she was teaching reading. The kids were fascinated by them."

At this point, Ani got on the phone, lest I get any weird impressions about her. She explained how the garden influenced her early impression of Rob. "I'm from Louisiana, Catahoula Parish. My family has a farm down there. A friend fixed me up with Rob, and I was thinking, 'I don't know about him. I don't know if I want to go out with this city slicker [Rob is originally from Long Island] who is an engineer. That's the worst of both worlds.'

"Then I came over to his house, and there were all these gorgeous berries all around the perimeter of the place. And the garden was so lush and beautiful. I thought, 'Oh, he isn't such a city slicker. He's a gardener and that's close to being a farmer.' So we had some common ground and I grew more and more comfortable around him."

Today, Ani and Rob garden in Palos Verdes, California, where the mild coastal climate is conducive to year-round growing. They erected a small greenhouse and are experimenting with growing tomatoes throughout the winter. Rob's favorite tomatoes are Brandywines and Purple Cherokees, both heirlooms. He also grows Japanese eggplant, bell peppers, cucumbers, lettuce, and herbs. In the winter he grows cabbages and broccoli. Although January and February are his least productive months, generally there is always something growing.

Year-round growing is such a foreign concept to me that I had to ask, "Don't you ever get tired of year-round gardening chores?"

Rob quickly denied the possibility. "No, I don't. It's something I look forward to after a day at work. It's relaxing. I work on the garden and there's nothing on my mind. My work is analytical, detail-oriented. The garden is relaxing. It's pleasant hanging out with plants."

Especially when those plants are responsible for bringing love into your life.

A Green in Many Colors

IF YOU CAN'T LOVE KALE FOR its hearty green flavor, super nutrition, and sheer beauty, then love it for its sheer perseverance. Here is a vegetable that holds its quality even after winter sets in. Brushing snow off the still-crisp leaves of this hearty green gives me a triumphant feeling of outsmarting Old Man Winter.

Staring at a bed of naked kale stems, however, reminds me that it is easier to outsmart Jack Frost than my neighbor's chickens. Chickens love kale! And they aren't particular about varieties. Personally, I prefer the flavor of the traditional "blue" Scotch curly-leaved kale, but I have admitted Red Russian kale and black "dinosaur" kale into my garden for their beautiful foliage.

There are many traditional Italian dishes that match kale with beans. It is also a star in a stir-fry. When the garden has given up on producing tender vegetables, its great to have fresh kale to cook with.

GROWING Cold-hardy kale will grow anywhere there are frosts. It does best in moderately warm weather (60° to 65°F) and does not do particularly well during the height of summer. Give it loamy soil with plenty of well-rotted organic matter.

SOWING Start transplants indoors 6 to 8 weeks before the frost-free date and set out 2 weeks before the frost-free date. Set transplants 12 to 15 inches apart in rows, 15 to18 inches apart in beds. Or sow seed 4 to 6 weeks before the frost-free date.

CULTIVATING Thin to keep plants 12 to 15 inches apart and add thinnings to salads. Keep well watered. Side-dress with nitrogen-rich fertilizer (manure or bloodmeal) when plants are 4 to 5 inches tall.

HARVESTING Cut the stems with a scissors or sharp knife about 1 inch above the ground. Harvest immature leaves for a "cut-and-come-again" crop — ornamental and Siberian varieties are particularly well suited for addition to salad mixes. For cooking, harvest outer leaves or full plants at full size. For best flavor, wait to harvest until after the first frost.

KALE MATH

1 pound fresh kale = 5 to 8 stems
= 12 cups stemmed and chopped

The curly leaves of kale will harbor grit from the garden, so wash thoroughly in several changes of water. Strip the leaves from the tough stems and discard the stems. Gather a handful of leaves and roll up like a cigar, then slice into ribbons.

Kale lends itself to steaming, braising, stir-frying, and sautéing. Ornamental varieties are tender and require less cooking than curly blue Scotch kale, so reduce cooking times accordingly. Blue Scotch kale and Lacinato kale (also called black kale, dinosaur kale, and Tuscan kale) share the same cooking requirements and can be used interchangeably. Oak-leaved Siberian or Russian types are best harvested as baby salad greens. Ornamental kale is best when harvested young for salads. After it has formed a head, it tastes more like cabbage than kale and is quite delicate and tender.

Kale is a hearty green that stands up to bold flavors. Use a liberal hand with whatever seasonings you choose to use.

TIMING

Steaming: 8 to 10 minutes
Sautéing and stir-frying: 6 to 10 minutes
Braising: 8 to 10 minutes

KALE NUTRITION NOTES

Kale's principle use in the United States seems to be as a decoration for deli counters and salad bars. This is most unfortunate, since kale is both delicious and nutritious. It provides the same cancer-preventing agents (indoles) as other cabbages. In addition, it is rich in vitamins A and C, potassium, and calcium. It is also a good source of iron. There are about 43 calories in a cup of cooked kale.

portuguese kale soup

Caldo verde ("green soup") is considered one of the national dishes of Portugal. I like it best when it is kept simple, made with homemade chicken stock, potatoes, sausage, and kale. The only seasoning needed is salt and pepper.

■ SERVES 4 ■

½ pound linguiça or chorizo sausage (or any garlicky smoked sausage), sliced

8 cups chicken broth (page 9)

3–4 medium-size potatoes (1 pound), peeled and diced

12 ounces kale, stems discarded and leaves chopped (8 cups lightly packed)

Salt and freshly ground black pepper

1 Combine the sausage and stock in a large saucepan. Bring to a boil, then reduce the heat and simmer while you prepare the potatoes.

2 Combine the potatoes with water to cover in a medium-size saucepan. Cover and bring to a boil. Boil until tender, about 8 minutes. Drain and briefly mash with a potato masher for an uneven, lumpy texture. Add to the chicken broth along with the kale.

3 Simmer for 10 to 15 minutes, until the kale is quite tender. Season with salt and pepper. Serve hot.

pasta with kale and beans

With canned beans, you can whip up this hearty vegetarian pasta dish in minutes. This is a bold dish, with bold flavors.

SERVES 4

3 tablespoons extra-virgin olive oil

4 large garlic cloves, minced

¼ teaspoon crushed red pepper flakes (optional)

1 can (15 ounces) cannellini beans, rinsed and drained, or 1½ cups cooked cannellini beans

1 pound kale, stems discarded and leaves shredded (about 12 cups lightly packed)

½ cup vegetable or chicken broth (see page 8 or 9)

1 pound bowties, penne, or other short pasta

1½ cups freshly grated Parmesan

Salt and freshly ground black pepper

1 Begin heating a large pot of salted water for the pasta.

2 Heat the oil over medium-low heat in a large saucepan. Sauté the garlic and hot pepper flakes, if using, in the oil until the garlic is fragrant, about 3 minutes. Stir in the beans, kale, and broth. Cover and simmer until the kale is partially wilted and almost tender, 5 to 8 minutes.

3 When the water boils, cook the pasta until al dente. Reserve 1 cup of the pasta cooking water and drain the pasta. Return the pasta to the pot, add the kale mixture, and toss well. Add as much of the reserved water as needed to moisten the pasta. Add 1 cup of the Parmesan, season with salt and pepper, and toss well.

4 Serve immediately, passing more Parmesan at the table.

tuscan kale
with white beans & garlic

A mess o' greens, Italian-style. This can be made extra-hearty with the addition of smoked turkey or ham, or it can be made as a vegetarian dish, omitting the meat. Either way, be sure to serve with plenty of bread to sop up the delicious pot liquor.

■ SERVES 4 ■

1 cup dried cannellini (white kidney) or great Northern beans

6 cups water

1 onion, halved

2 sprigs fresh thyme or 1 tablespoon dried

2 bay leaves

1½ pounds kale, stems removed and leaves chopped (16 cups lightly packed)

8 ounces smoked turkey or ham, diced (optional)

Salt and freshly ground black pepper

3 tablespoons extra-virgin olive oil

4 large garlic cloves, very thinly sliced

¼ teaspoon crushed red pepper flakes (optional)

1 Soak the beans for at least 8 hours in plenty of water to cover. Drain the beans.

2 In a large saucepan or Dutch oven, combine the beans with the water, onion, thyme, and bay leaves. Cover and bring to a boil. Reduce the heat and simmer, partially covered, until the beans are tender, approximately 1½ hours.

3 Remove and discard the onion, sprigs of thyme, and bay leaves. (At this point the beans can be refrigerated for up to 1 day before continuing the recipe.) Bring the beans and their liquid to a boil. Add the kale and the salt and pepper to taste. Simmer, stirring down the kale every few minutes, until the kale is tender, about 10 minutes. Stir in the smoked turkey, if using.

4 Meanwhile, heat the oil in a small heavy skillet over very low heat. Add the garlic and cook until fragrant and soft, stirring occasionally, about 5 minutes. Do not let the garlic brown. Mash the garlic with a fork. Add the hot pepper flakes, if using.

5 Pour the hot oil mixture over the beans and greens and serve immediately.

For adding to salads, the baby form of red Russian or Siberian kale and ornamental kale are the most tender and mild in flavor.

For cooking (steaming, braising, stir-frying, and sautéing), curly or blue Scotch kale and lacinato kale are best. Lacinato kale also goes by the names Tuscan kale, black kale, cavolo nero, and dinosaur or dino kale.

Calzone translates literally as "stuffed pants." Calzone as a relative of pizza is pizza dough folded over to encase a meat or cheese filling — in this case, kale and three cheeses.

SERVES 4

Basic Pizza Dough (page 12; while the dough is rising, prepare the filling as instructed in steps 1–3; see step 4 for exceptions to the recipe instructions)

2 cups ricotta cheese

2 tablespoons extra-virgin olive oil

4 cups packed chopped kale

4 garlic cloves, minced

1 cup grated mozzarella

½ cup freshly grated Parmesan

Salt and freshly ground black pepper

Heated seasoned tomato sauce, to serve (optional)

note If you can't serve the calzones soon after removing from the oven, lift onto wire racks so the bottom crust doesn't become soggy.

1 While the dough rises, prepare the filling. To begin, drain the ricotta in a fine-mesh metal sieve.

2 Heat the oil in a large skillet over medium-high heat. Sauté the kale in the oil until well coated and slightly wilted, about 3 minutes. Stir in the garlic, cover, and let steam until completely tender, about 2 minutes longer. Remove the cover and sauté for about 30 seconds to evaporate any liquid. Transfer to a medium bowl.

3 Add the drained ricotta, the mozzarella, and the Parmesan to the kale and mix well. Season to taste with salt and pepper.

4 Preheat the oven to 350°F. Follow the recipe instructions for stretching the dough onto two prepared pans, but be sure to use 10- to 12-inch pizza pans, not baking pans.

5 Spoon half the filling onto the middle of each dough round. Fold one end of the dough over onto the other to form a half-circle, and press closed with your fingertips.

6 Bake for 30 to 40 minutes or until well browned, rotating the pans halfway through for even baking. Serve hot or warm, passing the warm tomato sauce at the table, if using.

Kale ranks as one of the earliest of cultivated vegetables, though the writings of ancient Greeks and Romans don't distinguish among the various members of the cabbage family, which includes kale. The sarcophagus of Pharaoh Akhenaton's pyramid is decorated with kale leaves carved from jade.

According to Irish legend, fairies ride kale stalks instead of horses on moonlit nights. The Scots are less fanciful about kale, which has been a staple vegetable there for years. In Europe, kale is most likely found on tables in Italy and northern climates, including Denmark and Germany. In the United States, kale is more popular in the South, where cooked greens seemed to be more appreciated than elsewhere.

Kale is terrific in a stir-fry. Its hearty flavor stands up to a generous amount of garlic and ginger. If you like, substitute boneless chicken breasts for the pork.

SERVES 4

1 pound boneless pork tenderloin, cut into matchsticks

¼ cup soy sauce

3 tablespoons Chinese rice wine or sherry

3 tablespoons oyster sauce (available where Oriental foods are sold)

1 tablespoon sugar

1 piece fresh ginger, 1 inch long, peeled and minced

2 garlic cloves, minced

2 tablespoons peanut oil

1 pound kale, stems discarded and leaves shredded (12 cups lightly packed)

Hot cooked rice

1 Combine the pork with 2 tablespoons of the soy sauce, 2 tablespoons of the wine, the oyster sauce, sugar, ginger, and garlic in a nonreactive bowl. Set aside to marinate.

2 Heat a large wok over high heat. Add 1 tablespoon of the oil and swirl in the hot wok. Add the pork and marinade and stir-fry until the pork is cooked through, no pink shows, and the juices run clear, about 5 minutes. Remove the pork and sauce from the wok and keep warm.

3 Heat the remaining 1 tablespoon oil in the wok. Add the kale, the remaining 2 tablespoons soy sauce, and the remaining 1 tablespoon wine. Stir-fry for 1 minute, then cover and steam until the kale is barely tender, 3 to 5 minutes. Return the pork and sauce to the wok and stir-fry 2 to 3 minutes longer.

4 Serve at once over hot rice.

kale with sausage and garlic-roasted potatoes

Many of the classic kale dishes combine the green with potatoes and sausage. Think of kale as a common European vegetable for country folk, whose cooking was simple and hearty. This is a very simple and quick dish to make. As a bonus, if you use a low-fat turkey or chicken sausage, it is also very good for you.

■ SERVES 4 ■

4 medium potatoes (about 1 pound), sliced ¼ inch thick
2 garlic cloves, minced
2 tablespoons extra-virgin olive oil
Salt and freshly ground black pepper
1 pound hot or sweet Italian sausage, removed from its casing
2 cups chicken broth (page 9)
1¼–1½ pounds kale, stems removed and leaves chopped (about 16 cups)

1 Preheat the oven to 425°F. Brush a large baking sheet with oil or spray with nonstick cooking spray.

2 Combine the potatoes, garlic, and 1 tablespoon of the oil in a medium bowl. Season with a generous sprinkling of salt and a few grinds of pepper and toss to coat well. Spread the potatoes out in a single layer on the prepared baking sheet. Roast for 25 to 30 minutes, turning the potatoes a few times to brown evenly.

3 Heat the remaining 1 tablespoon oil in a large Dutch oven over medium-high heat. Sauté the sausage in the oil until no pink shows and the sausage is cooked through, about 8 minutes.

4 Stir in the broth and kale. Bring the broth to a boil. Cover and simmer, stirring occasionally, until the kale is wilted and tender but still bright green, 8 to 10 minutes.

5 Mix in the potatoes. Season with salt and pepper. Serve at once.

"I AM SO IN LOVE WITH MY WORK," says market gardener Rebecca Slattery.

Her small farm in Indianola, Washington, on the Olympic Peninsula is "as diverse a market garden as we can possibly be in this crappy climate" — on the west side of Puget Sound.

"Agriculture in this country is on the decline. But micro-farming is the one bright spot on the agricultural landscape. My farm is tiny but successful . . . We grow fifty-three varieties of vegetable crops, plus more than one hundred varieties of cut flowers and all the different berries and tree fruits." The marketing of these crops is also diverse. Persephone Farm is one of the oldest community-supported agriculture farms in the area, with 60 members. They also sell at two different farmers markets, as well as directly to a number of chefs. As a sideline, Slatterly is a floral designer, so she does a big business in wedding flowers.

Persephone Farm started in 1991 as a quarter-acre market garden with four partners in a collective. Today Persephone Farm has two acres in cultivation, including orchard land. It is now a sole proprietorship, with a neighbor who is folding in to become a full partner.

Greens are a particular specialty. "Our salad greens sell for ten dollars a pound and we always sell out. People are more than willing to pay for it. It contains sixty different varieties of greens, including tons of wild-crafted greens and edible flowers. I get a lot of the seeds from Europe," she says. "It's a very fancy mix."

What Slatterly calls "fringe" vegetables are the kinds of produce Persephone Farm focuses on: "We grow a lot of rapini [broccoli rabe]. In fact, we can't grow enough of it. We plant several different varieties so we can harvest through June." The farm also produces a lot of baby bok choy, arugula, specialty radishes, heirloom tomatoes, Jerusalem artichokes, and ground cherries.

Ground cherries, Slattery explains, are in the nightshade family, like tomatoes. They look like small tomatillos, encased in a similar husk. Ground cherries fall to the ground when they are ripe. The fruits within the husks are sweet enough to eat out of hand and make excellent jams and pies. They grow very well in "less than ideal climates." The Seed Savers Exchange, one of the many places from which Slattery acquires seeds, has seeds for ground cherries.

The crop in which Slattery takes the most pride is her yearly batch of apprentices. Slattery got her start in farming with a 6-month apprenticeship in ecological horticulture at the University of California at Santa Cruz. "A lot of what I do here is modeled on what I learned down there," she says.

Every year Persephone Farm receives about 100 applications for three apprenticeships. "These are people who want to come and learn and all they get paid is a small stipend, housing, and vegetables. In exchange I give them knowledge and skills — in everything from growing vegetables to marketing and bookkeeping. I've had wonderful luck with my apprentices — they have been of all ages and backgrounds, including one woman who was even older than me!" (Slatterly is in her early 40s.)

"My apprentices are definitely a key to what makes my farm work. It wouldn't work for me to hire out migrant farm labor. And teenagers can be such slackers! They get bored after twenty minutes and can't apply themselves."

The apprenticeships stretch from March to October, 8 months. "It runs the whole season to allow the apprentices to experience the whole cycle and the magic of the whole cycle, including seed saving, planting, cover crops, putting the garden to bed."

Persephone Farm's season actually starts in January, when Slatterly sows seeds for her specialty greens directly into the soil in her 25- by 50-foot greenhouse. This first crop is ready for harvest from April through June. Above the greens, on benches, seeds are started in March. By the time the greens are done, most of the seedlings have been planted outside, but there is space in the greenhouse for some peppers, tomatoes, and eggplant. These will keep producing until Thanks-giving: "One year the tomatoes continued to ripen fruit through January. It was so weird to be eating fresh tomatoes in the winter. I was actually happy to finally rip them out to get the greens started."

Succession planting is very important at Persephone Farm. "We are always looking for space to plant some quick-maturing crop. As soon as there is an empty spot, in goes another bed of baby bok choy or arugula."

In this unending treadmill of planting and harvesting, Slatterly finds that she likes planting the least, while her favorite job is keeping the tomato crop under control: "I follow a very strict practice of pruning and training my tomatoes. It's a crappy climate for tomatoes, wetter than they like it. I have a real problem with late blight. So pruning and growing the tomatoes on trellises is critical."

I mention that I have trouble ripening my tomatoes in my cold "crappy" climate, and Slatterly recommends Stupice, an heirloom variety from Eastern Europe: "It really likes a cool summer. It's a very reliable tomato, not very big but with delicious flavor. Its one of the workhorses of our tomato patch." I vow that next year I'll try it.

Then I realize that Slattery is correct when she says teaching is really what she loves best, and that her apprentices are her best crop. I've already learned something new, and I'm not even an apprentice.

Delicate Members of the Onion Family

WHEREAS WE GENERALLY THINK OF onions as aromatics that are used to season foods, leeks are definitely a vegetable to be enjoyed on their own. The flavor is much milder than that of bulb onions. They are also easier to grow than bulb onions, not requiring a specified number of hours of daylight. And, if you can keep the soil from freezing with a heavy layer of mulch, they can be harvested throughout the winter.

Leeks are called "poor man's asparagus" in Wales, where they are found in many dishes. What I like about leeks is that I can harvest them or ignore them in the garden as summer deepens into fall. Then, when the garden is past its prime and the only other greens that are vigorous are all in the cabbage family, I turn to leeks. They are as delicate as asparagus, but with a special affinity for potatoes. What a perfect fall vegetable.

GROWING Leeks require a long growing season. They like full sun but will tolerate partial shade. They do best with light steady water and fertile, well-drained soil.

SOWING Sow indoors in late winter and transplant to individual pots or growing cells when the plants are 2 inches tall. Transplant about 1 week after the last frost. Set the leeks in a trench about 8 inches deep.

CULTIVATING Keep the weeds down with mulch. As the leeks grow, hill up the soil around their base. This blanches and tenderizes the stems. You will use only the white and very pale green, tender stems.

HARVESTING Harvest as needed from late summer through winter. Protect from a hard freeze with a heavy layer of mulch. To harvest, loosen the soil gently with a garden fork and pull the plants from the soil.

Leeks often harbor soil between the leaves because of the way they have had soil hilled around their base. To prepare leeks, first cut away the tough green tops. Peel off any tough outer leaves. Trim off the root end. Make a long vertical slit through the center of the leek or slice in half vertically. Wash under cold running water, flipping through the leaves to expose the inner surfaces to the water. Pat dry.

TIMING

Sautéing or stir-frying: 5 minutes, sliced
Braising: 35 minutes, sliced
Grilling: 7 to 10 minutes
Roasting: 15 to 20 minutes at 425°F

LEEK MATH

1 large leek = ½ to ¾ pound
1 pound leeks = 6 cups sliced

Leeks and potatoes are often found together; it is one of those taste marriages that seem almost inevitable. This hearty side dish can be served with a simple roast or a broiled chop.

SERVES 4-6

2 pounds (about 6 medium) russet or Yukon gold potatoes, peeled and thinly sliced

2 garlic cloves, thinly sliced

2 cups milk

1 tablespoon fresh thyme leaves

Salt and freshly ground black pepper

4 slices (4 ounces) thick-cut bacon, preferably hardwood smoked

4 large leeks (2½–3 pounds), white parts only, thinly sliced

1 cup grated Gruyère

1 Combine the potatoes, garlic, milk, thyme, and salt and pepper to taste in a medium-size, heavy-bottom saucepan. Simmer over medium heat, stirring occasionally until the potatoes are tender, about 20 minutes. Taste and add more salt and pepper, if desired (unless the bacon is exceptionally salty, it will need plenty).

2 Preheat the oven to 350°F. Grease a 2-quart gratin dish with butter.

3 Cook the bacon in a large cast-iron skillet over medium heat until well browned, about 8 minutes. Drain on paper towels and reserve. Pour off all but 2 tablespoons of the bacon fat.

4 Return the skillet to medium heat. Add the leeks and sauté until tender, about 5 minutes. Crumble in the bacon.

5 Using a slotted spoon, remove about one third of the potatoes from the saucepan and make a single layer in the prepared gratin dish. Make another layer with one third of the leeks and bacon. Sprinkle one third of the cheese on top. Repeat the layers twice, ending with a final layer of cheese. Pour in the milk that the potatoes cooked in.

6 Bake for about 30 minutes, until a golden crust has formed on top and the potatoes are bubbling.

7 Let sit for about 10 minutes, then serve hot.

Variation
To make the dish vegetarian, omit the bacon and sauté the leeks in 2 tablespoons extra-virgin olive oil.

LEEKS IN HISTORY

Leeks rank among the most ancient of vegetables, perhaps dating as far back as the Bronze Age. Four thousand years ago, the Assyrians were growing leeks in their gardens and recommending them as a preventative for graying hair. The Bible notes that leeks were among the rations given to the pyramid builders in Egypt. In a guide to good eating written in China around 1500 BC, leeks were recommended. In AD 640, the Welsh wore leeks in their hats to distinguish themselves from the enemy during the battle between King Cadwallader of Wales and the Saxons. The leek became an emblem of pride in Wales, and the Welsh wear leeks on their hats to commemorate King Cadwallader's victory on St. David's Day, March 1.

roasted leek tart

It doesn't get any easier than this. Frozen puff pastry makes a spectacularly crispy, elegant, and easily handled crust. Roasting brings out the sweet mild flavor of leeks, and a touch of mustard and Gruyère adds a depth of flavor.

SERVES 4 AS A LIGHT MAIN COURSE, 9 AS AN HORS D'OEUVRE

6 leeks, white parts only, trimmed and cut into ½-inch slices

2 tablespoons extra-virgin olive oil

Salt and freshly ground black pepper

1 sheet frozen puff pastry (about 8 ounces)

1 egg, slightly beaten with 1 tablespoon water

2 teaspoons Dijon mustard

1 cup grated Gruyère

1 Preheat the oven to 425°F. Lightly grease a large sheet pan (preferred) or shallow roasting pan with oil.

2 Combine the sliced leeks and oil in a large bowl and toss to coat. Season with salt and pepper. Transfer the leeks to the prepared pan and arrange in a single layer.

3 Roast for 15 to 20 minutes, until the leeks are tender and lightly browned, shaking the pan occasionally for even cooking. Remove the pan from the oven and leave the oven on.

4 Roll out the pastry to an 8½-inch square about ¼ inch thick on a lightly floured surface. (For most commercial puff pastry sheets, this will simply involve unrolling or unfolding the sheet.) Cut and remove a ½-inch square from each corner of the pastry. Fold a ½-inch edge of pastry over toward the center of the pastry to form a raised border.

5 Transfer the pastry to an ungreased cookie sheet. Prick the bottom of the pastry with the tines of a fork at ½-inch intervals. Brush the egg over the bottom of the crust. Brush the mustard over the egg. Sprinkle the cheese in the pastry shell. Spoon the roasted leeks over the cheese.

6 Bake for 25 to 30 minutes, until the pastry is lightly browned. Serve hot or at room temperature.

pasta with leek-and-prosciutto sauce

In the time it takes to heat the water for the pasta, the sauce of leeks cooked to a point of melting tenderness is ready. The flavors are subtle, so make it with high-quality imported prosciutto and cheese. Serve with a green salad and Italian bread.

■ SERVES 4 ■

2 tablespoons extra-virgin olive oil

3 large or 6 medium leeks (2–3 pounds), trimmed, halved, and sliced

3 ounces prosciutto, diced

½ cup chicken broth (page 9)

¼ cup dry white wine

1 pound penne, rotini, or other short pasta

1 cup freshly grated Parmigiano-Reggiano, plus more to pass at the table

Salt and freshly ground black pepper

1 Heat the oil in a large saucepan over medium-high heat. Sauté the leeks and prosciutto in the oil until the leeks are wilted and softened, 4 to 5 minutes.

2 Add the chicken broth and wine. Cover, reduce the heat, and simmer until the leeks are meltingly tender, about 30 minutes.

3 Meanwhile, cook the pasta until just al dente. Reserve 1 cup of the pasta cooking water, then drain.

4 Add the pasta to the leeks and mix well. Add 1 cup of the cheese and toss. Add enough of the reserved water to moisten the pasta. Season generously with salt and pepper and serve immediately, passing additional cheese at the table.

snapper on a bed of leeks, provençal-style

Here is a terrific heart-healthy way to enjoy fish. Serve with a crusty loaf of French bread and a green salad.

SERVES 4

2 tablespoons extra-virgin olive oil
4–6 large leeks, white part only, sliced
2 garlic cloves, minced
2 cups seeded, peeled, and diced fresh or canned tomatoes
2 teaspoons dried herbes de Provence (page 7)
1½ pounds snapper or other firm white-fleshed fish
Salt and freshly ground black pepper
½ cup niçoise or other black olives, pitted
½ cup dry white wine
Hot cooked rice, to serve (optional)

1 Preheat the oven to 425°F. Lightly grease a 9- by 13-inch baking dish or large casserole dish with oil.

2 Heat the oil in a large skillet over medium-high heat. Sauté the leeks in the oil until slightly tender, about 3 minutes. Add the garlic and sauté for 1 minute longer. Add the tomatoes and herbs and simmer while you prepare the fish.

3 Wash and pat dry the fish. Season the fish on both sides with a generous sprinkling of salt and a few grinds of pepper.

4 Transfer the leek mixture to the prepared baking dish. Top with the fish, arranged in a single layer. Sprinkle the olives over the fish. Pour in the wine over the olives.

5 Bake for 10 to 15 minutes, until the fish flakes easily.

6 Serve hot on a bed of rice.

Fall is chicken potpie season in Vermont. At one time, fall was the season for slaughtering chickens that weren't worth feeding over the winter because their time of good egg production had passed. It turned out that "leaf peepers" coming to view the fall foliage were more than happy to eat chicken potpie at church suppers, enjoying the flavors of good old-fashioned Yankee home cooking. You won't find this particular recipe at a church supper. This potpie is rich in leeks and rutabagas, two favorite fall vegetables. Feel free to substitute whatever vegetables you have on hand.

SERVES 6

- 5 split chicken breasts (about 4 pounds)
- 6–8 cups water, or to cover
- 1 onion, quartered
- 2 garlic cloves, peeled and left whole
- 1 bunch flat-leaf parsley
- 1 teaspoon black peppercorns
- 1 medium rutabaga, peeled and diced
- 6 tablespoons extra-virgin olive oil
- 6 medium leeks, white and tender green parts only, sliced
- 6 tablespoons unbleached all-purpose flour
- 1 tablespoon chopped fresh dill or 1 teaspoon dried thyme
- Salt and freshly ground black pepper

Biscuit Topping

- 3 cups unbleached all-purpose flour
- 2 tablespoons baking powder
- 1½ teaspoons salt
- ⅔ cup butter, cut into pieces
- 1 cup buttermilk

1 Place the chicken in a large pot. Cover with the water. Add the onion, garlic, parsley, and peppercorns. Bring to a boil, then reduce the heat to maintain a slow simmer and simmer for 35 minutes, until the chicken is tender and no longer pink. Turn off the heat and allow the chicken to cool in the cooking liquid.

2 Cover the rutabaga with salted water in a small saucepan. Bring to a boil and boil until just tender, 5 to 8 minutes. Drain.

3 When the chicken is cool enough to handle, remove the chicken from the broth. Discard the skin and bones. Chop the meat into bite-size pieces.

4 Strain the broth and discard the solids. Skim off any fat that rises to the top. Reserve 3 cups broth for the potpie and refrigerate or freeze the remainder for other recipes.

5 Heat the oil in a large saucepan over medium heat. Sauté the leeks in the oil until tender, about 5 minutes. Sprinkle in the flour and stir until all the flour is absorbed into the oil. Whisk in the 3 cups reserved broth and stir until thickened and smooth. Stir in the chicken, rutabagas, and dill. Season with salt and pepper. Bring to a boil. Keep hot while you prepare the biscuits.

6 Preheat the oven to 450°F. Set out an ungreased 9- by 13-inch baking pan.

7 Combine the flour, baking powder, salt, and butter in a food processor and process until the mixture resembles coarse crumbs. Pour in the buttermilk and process to make a soft dough. Knead a few times on a lightly floured board. Pat out the dough to a thickness of about ½ inch. Cut into 3-inch rounds. By gathering the scraps and patting out again, you should get 12 biscuits.

8 Pour the chicken mixture into the baking pan. Place the biscuit rounds on top. Bake for about 18 minutes, until the biscuits are golden and the chicken mixture is bubbling.

9 Let stand for a few minutes before serving.

stir-fried lamb and leeks

In northern China, lamb appears frequently on the menu. It combines beautifully with leeks. Serve over rice.

■ **SERVES 4** ■

Lamb and Marinade

2 pounds boned leg of lamb, cut into matchsticks

2 tablespoons soy sauce

2 tablespoons rice wine

1 tablespoon cornstarch

2 teaspoons sugar

Sauce

2 tablespoons soy sauce

2 tablespoons rice wine

1 tablespoon dark sesame oil

1 teaspoon rice vinegar

6 tablespoons peanut or canola oil

6 leeks, white and tender green parts, trimmed and sliced

1 red bell pepper, cut into matchsticks (optional)

6 garlic cloves, minced

1 can (8 ounces) sliced water chestnuts, rinsed and drained

1 Combine the lamb, soy sauce, wine, cornstarch, and sugar in a large bowl. Stir to mix well. Set aside for 30 minutes to marinate.

2 Stir together the soy sauce, rice wine, sesame oil, and vinegar in a small bowl. Set aside.

3 Heat a wok or large skillet over high heat until very hot. Add 2 tablespoons of the peanut oil and heat. Add half the lamb and stir-fry until the lamb changes color, about 4 minutes. Use a heat-proof rubber spatula to scrape the lamb and sauce into a bowl to keep warm. Heat 2 tablespoons of the remaining oil in the wok. Add the remaining lamb and stir-fry until the lamb changes color, about 4 minutes. Scrape out and add to the first batch of lamb.

4 Reheat the wok with the remaining 2 tablespoons oil. Add the leeks and red bell pepper, if using, and stir-fry until tender, 5 to 6 minutes. Push the leeks to the side of the wok and add the garlic. Cook until fragrant, about 30 seconds, then toss with the leeks. Add the lamb and water chestnuts and toss to mix.

5 Add the soy sauce mixture and toss to mix well. Stir-fry just long enough to heat through, 1 minute, and serve hot.

A Flavoring
Worth Savoring

My mother started every dish she made, with the possible exception of chocolate cake, by sautéing an onion. An Indonesian friend tops every dish she makes with fried shallots. A Cajun friend starts every dish she makes with what she calls the holy trinity — celery, peppers, and, of course, onions. Take away onions and many great dishes lose their essence.

While we usually think of onions as flavoring ingredients, they can also be savored as vegetables. Indeed, a roasted onion, sweetened by caramelizing its natural sugars, is a delicious vegetable to serve with any dish and makes a terrific, simple topping for pasta. French onion soup is nothing more than broth and slowly cooked onions, but what a fine soup it is.

The trick to growing onions successfully is to follow the rules. With some vegetables, you can broadcast the seeds or stick transplants into a barely prepared seedbed, leave it up to nature to provide sun and rain, and you will get a harvest — nothing like the harvest of a well-nurtured garden, but a harvest nonetheless. Not so with onions. If you want to harvest nice big bulbs, you must choose the proper variety for your climate, plant in a timely fashion to allow for the necessary day length and night length, provide adequate moisture and nutrition, harvest on time, and store well.

The good news is that there are plenty of growers willing to do what is necessary to get a good crop, and you will probably never be faced with a shortage of onions. Still, there's nothing more satisfying than growing your own, no?

GROWING Most seed catalogs indicate whether a particular onion variety is an (S) short-day or (L) long-day type. Imagine a line drawn between San Francisco and Washington, D.C. North of the line, you should grow long-day onions. South of the line, choose short-day onions. Usually, short-day types are planted in the fall, long-day types in the late winter or early spring. Onions do best in fertile, loose, friable, well-drained soil.

SOWING Direct seed in the spring when the soil temperature reaches 50°F, or transplant plants or sets 3 to 4 inches apart in the garden 4 weeks before the last expected frost.

CULTIVATING Thin directly seeded plants to 3 to 4 inches apart. Keep well weeded and mulch heavily. Alternatively, control weeds with companion plants, such as beets. Water regularly.

HARVESTING When most of the tops fall over, the onions are ready to harvest. Gently pull the onions from the ground and leave to cure in the sun for at least a week. Or cure for a few days, then braid and hang the braids where they will receive good air circulation to finish curing. Sweet onions should be used within a few weeks of harvest.

TIMING

Sautéing or stir-frying: 3 to 5 minutes over medium-high until tender; 10 to 15 minutes over low heat until caramelized
Boiling: 15 minutes for small onions
Roasting: 20 to 30 minutes at 400°F
Grilling: 10 to 15 minutes for thick slices
Braising: 15 to 25 minutes, small whole onions

Green onions and scallions are excellent to use as flavorings added raw to salads, spreads, and sauces. Or you can add them during the last few minutes of cooking to stir-fries, soups, sauces, sautés, and stews. Grilled green onions and scallions are excellent accompaniments to many grilled dishes.

Small onions go by various names including pearl, boiler, baby, mini, creamer, and pickling onions. All of them are regular onions, harvested small; none is a distinctive variety. To peel small onions easily, place in a bowl and add boiling water to cover. When the water is cool enough to plunge your hand into, the skins should slip off readily.

Sweet onions are not really sweeter than standard storage onions; they just have less heat and "bite" (pyruvic acid). An onion grown in low-sulfur soils, in cool weather, with adequate moisture will be sweet and mild. Even if you choose a sweet variety to grow, if you can't provide the optimal growing conditions, the onions may have more bite than you expected. These onions do have a higher moisture content than regular storage onions and so are more prone to rot. Keep in a cool, dry place and use quickly. Sweet onions are the best onions to use raw.

Onions make people cry because the cells damaged by cutting release sulfuric compounds that, when combined with air, activate and release a compound called thiopropanal sulfoxide. To avoid crying, you have to avoid the compound by wearing goggles. *Cook's Illustrated* reports that a flame from a candle or gas burner will oxidize the thiopropanal sulfoxide, thereby reducing crying.

ONION MATH

1 pound onions = 4 cups diced

creamed onions

Creamed onions are not a holiday tradition in my house, but some people just don't think it is Thanksgiving without them. Creamed onions is a wonderful side dish to serve alongside all kinds of roasts and simply broiled meats.

■ SERVES 4 ■

1½ pounds small boiling or pearl onions
3 tablespoons butter
2 teaspoons sugar
⅓ cup light cream
Salt and freshly ground black pepper
2 tablespoons chopped freshly parsley

1 Place the onions in a medium bowl. Add boiling water to cover and let stand until cool enough to handle. Drain the onions. You should be able to squeeze the onions right out of their skins.

2 Arrange the onions in a single layer in a large skillet. Add the butter and sprinkle with the sugar. Add enough water to come halfway up the sides of the onions. Partially cover the skillet, leaving the lid askew. Bring the water to a simmer over high heat, reduce the heat to medium, and simmer the onions until tender when poked with a knife, 15 to 25 minutes, depending on the size of the onions.

3 Add the cream and simmer for 2 to 3 minutes, shaking the pan to coat the onions thoroughly. Season with salt and pepper.

4 Transfer to a serving dish, sprinkle with the parsley, and serve hot.

caramelized onions

Roasted onions make a delicious vegetable dish, especially as an accompaniment to meat. They are also a delicious addition to an antipasto platter. The trick is to brown the onions thoroughly without blackening them, which will create a bitter flavor. Flat or saucer-shaped onions, such as cipollini, or torpedo-shaped onions are the best choice for this because you can get more surface area for good browning.

■ **SERVES 4** ■

2 pounds small flat or torpedo-shaped onions, peeled
2 tablespoons extra-virgin olive oil
2 tablespoons chopped fresh thyme
Salt and freshly ground black pepper
High-quality balsamic vinegar (optional)

1 Preheat the oven to 400°F. Grease a large baking sheet (preferred) or shallow roasting pan with oil.

2 Cut the onions in half to achieve the maximum amount of surface area. Flat onions should be sliced horizontally, but torpedo-shaped onions should be sliced vertically. Arrange the onions cut-side down on the prepared baking sheet. Brush with the oil. Sprinkle with the thyme and salt and pepper to taste.

3 Roast for 20 to 30 minutes, until the onions are well browned and tender. Check often and remove the onions before they char.

4 Drizzle with a little of the vinegar, if using. Serve hot or warm.

"You should grow like an onion with your head in the ground."

—*Favorite Yiddish curse*

grilled onion slices

Grilled onions are the best possible accompaniment for burgers, whether they be hamburgers, veggie burgers, or turkey burgers. I prefer sweet onions for this recipe, but any onion will do, the larger the better.

SERVES 4

1–2 large onions, sliced ½ inch thick
Extra-virgin olive oil or Italian-style salad dressing
Salt and freshly ground black pepper

1 Prepare a medium-hot fire in the grill. Place a vegetable grill rack on the grill. If you don't have a grill rack, thread a presoaked bamboo skewer horizontally through each onion slice.

2 Brush the onion slices with the oil.

3 Grill for 10 to 15 minutes, turning once, until the slices are tender and browned. Sprinkle with the salt and pepper to taste and serve hot.

Onion's skin, very thin
Mild winter's coming in.
Onion's skin, thick and tough
Coming winter cold and rough.

—Yankee weather wisdom

oven-steamed chinese-style fish with scallions

The steaming liquid provides plenty of sauce, so serve with rice. A lightly cooked green vegetable — steamed or stir-fried asparagus, broccoli, green beans, or snow peas — makes the perfect accompaniment. This dish is so easy to put together, it practically makes itself.

■ SERVES 4 ■

- 6–8 scallions or spring onions, julienned
- 1 piece fresh ginger, 2 inches long, julienned
- 2 garlic cloves, minced
- ¼ cup soy sauce
- 2 tablespoons rice wine
- 2 teaspoons dark sesame oil
- 1 teaspoon sugar
- ¼ teaspoon freshly ground black pepper
- 1½–2 pounds firm white fish fillets, such as cod, halibut, tilapia
- 2 tablespoons chopped fresh cilantro

1 Preheat the oven to 450°F.

2 Scatter half the scallions, ginger, and garlic in a shallow roasting pan.

3 Stir together the soy sauce, rice wine, sesame oil, sugar, and black pepper in a small bowl. Pour half into the roasting pan.

4 Arrange the fish fillets in the pan. Cover with the remaining scallions, ginger, and garlic. Pour the remaining steaming liquid over the top. Seal the pan with aluminum foil.

5 Bake for about 20 minutes, or until the fish flakes readily with a fork.

6 Scatter the cilantro on top and serve hot.

crispy fried shallots

Indonesian dishes are frequently garnished with crispy deep-fried shallots. You may even be able to find packages of fried shallots in specialty food stores where Asian foods are sold. These are terrific to have on hand for garnishing vegetable dishes. Be forewarned: These crispy bits are so delicious, it is best to make them when you are alone in the house.

■ **MAKES 2 CUPS** ■

1 pound shallots, sliced into ¼-inch rings
Oil for deep-frying
Coarse sea salt

1 Heat 2 inches of oil in a medium saucepan over medium-high heat until shimmering. Add about one quarter of the shallots and fry, stirring occasionally until browned, 4 to 5 minutes. (If the shallots brown in less time, the oil is probably too hot and the temperature should be reduced.) Using a slotted spoon, transfer the shallots to paper towels to drain.

2 Repeat until all the shallots have been fried.

3 Season generously with the salt. Use immediately or store for up to 1 week in an airtight container in the refrigerator, or up to 1 month in the freezer. Reheat in a 350°F oven for 10 minutes to restore the crunch, if needed.

THE ONION FAMILY IS A BIG GROUP. Some onions, like leeks, deserve their own chapter because they are so versatile as vegetables. Others, like shallots and scallions, add flavor, but are used mostly as aromatics or herbs. Here's a guide to using onions as flavorings and accents.

Chives (*Allium schoenoprasum*) The leaves of the chive plant are used to give a mild onion flavor. Chives grow quickly and multiply readily. If you dig a clump from a friend's garden and plant the clump (or separate the tiny bulbs and plant a few clumps), you should have chives for the rest of your life. Harvest with scissors whenever you need them. The flavor is best before the chives start to flower, so to extend the season, cut off the flower stems as they appear. The purple flowers, however, are edible and make a striking addition to salads.

Egyptian Onions (*Allium cepa* var. *viviparum*) Also known as tree onions, multiplier onions, and winter onions, these produce clusters of small bulbs called bulbils at the top of the seed stalk in late summer. The bulbils are used to produce very early green onions. These are odd plants, but they grow as perennials and dependably produce greens that can be used as scallions very early in the spring. They are said to do a great job of controlling aphids.

Garlic Chives (*Allium tuberosum*) Also known as Chinese leeks, their flavor is reminiscent of garlic and chives. You can use the leaves — and flowers — any way you would use chives. Garlic chives grow and multiply like ordinary chives; digging a clump from a friend's garden will keep you in garlic chives forever. The flowers are white and lovely, and the leaves are flat like garlic and leeks, not round like onions and chives.

Scallions (*Allium fistulosum*) A scallion is an onion that produces a bulb no larger in width than the base of the leaves. Sometimes these are called bunching onions or green onions. The root end may be white or red. Scallions are used extensively in Asian cooking, added at the last minute to stir-fries, or finely chopped and added to salad dressings. To prepare, trim off the root end and strip away any damaged leaves. Then chop or julienne. Scallions can be added raw to salads. The flavor is quite mild.

Shallots Shallots look like miniature red-skinned or brown-skinned onions. The flesh is milder than onions, and can be used interchangeably with onions.

Spring Onions A spring onion is any onion that is harvested before the bulb forms. These are used as scallions (and some cookbooks use spring onions, green onions, and scallions interchangeably), but the flavor is sharper.

Who'd Have Thought They Could Be This Good?

M. F. K. FISHER, PERHAPS THE MOST famous and well loved of food writers, wrote, "Almost all vegetables are good, although there is some doubt still about parsnips."

It was a sentiment I shared until my friend Steve Worthen brought parsnips to a potluck, newly harvested. "Are these white carrots?" I asked, more ready to believe these delicious vegetables were some rare exotica than the lowly parsnip.

"If you haven't had parsnips when they are first harvested," explained Steve, "you've never experienced what they are supposed to taste like." Neither Steve nor I can remember exactly what parsnip dish he prepared that night. But I have been experimenting with this humble vegetable ever since, and I am prepared to state categorically that if you haven't tasted a properly roasted fresh parsnip, then you haven't tasted a parsnip. Roasting brings out the hidden nutmeg and sweet nuances of parsnips. It's a flavor everyone likes — even the doubters. Just don't tell them they are about to try parsnips.

GROWING Parsnips do best in loose, moderately fertile soil. They yield best in full sun but can tolerate light shade. They don't develop their characteristic sweet flavor until after they have been through some hard frosts.

SOWING Sow outdoors as soon as the soil can be worked.

CULTIVATING When parsnips are 4 to 6 inches tall, thin the plants to 3 to 4 inches apart. Mulch heavily, then neglect until harvest.

HARVESTING They are best if harvested in early spring after staying in the ground through the winter. Store in the refrigerator or root cellar.

Parsnips really are best when roasted, but braising also works well. There is little point in preparing them by other methods, unless it is to prevent famine. Parsnips can be sautéed in butter, but the flavor is somewhat anemic and bitter.

Parsnips should be peeled, like carrots. If the cores are pithy or woody, they should be removed and discarded.

TIMING
Steaming: 10 to 20 minutes, chunked
Roasting: 20 minutes at 425°F, sliced
Braising: 20 to 30 minutes

PARSNIP MATH
1 pound parsnips = 3 cups sliced or diced

world's best parsnips

Joining "world's best" and "parsnips" is not an oxymoron. Roasting brings out flavors in parsnips I never knew existed. The flavor is sweet, nutty, and aromatic. It is critical to slice the parsnips uniformly so they roast evenly — and ¼-inch thickness works best.

■ SERVES 4 ■

2 pounds parsnips, peeled and sliced into ¼-inch rounds
2 tablespoons extra-virgin olive oil
2 teaspoons chopped fresh thyme (optional)
Salt and freshly ground black pepper

1 Preheat the oven to 425°F. Grease a baking sheet with oil.

2 Toss together the parsnips, oil, and thyme in a medium bowl. Season with salt and pepper. Transfer to the prepared baking sheet and arrange in a single layer.

3 Roast for about 20 minutes, shaking the pan occasionally, until the parsnips are well browned and tender. Serve hot.

ROOTING FOR PARSNIPS IN HISTORY

THAT CULTIVATED PARSNIPS ORIGINATED FROM wild ones is a fact no historians doubt, though where wild parsnips originated is under debate; they are found quite commonly throughout northern Europe and Asia and western North America. Cultivated parsnips date as least as far back as the first century AD, when Lucius Junius Moderatus Columella mentioned cultivated parsnips in print.

It wasn't until the Middle Ages that a fleshy parsnip was developed; earlier parsnips tended to be skinny roots, not much different from wild parsnips. Parsnips were often used in sweet dishes and were especially enjoyed during Lent, when meat was forbidden. As a starchy root, parsnips were filling and relatively nutritious. The wealthy enjoyed them in cream sauces, especially with salt cod, while the poor ate them in fritters. Once the potato was introduced from the New World, however, the parsnip started its decline in popularity as a cheap, versatile starch. As far as I can tell, it is still declining.

mapled parsnips

If you already love parsnips, this dish will strike you as pure comfort food.

SERVES 4–6

1½ pounds parsnips, peeled and cut into 2-inch chunks (about 5 cups)
2 tablespoons butter
Salt and freshly ground black pepper
Pinch nutmeg
Pure maple syrup

1 Place the parsnips in a steamer basket and steam over boiling water until tender, 10 to 20 minutes. Reserve the water.

2 Purée in a food processor, adding the butter and as much of the water as needed to make a smooth purée.

3 Transfer to a saucepan. Season with salt, pepper, and nutmeg. Add maple syrup. Reheat over medium heat until hot, stirring occasionally. Serve hot.

balsamic-glazed parsnips

A dissenter in my family claims this is the best way to prepare parsnips. The vinegar combines with the natural sweetness of parsnips to create a slightly sweet-and-sour dish of glazed parsnips. As this recipe clearly demonstrates, braising is a simple, rewarding way to prepare flavorful vegetables.

SERVES 4–6

6–7 parsnips (about 2 pounds), peeled and thinly sliced on the diagonal

½ cup vegetable or chicken broth (page 8 or 9)

¼ cup extra-virgin olive oil

¼ cup balsamic vinegar

1 tablespoon soy sauce

1 Combine the parsnips, broth, oil, vinegar, and soy sauce in a large nonreactive skillet or Dutch oven. Bring to a boil.

2 Reduce the heat and simmer, stirring occasionally, until the parsnips are tender-crisp, 20 to 30 minutes. The parsnips will absorb the liquid and become glazed. Serve hot.

Baked, Boiled, & Knished

I LIKE TO EXPLAIN MY SHORT, sturdy stature by saying I come from potato peasant stock, implying that my ancestors in the Old Country (Russia) subsisted on their meager crop of tubers.

Actually my immigrant grandparents were quite urbanized. But, as far as I can remember, neither grandmother ever served a meal without potatoes, boiled, mashed, baked, or occasionally knished — that is, mashed and seasoned and used as a filling for a savory Jewish pastry known as a knish.

My mother followed the culinary custom, but as an American mom, she also served Rice-a-roni and a packaged noodle dish now and then. I thought *that* stuff was marvelous and grew up craving pasta. But I married a man with Irish potatoes in his heritage and I was forced to reconsider the humble spud.

The humble spud is no longer so humble. With so many varieties, colors, and shapes to choose from, potatoes can take center stage on the plate.

GROWING Potatoes grow best in cool soils enriched with compost, with adequate moisture.

SOWING In warm climates, plant in the fall. In warm-temperate climates, plant potatoes in late winter. In cool climates, plant in early spring, 3 weeks before the last frost. Plant tubers in trenches 3 inches deep and 1 foot apart.

CULTIVATING When the plants are a few inches tall, apply 1 inch of compost topped by a layer of straw mulch so about half the plant is covered. Continue to add mulch as the plant grows. Keep well watered from the time they flower until 2 weeks before harvest.

HARVESTING Within 2 months of planting, begin harvesting new potatoes by reaching in the soil and pulling out one or two from each plant. Harvest the main crop when the foliage dies back. Use a garden fork to loosen the soil, then remove the potatoes by hand. Brush off the soil, let cure for 2 weeks in humid conditions, then store in a root cellar.

POTATO MATH

1 pound potatoes = 3 russet-type potatoes or
8 to 10 new potatoes
= 4 cups grated or diced
= 3 cups sliced or chopped
= 2 cups cooked and mashed

From a cook's perspective, there are basically three types of potatoes. Starchy or baking potatoes, like the classic Idahos or russets, are best for baking, mashing, and deep-frying. (British cookbooks call this type of potato "floury.") "Waxy" potatoes hold their shape well and are good for boiling, roasting, and pan-frying. Examples of these are Red Bliss, Red Creamer, and White Rose. These are the potatoes to use in potato salads. All-purpose potatoes include Yukon golds, Yellow Finn, and Purple Peruvian potatoes. These potatoes can be mashed or baked, but they don't have as fluffy a texture as the russets. New potatoes are any potato harvested young, when the size is small and the skin is tender.

These days there are numerous potato varieties in a rainbow of colors. Do not expect the colors to remain true once the potato is cooked. This quality varies from variety to variety. Also, soil conditions greatly affect how the potato develops. A tuber grown in Maine may differ considerably from the same variety grown in California.

TIMING

Baking: 1 to 1¼ hours at 350°F
Boiling: 15 to 25 minutes
Steaming: 15 to 25 minutes (new potatoes)
Roasting: 25 to 30 minutes at 425°F, cut into wedges
Grilling: 15 to 25 minutes, sliced;
60 to 90 minutes, foil-wrapped whole potatoes

indian-spiced potato balls

Serve as an appetizer or side dish with a cooling raita (page 137) and a sweet chutney, such as Major Grey's.

MAKES 36 BALLS

2 pounds baking potatoes, peeled

2 tablespoons canola oil

1 onion, minced

3 jalapeños or other fresh green chiles, minced

1½ tablespoons curry powder, or to taste

1 cup finely diced red bell pepper or frozen peas

1 teaspoon garam masala (available wherever Indian spices are sold)

Salt

Oil for deep-frying

Batter

1 cup unbleached all-purpose flour

½ teaspoon baking soda

½ teaspoon salt

1 large egg yolk, lightly beaten

1 cup ice water

1 Put the potatoes in a medium saucepan with salted water to cover. Bring to a boil and boil until tender, 10 to 15 minutes. Drain well and mash or pass through a ricer.

2 Heat the canola oil in a medium skillet over medium heat. Add the onion, jalapeños, and curry powder. Sauté until the onion is tender, 3 to 5 minutes. Scrape the mixture into the potatoes, along with the bell pepper, garam masala, and salt to taste. Mix well and allow to cool to room temperature.

3 Pinch off pieces of the potato mixture the size of a walnut and roll into a smooth ball. Refrigerate for at least 30 minutes.

4 Preheat about 2 inches of oil in a tall saucepan to 375°F.

5 While the oil heats, prepare the batter. Mix together the flour, baking soda, and salt in a shallow bowl. Make a well in the center and pour in the egg yolk and water. Stir to combine. The batter should be lumpy.

6 Dip each potato ball into the batter and carefully add to the hot oil. Fry a few balls at a time for about 2 minutes each, or until golden. Drain well on paper towels and continue frying until all the potato mixture is used. Serve hot.

POTATO TIPS

- Storage conditions affect potato flavor. At 50°F, potatoes will keep for up to 3 months. Cold temperatures cause potatoes to convert starches to sugar and to darken when cooking. Warm temperatures encourage sprouting and shriveling. Potatoes that have been exposed to light develop green patches. Cut these away.
- Peeled potatoes discolor readily, so keep them covered with acidulated water (1 tablespoon lemon juice or vinegar to 4 cups water) once you have peeled them.
- Never mash potatoes in a food processor; the cutting blades turn the potatoes into a gummy mess.
- Russets are the best potatoes for mashing.
- Rubbing butter or oil onto the skin of potatoes to be baked will make the skin crisper and cause the potatoes to bake a little faster.

classic potato salad

I sought for years to re-create the deli potato salad I grew up with — one that I far preferred to my mother's homemade version. One day I tasted it at a church supper and had to track down the lady who had brought the salad. She was amused at my enthusiasm. "Why, honey," she said, "it's just Miracle Whip that makes it taste so good."

■ SERVES 6–8 ■

2½ pounds waxy or all-purpose potatoes

3 hard-cooked eggs, chopped

2 large celery stalks, finely chopped

½ red bell pepper, finely chopped

½ large sweet onion or small yellow onion, finely chopped

1 cup boiled salad dressing, such as Miracle Whip, or more to taste

2 tablespoons chopped dill pickle or sweet pickle relish, or more to taste

Salt and freshly ground black pepper

Paprika, to garnish

1 Put the potatoes in a large saucepan and fill with enough cold water to cover the potatoes by 1 inch. Bring to a simmer and cook until the potatoes are tender, 15 to 30 minutes, depending on the size. Don't overcook. Drain well and let cool.

2 When the potatoes are cool enough to handle, peel and slice them into ½-inch cubes.

3 Combine the potatoes, eggs, celery, bell pepper, and onion in a large mixing bowl. Add the dressing and pickles. Season with salt and pepper. Mix well. Add more dressing if the salad seems dry. Adjust the flavor with additional pickles and salt and pepper, if desired. Chill well. The salad will develop flavor as it sits.

4 Just before serving, taste and adjust the seasoning. Sprinkle paprika on top to garnish.

german potato salad

Everything tastes better with bacon, no? The hot dressing soaks into the warm potatoes.

SERVES 4–6

2 pounds waxy potatoes, scrubbed, halved, and sliced ¼ inch thick

4 ounces bacon, diced

1 shallot, minced

2 tablespoons extra-virgin olive oil

5 tablespoons white wine or red wine vinegar

1 teaspoon sugar

2 celery stalks, diced

¼ cup minced fresh parsley

Salt and freshly ground black pepper

1 Combine the potatoes with 6 cups salted water in a medium saucepan. Bring to a boil, then reduce the heat and simmer until the potatoes are tender, 5 to 10 minutes. Reserve ¼ cup of the cooking liquid and drain. Transfer the potatoes to a large mixing bowl and keep warm.

2 Meanwhile, in a large skillet, cook the bacon over medium heat until brown and crisp, about 4 minutes. Remove the bacon with a slotted spoon and transfer to the bowl with the potatoes. Drain off all but 2 tablespoons of the bacon grease.

3 Add the shallot to the skillet and cook until slightly softened, about 3 minutes. Stir in the reserved cooking liquid, oil, vinegar, and sugar. Bring to a boil. Pour the mixture over the potatoes and toss to coat. Add the celery, parsley, and salt and pepper to taste. Mix well. Serve immediately.

herbed new potatoes

There's no better way to treat creamy new potatoes than with a gentle steam bath and a delicate coating of butter, fresh herbs, and sea salt. Steaming is essential; boiling will drown the subtle flavor of new potatoes. Unsalted butter usually is fresher than salted butter, so it is recommended here. If you have sea salt, you'll want to use it to work with the delicate flavors of these fresh, fresh ingredients. The herbs can be a mixture of what you have in the garden.

SERVES 4–6

2 pounds new potatoes, scrubbed

3 tablespoons unsalted butter, melted

3 tablespoons chopped fresh herbs (dill, oregano, chives, savory, chervil, tarragon, parsley, marjoram, alone or in any combination)

Sea salt and freshly ground black pepper

1 Bring about an inch of water to a boil in a saucepan. Add the potatoes in a steaming basket, cover, and steam for 25 to 35 minutes, until the potatoes are tender when pierced with a knife.

2 Transfer the potatoes to a warmed serving bowl. Pour in the butter, and sprinkle the herbs and salt and pepper over the butter. Toss gently. Serve immediately.

fraked potatoes

In certain parts of Vermont, these potatoes are known as Annie Harlow's Famous Fraked Potatoes. She developed the recipe and often takes the dish to potlucks, which is where I first encountered them. Her method of first frying, then baking new potatoes (hence the term "fraked") creates a wonderfully crusty roasted potato with a minimum amount of oil. The odd thing about these potatoes is that they are best made ahead and reheated. I can't figure out why, but I do know that this makes them perfect for parties.

SERVES 6

Extra-virgin olive oil

3 pounds small new potatoes, cut into halves (see Note)

Coarse sea salt and freshly ground pepper

1 Preheat the oven to 475°F.

2 Pour enough oil into a large cast-iron skillet to generously coat the pan and heat over high heat until quite hot. Add a single layer of potato halves, cut-side down. Fry until the potatoes are beginning to brown, 4 to 5 minutes. Transfer the potatoes to a large, ungreased baking sheet and repeat with the remaining potatoes. Continue until all the potatoes have been browned on the cut side.

3 Place the potatoes in the oven and bake until completely tender, about 20 minutes longer.

4 Season generously with salt and pepper. Serve immediately or hold in the refrigerator for 1 to 2 days.

5 Reheat at 400°F until hot throughout, about 20 minutes. Taste and adjust the seasonings if desired.

note The recipe requires small potatoes, no bigger than a Ping-Pong ball. If your potatoes are bigger, use a different recipe.

spicy skillet potatoes

A step above ordinary hash browns, these potatoes are just about perfect when made with new Yukon golds. The method, a little fussy perhaps, makes terrific well-browned potatoes that can be adapted to different flavor combinations or stripped down to make simple, but perfect, hash browns. The secret is browning the potatoes in batches.

■ SERVES 4 ■

1½ pounds mature all-purpose potatoes (peeling optional), cut into ½-inch cubes, or new potatoes (not peeled), cut into bite-size pieces

3 tablespoons canola oil

1 teaspoon ground cumin

1 teaspoon sweet paprika

Salt and freshly ground black pepper

1 onion, diced

1 red or green bell pepper, diced

1 jalapeño or other chile, seeded and diced

1 Put the potatoes in a saucepan and cover with salted water. Bring to a boil over high heat. As soon as the water begins to boil, drain the potatoes.

2 Preheat the oven to 300°F.

3 Heat 2 tablespoons of the oil in a large skillet over medium-high heat. Add half the potatoes to fit in a single layer in the skillet. Season with ½ teaspoon of the cumin, ½ teaspoon of the paprika, a generous pinch or two of salt, and a several grinds of pepper. Cook until the bottom sides of the potatoes are brown, 3 to 5 minutes, then turn the potatoes and brown on another side, without stirring, 3 to 5 minutes. Repeat until all the sides are browned. New potatoes will brown more quickly than mature potatoes. Remove the potatoes from the skillet with a slotted spoon and spread out in a single layer on a large baking sheet. Keep warm in the oven.

4 Heat the remaining 1 tablespoon oil in the skillet and cook the second half of the potatoes as you did the first half. Remove from the skillet and add to the potatoes in the oven.

5 Add the onion, bell pepper, and jalapeño to the skillet and sauté until softened, 4 to 5 minutes. Add the potatoes and mix gently. Season with more salt and pepper, if desired, and serve immediately.

Garlic mashed potatoes have many different interpretations. For some people, it means adding roasted garlic to the mashed potatoes, which gives a nutty, garlicky flavor. Others like the punch of garlic sautéed with butter. In this version, the garlic is tamed by cooking with the potatoes, creating a subtle background flavor.

SERVES 4-6

3 pounds baking potatoes, peeled and cut into chunks
4 garlic cloves, peeled and left whole
¾ cup milk
3 tablespoons butter
Salt and freshly ground black pepper

1 Cover the potatoes and garlic with cold salted water in a saucepan. Cover and bring to a boil. Partially remove the lid and boil until the potatoes are tender, about 25 minutes. Meanwhile, heat the milk and butter in a small saucepan until steaming.

2 Drain the potatoes. Mash the potatoes in a mixing bowl or pass through a potato ricer into a mixing bowl. Beat the potatoes as you pour in the heated milk mixture. Season generously with salt and pepper. Serve hot.

OTHER POTATO RECIPES

tex-mex potato cake

Most of the time, I'm not one for weird fusion cooking, but I thought my grandmother's potato kugel could use a little sparking up. Potato kugel (kugel means pudding in Yiddish) is a traditional Jewish dish of grated potatoes flavored with onion and baked in a casserole. In this version, there is additional flavor from chiles and cheese. If you have a food processor, the dish comes together in minutes, which is good because I've seen people devour the finished product in minutes. This is a great dish to have in your repertoire; it is very quick to make, holds up well on a buffet table, transports easily to a potluck, and can even be made ahead and reheated.

SERVES 6–8

10 medium potatoes (about 3 pounds), peeled and grated
2 onions, grated
1 can (4 ounces) diced roasted green chiles, drained
2 tablespoons unbleached all-purpose flour
2 large eggs, lightly beaten
¼ pound Cheddar, grated
Salt and freshly ground black pepper

1 Preheat the oven to 350°F. Grease a 9- by 13-inch baking dish with butter or oil.

2 Combine the potatoes, onions, chiles, flour, eggs, and cheese in a large bowl. Season with a generous pinch of salt and a few grinds of pepper. Mix well. Spoon into the prepared baking dish.

3 Bake for 1 to 1¼ hours, until golden and firm.

4 Cut into squares and serve.

potato latkes

The Jewish holiday of Hanukkah falls sometime in December. It is traditional to eat fried foods, commemorating the lamp oil in the Temple in Jerusalem that burned for eight days. Fried potato pancakes, or latkes, are probably the most famous of the traditional foods. Latkes are often mistreated in the kitchen, and the result is a greasy pancake, gray on the inside, soggy throughout. The perfect latke is crisp on the outside, tender and snowy white on the inside. There are a few extra steps in this recipe as part of my never-ending quest to get the dish right.

■ SERVES 4–6 ■

3 pounds russet or baking potatoes, peeled
1 large onion
Fresh lemon juice or vinegar
2 large eggs, lightly beaten
2 teaspoons salt
¼ teaspoon freshly ground black pepper
Canola oil, for frying
Applesauce, to serve
Sour cream, to serve

1 Coarsely grate the potatoes and onions by hand or in a food processor.

2 Transfer the potato mixture to a large bowl filled with acidulated water (1 tablespoon lemon juice or vinegar to 4 cups water). Swish around with your hands for 1 minute. Pour into a strainer and drain well. Place a clean kitchen towel on the counter. Dump the potatoes onto the towel and pat dry. This step will keep the potatoes from turning pink, then gray as they are exposed to air.

3 In the food processor, pulse the potato mixture until finely chopped but not puréed.

4 Transfer the potato mixture to a large mixing bowl and add the eggs, salt, and pepper, and mix well.

5 Preheat the oven to 300°F.

6 Heat 1 inch of oil in a frying pan over medium-high heat. Drop the potato mixture, ¼ cup at a time, into the pan and fry until golden on the bottom, 1½ to 2 minutes. Do not crowd the pan. Turn and fry on the other side, about 1½ minutes. Drain on paper towels.

7 Keep the latkes warm in the oven while cooking the remaining potato mixture, but serve as soon as possible. Pass the applesauce and sour cream at the table.

Potatoes were cultivated in the Andes Mountains of Peru at least as far back as 3000 BC. The Spanish conquistador Gónzalo Jiménez de Quesada was one of the first Europeans introduced to what the Natives called *papas*. But since they grew underground, the Spanish mistook them for a kind of truffle and called them *tartuffo*.

They Aren't Turnips

THE BEST THING I CAN SAY about the rutabaga is that it is not a turnip. So when an old-timer told me that the best turnip he ever tasted was the heirloom Gilfeather, I thought to myself that Gilfeather may be the best-tasting turnip, but that isn't saying much. Meanwhile I was conducting a kitchen romance with rutabagas, blithely unaware that the Gilfeather is a rutabaga.

So, sure, a rutabaga is called a yellow turnip. But a turnip is sharp and pungent, where a rutabaga is sweet and mild. A turnip is best grown in early spring and harvested before temperatures sharpen the flavor. A rutabaga savors a few fall frosts. And let's face it, rutabaga is a great name.

Carl Sandburg, one of America's finest poets and writers, celebrated the rutabaga in his *Rootabaga Stories,* published in 1922. The book is collected stories he told his granddaughter as they sat together on his front-porch swing. They tell the tale of Gimme the Ax and his two children — Please Gimme and Ax Me No Questions — and how they packed up everything they owned and headed off to see the world riding on the Zig-Zag Railroad. There's no finer way to spend a frosty evening than curled up by the fire with the *Rootabaga Stories* in your hand and a fine meal of rutabagas in your belly.

GROWING Rutabagas, like other root vegetables, do well in a fertile soil with an ample supply of potassium and phosphorus. They do best in full sun but will tolerate some shade. Leaving the roots in the ground for a few fall frosts helps to develop flavor.

SOWING Sow directly outdoors in early to mid-summer (90 days before the intended harvest).

CULTIVATING Fertilize with compost tea throughout the growing season.

HARVESTING Harvest after a few frosts. Cut the tops off about an inch from the root. Store in a humid root cellar with the temperature just above freezing, or place in a plastic vegetable storage bag in the refrigerator.

TIMING
Steaming: 30 minutes, cubed
Roasting: 25 minutes at 450°F, cubed

Rutabagas have a tough, tan-to-purple, inedible skin that should be peeled away with a knife.

Some people add raw rutabagas to crudités platters, but I don't think the raw rutabaga is likely to win over any new friends. Like most root vegetables, roasting is the very best way to bring out its nutty, sweet flavors.

Mashed rutabagas is a traditional dish. The rutabagas will make a tighter, less watery purée if they are steamed rather than boiled.

During the winter months, I throw diced or cubed rutabagas into many, many dishes, including beef stew, chicken potpie, vegetable soups, and any combination of roasted root vegetables — served as a side dish or used in tarts, salads, pasta dishes, pizzas, and sandwiches.

RUTABAGA MATH
1 pound rutabaga = 3½ cups cubed
= 2 to 3 cups finely diced
= 2 cups steamed and puréed

mashed rutabagas

If you didn't grow up with mashed rutabagas, you might be reluctant to try them. But let me assure you, they are delicious — especially if you use freshly harvested vegetables. The tiny amount of maple syrup is key to smoothing out the rough edges of this vegetable.

SERVES 4

2–3 rutabagas (2 to 3 pounds)
2 tablespoons butter, or more to taste
2 tablespoons milk or light cream
1 tablespoon pure maple syrup, or more to taste
Salt and freshly ground black pepper
Freshly grated nutmeg

1 Peel the rutabagas with a paring knife, cutting away any green flesh. Cut the rutabagas into 2-inch cubes and place in a steamer over a few inches of water in a medium saucepan. Cover and bring the water to a boil over high heat. Steam until the rutabagas are tender when poked with the tip of a knife, about 30 minutes.

2 Press the rutabagas through a ricer or food mill. Put into a saucepan and cook over medium heat for 2 to 3 minutes, until the purée is slightly dry. Stir in the butter, milk, and maple syrup. Season with salt, pepper, and nutmeg. Serve hot.

roasted spiced rutabaga sticks

The treatment here is similar to what I do with sweet potatoes — slick matchsticks of rutabaga with a spiced oil, then roast in a hot oven. The result is a spicy, sweet vegetable treat. If you want to multiply the recipe, use two baking sheets, rotate them every 10 minutes or so and increase the roasting time as needed.

SERVES 2–4

2 tablespoons canola oil

1 teaspoon ground cinnamon

1 teaspoon ground cumin

1 teaspoon salt, or more to taste

¼–½ teaspoon ground chipotle chile (or substitute another ground chile)

1 large or 2 medium rutabagas, peeled and cut into matchsticks

1 Preheat the oven to 450°F. Lightly grease a large sheet pan (preferred) or shallow roasting pan with oil.

2 Combine the oil, cinnamon, cumin, salt, and ground chipotle in a large bowl. Add the rutabaga and toss to coat. Transfer to the prepared pan and arrange in a single layer.

3 Roast for about 25 minutes, until tender and lightly browned, stirring or shaking the pan occasionally. Serve hot.

roasted chicken
with rutabagas

Rutabagas are a favorite in my family, but just about any root vegetable will work here. Mashed potatoes are a great accompaniment to this wonderfully rustic, satisfying dish.

SERVES 4–6

2 tablespoons extra-virgin olive oil

3–3½ pounds chicken parts or bone-in thighs

Salt and freshly ground black pepper, plus more to taste

2–3 rutabagas (about 3 pounds), peeled and cut into ½-inch cubes

3 heads garlic, cloves separated and peeled

2 tablespoons chopped fresh thyme

2 tablespoons unbleached all-purpose flour

1 cup dry white wine

1 cup chicken broth (page 9)

1 Preheat the oven to 350°F.

2 Heat the oil in a large skillet over medium-high heat. Add the chicken pieces in a single layer, season with a generous pinch of salt and a few grinds of pepper, and cook until well browned, about 10 minutes, turning as needed. Work in batches, if necessary, to avoid crowding the pan. Arrange the chicken in a single layer in a large roasting pan.

3 Add the rutabagas and garlic to the skillet and sauté over medium-high heat until lightly coated in oil, about 2 minutes. Season to taste with salt and pepper. Scatter the rutabagas and garlic cloves over and around the chicken. Sprinkle the thyme over all. Set the skillet aside, but do not wash.

4 Roast the chicken and vegetables for 45 to 50 minutes, until the chicken is no longer pink and the vegetables are tender.

5 Meanwhile, to make the sauce, pour off all but 2 tablespoons fat from the skillet. Whisk in the flour. Whisk in the wine and broth, scraping the bottom of the pot to dislodge any brown bits. Bring to a boil and stir until smooth and thickened. Season to taste with salt and pepper. Keep warm.

6 To serve, arrange the chicken and vegetables on a large platter and pass the sauce on the side. Serve hot.

RUTABAGA FACTS & FICTIONS

There's some question of the rutabaga's origin, but it is generally accepted to be a turnip cabbage cross that originated in Bohemia (part of Slovakia) in the early 1600s. Well suited to northern climates, it spread to Britain and Scandinavia. The name comes from the Swedish *rotabagge*, or "red bags," referring to its shape.

In Scotland, rutabagas are more popular than turnips and are called "neeps," an early form of the word turnip. They are a popular accompaniment to haggis (haggis and bashed neeps). Rutabagas are said to make a fine vodka in Poland.

In the United States, the rutabaga was particularly important in the North, where its ability to keep its quality during the winter in root cellar storage made it an important foodstuff. It was called the "big yellow" and "Canadian turnip" by early settlers.

In addition to being a rich source of beta-carotene, rutabagas are high in vitamin C, the B vitamins, calcium, potassium, and fiber.

The Pumpkin's in the Pie

THIS IS THE TIME OF YEAR when New Englanders count our blessings. It's hard not to, with the leaves so colorful, the weather so bracingly crisp, and the harvest so bountiful. Of course, not every harvest is bountiful. Summer may have brought bugs, intractable weather, a glut of zucchini, or a shortage of ripe tomatoes. But pumpkins and winter squash are a crop all Yankees can depend on — and have depended on since our earliest days.

Native Americans introduced the first European settlers in New England to beans, corn (maize), and pumpkins and winter squash. They treated them to a seafood chowder made with "Indian squash" that at least one writer condemned as "the meanest of God's blessings." But after a taste of New England winter, the Pilgrims came to appreciate pumpkin and squash for prolific harvests that staved off starvation.

Native Americans didn't distinguish between pumpkins and winter squash, and neither do botanists. According to the scientists, there are four basic types of edible squashes. *Cucurbita pepo* is noted for its pentagonal stems with prickly spines. This group includes pumpkins and acorn squash, as well as all the summer squashes, spaghetti squash, and numerous gourds. Butternut squash, which is one of the best replacements for pumpkin in any recipe, is in another grouping entirely, *C. moshata. C. maxima* (round stems) includes buttercup, Hubbard, and turban squashes.

In the kitchen, what we can say is that summer squash is eaten when immature. Winter squash and pumpkins are eaten fully mature after seeds and a hard shell have developed.

GROWING Most winter squash and pumpkins grow on vines that may extend 20 feet or more. Vining squash can be trained to grow on a trellis or tepee. The expansive growth can be curtailed by pinching back the growing tips. They require full sun, steady and even moisture, and relatively rich soil. They need 3 months or more of frost-free growing.

SOWING Direct-seed in warm areas once the soil has warmed in the spring and the danger of frost is past. In cooler regions, direct-seed or set out transplants after soil has warmed.

CULTIVATING Row covers will maintain the necessary warm temperatures and protect from insects when the plants are small. Remove when blossoms appear. Keep well watered.

HARVESTING Winter squash must be allowed to reach maturity before it is harvested. At that point, its thick, tough skin makes it a candidate for winter storage. The squash sweetens with age as the starches turn to sugars. If picked before reaching its prime, the squash will be watery and lacking in flavor.

After harvest, winter squash should be allowed to cure at room temperature for a couple of weeks. This hardens the skin. Then it should be stored in a cool airy space; 50°F is the ideal temperature for storage. Squash will keep for several months at this temperature.

WINTER SQUASH & PUMPKIN NUTRITION NOTES

Winter squash and pumpkin are rich in beta-carotene. One cup provides all the daily requirements for vitamin A, plus a healthy dose of vitamin C and potassium. All this for only 82 calories.

Most recipes call for cutting winter squash into pieces. This may be easier said than done. Some winter squash, like blue Hubbard, require a heavy cleaver (or ax) to do the job, while others, such as delicata, have skins that are easily cut or are even edible. Butternut can be peeled with a swivel-bladed vegetable peeler. For very hard squash, the best thing to do is drop it on a concrete floor or a paved driveway. Another way is in the microwave. Place the whole squash in the microwave and cook on high for 2 minutes. Allow the squash to stand for several minutes, then cut in half for further cooking. After cutting the squash, remove the fibers and seeds.

Winter squash is usually cooked until it is completely tender. You can't really overcook winter squash, unless you are serving it stuffed, in which case you do want the shell to remain intact. Test with a fork through the skin. The fork should meet with little or no resistance.

TIMING

Steaming: 15 minutes for halves or pieces
Baking: 45 to 90 minutes at 350°F with 1 inch water in pan
Grilling: Steam slices until tender (15 minutes), then brush with oil and grill about 5 minutes per side
Roasting: 20 to 30 minutes at 425°F, peeled and sliced or cubed
45 to 60 minutes at 425°F for halves or quarters

WINTER SQUASH & PUMPKIN MATH

1 pound winter squash = 4 cups cubed or or pumpkin   3 cups diced

1 pie pumpkin, 6 pounds = 2 cups cooked & strained puree

spaghetti squash salad with citrus dressing

After much consideration (and consumption), I have concluded that the very best way to enjoy spaghetti squash is in a salad. In this version, the citrus dressing enhances the sweetness of the squash, and the almonds add a pleasant crunch. You won't think of pasta or pasta salads while you enjoy this, but you may think of rice noodles.

SERVES 6

1 spaghetti squash, 3½ pounds, halved lengthwise and seeded

3 tablespoons canola oil

2 tablespoons fresh lime juice

2 tablespoons fresh orange juice

1 tablespoon fresh lemon juice

½ teaspoon fresh lime zest

Salt and freshly ground black pepper

1 carrot, grated

1 cup flaked almonds, toasted

3 scallions, white and tender green parts, chopped, or ⅓ cup diced sweet onion

2 tablespoons chopped fresh cilantro

2 tablespoons chopped fresh mint

1 Place the squash halves in a large pot, cover with water, salt generously, and bring to a boil. Boil the squash until just tender, 12 to 15 minutes. Drain well and let cool.

2 Meanwhile, combine the oil, lime juice, orange juice, lemon juice, and lime zest in a small bowl. Whisk well. Season with salt and pepper.

3 When the squash is cool enough to handle, scrape out the strands of squash with a fork. Toss, pat dry, add the carrot, almonds, scallions, cilantro, and mint, and toss again. Pour the dressing over the salad and toss well. Taste and adjust the seasoning.

4 Let the salad stand for at least 30 minutes to allow the flavors to blend. Serve at room temperature.

Delicata squash — the name says everything. The flavor is delicate and sweet. The size is delicate and dainty. A large one serves four, a small one two. The skins are delicate enough in texture to eat. They don't add flavor, but they help the squash retain its shape and make its preparation very convenient for the cook.

SERVES 4

1½–2 pounds delicata squash (about 2 medium)
3 tablespoons butter, melted
2 garlic cloves, minced
1 teaspoon minced fresh ginger
1 tablespoon honey

1 Preheat the oven to 350°F.

2 Slice off the ends of the squash and scoop out the seeds and fibers with a spoon. Cut the squash into ¾-inch rings.

3 Stir together the butter, garlic, and ginger in a small bowl. Brush on both sides of the squash, reserving 1 tablespoon of the butter mixture, and place the rings on a rimmed baking sheet.

4 Roast for 15 minutes, turning the rings once halfway through.

5 Add the honey to the remaining butter. Brush the honey-butter mixture over the squash and return to the oven to roast for another 5 minutes, or until completely tender and lightly browned. Serve hot.

If you want to serve the squash stuffed, cut in half and bake it skin-side up for about 45 minutes. Then turn the squash skin-side down. Loosen the squash pulp with a fork and add the stuffing ingredients, or remove the squash flesh and combine it with the filling ingredients, then return it to the squash shell. Bake for another 15 minutes, until the filling is heated through.

Cabin fever comes in many forms, and exotic flavors can be one of its cures. Sweet winter squash can offer a blank palette for some toothsome combinations. In this version, brown sugar and rum provide a welcome tropical flavor breeze.

SERVES 4–6

1 large buttercup, butternut, or red kuri squash, or ½ small baby blue Hubbard squash

2 tablespoons butter

2–4 tablespoons dark or light brown sugar

1 tablespoon dark or light rum

1 tablespoon milk

Salt and freshly ground black pepper

1 Preheat the oven to 400°F.

2 Cut the squash into halves if small or into quarters if large. Remove and discard the seeds and fibers. Place skin-side up in a baking dish and add about 1 inch water to the dish.

3 Bake until completely tender when pierced with a skewer, 60 to 90 minutes, depending on the size of the pieces.

4 Drain off the water. Turn the pieces flesh-side up and allow to cool enough to be easily handled. Scrape the flesh from the skins into a mixing bowl and discard the skins. Add the butter, brown sugar, rum, and milk and mash or beat until smooth. Season to taste with the salt and pepper.

5 If desired, reheat in a microwave or in the top of a double boiler set over boiling water. Serve hot.

Blue hubbards and butternut squash are my favorites for this basic recipe.

SERVES 4–6

1 large buttercup, butternut, or red kuri squash or
½ small baby blue Hubbard squash
4–6 tablespoons butter
4–6 tablespoons pure maple syrup
3–4 tablespoons half-and-half or light cream
Salt and freshly ground black pepper

1 Preheat the oven to 400°F.

2 Cut the squash into halves if small or into quarters if large. Remove and discard the seeds and fibers. Place skin-side up in a baking dish and add about 1 inch water to the dish.

3 Bake until completely tender when pierced with a skewer, 60 to 90 minutes, depending on the size of the pieces.

4 Drain off the water. Turn the pieces flesh-side up and allow to cool enough to be easily handled. Scrape the flesh from the skins into a mixing bowl and discard the skins. Add the butter and beat until smooth. Beat in the maple syrup and half-and-half. Season with salt and pepper.

5 If desired, reheat in a microwave or in the top of a double boiler set over boiling water. Serve hot.

For pottage and puddings, custards and pies,
Our pumpkins and parsnips are common supplies.
We have pumpkins at morning and pumpkins at noon;
If it were not for pumpkins, we should be undoon.

—Anonymous (c. 1630)

roasted butternut squash with apple cider glaze

While the squash roasts, apple cider is reduced on top of the stove to a syrupy consistency. When the two ingredients are combined, the result may be the best winter squash you've ever enjoyed. The glazed squash tastes rich and buttery, an almost magical enhancement of the sweet butternut flavors.

SERVES 4–6

2–3 pounds butternut or other easy-to-peel, smooth-skinned winter squash

2 tablespoons canola oil

Salt and freshly ground black pepper

2 cups apple cider

1 shallot, minced

4 sage leaves, minced

1 Preheat the oven to 350°F. Lightly grease a large sheet pan (preferred) or large shallow roasting pan with oil.

2 Peel the squash; a sharp swivel-bladed vegetable peeler will do the job. Slice the squash in half and scoop out the fibers and seeds. Cut into ½-inch cubes. Combine the squash, oil, and salt and pepper to taste in a large bowl and toss to coat. Arrange in a single layer in the prepared pan.

3 Roast for 30 minutes, until the squash is tender, stirring every 10 minutes or so for even cooking.

4 While the squash is roasting, combine the cider and shallot in a small saucepan. Bring to a boil over medium-high heat and boil until reduced by two thirds, about 20 minutes. Remove from the heat, stir in the sage, cover, and keep warm.

5 Transfer the squash to a serving bowl. Pour the cider mixture over the squash, toss gently, and serve.

caramelized winter squash and onion pizza

Roasted winter squash with roasted onions and goat cheese is one of my favorite flavor combinations. The sweet vegetables make a delicious foil for the earthy goat cheese. The timing works out for the dough to rise while you prepare and roast the vegetables.

■ SERVES 4 ■

½ recipe Basic Pizza Dough (page 12; while the dough is rising, follow steps 1–4)

1 medium-size butternut squash (1½ pounds) peeled, seeds and fibers discarded, and diced

2–3 onions, diced

2 tablespoons extra-virgin olive oil

1 teaspoon crumbled dried rosemary or thyme

Salt and freshly ground black pepper

6 ounces fresh goat cheese, crumbled

2 tablespoons pine nuts

1 While the dough is rising according to the recipe instructions, preheat the oven to 425°F. Lightly grease a large sheet pan (preferred) or shallow roasting pan with oil.

2 Combine the squash and onions on the prepared pan. Drizzle with the oil and toss to coat. Arrange in a single layer. Sprinkle with the rosemary and season generously with salt and pepper.

3 Roast for about 30 minutes, until the vegetables are well browned and tender, stirring or shaking the pan occasionally for even cooking.

4 When the vegetables are done, remove from the oven and increase the oven temperature to 500°F.

5 With the dough stretched over the pizza pans or baking sheets according to the recipe instructions, scatter half the goat cheese over the top. Scatter the vegetables on top of the cheese. Top with the remaining goat cheese and the pine nuts.

6 Bake on the bottom shelf of the oven for 10 to 12 minutes, until the crust is golden brown.

7 Slice and serve warm.

PUMPKIN & WINTER SQUASH SEEDS

NATIVE AMERICANS who met the Spanish invaders on the Rio Grande included pumpkin seeds among their gifts of peace. The conquistadors willingly adopted the pumpkin seeds, and a dish of chicken cooked in a sauce of blanched almonds, pumpkin seeds, cumin seeds, chiles, and garlic is a legacy of that time.

If pumpkin seeds are your weakness, you may want to grow a variety that produces hull-less seeds. Johnny's Selected Seeds (see Sources) offers Kakai, a small black-striped pumpkin that is particularly prized for its seeds. Some people find winter squash seeds to be even more delicious than pumpkin seeds.

To prepare seeds for roasting, just wash the seeds in a bowl of water to separate the seeds from the stringy fibers to which they are attached. Then pat dry. Fill a medium saucepan with salted water and bring to a boil. Add the seeds, reduce the heat, and simmer gently for 1½ to 2 hours. Drain in a colander.

Preheat the oven to 250°F. Spread out the seeds on a baking sheet. Using a pastry brush, coat the seeds in olive oil. Season generously with salt. Bake until the seeds are browned and crunchy, about 45 minutes. Sprinkle with coarse salt and let cool thoroughly. Store in an airtight jar in a cool, dry place for up to 2 weeks.

easy pumpkin cake

At my children's elementary school, this recipe was passed from mother to mother and from class to class. It was featured at the school's annual Thanksgiving feast, a meal prepared by parents and school children and shared with all the school families and the town elders each year. It has become the cake I am most likely to whip up when a bake sale or potluck dinner catches me unprepared. And it is absolutely foolproof.

■ SERVES 12–15 ■

> "To dream of pumpkins is a very bad omen."
>
> —Richard Folkard,
> *Plant Lore* (1884)

Cake

- 2 cups unbleached all-purpose flour
- 2 teaspoons baking powder
- 2 teaspoons ground cinnamon
- 1 teaspoon baking soda
- 1 teaspoon salt
- 1½ cups granulated sugar
- 1 cup canola oil
- 4 large eggs
- 1¾ cups cooked and mashed pumpkin or winter squash or canned pumpkin purée

Cream Cheese Frosting

- 8 ounces cream cheese, softened
- ½ cup butter, softened
- 1 teaspoon pure vanilla extract
- 2–2½ cups confectioners' sugar, sifted

1 Preheat the oven to 350°F. Grease a 9- by 13-inch baking pan with butter and dust with flour.

2 To make the cake, combine the flour, baking powder, cinnamon, baking soda, and salt. Mix well.

3 Combine the sugar and oil and beat until light. Add the eggs, one at a time, beating well after each addition. Beat in the pumpkin. Add the flour mixture and beat just until thoroughly blended. Pour the batter into the prepared pan.

4 Bake for 30 to 35 minutes, until the top springs back when lightly touched.

5 Cool completely on a rack.

6 To make the frosting, beat together the cream cheese, butter, and vanilla. Add 2 cups of the sugar and beat until smooth. If the frosting is too thin, add the additional ½ cup sugar and beat until smooth.

7 Spread evenly over the cooled cake.

JACK-O'-LANTERNS

The tradition of carving pumpkins to make jack-o'-lanterns came from Ireland in the mid-19th century. It seems that a blacksmith named Jack sold his soul to the devil for financial gain. When it came time to pay the devil with his soul, he weaseled out of the deal by trapping the devil in a pear tree. Barred from Heaven for his deal with the devil, Jack was sent straight to Hell. The devil, still unhappy about the pear-tree incident, kicked him out of Hell. On his way out, Jack scooped up a lump of burning coal and placed it in a pumpkin. He used this as a lantern while roaming the world, waiting for Judgment Day.

THERE ARE DEFINITE DIFFERENCES among winter squash. While most varieties can be used interchangeably, there are some squash that require special attention.

Acorn Shaped like an acorn, this squash comes in three colors: green, orange, and white. The flesh is somewhat drier and stringier than other varieties, but it is a convenient size for stuffing and for serving in baked or roasted wedges.

Banana A monster of a squash, these can grow up to 100 pounds with mild, sweet, and very creamy pink flesh. Banana squash is more commonly grown in the West than in the East.

Buttercup Fans of the buttercup claim that this squash is so sweet, it doesn't need a sweet glaze. (Take that advice with a grain of salt.) It has a dark green round shape, with a pale green "cap."

Butternut The one winter squash that is easily peeled, butternut has moist, rich, smooth flesh. It makes a delicious purée and its cubes and slices also can be grilled or roasted. Butternut squash can be grated raw and used as a stand-in for grated carrots in baked dishes. This is a very good, all-purpose squash that is usually available year-round.

Calabaza Caribbean recipes calling for "pumpkin" are inevitably referring to the calabaza. It is usually rounded or pear shaped and fairly large, with mottled skin that may be green, orange, amber, or cream, speckled or striped. It is the one "winter squash" that is grown year-round in warm climates.

Delicata Also known as "sweet potato squash," this squash is shaped like a long, ridged tube, with cream, orange, and green stripes. Delicata should be sliced in half lengthwise, seeded, then cut into crescent-shaped pieces. The peel is edible. One delicata squash serves two.

Hubbard Hubbards present a grand challenge in the kitchen. They can weigh anywhere from 8 to 40 pounds, and their skins are extremely hard to cut through. But once wrestled into manageable pieces, the light orange flesh is sweet and moist. This squash makes excellent baby food.

Pumpkin Pie pumpkins, also know as "sweet" pumpkins or "cheese" pumpkins, are smaller than those cultivated for jack-o-lanterns. They can be cooked like any other winter squash.

Red Kuri Recognize red kuri by its brilliant orange color. The flesh is rather bland compared to other winter squash, but its brilliant deep orange flesh is extremely attractive on the plate. Red kuri is often used to make soup.

Spaghetti Yellow and football shaped, spaghetti squash has turned the distressing tendency of winter squash to be stringy into a virtue. When cooked, the flesh of the spaghetti squash turns into long, spaghetti-like strands. Although many suggest serving spaghetti squash as a pasta substitute, it is probably better to acknowledge its sweet flavor and work with it as a winter squash.

Sweet Dumpling Small and pumpkin shaped, sweet dumplings are cream colored with dark green stripes. Like delicata squash, the skin of the sweet dumpling squash is edible. The flesh is smooth, sweet, and moist. One sweet dumpling serves one.

Turban As much prized for its decorative appearance as its flavor, the turban is indeed shaped like a turban. It can be used like any other winter squash. The skin is tough and difficult to cut into.

BEST OF THE SEASON:

FALL INTO WINTER

How CONVENIENT that vegetables that lend themselves to longer, slower cooking are harvested for the fall. Now we welcome the opportunity to make slow-cooking stews and long-roasted root vegetables. As we spend more and more time indoors, there is time to experiment in the kitchen and think about next year's garden. Maybe more rutabagas?

sage-roasted fall vegetable salad

The very best flavors of fall and come together in this salad — roasted root vegetables, nutty wild rice, and cranberries. It tastes like Thanksgiving all over again.

■ SERVES 6 ■

Salad

1 cup wild rice

3 cups water

1 teaspoon salt, plus more to taste

12 cups peeled and diced fall vegetables (any combination of winter squash, carrots, beets, rutabagas, turnips, parsnips)

1 onion, diced

1 tablespoon chopped fresh sage

3 tablespoons extra-virgin olive oil

Freshly ground black pepper

2 cups sliced Belgian endive, radicchio, or other fall green

Cranberry Vinaigrette

2 shallots, chopped

1 cup homemade or canned cranberry sauce

2 tablespoons raspberry vinegar or other fruited vinegar or red wine vinegar

2 tablespoons fresh orange juice

¾ cup walnut oil or extra-virgin olive oil

Salt and freshly ground black pepper

1 Combine the wild rice, water, and salt in a small saucepan. Cover and bring to a boil. Reduce the heat and simmer until the rice is tender and most of the grains have burst open, 40 to 60 minutes. Drain off any excess water. Let cool.

2 Meanwhile, preheat the oven to 450°F. Lightly grease a large shallow roasting pan or half-sheet pan with oil.

3 Combine the diced fall vegetables, onion, and sage in a large bowl. Add the oil and toss gently to lightly coat the vegetables. Transfer to the prepared pan and arrange in a single layer.

4 Roast for 30 to 40 minutes, stirring occasionally, until the vegetables are tender and lightly browned. Let cool.

5 To make the vinaigrette, finely chop the shallots in a blender. Add the cranberry sauce, vinegar, orange juice, and oil and process until smooth. Season with salt and pepper.

6 Combine the roasted vegetables, sliced Belgian endive, and vinaigrette in a large bowl. Toss gently to mix. Taste and add salt and pepper if desired. Serve at room temperature.

colcannon

Some combinations are just so inevitable that it hardly seems necessary to provide a recipe. Still, colcannon, an Irish dish, isn't served that often, considering its terrific flavor and the healthy way it upgrades mashed potatoes. In Ireland, it is a traditional Halloween dish. It is important to cook the cabbage slowly to coax all the sweetness out of the vegetable. If you like, grate a large carrot and add it to the cabbage mixture for color and more vegetable goodness.

■ SERVES 4 ■

6 tablespoons butter

½ head green cabbage, shredded

2 medium leeks, trimmed and sliced, or 1 large onion, halved and thinly sliced

2 pounds baking or russet potatoes, peeled and cut into large pieces

½ cup milk or cream, warmed

Salt and freshly ground black pepper

1 Melt 3 tablespoons of the butter over medium heat in a large skillet. Add the cabbage and leeks and sauté until very tender and sweet, about 30 minutes, stirring frequently.

2 Meanwhile, combine the potatoes with salted water to cover in a small saucepan. Cover and bring to a boil over high heat. Reduce the heat and boil gently until completely tender, 15 to 25 minutes.

3 Drain the potatoes well. Mash the potatoes with a potato masher, press through a ricer, or whip in a standing mixer until you have a light texture. Beat in the remaining 3 tablespoons butter and the milk.

4 Fold in the cabbage mixture. Season generously with salt and pepper. Transfer to a serving dish and serve hot.

RADICCHIO: THE PERFECT FALL "GREEN"

Although radicchio can be green, most gardeners and growers in the United States grow the maroon-and-white variety. Most varieties require cool temperatures to produce the characteristic red color. And most varieties will taste bitter if grown in warm weather. So radicchio is generally considered a fall or very early spring crop. However, you can find some varieties that will tolerate warmer temperatures. The slightly bitter flavor and beautiful color of radicchio make it an excellent addition to salads. Cooking brings out more flavor, but the color does turn brown. Most recipes for Belgian endive (pages 334 to 338) can be made with radicchio.

beef stew with root vegetables

Late fall is the time for slow-cooked foods and long-keeping vegetables. The long-keeping root vegetables in this stew offer up an appealing sweetness, with the flavor of the Jerusalem artichokes dominating. If you aren't certain everyone likes Jerusalem artichokes, you might want to substitute potatoes.

■ SERVES 6 ■

⅔ cup unbleached all-purpose flour

2 tablespoons chopped fresh thyme leaves

1 tablespoon chopped fresh oregano leaves

Salt and freshly ground black pepper

2 pounds stew beef, cut into bite-size pieces

4 tablespoons extra-virgin olive oil

1 large onion, thinly sliced

1½ cups beef broth

2 cups diced canned tomatoes with juice

1 cup red wine

2 garlic cloves, minced

1 pound rutabagas or turnips, peeled and cut into 1-inch cubes

1 pound carrots or parsnips, cut into 1-inch slices

2 pounds Jerusalem artichokes, scrubbed and cut into 1-inch pieces

1 Combine the flour, 1 tablespoon of the thyme, and the oregano in a shallow bowl. Season generously with salt and pepper. Add the beef and toss to coat.

2 Heat 3 tablespoons of the oil in a large Dutch oven over medium-high heat. Lift the beef pieces out of the flour, shaking off the excess, and add in a single layer to the pot. Do not crowd the pot. Let the meat brown, turning as needed, about 5 minutes. Remove the meat as it browns and set aside. Repeat until all the meat is browned.

3 Add the remaining 1 tablespoon oil and the onion to the Dutch oven and sauté until the onion is soft, about 3 minutes. Add the broth, tomatoes, wine, and garlic. Stir to scrape up any stuck bits from the bottom of the pot. Bring to a boil, then reduce the heat to a slow simmer. Return the meat to the pot. Partially cover the pot and let simmer until the meat is tender, about 2 hours.

4 Add the rutabagas, carrots, and Jerusalem artichokes to the pot and let simmer until the vegetables are tender, about 1 hour.

5 Taste and add salt and pepper as needed. Serve hot.

ONE OF MY FAVORITE SPOTS in the entire world is the backyard garden of Jane and Marshall Eddy in downtown Middlebury, Vermont. On the banks of the Otter Creek, the Eddy garden lies on a floodplain behind an old carriage barn. These two artists have painstakingly transformed the barn into a beautiful home, but their artistry is nowhere more apparent than in the garden.

Thirty years ago, when Jane and Marshall first established the garden, they had to bring in soil to make the beds. The garden was a stony, rubble-strewn field. Today, the long rectangular garden (about 40 by 60 feet) stretches down a narrow yard, bordered by cedar trees, flowers, and trellised grapevines. The vegetable garden is enclosed in a fence that is buried 10 inches deep and about a foot horizontally as protection against wood-chucks, but the fencing also makes it safe for tod-dlers to play in the garden while the adults enjoy dinner at the picnic table at the head of the garden.

The vegetable garden is divided in half, with a long grass path down its entire length. On each side are long beds — his and her beds, as it turns out. To the right are Marshall's beds. Marshall's garden beds are as precise as the geometric pat-terns he carves on his instantly recognizable pot-tery vases. He is the only vegetable gardener I know who uses landscape cloth on his beds, cov-ered by straw (never hay), to keep the weeds down. Every row is immaculately straight, every tomato centered within its cage, every path com-pletely weed-free.

Marshall is a busy man, and fall is a particularly busy time when he returns to school to teach art. Therefore, he specializes in early crops. His garden beds are hand-dug in the spring and enriched with manure trucked in from a local farm. His peas are planted by April 15. Then he plants early spinach, early carrots, early lettuce, early Swiss chard. His tomatoes are planted three by four: three romas, three Early Girls, three yellow table tomatoes, and three yellow pear tomatoes. His basil must be planted quite early, because in September it is about 5 feet tall. Ever since woodchucks devoured his garden one year, he plants nothing that is particularly attractive to them — meaning no cole crops.

To the right are Jane's beds, free-form, flowing. Here there is a patch of parsley, there some leeks. Beans grow along trellises here, there a colossal bunch of white-ribbed Swiss chard flourishes. There is waist-high bunch of red-ribbed Swiss chard on the other side of the garden. Jane harvests only the outer ribs, and the plants grow vigorously. Here leeks have seed heads; dill, cilantro, and Johnny-jump-ups are everywhere. Where a lettuce sprouted, it grows — a head here, a head there. Where a pole bean sprouted, she set up a tepee and planted more beans, yellow-podded, purple-podded, green. It is a riot of color and form.

Jane's garden isn't so much planned as it is encouraged. Bunches of yellow coreopsis arc over the cabbages, tall cosmos border the edamame, apple-blossom hollyhocks grow next to the Japanese radishes. "I used to think flowers were self-indulgent," says Jane. "But I've fallen in love with them as I mature." Flower beds conceal the fencing around the garden. There are also beds of flowers all around the house, and flowers in beds here and there. In Jane's vegetable garden, if a flower sows itself, it is welcome to stay.

Jane's gardening practices are very much influenced by gardens they visited in Barcelona, when their daughter, Serena, competed as a rower in the 1992 Olympics: "Everything was trellised, everything was grown vertically. And it was all so beautiful." Her yellow pear tomatoes, an heirloom variety that gets quite leggy, are trellised on a structure made of pine and bamboo. Her yard-long beans and cucumbers are trellised, as were the peas that grew to a height of 7 to 8 feet.

Jane grows kale, broccoli, and cabbages — all plants banished from Marshall's garden. She also grows melons because that is what the grandchildren like to eat most, and she has taught them how to judge when the melons are mature. She has paths made of straw, of wooden planks, and of dirt.

"Paths are crucial to a garden," says Jane. "They are very inviting. Kids love to follow them."

Making the grandchildren welcome in the garden is important to both Jane and Marshall. Near the gate to the garden is the grandchildren's sunflower house. Around the outside of the bed are planted Mammoth sunflowers, with a single gap for a door. These are the walls of the sunflower house, and the flowers are a good 10 feet tall. Scarlet runner beans are planted at the base of each sunflower. They climb up the sturdy stems, then run along strings woven between sunflowers at about 5 feet to form a roof. Inside the little house, the children have laid stones to create paths, installed two mini Adirondack chairs and tables, and planted shade-tolerant flowers. Flowers also grow outside of the sunflower walls. An asparagus plant anchors one corner of the bed — it is the "pine tree." It is as cozy a garden house as one could want.

"Both sets of my grandmothers and my great-grandmother had gardens and they hoed and planted right into their nineties," says Jane. "They gave me beds of my own starting when I was nine, so I've had a garden practically my whole life. I hope I'm still gardening in my nineties." She probably will be, and by then grandchildren Kess, Max, and Tuck will be old enough to do a little of the heavy lifting.

PRESERVING THE HARVEST

IF YOU GARDEN, IT IS ALMOST INEVITABLE that you will be faced with a surplus of vegetables from time to time. One way to deal with the overabundance is to preserve your bounty for later consumption.

Many of us have negative associations with preserving because it seems to involve so much time in the hot kitchen on hot summer days. But that image may be a little outdated. If you focus your efforts on just a few vegetables, or just a few different techniques, and not attempt to preserve enough to survive on for the rest of the year, then preserving may become part of the pleasure of gardening.

What I preserve varies from year to year. Sometimes I find myself making a lot of pickles, other years I do a fair amount of freezing. Some years I make a few fruit jams and salsas and not much else. But I always, always make pesto for the freezer. And I always use it all, because we love pesto in my house. When you think about preserving, give some thought to what you and your family will eat. There's no point in, say, spending hours blanching pounds of green beans if no one will touch a frozen bean.

This chapter provides a brief overview of the techniques of cold storage, freezing, canning, and drying — enough to get you started. If you are serious about food preserving, you may want to consult a book devoted to the subject. Your local county agricultural extension agent also should be knowledgeable on the subject.

COLD STORAGE

Storing vegetables in a root cellar is the oldest, fastest, and easiest method of storing food. But few people, including myself, have homes with root cellars. Root cellars differ from refrigerators in that they provide moist, cold storage — the refrigerator is too drying. If you have an unheated basement with a dirt floor, you may be able to provide root cellar conditions. Pumpkins, winter squash, and onions require relatively dry conditions; shell beans, beets, cabbages, carrots, cauliflower, celery, kohlrabi, peppers, potatoes, and green tomatoes should be stored in relative moist conditions — packed in barrels of moist sand or sawdust.

Here are the general guidelines.

- Clean your storage area once a year. Sweep out all debris and scrub all containers with hot, soapy water.

- Each vegetable should be stored in a separate container. Containers can be sturdy cardboard boxes, barrels, large plastic bags, or bins.

- Vegetables should be packed in layers of dried leaves, straw, crumpled or shredded newspapers, or sawdust.

- Vegetables should be clean and dry before packed into storage. Onions should be dried before storing. Winter squash and pumpkins should be cured in the sun before they are packed away.

- Harvest green tomatoes before the first frost with the stems attached. Wash and dry thoroughly. Discard any with bruises. Pack the green tomatoes in shallow cartons packed with straw, leaves, or shredded paper. Keep in a cool place where the temperature ranges between 55° and 70°F — often a back porch or an unheated attic provides the best conditions. Check the tomatoes every few days, and remove the tomatoes as they ripen.

FREEZING

Freezing is an easy way to preserve, if you have the freezer space. Most vegetables require blanching first. A few vegetables, including tomatoes, can be frozen without blanching. Many vegetables freeze beautifully, especially if prepared in a ready-to-serve soup or sauce before freezing.

Here are general guidelines.

- For the best finished product, blanch vegetables before freezing. Trim or slice the vegetables into uniform-size pieces. Plunge the vegetables into boiling water and boil until just barely tender (see blanching times for each vegetable in the individual chapters). Plunge into ice water to stop the cooking. Drain well. Pat dry with clean kitchen towels.

- Pack vegetables in plastic bags or containers. Seal, label, and freeze.

- You can freeze the tomatoes whole, without blanching. Just wash the tomatoes and dry thoroughly. Remove the cores and place on a cookie sheet. Freeze until solid, then bag the tomatoes in resealable plastic bags and remove as needed. Thaw the tomatoes in a nonreactive metal sieve set over a bowl. As the tomatoes thaw, the skins should slip off easily and the tomatoes will release water. Save the water and add back as much or as little as needed for the dish you are making.

- If you prefer, you can peel the tomatoes before freezing. Plunge the tomatoes into boiling water for 30 to 60 seconds, then slip off the skins. Freeze the tomatoes in plastic containers. Then thaw the tomatoes in a sieve, or add them still frozen to sauces and soups and just cook off the excess water.

- Alternatively, you can freeze tomatoes already made into salsas or soups. If you freeze an uncooked sauce, such as salsa, let it thaw in a sieve set over a bowl and add back just enough of the thawed juices to achieve a good consistency.

- For cooked sauces, wash, core, and quarter the tomatoes. Simmer, covered, in a heavy saucepan until soft, then remove the lid. Add seasonings as desired. For stewed tomatoes, simmer for 15 to 30 minutes. To make a sauce, continue to simmer until the tomatoes are cooked down to a pleasing consistency, for 2 to 6 hours, depending on how big a batch you are working with.

- Use home-frozen vegetables within 10 months.

DRYING

Unless you live in the American Southwest, where the temperature can read about 100°F and the humidity is below 60 percent, you will find drying works best in a dehydrator. I have had some success with oven-drying tomatoes, but the quality of oven-dried foods is generally lower than of those dried in a dehydrator. Vegetables, with the exception of tomatoes, should be blanched before drying.

- To dry in the sun, stretch clean, 100 percent cotton sheeting or cheesecloth over wooden frames and secure with staples. You can use window screening, as long as it isn't made from galvanized metal, which will impart "off" flavors to the food. Arrange the food on the screens and cover with a second screen or cheesecloth to protect from insects.

- Trim or slice the vegetables into uniform-size pieces. Plunge the vegetables into boiling water and boil until just barely tender (see blanching times for each vegetable in the individual chapters). Plunge into ice water to stop the cooking. Drain well. Pat dry with clean kitchen towels.

- Green beans and tomatoes should be dried until they are leathery but still pliable. Beans, corn, okra, and peas should be dried until they are hard and brittle.

One can pasteurize dried vegetables for long-term storage by one of two methods. Arrange the dried vegetables on trays in a thin layer and leave in a 175°F oven for 10 to 15 minutes, then cool. Or place the dried vegetables in a 0°F freezer for 2 to 4 days.

Oven-Drying Tomatoes

Any type of tomato can be dried, but typically paste or plum tomatoes are used.

1. Wash and dry the tomatoes. Cut them in half and scoop out the seeds and cores. Pat the interior dry with paper towels.
2. Preheat the oven to 150°F. If your oven has an upper broiler element, turn it off. Cover the oven racks with clean sheeting, cheesecloth, or thin kitchen towels to hold the tomatoes while allowing air to circulate. Place the tomatoes on the cloth so they are not touching. Do not attempt to dry more than two racks of tomatoes at a time. Place the racks in the oven. Close the door and bake for 30 minutes.
3. Open the oven door to let out the moisture. Leave the door propped open with a wooden spoon or something similar that will allow the door to remain ajar. Continue drying for 6 to 8 hours, until the tomatoes are pliable and slightly leathery.
4. Transfer the tomatoes to a dry ceramic or glass (not aluminum) container and leave it uncovered in a dry and airy place for 10 days. Stir the tomatoes at least once a day.

5. Pasteurize the tomatoes as described earlier.
6. Store in an airtight container at room temperature and use as needed.

BOILING-WATER-BATH CANNING

Boiling-water-bath canning is a safe way to can pickles, tomatoes with added acid, and fruits. Canning preserves food by processing it at high temperatures for long enough to kill bacteria, molds, and other organisms that cause spoilage. During processing, air is forced out of the jars, leaving a vacuum sealed by the lid. As long as the jars remain airtight, the vacuum protects the food inside from harmful organisms. Low-acid vegetables require pressure canning, a process that requires special equipment and very careful attention to detail. The process is covered in other books devoted exclusively to methods of preservation.

Canning Equipment

Apart from ladles, funnels, and sieves, which you may already own, you need the following items. Most supermarkets and hardware stores stock canning equipment, especially in late summer.

1. A boiling-water-bath canner with a wire rack to hold the jars.
2. Canning jars in quart, pint, and half-pint sizes. Canning jars are made from glass tempered to withstand high heat during

processing. They can be reused year after year if undamaged. Do not use jars in which you bought commercially prepared sauce or jam because the glass may not be strong enough.

3. Two-piece lids comprising a flat disk called a dome lid that sits on top of the jar and a screw ring to hold it in place. The lid cannot be reused, but undamaged screw rings can be.

4. A jar lifter so you can handle hot jars.

The Rule for Tomatoes

Because the acidity of the tomatoes varies, safe canning requires that the tomatoes be acidified. In the case of many preserves, the acid is part of the recipe — as in the case of ketchup, which contains vinegar. Otherwise, acidify the tomatoes by adding 2 tablespoons bottled lemon juice or a ½ teaspoon citric acid to each quart jar.

Steps for Canning

For safe canning, follow these directions, based on USDA recommendations.

1. Prepare the pickles or tomatoes or the sauce according the recipe.

2. Prepare the lids and rings by putting them in a pan of water and heating it to boiling point. Keep them in boiling water for 10 minutes. Do not remove them until you are ready to put them on the jars.

3. Prepare the jars. You do not have to sterilize jars used for food processed in a boiling-water bath for more than 10 minutes. Simply wash them in soapy water or a dishwasher, then rinse thoroughly to remove all traces of soap. For boiling-water-bath processing times of less than 10 minutes, sterilize the washed jars by submerging them in a canner filled with hot (not boiling) water, making sure the water rises 1 inch above the jar top. At sea level, boil the jars for 10 minutes; at higher elevations, boil for an additional minute for every 1,000 feet, as indicated in the table on page 477. Some dishwashers have a sterilizing cycle.

4. Fill the jars leaving a ½-inch headspace or the headspace indicated in your recipe. Wipe away any drips on rim. If bubbles appear as you fill the jars, run a clean spatula or chopstick inside the jar to release them. Do not stir, which could create more bubbles.

5. Place the lids on top and secure with a metal ring, tightening it so it grips. (You do not need to exert extra pressure to make it extremely tight.) Load the jars into the rack.

6. Fill the canner half full with water and pre-heat to 180°F. Lift the rack by its handles and set it in the canner.

7. Add more boiling water if necessary to bring the water level to 1 inch above the jars.

8. Turn the heat as high as possible and wait until the water is boiling vigorously. Cover the canner with the lid. Reduce the heat to maintain a moderate boil. As soon as you have

covered the canner, set a timer for the recommended processing time. If you live at a high elevation, increase the processing time as necessary, using the table below.

9. Have more boiling water on hand so you can add it to the canner, should evaporation make the water fall below the recommended level. Arrange folded towels on a counter where you can place the finished jars for cooling.

10. When the jars have boiled for the recommended time, remove them from the canner using a jar lifter. Set them on the towels, placing them at least 1 inch apart.

11. Let the jars cool for 12 hours, then test to establish that you have a good seal. Look at the middle of the lid; it should be slightly concave. Press the center hard with your thumb; if it does not move downward or "give," it is sealed. You can also tap the lid with the rounded bowl of a teaspoon. If it is correctly sealed, it will ring clearly; if not, it will sound dull. If the seal is faulty, the tomatoes or pickles inside the jar are not spoiled, but they cannot be kept for a long period. Store them in the refrigerator and use within a week.

CANNING TIMES FOR ALL ALTITUDES

At sea level, water boils at 212°F. At higher elevations, it boils at lower temperatures; therefore, in these regions foods must be processed for longer to ensure that harmful organisms are destroyed. The USDA recommends that you add 1 minute for every 1,000 feet above sea level when processing foods that require less than 20 minutes in the boiling-water bath. Add 2 minutes for every 1,000 feet for foods that must be processed for more than 20 minutes. The table illustrates these times.

ALTITUDE IN FEET	FOR PROCESSING TIMES OF 20 MINUTES OR LESS, ADD	FOR PROCESSING TIMES OF 20 MINUTES OR MORE, ADD
1,000	1 minute	2 minutes
2,000	2 minutes	4 minutes
3,000	3 minutes	6 minutes
4,000	4 minutes	8 minutes
5,000	5 minutes	10 minutes

RESOURCES

You can contact *The Art of Eating* at Box 242, Peacham, VT 05862, or at www.artofeating.com.

For **seeds** or to order Ellen Ogden's cookbook, *From the Cook's Garden,* contact The Cook's Garden at 1-800-457-9703 or www.cooksgarden.com

To find a **CSA** near you, search the database at www.nal.usda.gov/afsic/csa

The Food Bank Farm is located at 121 Bay Road (Route 47) in Hadley, Massachusetts. For more information about The Food Bank Farm, call (413) 582-0013 or send an e-mail to foodbankfarm@yahoo.com.

To order *The Joy of Pickling* by Linda Ziedrich, contact your local bookstore. To order directly from the publisher, contact Harvard Common Press, 535 Albany Street, Boston, MA 02118; 617-423-5803.)

To learn more about **Kitchen Gardeners International,** check out the Website at www.kitchengardeners.org.

For more information about **Plant A Row,** visit the Garden Writers of American web site at www.gwaa.org. Call FoodChain at (800) 845-3080 or Second Harvest at (800) 771-2302 to locate donation agencies for your extra produce.

SUPPLIERS

Burpee Seeds & Plants
300 Park Avenue
Warminster, PA 18974

Phone: (800) 888-1447

Fax: (800) 487-5530

E-mail: custserv@burpee.com

Web site: www.burpee.com

Seeds, plants, gardening supplies and decorative accents

The Cook's Garden
PO Box C5030
Warminster, PA 18974

Phone: (800) 457-9703

E-mail for customer service:
    cooksgarden@earthlink.net

E-mail for plant questions:
    gardener@cooksgarden.com

Web site: www.cooksgarden.com

Seeds, some tools and garden supplies

Fedco Seeds
PO Box 520
Waterville, ME 04903

Phone: (207) 873-7333

Web site: www.fedcoseeds.com

Cold-hardy varieties shipped in season and gardening supplies year round

Harris Seeds
PO Box 24966
Rochester, NY 14624-0966
Phone: (800) 514-4441
Fax: (877) 892-9197
Web site: www.harrisseeds.com
Seeds, tools, gardening supplies

Heirloom Seeds
PO Box 245
West Elizabeth, PA 15088-0245
Phone: (412) 384-0852
E-mail: mail@heirloomseeds.com
Web site: www.heirloomseeds.com
Seeds, tools and books

High Mowing Seeds
813 Brook Road
Wolcott, VT 05680
Phone: (802) 888-1800
Fax: (802) 888-8446
E-mail to request catalog:
    catalogs@highmowingseeds.com
E-mail for inquiries:
    questions@highmowingseeds.com
Web site: www.highmowingseeds.com
Certified organic seeds

Johnny's Selected Seeds
955 Benton Avenue
Winslow, ME 04901
Phone: (207) 861-3999
E-mail: rstore@johnnyseeds.com
Web site: www.johnnyseeds.com
Seeds, tools, gardening supplies, cold frames, compost bins

Pinetree Garden Seeds
PO Box 300
New Gloucester, ME 04260
Phone: (207) 926-3400
Fax: (888) 527-3337
E-mail: pinetree@superseeds.com
Web site: superseeds.com
Seeds

Seeds of Change
PO Box 15700
Santa Fe, NM 87506-5700
Phone: (888) 762-7333
Web site: www.seedsofchange.com
Organically grown seeds

Shepherd's Garden Seeds
30 Irene Street
Torrington, CT 06790
Phone: (860) 482-3638
E-mail: hort@shepherdseeds.com
Web site: www.shepherdseeds.com
Seeds, tools, garden supplies

White Flower Farm
PO Box 50
Litchfield, CT 06759-0050
Phone: (800) 503-9624
Web site: www.whiteflowerfarm.com
Ornamental and edible plants, tools, supplies

INDEX

OTHER STOREY TITLES YOU WILL ENJOY

The Classic Zucchini Cookbook, by Nancy C. Ralston, Marynor Jordan, and Andrea Chesman. This completely revised and updated edition contains 225 through-the-menu recipes; an illustrated zucchini and squash primer; and information on how to select, store, clean, preserve, and substitute. 320 pages. Paperback. ISBN 1-58017-453-1.

Mom's Best Desserts, by Andrea Chesman and Fran Raboff. Nothing says "home" like Mom's old-fashioned home cooking. Here are 100 foolproof recipes for the desserts you've loved all your life with practical advice on how to bake just like Mom does. 208 pages. Paperback. ISBN 1-58017-480-9.

Carrots Love Tomatoes, by Louise Riotte. This classic companion-gardening guide has taught generations of gardeners how to use the natural attributes of wild plants, vegetables, and herbs to strengthen and support each other. With this enduring gardening reference, learn which plants nourish the soil, which keep away bugs and pests, and which just don't get along. 224 pages. Paperback. ISBN 1-58017-027-7.

The Tomato Festival Cookbook, by Lawrence Davis-Hollander. For the millions of people who love warm, lush, juicy, vine-ripened tomatoes, here is a stunning collection of 150 recipes that highlight glorious summer tomatoes as well as history; folklore; and growing, preserving, and seed-saving advice. 320 pages. Paperback. ISBN 1-58017-498-1.

The Gardener's A-Z Guide to Growing Organic Food, by Tanya L.K. Denckla. This invaluable resource for organic gardeners provides in-depth growing, harvesting, and storing information for 765 varieties of vegetables, fruits, herbs, and nuts. To keep the crop healthy, organic remedies for 201 garden pests and diseases are included. 496 pages. Paperback. ISBN 1-58017-370-5.

The Vegetable Gardener's Bible, by Edward C. Smith. By integrating four principles — Wide rows, Organic methods, Raised beds, and Deep soil — Smith reinvents vegetable gardening, showing everyone how to have their most successful garden ever. 320 pages. Paperback. ISBN 1-58017-212-1.

Deerproofing Your Yard & Garden, by Rhonda Massingham Hart. In this completely revised and updated edition of her bestselling classic, Hart shares the latest research on deer behavior and food preferences, as well as her hands-on experience in successfully combatting deer, from choosing the best fence to planting the most deer-detested plants. 224 pages. Paperback. ISBN 1-58017-585-6.

These and other books from Storey Publishing are available wherever quality books are sold or by calling 1-800-441-5700. Visit us at www.storey.com.